# THE ROUGH GUIDE TO
# CYPRUS

ROUGH
GUIDES

# Contents

CHAPEL IN THE HARBOUR OF FAMAGUSTA, PROTARAS

# Introduction to

# Cyprus

Birthplace of Aphrodite and crossroads between three continents, Cyprus has seduced and inspired generations of travellers for hundreds of years. And it continues to do so today. The promise of Cyprus is one of dazzling beaches, shimmering blue seas, endless summers and tables groaning under heaped platters of mezé and bottles of sweet chilled wine. On the cusp between West and East, between Christian and Muslim, and with towns and cities that are vibrantly modern yet bear witness to the island's long and culturally diverse history, Cyprus is blessed with a balmy climate and a rugged landscape of coast and mountains dotted with vineyards, villages and monasteries.

Cyprus has earned its place as one of Europe's tourist hotspots. From quaint rustic cottages to luxury hotel complexes, from welcoming village tavernas to burgeoning fine-dining restaurants, from coastal resorts with all the tourist bells and whistles to empty wilderness peninsulas and forested mountains, Cyprus can cater for all tastes. And native Cypriots, whether Greek or Turkish, are famous for the warmth of their hospitality.

Venture beyond the resorts, with their karaoke bars and restaurants knocking out fish and chips, pizza and, more recently, Russian stroganoff, and it's not hard to find another Cyprus. Traces of the exotic and Levantine are never far away, from ruined Lusignan and Venetian castles and elegant Islamic minarets to cool mountain villages hiding sacred icons from the very first days of Christianity.

No stranger to turbulence and strife, Cyprus has suffered waves of foreign invaders, from Mycenaean Greeks and Persians to sunburnt Crusaders, Ottoman pashas, and British Empire-builders. More recently, it has attracted numerous Russian expats. Internal division too has left its mark on the island. First, in the 1950s and 60s, came the struggle by Greek Cypriots for independence and **union with Greece**, then intercommunal violence prompted by fears among the minority Turkish Cypriots

## FACT FILE

- Cyprus, with a land area of 9251 square kilometres, is the **third largest island** in the Mediterranean. Its nearest neighbours are Turkey (75km) and Syria (105km) respectively. The capital, once Nicosia, now **Lefkosia** and **Lefkoşa**, is over 900km from Athens and only 250km from Beirut. The island's highest point, at 1952m, is **Mount Olympos**.

- The official **population** (of the whole island) stands at just above 1,000,000, of which the majority (around 70 per cent) are **Greek Cypriot** (and therefore Orthodox Christian), while **Turkish Cypriots** (and therefore Muslims) are in the minority (around 10 per cent). There's also a significant expat community based on the island.

- The **government** of the Republic of Cyprus (and therefore de jure of the whole island) is a democracy which, since 2004, has been a member of the EU. **North Cyprus**, occupied by Turkey since 1974, has declared itself to be the "Turkish Republic of North Cyprus", but is recognized internationally only by Turkey. Since 2003 the number of crossing points on the dividing (and UN-administered) **Green Line** has increased to seven, with two more in the pipeline. Attempts to reunite the island are ongoing, reinvigorated by a new negotiating process introduced in February 2014.

- Over 1 million **Britons** visit Cyprus each year (42 percent of total arrivals) and the fastest growing group of visitors are Russians. Overall, the total arrivals are at a constant increase.

- **Famous people** of Cypriot origin include singers George Michael, Yusuf Islam (Cat Stevens), Peter Andre and Tulisa Contostavlos (N-Dubz), actress Angela Bowie (ex-wife of David), sportspersons Marco Baghdatis (tennis) and Muzzy Izzet (Premiership football), celebrity chef George Calombaris (Masterchef Australia), businessmen Stelios Haji-Ioannou (founder of easyJet) and Asil Nadir (of Polly Peck fame) and artist Tracey Emin.

regarding what union with Greece might mean for them, and finally the Turkish invasion of the island in 1974 which resulted in its de facto partition between a Turkish Cypriot north and a Greek Cypriot south. Bitterness caused by the split lives on today. However, in recent years the easing of tensions and the gradual **opening up of the Green Line** has made it easier for travellers to explore the island as a whole. It is now possible to experience both sides of the divide in one day, and in the capital you can immerse yourself in two distinct cultures – Greek and Turkish, Christian and Muslim – simply by walking down a street and crossing between the two halves of the city.

Cyprus, then, offers the traveller not only a welcome whose warmth is legendary, but both hedonistic pleasure and cultural diversity out of all proportion to its size.

# Where to go

One of the great advantages of Cyprus as a holiday destination is that it's a relatively small island offering a huge variety of attractions, scenery and activities linked together by an **excellent road system**. Wherever you stay, you can get to pretty much anywhere else in a day.

The vast majority of tourists begin their trip on the narrow coastal strip in the south, which hosts the main towns of **Larnaka**, **Lemesos** and **Pafos**, each with a historic old town, promenade and popular beaches. Beyond them, to the north, foothills rise to the island's main mountain range, the **Troodos Massif**, dotted with villages, churches and monasteries. To the west of the island is a plateau covered in **vineyards**, the great wilderness forest of

**Tiliria** and the stark empty beauty of the **Akamas Peninsula**. North of the Troodos (and lying within Turkish-occupied north Cyprus), lie the more impressive but less lofty mountains of the **Kyrenia Range**. Beyond here is the even narrower northern coastal strip on which **Girne/Kyrenia** is by far the most important and most beautiful town. To the east is the broad and largely flat **Mesaorian Plain** on which stands the island's divided capital **Nicosia**, known today as **Lefkosia** (south) or **Lefkoş** (north); further east is the crumbling port city of **Gazimağusa/Famagusta**, with its range of pretty and not-so-pretty ruins, and the long, tapering **Karpaz Peninsula**, home to wild donkeys and far-flung villages.

For traditional sun, sea and sand holidays, you have an extensive choice – in the south, **Protaras** and **Agia Napa** east of Larnaka, the beaches either side of Lemesos, Pafos and its satellite **Coral Bay** – which are packed with **resorts** offering a range of activities; in the north, the coast either side of Girne and north of Gazimağusa offers more of the same. For smaller hotels with a more individual character, try the north coast around **Polis** and the Akamas Peninsula, or the **hill villages** of the Troodos Mountains which offer traditional homes converted into guest houses.

For a taste of Cyprus's newly developed **restaurant scene** head to Lemesos, the island's gastronomic capital. Lefkosia also boasts several cool cafés and Cyprus's best **shopping**, while the northern towns of Girne and Gazimağusa provide a relaxed harbour-

OLD TOWN, LEFKOSIA

side ambience. Wine lovers are particularly well-catered for by the wine museum and wine festival in Lemesos, and by six well-signposted **wine routes** in Pafos and Lemesos districts.

Cyprus has a rich **history**, and virtually every region has its Roman (or earlier) ruin, its Byzantine church, a Crusader castle or Ottoman mosque, plus some grand British colonial architecture. Standout sights include the **prehistoric villages** at Tenta and Choirokoitia, the **ancient cities** of Kourion and Salamis, **crusader castles** such as those at Kolossi and Lemesos in the south and St Hilarion, Buffavento and Kantara in the north, **monasteries** like Kykkos and Machairas, and the beautiful **UNESCO World Heritage painted churches** of the Troodos Mountains. **Ottoman architecture** can be admired in Lefkoşa's Büyük Han, and Muslim **mosques** in Hala Sultan Tekke in Larnaka or Hazret Omer Tekke east of Girne. For **nature** and the great outdoors, the Troodos and Kyrenia mountains offer superb climbing, hiking and cycling, the seas around the island provide stimulating dive sites, and the beaches at Lara Bay in the west and Algadi in the northeast are great for turtle-watching. Golfers will enjoy the fine courses in Pafos and Girne. Across the island look out for the colourful religious and village **festivals** that take place in spring, summer and autumn.

In terms of what to avoid, be aware that certain southern resorts (especially parts of Lemesos) can be quite sleazy (dominated, it's said, by the Russian mafia), with dubious "gentlemen's clubs" and working girls operating openly in the streets. North Cyprus has also developed a reputation for vice and more obviously gambling; driven by Turkish organized crime, its dozens of **casinos** attract not only Turks from the mainland but also, perhaps surprisingly, hedonists from the south.

# When to go

The **tourist season** in Cyprus lasts from April to October. During this time there should be no trouble getting flights and hotels; all the attractions, restaurants and so on will be open, and there should be numerous activities and festivals to keep you occupied. The downside is, of course, overcrowding and inflated prices. Given a choice, try to avoid the fierce **August heat**. If high summer is unavoidable, make sure your hotel/car has air conditioning. The **autumn**, too, can be remarkably hot and humid, so don't bank on cool, pleasant weather in September or even October. The best time to visit Cyprus, as a tourist, hiker, cyclist or lover of nature, has got to be the **spring**, when skies are blue, the air is warm and balmy, the uplands are a luxuriant green, the streams and reservoirs are full of water, migrating birds fill the air and there are wild flowers everywhere. To further refine your choice, try if possible to be in Cyprus during the **Greek Easter** – it's a major celebration in the Orthodox calendar, and there are colourful events going on in towns and villages across the island. Much of this advice applies to the **north** as well as the south, though festivals will in general be Muslim rather than Christian, and the north coast can be cooler than the rest of

## AVERAGE MONTHLY MAXIMUM TEMPERATURES

|  | Jan | Feb | March | April | May | June | July | Aug | Sept | Oct | Nov | Dec |
|---|---|---|---|---|---|---|---|---|---|---|---|---|
| **COASTAL (LEMESOS)** | | | | | | | | | | | | |
| Max °C | 17 | 17 | 19 | 22 | 25 | 29 | 31 | 31 | 29 | 27 | 22 | 18 |
| Max °F | 63 | 62 | 66 | 80 | 77 | 84 | 88 | 88 | 84 | 81 | 72 | 65 |
| **INLAND (LEFKOSIA)** | | | | | | | | | | | | |
| Max °C | 15 | 16 | 19 | 24 | 29 | 34 | 37 | 37 | 33 | 29 | 22 | 17 |
| Max °F | 60 | 60 | 66 | 75 | 85 | 94 | 99 | 98 | 92 | 84 | 72 | 63 |
| **HILLY AREAS (AGROS)** | | | | | | | | | | | | |
| Max °C | 10 | 11 | 14 | 19 | 24 | 29 | 32 | 32 | 28 | 24 | 17 | 12 |
| Max °F | 51 | 51 | 58 | 66 | 75 | 84 | 89 | 89 | 83 | 75 | 63 | 54 |

the island thanks to mountain breezes from the Kyrenia Mountains. During **winter** your experience of Cypriot life is likely to be far more authentic and less touristy, but a lot of places will be shut, and the weather will be more unsettled and even quite cold. That said, during the winter you can head to the slopes to enjoy the island's limited skiing opportunities.

BÜYÜK HAN, LEFKOŞA

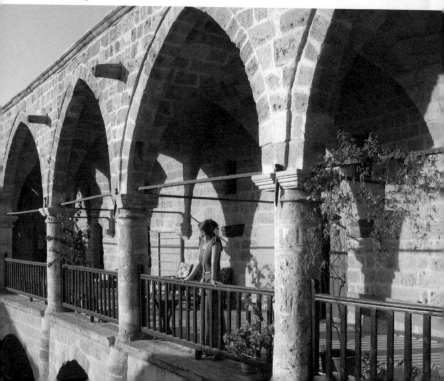

# Author picks

Our intrepid author has visited every corner of Cyprus, north and south, to bring you some unique travelling experiences, from the white sandy beaches of the coast to the forest hiking trails of the high mountains. These are some of his personal favourites.

**Spectacular ruins** On headlands high above the azure Mediterranean, the Palace of Vouni in the north (see page 230) and Ancient Kourion in the south (see page 100) take some beating.

**Unexpected pleasures** The naive sculptures and paintings of Costas Argyrou in the village of Mazotos (see page 72) are a delight. Don't miss, also, the quirky folk museums housed in many Cypriot villages: two of the best are to be found in Agia Varvara, south of Lefkosia (see page 193), and Steni, south of Polis (see page 141).

**Waterfall walk** The Kaledonia Trail in the lofty Troodos Mountains (see page 150) takes you to the highest waterfall on the island – a welcome escape from the heat.

**Castle heaven** St Hilarion (see page 220), with its sheer wow factor, is one of the island's highlights (and busiest sights), while little-visited Buffavento Castle (see page 222) can't be beaten for atmosphere.

**Marvellous marinas** Small boat harbours, often hosting a colourful collection of fishing vessels and lined with seafood restaurants are a pleasure to visit. Try low-key Lakki (see page 139) or picturesque Potamos Liopetriou (see page 62).

**People-watching** Cyprus is a great place for sipping a frappe (iced coffee) and watching the world go by. Try Gazimağusa's central square (see page 230), Lemesos's newly remodelled town centre (see page 82), the cafés around stunning Bellapais Abbey (see page 224), or Lefkoşa's renovated Büyük Han (see page 205).

**Sweet treats** Cypriots have a notoriously sweet tooth – try the local version of Turkish Delight, *loukoumia*, on sale in Geroskipou (see page 124), unbeatable ice cream at McKenzie Beach in Larnaka (see page 53) or heavenly baklava at *Petek* in Gazimağusa (see page 238).

> Our author recommendations don't end here. We've flagged up our favourite places – a perfectly sited hotel, an atmospheric café, a special restaurant – throughout the Guide, highlighted with the ★ symbol.

ANCIENT KOURION
LOUKOUMIA ("CYPRUS DELIGHT")

# 20
## things not to miss

It's not possible to see everything that Cyprus has to offer in one trip – and we don't suggest you try. What follows is a selective and subjective taste of the island's highlights: superb ancient and religious sites, unforgettable scenery and a variety of activities. All highlights are colour-coded by chapter and have a page reference to take you straight into the Guide, where you can find out more.

1

### 1 NORTH COAST BEACHES
See page 244
Cyprus has hundreds of beaches, though arguably the finest – such as Golden Sands – are strung along the north coast and Karpaz Peninsula.

### 2 WINE TASTING
See pages 90 and 98
Follow one of six wine-tasting routes, drop into the Cyprus Wine Museum or throw yourself into the bacchanal of the Lemesos Wine Festival.

### 3 BELLAPAIS
See page 223
Made famous by Lawrence Durrell, who once lived here, Bellapais is beautifully set around its medieval monastery.

### 4 TURTLE-WATCHING
See pages 133 and 219
In both the south and north of the island are beaches which are some of the last Mediterranean nesting places of green and loggerhead turtles.

### 5 GIRNE (KYRENIA)
See page 211
Undoubtedly the most picturesque port on the island, with a perfect harbour backed by the majestic Kyrenia Mountains.

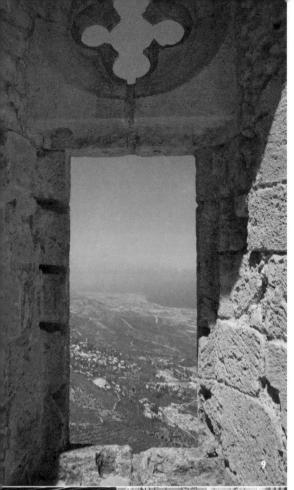

**6 LEMESOS RESTAURANTS**
See page 94
The south's great multicultural port is developing a reputation as the gourmet capital of the island.

**7 PAINTED CHURCHES OF THE TROODOS MOUNTAINS**
See page 156
These beautifully painted wooden churches have been granted UNESCO World Heritage status.

**8 OMODOS**
See page 105
A wonderful hill village boasting not only a winery but also a pretty, cobbled central square, a venerable monastery, and a range of restaurants and shops.

**9 ST HILARION**
See page 220
A fantastical castle whose crumbling walls, meandering steps and ruined buildings blend into the craggy heights upon which it is built, offering spectacular views of the coast and mountains.

**10 KYKKOS MONASTERY**
See page 157
Of the dozens of monasteries in Cyprus, Kykkos, though not the oldest, is the most captivating.

## 11 THE AKAMAS PENINSULA

See page 133

With no main roads, few people and a spectacular coastline, this area is a refreshing contrast to the more developed and crowded parts of the island.

## 12 ANCIENT SALAMIS

See page 238

In an idyllic setting lapped by the sea, ruined Salamis is at once one of the most impressive and most significant archeological sites anywhere on the island.

## 13 MOUFLON

See page 143

The impressively horned and increasingly rare mouflon, a subspecies of a wild sheep found across the Middle East, can be seen at Stavros tis Psokas in the Tilirian forest.

## 14 DIVING

See page 56

The wreck of the *Zenobia*, a modern car ferry which sank in mysterious circumstances off Larnaka, is one of the Mediterranean's premier dive sites.

## 15 THE CYPRUS MUSEUM

See page 179

The best museum in Cyprus, just outside the walls of Lefkosia, containing treasures from across the island and the ages.

13

14

15

### 16 HIKING
See page 33

Cyprus has some top-quality hiking trails, particularly in the Troodos Massif – even in high summer, the altitude makes for a pleasant walking climate.

### 17 CAFÉ CULTURE
See page 29

From small village *kafenía* occupied by old men sipping strong Greek coffee to smart Lefkosia establishments packed with the young and stylish, the imbibing of caffeine and its associated rituals flourish across the island.

### 18 PAFOS MOSAICS
See page 113

These stunningly vivid mosaics give an insight into the life of the Roman elite on the island.

### 19 GAZIMAĞUSA (FAMAGUSTA)
See page 230

One of Cyprus's great cities, where modern life takes place among ruins generated by the Ottoman siege of the city over four centuries ago.

### 20 HALA SULTAN TEKKE
See page 54

A perfectly proportioned mosque, sitting among elegant palm trees on the edge of Larnaka's blinding-white salt lake.

# Itineraries

Despite its relatively compact size, Cyprus rewards those with a sense of wanderlust. Within an hour's drive you can leave the beach and find yourself exploring a cool mountain monastery or wandering the streets of an ancient Roman city. The following itineraries can all be done within a fortnight, giving you a taste of both sides of the island.

## THE GRAND TOUR

Two weeks in Cyprus and not sure where to start? Our Grand Tour puts you on the right track.

❶ **Larnaka** Home to the island's biggest airport, Larnaka is the inevitable starting point for many visitors to Cyprus. However, its elegant promenade, beautiful Agios Lazaros cathedral, ancient ruins, and a vibrant resort are reason to linger. See page 44

❷ **Lemesos** Cyprus's second city, with a reputation for great restaurants, has transformed itself recently into the definition of laidback Mediterranean living. See page 82

❸ **The Troodos Mountains** Small villages, lovely monasteries and churches, cool mountain air, the Troodos Massif offers a startling contrast to the more hectic coast. See page 146

❹ **Pafos** Known for its family-friendly resorts, Pafos has, among the hotels, shops and restaurants, a pretty harbour, some world-class historical monuments and a fascinating hinterland of small villages. See page 110

❺ **Girne (Kyrenia)** The most beautiful harbour town on the island, and a good introduction to life in north Cyprus, Girne has a stunning castle, a relaxed atmosphere and offers wonderful days out to St Hilarion Castle and Bellapais Abbey. See page 211

❻ **Nicosia (Lefkosia/Lefkoşa)** Cyprus's capital, with a wealth of monuments, museums and good shopping and eating, offers a taste of both north and south Cyprus – you can cross from one side to the other in a matter of minutes. See pages 170 and 196

❼ **Gazimağusa (Famagusta)** An ancient port city defined by its elegantly ruined old town, pounded by the Ottomans in 1571. Nearby are the magnificent ruins of Ancient Salamis and also the unsettling sight of Varosha, derelict since 1974. See page 230

## EAST CYPRUS

East Cyprus, particularly Larnaka district, boasts some of the island's finest beaches, liveliest resorts and several crossing points to the north.

❶ **Agia Napa** Once the archetypal 18–30 resort, Agia Napa has morphed into a more sophisticated destination with a surprising smattering of museums, street art and other attractions. See page 58

❷ **Larnaka** Worth a day or two for its promenade, town centre beach and marina, and also its old fort, Pierides museum and Agios Lazaros Church. See page 44

❸ **Nicosia (Lefkosia/Lefkoşa)** Take a walking tour of both north and south sides of the city, then drive across the Green Line and north to

Girne, stopping off at St Hilarion Castle on the way. See pages 170 and 196

**❹ The Karpaz Peninsula** Explore the villages and small-scale sights of the Karpaz Peninsula. Look out for its wild donkeys, and press on to lonely Apostolos Andreas monastery, both the easternmost and the northernmost point on the island. See page 244

**❺ Salamis** You could spend an entire day exploring the ancient city of Salamis, the nearby Royal Tombs, Monastery of St Barnabas and the ruins of Enkomi-Alasia – all within a couple of kilometres of each other. See page 238

**❻ Gazimağusa (Famagusta)** A modern city with an old town at its heart, a place for strolling, sitting in cafés, and admiring the historical ruins. See page 230

**❼ Deryneia** Cross back into the republic at Strovilia, drive around the Kokkinochoria (red villages), and drop into the Cultural Centre of Occupied Famagusta to view the ruins of Varosha on the outskirts of Gazimağusa, a ghost town abandoned since the invasion of 1974. See page 70

## WEST CYPRUS

The west side of the island presents untouched wilderness, lively resorts and some of the island's most important archeological sites.

**❶ Pafos** With an airport second in importance only to Larnaka, Pafos is the best place to start a tour of the west. Don't miss the town's spectacular UNESCO-listed Roman mosaics, important early Christian remains, eerie Tombs of the Kings or, just to the southeast, the ruins of Palaipafos and pretty Petra tou Romiou, the birthplace of Aphrodite. See page 110

**❷ Polis** Driving from Pafos to Polis, take time to look at the Monastery of Agios Neofytos, Pafos Zoo, and the numerous villages, known for their traditions and their wine, in between. Polis is also the gateway to the Akamas Peninsula. See page 136

**❸ Kato Pyrgos** Having driven northeast around Chrysochou Bay, through the villages of Pomos and Pachyammos, stay for a while in quiet Kato Pyrgos, from where you can explore the forests of Tiliria. See page 140

**❹ Vouni and Soli** Cross the Green Line into north Cyprus at Limnitis/Yesilirmak, and take time to look first at the remains of the Palace of Vouni, then of Soli. Continue to Güzelyurt, an unpretentious market town with an interesting museum. See pages 230 and 228

**❺ The northern Troodos** After Güzelyurt, cross back into the south at Zodeia/Astromeritis and head up into the northern Troodos regions of Marathasa and Solea, staying perhaps in Kakopetria. Head south to the coastal motorway, then west to Pafos Airport and your flight home. See pages 154 and 159

GOATS CROSSING, TROODOS FOOTHILLS

# Basics

# Getting there

Although the bulk of foreign visitors to Cyprus arrive on package tours, you can find competitive deals by arranging your own flights and accommodation. The republic has two international airports (Larnaka and Pafos), and there are frequent direct flights to both these airports from London, Manchester and numerous regional airports in the UK. Other major hubs for Cyprus include Athens, Amsterdam and Brussels. Turkish-occupied north Cyprus (the "TRNC") has one international airport at Ercan to which there are no direct flights other than through Turkey. A ferry service also links Turkey with north Cyprus.

Since Cyprus is a smallish island, and has an excellent motorway system joining all the main towns and holiday areas, price can be as much of a factor as transfer times in choosing your airport. However, Larnaka is the biggest and busiest, and therefore offers the widest choice of flights and arrival times and links with the rest of the island.

There are no direct flights to Cyprus from the US, Canada, South Africa, Australia or New Zealand, so journeys involve at least one change of plane, often in London, Athens or Dubai.

## Flights from the UK and Ireland

Many British airports offer flights to Larnaka, Pafos or both, though some are restricted to the summer months. **Flight times** to Cyprus from London are usually around 4hr 30min. Flights from Ireland require at least one, and often two, stops, and therefore take the best part of a day. Add another 40min for flights to Ercan in north Cyprus which must touch down in Turkey first. **Fares** can vary enormously, coming in as low as £150 return during low season, but soaring in summer to £300 or more, though with an average of £250–300. Prices can also jump during the Greek Orthodox Easter (not always the same as the Western

European Easter) as expats flood home for this most important of festivals.

### TO LARNAKA AND PAFOS

**British Airways** Ⓦ britishairways.com. London Heathrow and Manchester to Larnaka (and Pafos in the summer).
**easyJet** Ⓦ easyjet.com. Larnaka from London Gatwick and Pafos from London Gatwick, Luton, Manchester, Bristol and Edinburgh.
**First Choice Airways** Ⓦ firstchoice.co.uk. Pafos from Gatwick, Manchester, Birmingham, Glasgow, Doncaster (all year). Larnaka from Bristol, Gatwick, Manchester and Newcastle (April–Oct).
**Jet2** Ⓦ jet2.com. Flights to Larnaka and Pafos from East Midlands, Manchester, Leeds Bradford, Newcastle, Glasgow, and from Edinburgh to Pafos.
**Monarch Airlines** Ⓦ monarch.co.uk. Larnaka (from Birmingham, Leeds Bradford, Luton and Gatwick) and Pafos (from Birmingham and Gatwick).
**Ryanair** Ⓦ ryanair.com. Pafos from Stansted.
**Thomas Cook Airlines** Ⓦ thomascook.com. Larnaka and Pafos from London Gatwick and most regional airports: Aberdeen, Belfast, Birmingham, Bristol, Cardiff, East Midlands, Glasgow, Leeds Bradford, Manchester and Newcastle.
**Thomson** Ⓦ thomson.co.uk. To Larnaka and Pafos from London Gatwick and Stansted plus many UK regional airports: Aberdeen, Belfast, Birmingham, Bristol, Cardiff, Doncaster, East Midlands, Exeter, Glasgow, Leeds Bradford, Manchester and Newcastle. Also from Dublin.

### TO ERCAN (NORTH CYPRUS)

**Atlas Global** Ⓦ atlasglb.com. Luton to Ercan via Istanbul.
**Pegasus** Ⓦ flypgs.com. Gatwick or Stansted to Ercan via Istanbul.
**Turkish Airlines** Ⓦ turkishairlines.com. Ercan via Istanbul from London Gatwick and Heathrow plus Manchester, Birmingham and Edinburgh.

## Flights from the US and Canada

There are **no direct flights** from the US and Canada to Cyprus. North American visitors must therefore travel via London, Athens, or other European hub airports. Numerous airlines offer one- or two-stop flights, and round-trip **fares** can vary between US$650 and US$3000 from New York and US$1100 to US$380 from Los Angeles, though the cheapest fares tend to be from the smaller airports – Newark, New Jersey, for example, has

---

## A BETTER KIND OF TRAVEL

At Rough Guides we are passionately committed to travel. We believe it helps us understand the world we live in and the people we share it with – and of course tourism is vital to many developing economies. But the scale of modern tourism has also damaged some places irreparably, and climate change is accelerated by most forms of transport, especially flying. We encourage our authors to consider the carbon footprint of the journeys they make in the course of researching our guides.

## THE NORTH/SOUTH DIVIDE AND THE "TRNC"

After its occupation by the Turkish army, the north declared itself to be the "Turkish Federated State of Cyprus" before unilaterally declaring independence in 1983 as the "Turkish Republic of North Cyprus". This title has no international validity, and is strongly resented by the Republic of Cyprus, the only legitimate government of the whole island. For ease of reference we have largely referred to the TRNC as "**the north**" and the rest of the island, that controlled by the republic government, as "**the south**". Where the title TRNC is used it is for convenience, and implies no endorsement of the Turkish occupation.

fares that start at around US$630. Flights from Toronto, Montreal and Vancouver start at under CAN$1180. The best deals from North America to Cyprus seem to be from American Airlines (Ⓦ americanairlines.co.uk), Austrian Airlines (Ⓦ austrian.com), Delta (Ⓦ delta.com), Air Canada (Ⓦ aircanada.com), Lufthansa (Ⓦ lufthansa.com) and British Airways (Ⓦ britishairways.com).

### Flights from Australia, New Zealand and South Africa

Travelling from Australia, New Zealand or South Africa to Cyprus involves at least one **stopover**, usually via a Middle Eastern hub such as Dubai. One-stop flights from Australia start at around AUS$1580; from New Zealand NZ$2640. The cheapest route from South Africa is Johannesburg via Dubai with prices starting at ZAR10,300. Emirates (Ⓦ emirates.com), code-sharing with BA and Qantas, appear to offer the most competitive deals.

### Ferries

Since concerns about international terrorism closed its ferry ports back in 2001, the only viable way of visiting the south, unless you have access to an ocean-going yacht, is by air. However, there are several sea routes between the Turkish mainland and north Cyprus, with passenger-only ferries being a lot quicker than car ferries: Mersin–Gazimağusa (Mon, Wed & Fri, with return trips on Tues, Thurs & Sun); Tasucu–Girne (daily); Alanya–Girne (Mon & Thurs).

### Travel agents and tour operators

#### GENERAL TRAVEL AGENTS

**North South Travel** Ⓦ northsouthtravel.co.uk. Friendly, competitive travel agency, offering discounted fares worldwide. Profits are used to support projects in the developing world, especially the promotion of sustainable tourism.
**STA Travel** Ⓦ statravel.co.uk. Worldwide specialists in independent travel; also student IDs, travel insurance, car rental, rail passes, and more. Good discounts for students and under-26s.

**USIT** Ireland Ⓦ usit.ie. Ireland's main student and youth travel specialists.

#### CYPRUS SPECIALISTS

**Amathus Holidays** Ⓦ amathusholidays.co.uk. Hotel packages for all the main resorts, including Lakki, Polis and Pissouri.
**Cyplon Holidays** Ⓦ cyplon.co.uk. Wide choice of resort packages across the south.
**Cyprus Active** Ⓦ cyprusactive.com. Range of activities – walking, cycling, horseriding, paragliding, scuba diving, cooking.
**Cyprus Direct** Ⓦ cyprusdirectholidays.com. North Cyprus specialist offering flights to Ercan and hotels located mainly but not exclusively in the Girne area.
**Cyprus Villages** Ⓦ cyprusvillages.com.cy. Offers not only traditional accommodation, but also activity-based holidays including cycling, walking and yoga.
Planet Holidays www.planet-holidays.co.uk Bespoke holidays, honeymoon choices and even wedding venues - if you're in for a beach wedding.
**Sun Island Tours** Ⓦ sunislandtours.com.au. Australian-based company specializing in Middle Eastern and Mediterranean holidays including packages to the most popular Cypriot holiday areas.
**Sunvil** Ⓦ sunvil.co.uk. The premier tour operator for Cyprus, offering mainly self-catering villa and agrotourism holidays.

# Getting around

**The bulk of visitors to Cyprus rely on tour-company coaches to get around. Independent travellers have a choice of renting vehicles, catching buses, or taking taxis. For the more intrepid, walking and cycling are also options. The transport system in the north is nowhere near as well developed as that of the south, and your best bet here is to rent a car or book a tour.**

## By bus

Following reorganization in 2010, the south now has a good urban and **intercity bus system**. Buses are modern, usually on time, and although run by different companies in each district (Zinonas in Larnaca, OSEA in the Agia Napa/Protaras area – sometimes called "free Famagusta", EMEL in Lemesos, OSYPA in Pafos, and OSEL in Lefkosia), fares are standard and simple: single journey €1.50, daily ticket €5, weekly ticket €20, monthly ticket €40, daily intercity €15). Each company has its own contact number and website: Lefkosia (☎77777755, 🖥osel.com.cy), Lemesos (☎77778121, 🖥limassolbuses.com), Larnaka (☎80007744, 🖥zinonasbuses.com), Pafos (☎80005588, 🖥pafosbuses.com), Gazimağusa (☎80005200, 🖥osea.com.cy). You can also access information about Intercity Buses and airport shuttles on ☎80007789, 🖥intercity-buses.com. A very useful combined website at 🖥cyprusbybus.com pulls all the information together. **Rural buses**, especially in the Troodos Mountains, are less frequent and less reliable.

Bus services in **the north** are unreliable, don't seem to follow a timetable, will often wait until the bus is full before setting off, and are little used by visitors. Indeed, native Turkish Cypriots rarely use them either, so you're likely to find yourself sitting next to Turkish mainland settlers or Turkish army personnel. If you decide to brave this rather chaotic system, note that fares fall into the 3 and 4 range.

## By car and motorcycle

The best and most efficient way of getting around Cyprus is to **rent a car** or, if you're not put off by their poor safety record, motorcycles, quad bikes, scooters or beach buggies. Car rental starts at around €50 per day in summer, €25 per day in winter – the longer the rental period, the lower the rate – but it's worth prebooking and shopping around. And if you intend exploring the remoter parts of the island, it is well worth splashing out on a **4WD**, especially as normal rental agreements often exclude driving on dirt roads. Petrol and diesel costs around €1.40 per litre, and there are plenty of filling stations. Bear in mind, though, that some may be closed in August, so it pays to keep your tank as full as you can.

Motorways (prefix "A") and main roads (prefix "B") are of good quality, but side roads, especially in the mountains, might be unsurfaced. Visitors from the UK will feel particularly at home because driving is on the left, cars are right-hand drive, and there's a whole host of familiar street furniture, from Belisha beacons to zebra crossings. **Speed limits** (strictly enforced) are as follows: motorways max 100km/h, min 65km/h. Unless otherwise indicated, main roads have a limit of 80km/h; built-up areas 50km/h.

**Parking** is free in many villages, while town-centre car parks charge €2 to €3 for half a day. On-street parking in major towns is meter controlled, falling in the range €1–2 during office hours. Parking is free on Saturday afternoons, Sundays and public holidays.

Driving in the **north** is similar to driving in the south: cars keep to the left, signs are international, there are plenty of petrol stations, road signs are usually in kilometres, though sometimes in miles. Because development has been patchy, you might well come across bottlenecks where good new roads disgorge traffic onto narrow unimproved ones.

### Car rental in the south

Main towns and cities are well served by **rental agencies**, both local and international. Those in holiday areas like Pafos and Agia Napa offer a range of vehicles in addition to cars, such as scooters, motorcycles, quad bikes and buggies.

### SOUTH CYPRUS DISTANCE CHART (KM)

|  | Lefkosia | Lemesos | Pafos | Larnaka | Troodos Resort | Agia Napa | Polis |
|---|---|---|---|---|---|---|---|
| Lemesos | 86 | | | | | | |
| Pafos | 149 | 68 | | | | | |
| Larnaka | 45 | 71 | 139 | | | | |
| Troodos Resort | 71 | 45 | 113 | 111 | | | |
| Agia Napa | 80 | 106 | 175 | 41 | 152 | | |
| Polis | 176 | 98 | 35 | 165 | 148 | 197 | |
| Paralimni (Protaras) | 83 | 110 | 179 | 45 | 156 | 9 | 201 |

### NORTH CYPRUS DISTANCE CHART (KM)

|  | Lefkoşa | Girne | Gazimağusa | Güzelyurt |
|---|---|---|---|---|
| Girne | 26 | | | |
| Gazimağusa | 61 | 73 | | |
| Güzelyurt | 40 | 48 | 94 | |
| Dipkarpaz | 123 | 133 | 80 | 158 |

## DRIVING TIPS

Contrary to popular belief, Cypriots are usually courteous drivers. However, some drive very fast, while others, especially in rural areas, drive insanely slowly. While the fatality rate on Cyprus's roads is higher than the UK's (particularly low) figure, it still compares well with, for example, Greece and the US.

• Alcohol limits are low – 50mg of alcohol per 100ml of blood (compared with 80mg per 100ml in the UK) – and punishment for exceeding them severe. The only way to be sure of not falling foul of the law is not to drink at all if you're driving.

• Children must use restraints appropriate to their height and weight. In taxis, they can use rear-seat adult seat belts if that's all that's available. Rear-facing baby seats must not be used in front seats protected by air bags, unless the air bags have been deactivated.

• Jaywalking in towns seems to be endemic, often because the pavement is obstructed by telegraph poles, restaurant tables and chairs, eccentrically parked vehicles and so on.

• You'll often see several people crammed onto a single moped – treat them with caution.

• Donkeys (often heavily laden) and goats can be a hazard on country roads.

• Don't cross double lines to overtake.

• Don't acknowledge courtesy by holding out your hand palm outwards. This is, in Cyprus as in Greece, a very rude gesture.

• For roadside assistance call the Cyprus Automobile Association (☏ 22313233, ⓦ caa.com.cy). In case of accidents, call ☏ 112.

Drivers under 25 who have been driving for less than three years must inform the rental agency so that special under-age insurance can be provided.

If you rent a car in the south, many companies will not allow you to **cross to the north** – check when arranging the rental. Where companies do allow you to cross into the north, most will not arrange insurance – you'll need to arrange your own at the crossing point – there will be a booth where you can do this. Petsas Rent a Car (see below) will, however, arrange insurance for the north on your behalf.

### RENTAL AGENCIES IN THE SOUTH

**Alamo** ⓦ alamo.com. Larnaka and Pafos airports.
**Auto Europe** ⓦ autoeurope.com. All main towns.
**Avis** ⓦ avis.com. All main towns.

**Budget** ⓦ budget.com. Larnaka and Pafos airports.
**DriveCyprus** ⓦ drivecyprus.com. Online broker which can arrange car rental in any of the republic's main towns.
**Europcar** ⓦ europcar.com. All main towns.
**Hertz** ⓦ hertz.com. All main towns.
**Holiday Autos** ⓦ holidayautos.co.uk. All main towns.
**National** ⓦ nationalcar.com. Larnaka and Pafos airports.
**Petsas Rent a Car** ⓦ petsas.com.cy. Larnaka, Pafos and Ercan airports, and will also arrange insurance for north Cyprus.
**Rental Car Group** ⓦ rentalcargroup.com. All main towns.
**SIXT** ⓦ sixt.com. All main towns.

### Car rental in the north

Since none of the big international car rental companies covers **north Cyprus**, you're limited to local firms. However, most will deliver and pick up from your hotel, or from Ercan Airport, and some now include that service for Larnaka. Note that to rent a car in north Cyprus you must be at least 25 years old.

The TRNC Rent a Car Association produces a booklet annually with advice on renting cars in the north, and the phone numbers of about forty rental companies. Otherwise, try British Rentacar (ⓦ britishrentacar.com) or Sun Rent a Car (ⓦ sunrentacar.com).

# By taxi

In the **south** taxis are numerous in larger towns and cities and can either be hailed from the street or picked up at ranks. All **urban taxis** should have meters and fares that are controlled by the government. In rural areas taxis do not have meters, so it's as well to agree a fare before setting off. The fare structure for urban taxis is complicated: it is divided into day (6.01am–8.30pm) and night tariffs, with an initial charge (day €3.42, night €4.36) and a fare per km (day €0.73, night €0.85). There are also charges for waiting (per hour), for luggage (per item) and during public holidays. In **the north**, taxis (marked by a "Taksi" sign on the roof) do not have meters in the rural areas, so you should agree a price before getting in. Taxis are not allowed to cruise, and operate from official ranks which are closed at night. In both the south and the north you can also use **shared taxis**, which carry between four and eight passengers, between main towns. In the south (where they are also called Transurban Taxis) these operate on a fixed half-hourly timetable from 6am to 6pm (Sundays 7am to 5pm); in the north (where they are known as *dolmuşes*), they usually wait until they are full.

# By bike

Cyprus's mild climate is ideal for cyclists, though during midsummer the obvious precautions

## FIVE GREAT DRIVES

For such a small island, Cyprus offers a remarkable variety of exhilarating drives, from the ups and downs of the Troodos Massif to the off-road excitement of the Akamas Peninsula.

**Lemesos to Pafos** Take the old road B6 west from Lemesos, first through the Home Counties tidiness of the British Akrotiri base, then past the castle at Kolissi and the ancient sites at Kourion and the Sanctuary of Apollon Ylatis, to the beautiful coast at Petra tou Romiou.

**Pafos to Pano Panagia** A steep climb up from Pafos, along the E606, brings you to rolling upland vineyards, pretty villages and monasteries, and the birthplace of Archbishop Makarios III.

**The Akamas Peninsula** The empty wilderness of the Akamas Peninsula can be explored by car (though only a 4WD will do), from the Avagas Gorge in the south to Lara Bay in the middle and the Baths of Aphrodite in the north.

**Güzelyurt to Kykkos Monastery** Experience both sides of the Green Line by driving through the orange groves of Güzelyurt, along the pretty north coast past the ancient sites of Soli and Vouni, across to Kato Pyrgos then south through the dense forests of Tilliria via beautiful Cedar Valley to lofty Kykkos, Cyprus's most famous monastery.

**Lefkoşa to Girne** This north Cyprus loop takes you north from the capital through the Kyrenia Mountains to the coast and west to Girne. Diversions off this route allow you to take in Buffavento and St Hilarion castles and the superb Bellapais Abbey.

– helmet, sun cream, plenty of drinking water – should be taken. Most towns in the south have **bike rental** companies, and mountain and road bikes are readily available, with charges usually being around €50 for three days, €100 for a week. A new cycle track has recently been established in the Troodos Mountains, with nearly 60km of well-signposted surfaced and unsurfaced track. For information on cycling in Cyprus, contact the Cyprus Cycling Federation, 21 Amphipoleos Street, Lefkosia ☎22449870, ⓦcypruscycling.com. The renting of bikes in the north is less developed than in the south, but a number of hotels will be able to help arrange this.

## CROSSING THE GREEN LINE

With seven **crossing points** now open across the **Green Line** – the de facto division between the northern and southern sectors of Cyprus – visitors can stay in the south and cross to the north as often as they like. It's not yet quite as straightforward the other way around (cars rented in the north, for example, are not allowed to cross to the south), but things appear to be becoming more relaxed each year. Visitors accustomed to heavily signposted checkpoints elsewhere in the world will be surprised at how anonymous these Cypriot ones are – on both sides of the Green Line. If you're not careful, you can find yourself stumped as to how to get back, so be sure to take a note of landmarks and directions and take a map (preferably two, owing to the different place names used either side of the line). The crossing points (west to east) are:

**Limnitis/Yesilirmak** The most recent (and prettiest) crossing, in the hills above Kato Pyrgos. This represents the westernmost part of north Cyprus (apart from the militarized Kokkina Enclave). The best crossing for visiting the Palace of Vouni and Soli from the west.

**Astromeritis/Zodhia** The best crossing for Morphou/Güzelyurt from the main Lefkosia–Troodos road. Cars only.

**Agios Dometios/Metehan** The closest vehicle crossing point to Lefkosia, ideal for Kyrenia and the north coast.

**Ledra Palace, Lefkosia** Pedestrians only, just outside the Venetian walls on the western side of the city.

**Ledra Street, Lefkosia** Pedestrians only. At the top of Lefkosia's main shopping street, and therefore the best for exploring Lefkoşa.

**Pyla/Beyarmudu** Best place to cross into the north from Larnaka.

**Strovilia** The easternmost crossing point, and the most convenient for visiting Gazimağusa (Famagusta) from Agia Napa, Paralimni and Deryneia.

Four more are planned at the rime of writing this book:

Kato Pyrgos-Kokkina, Kokkina-Pachyammos, Lefka-Apliki and Deryneia.

# Accommodation

**Cyprus, north and south, has a huge choice of hotels, hotel-apartments and villas, ranging from the palatial to the cheap-and-cheerful. There is also a growing number of "agrotourism" options – village houses, barns, small public buildings adapted and renovated to provide modern comforts and facilities. However, unlike in Greece for example, the renting of rooms in the homes of local people does not feature strongly.**

## The south

All tourist accommodation in the republic is registered with, and classified by, the Cyprus Tourist Organisation (CTO), listed in their annual *Guide to Hotels and Other Tourist Establishments* (available at Ⓦ visitcyprus.com). Although attempts by the CTO to standardize accommodation have been largely successful, there is still a big gap between the best and the worst – it's always worth checking your proposed accommodation online.

In all establishments **rates** are approved by the CTO, and guaranteed for the range of dates specified. Rates should be displayed in the room or apartment, and include overnight stay, breakfast, VAT and ten-percent local taxes. Air conditioning is compulsory in three- to five-star hotels and "category A" apartments and villas in the big resorts on the coast, though not in the Troodos Mountains. There are reduced rates per person for single occupancy, and for children sleeping in parents' rooms.

## The north

Partly because of the isolation of the north since 1974, and partly because of the lack of investment caused by this, **north Cypriot hotels** can often seem old-fashioned and down at heel, particularly outside

---

### ACCOMMODATION PRICES

Accommodation prices given in this Guide are for the **cheapest double room in high season** (ie July and August). This is the "rack" rate and does not take into account discounts or "web only" deals. An up-to-date list of maximum prices agreed by the CTO is available on its website Ⓦ visitcyprus.com. Rates include service charges and VAT, and usually breakfast – if breakfast is not included, this is stated in the review. For ease of comparison, hotel prices in north Cyprus are given in euros.

---

the main tourist areas of Girne and Gazimağusa. Staff, though often friendly enough, can appear poorly trained and may speak only Turkish. However, it must be taken into account that many such hotels are aimed primarily at Turkish businessmen or gamblers while some operate as thinly disguised brothels. Therefore, families or solo female travellers can find themselves feeling uncomfortable. On the other hand, rates are generally lower than in the south.

Bear in mind also that **land ownership** in the north is still extremely controversial. Many of the north's hotels and villas, once owned by Greek Cypriots, are regarded in the south as stolen property. The Cypriot Ministry of Foreign Affairs publishes a list giving the ownership status of every hotel in the occupied north – only sixteen are considered legitimate, since they were owned by Turkish Cypriots before 1974, or are built on land owned by Turkish Cypriots (Ⓦ mfa.gov.cy/occupiedarea-properties). While this is extremely unlikely to affect the casual visitor, it is worth bearing in mind for those considering buying or leasing property in the north.

Tourist accommodation in the north is listed in the *North Cyprus Hotel Guide*, available at tourist offices and Ⓦ northcyprus.net. Though the guide offers no guarantees regarding standards or prices (it is produced by the hotel owners themselves, after all), it is a useful summary and provides helpful lists of travel agencies, taxi and car rental firms, restaurants, festivals and museums.

## Hotels and apartments

The bulk of the island's accommodation is dominated by big full-service **resort hotels** and holiday villages, concentrated in Agia Napa, Protaras, Larnaka, Lemesos and Pafos in the south and Girne and Gazimağusa in the north. Most include a choice of rooms, apartments and villas, restaurants, bars and shops, spas, sports facilities and kids' clubs, with access to private beaches. These are supplemented by apart-hotels where services are limited (though some do have swimming pools, café/restaurants and kitchen facilities). Far less common are the smaller town-centre hotels and **guest houses**, which should appeal to those who like to be in the thick of things, but they can be very noisy, are less well organized than the big establishments and, in the north especially, quality can't be assumed. In the Troodos Mountains, small hotels might be the only option. A range of private apartment rentals can also be found at Ⓦ airbnb.com.

## Self-catering villas

An increasingly popular accommodation type across the island is the **self-catering villa**, either purpose-built for the tourist trade or privately owned by those (often Brits) who wish to offset part of the cost of their place in the sun by letting it out. Lettings are usually for one or two weeks, and are often part of a package which includes flights, the services of a courier and, in some cases, the use of a car. On average, you could expect to pay €900 (one week) to €1400 (two weeks) per person with flights and car rental included, varying according to season and how many people are in the party. Sunvil Holidays (see page 24) offers perhaps the widest choice of villas on the island.

## Agrotourism

A similar sort of self-catering experience can be obtained by taking advantage of the burgeoning **agrotourism** industry, where traditional houses are modernized and rented out (see page 30). These are frequently in rural villages, and so are ideal for people who want something a bit different – peace and quiet and an insight into traditional Cypriot life. In some, guests might even be allowed to help with the harvest, or with milking the odd goat. For the full range of properties check out the excellent *Guide to Traditional Holiday Homes* published by the Cyprus Agrotourism Company (☎22340071, ⓦagrotourism.com.cy).

## Hostels and campsites

Finally, there are hostels and campsites, though their numbers are severely limited. There are official CTO-approved **campsites** at Governor's Beach, Geroskipou, Coral Bay and Polis, with two more in the Troodos Mountains, plus four **HI hostels** (ⓦhihostels.com) at Girne, Pafos, Larnaka and Protaras. However, the only hostel that can be unreservedly recommended is the forest station hostel at Stavros tis Psokas deep in the Tillirian forest. Wild camping, while not specifically illegal (except on picnic grounds), is viewed with suspicion in both north and south.

# Food and drink

**Greek-Cypriot food and drink is largely identical to Greek food. However, Cypriots themselves consider their cuisine to be far superior and point out differences, both in quality and sometimes in ingredients. So, for example, the Cypriot *koupepia* (stuffed vine leaves) contain minced meat as well as rice, whereas the Greek equivalent (dolmades) don't. That said, all the old**

### SPECIAL PLACES TO STAY

**Aunt Maria's, Lefkara** A good example of the type of renovated traditional building being increasingly provided by the agrotourism industry, in this case in one of Cyprus's most famous villages. See page 79.

**Gardens of Irini, Bellapais** Tiny guest house run by artistic expats. See page 225.

**Hostel at Stavros tis Psokas** You can't get further away from it all than the hostel in the forest station at Stavros tis Psokas in the Tillirian forest. See page 143.

**Kiniras Hotel, Ktima Pafos** Bright modern accommodation in a Venetian mansion. See page 122.

**Library Hotel, Kalavassos** Luxurious facilities contained in a nineteenth-century building. And yes, it does have its own library. See page 79.

**Linos Inn, Kakopetria** Accommodation in restored village homes in the old part of one of the Troodos Massif's most interesting villages. See page 160.

**Nostalgia, Girne** Old-fashioned (the clue's in the name) and quirky hotel in the centre of Cyprus's most beautiful town. See page 217.

**Greek favourites will be found in most restaurants on the island – moussaka, souvlakia, stifado, kléftiko, sheftalia, keftedes, goubes, godopoulo (see page 266) and above all mezé, together with dips such as tzatziki, taramasalata and humus. If you're after traditional Greek food, look out for the presence of a large domed oven at the back of the restaurant, and/or a charcoal grill or "souvla". Fish is often of good quality and freshly caught – you might well be invited to the kitchen to choose from that day's catch.**

The cuisine of north Cyprus is very similar to that of the south – after all, both communities had a shared history before 1974. The only gastronomic effect of the Turkish invasion of 1974 seems to be that international fast-food chains have been replaced by Turkish ones (the absence of McDonald's, Starbucks and their ilk is particularly noticeable). International wines and beers have been replaced by local or Turkish equivalents, and Greek brands have been replaced by Turkish ones. Ordering food in restaurants and buying it in supermarkets is getting easier as the practice of labelling in English as well as Turkish spreads.

## AGROTOURISM

Faced with the challenge of rural depopulation, Cypriots on both sides of the Green Line have come to the conclusion that one way of safeguarding their traditional lifestyles is to encourage the growth of **agrotourism**. This involves renovating attractive old buildings and farms to create atmospheric apartments, villas and small hotels, reviving rural crafts, and promoting local festivals. For more information check out the following organizations:

### SOUTH CYPRUS

**Cyprus Agrotourism Company** ☎ 22340071, �ⓦagrotourism.com.cy. Supported by the Cyprus Tourism Organization, the Cyprus Agrotourism Company handles properties across the island including Choirokoitia, Kalopanayiotis, Omodos and Arsos.

**Cyprus Villages** ☎ 24332998, ⓦcyprusvillages.com.cy. Established by a Greek Cypriot in 1987, Cyprus Villages offers apartments and villas in Tochni and the nearby villages of Kalavasos and Psematismenos.

**The Laona Foundation** Lemesos ☎ 25358632, ⓦlaona.org. The Laona Foundation promotes and supports agrotourism projects and rents villas through Sunvil Holidays.

**Skarinou Agrotourism** 7731 Skarinou, Larnaka ☎ 24322089, ⓦagrotourismincyprus.com. A small company which deals exclusively with five properties in the village of Skarinou, conveniently located close to the Larnaka–Lemesos motorway.

### NORTH CYPRUS

Though the potential benefits of agrotourism are beginning to be recognized in the north, little headway has yet been made into actual provision. For a glimpse of things to come, take a look at EcoTourism Cyprus (ⓦecotourismcyprus.com), a local association trying to develop the village of Büyükkonuk at the base of the Karpaz Peninsula, offering cheap accommodation in traditional houses, craft, art and cookery activities, and putting on such things as donkey days, outdoor fests and, in late spring, an eco-day festival.

## Cypriot specialities

Look out for **halloumi**, goat- or ewe's-milk cheese soaked in brine. Rubbery when raw, but lovely when fried or grilled, it has found its way into many Middle Eastern and Mediterranean dishes. Meat products to look out for include *lountza*, beautifully lean pork fillet, and *loukanika*, a spicy and very fatty smoked sausage; *loukanika* is something of an acquired taste – if you cook it in your apartment, you'll be able to smell it for days.

For street food, go for *tiropittes* (flaky pastry cheese pies), *spanakopittes* (similar, but with spinach), *souvlakia* wrapped in pitta bread, or corn on the cob.

For those with a **sweet tooth** there's *daktyla* (almond fried pastry), *lokmades* (fried pastry balls in syrup), *loukoumi*, known to the rest of the world (to the disgust of Greeks) as Turkish Delight, and "spoon" sweets such as preserved quince, walnut or orange. **Soutzioukos**, made of grape juice and almonds or walnuts, is supposed to be good for the libido. Cake and ice cream are also very popular – people often go out in the late evening, Italian style, just to visit *sacharoplasteia* for a wide choice of cakes, or gelato cafés for ice cream.

Cypriots love their **fruit** (fresh, dried and preserved), olives and nuts – you'll find a variety on sale in any market or greengrocers. Indeed, for visitors in self-catering accommodation, shopping in Cypriot supermarkets, specialist shops and open-air markets is a highlight of their trip.

## Breakfast and lunch

In the past, for breakfast Cypriots would help themselves to leftovers from the previous night. Today, **breakfasts** differ little from those favoured by the rest of Europe. Most hotels will offer the "continental breakfast" of croissants, bread and preserves, often supplemented with eggs, cheese and cold meats. Most will also put on a "full English", though any similarities between Cypriot and English bacon are coincidental. **Lunch** is served in most restaurants between noon and 2.30pm, and can vary from a light snack to a full meal.

## Restaurants and eating out

Except for Sundays, Cypriots prefer to take their main meal in the evening, when it's cooler. And because of the practice of having a siesta, they tend to **eat late**: restaurants rarely open before 7pm, and most customers will arrive at any time from 8pm onwards. Restaurants can get very busy in high season, especially at weekends, so it's a good idea to make a reservation. Prices vary, but allow for perhaps €50 for mezé for two, with a bottle of wine, €60 for a three-course meal with wine.

The variety of restaurants in Cyprus has increased exponentially during the last decade or two. Most popular are still the traditional **tavernas** (still the only option in many rural areas), or the slightly more formal *estiadoria*. But these have been joined by a host of restaurants offering cuisine from around the world: Italian, French, Chinese, Indian, Japanese, Thai, Lebanese, Arabic, Mexican, Russian and Armenian restaurants can all be found across the island. Fast food and "international cuisine" is ubiquitous, served up not only by the likes of Pizza Hut, McDonald's and KFC, but by local equivalents – Goody's, for example – and by the hundreds of restaurants aimed squarely at tourists (often recognizable by the photographs of the food outside). Though Cypriot restaurants are usually locally owned, a recent change has been that serving staff now often hail from Eastern Europe.

## Drink

Cyprus has a long history of **winemaking**, thanks to its period under Lusignan (originally French Crusader) rule. The bulk of its wine is produced in Lemesos and Pafos districts by four large wineries (ETKO, KEO, LOEL and SODAP). By far the most famous variety is the sweet dessert wine Commandaria, but a whole range of reds, whites and rosés, varying from very dry to very sweet, can be experienced on the six wine routes assembled by the tourist board (see page 105). Most wineries have tastings, and you can learn all you need to know about Cypriot wine at the Cyprus Wine Museum (see page 98).

For those looking for something a little stronger, the famous anise-flavoured **ouzo**, produced by distilling grape juice, is a popular aperitif, drunk neat and ice-cold, or with water and/or ice (which makes the clear liquid turn milky). Stronger still is *zivania*, distilled from grape skins and local wines (tip: if mosquito bites are keeping you awake, alternately dab *zivania* on the bites and take a swallow – you'll be asleep in no time). Cyprus has long been renowned for its inexpensive **sherry** (many British drinkers of a certain age will have cut their teeth on Cyprus sherry from the local off-licence) and its brandy.

The needs of **beer** drinkers are met by locally brewed Carlsberg and Keo, though a wide range of imported beers is available in many bars. Fruit juices in Cyprus are good value, as is the local **coffee** (call it Turkish at your peril) – it is served in tiny cups which are half-full of grounds, and you must specify the degree of sweetness when you order (*glyco* – sweet, *metrio* – medium, *sketo* – unsweetened): sugar cannot be added once it's made. Ordinary instant coffee is also widely available (called "Nes" after "Nescafé"), and a refreshing variant on a hot day is frappé, or iced coffee (check out ⓦcyprus.com/how-to-make-the-perfect-frappe.html for the lowdown on making your own).

# Festivals and public holidays

**In both north and south Cyprus there are two types of festivals and public holidays – those associated with religion or politics, and local festivals. The former are covered below, while a list of local festivals will be found in the relevant chapters in the Guide.**

## The south

Inevitably, given the importance of **Easter** in the **Greek Orthodox Church** (much more important, for example, than Christmas), a lot of the festivals relate to Easter – the run-up to it, the day itself, and its aftermath. This is why Easter flights to Cyprus can be so expensive – there'll be competition from Cypriots wanting to go home for the holiday, and it's a great

---

### SIX GREAT RESTAURANTS

**Militzis, Larnaka** Cypriot food, knowledgeable Greek-Cypriot waiters, and a setting beside the sea. See page 57.

**Aliada, Lemesos** Mixture of traditional and international food served in an atmospheric old mansion in the Old Town. See page 94.

**Mylos Restaurant, Kakopetria** Wide-ranging menu in imposing mill building overlooking one of the prettiest villages in the Troodos. See page 160.

**Yiannakos, Fikardou** Greek-Cypriot dining as it used to be in a picture-perfect restored mountain village. See page 167.

**Fanous, Lefkosia** Hotel restaurant tucked away in one of the city's narrow lanes, with Lebanese food, hookah pipes and belly dancing. See page 189.

**Tree of Idleness, Bellapais** Atmosphere in abundance. Turkish-Cypriot food on the main square, opposite floodlit Bellapais Abbey. See page 225.

## SIESTA TIME

Many Cypriots still follow the practice of taking a long lunch/**siesta break** in the middle of the day, then working well into the evening, though there are signs that the Western European/American regime of a shorter break and an earlier finish is creeping in. Summer visitors would be well advised to follow the traditional practice – divide the day into morning and evening, and have a nap during the searing heat of the afternoon.

time to visit the island, with weather that's not too hot and lots of spring flowers.

The main festivals that are celebrated across the republic are listed below.

### A FESTIVAL CALENDAR

**January 1** New Year's Day. The feast day of Agios Vassilos, New Year's Day is celebrated by the eating of a special cake called "vassilopitta" baked the previous evening, and containing a coin which confers good luck on the person who finds it in their share.

**January** Epiphany (Phota). Together with Easter, one of the biggest religious festivals in the Greek Orthodox calendar. Epiphany celebrates the baptism of Christ, and the festivities culminate on Jan 6 with the "blessing of the water" – a religious procession walks through the streets to the sea or nearest lake, a cross is ceremonially baptized by being thrown into the water, then young men dive to try to retrieve it.

**February/March** Green Monday. Green Monday (also known as "clean Monday" or "pure Monday") marks the beginning of Lent, and is celebrated across the island with outdoor music, dancing, vegetarian food and kite flying. In Lemesos the period is celebrated by a full carnival lasting a fortnight, with parades and fancy-dress parties, and much drinking and eating – meat during the first week, cheese during the second.

**April/May** Easter. The biggest event in the Greek Orthodox calendar. There are processions on the evening of Good Friday, midnight Mass on Easter Saturday, and lots of eating and drinking and games on Easter Sunday and Monday. Note that the Greek Orthodox Easter doesn't always coincide with that in the rest of Europe.

**First Sunday in May** Anthestiria. Probably with pagan roots going back to Ancient Greece, Anthestiria celebrates the arrival of Spring with parades of floats where the emphasis is on fresh flowers.

**May 1** EU Accession Day. Public holiday marking the republic's accession to the European Union in 2004.

**June** The Flood festival (Kataklysmos). A day of celebration of the Holy Spirit which takes place fifty days after the Greek Easter, Kataklysmos has a complicated relationship with the New Testament, the Old Testament (in particular the Flood, hence the name) and even Greek mythology's Aphrodite and Adonis. As with many Cypriot festivals, it is strongly related to the sea, with

religious ceremonies on the coast, concerts, boat races, swimming galas and water-throwing activities, all connected with Pentecost and the purification of both body and soul.

**August** August Village Festivals. Look out for village festivals throughout the region – live music, traditional Greek dancing and lots of food and wine.

**December 25** Christmas. Although never as important as Easter in the Greek Orthodox Church, Christmas is increasingly celebrated as in the rest of Europe with church services and feasting. Children go from door to door, singing the traditional "Kalanda" Christmas songs in return for small sums of money, and special Christmas sweets (such as *kourabiedes* and *melomakarona*) are eaten.

# The north

North Cyprus uses the same Gregorian calendar as the rest of Europe, but its main religious festivals, shared with the rest of Islam, change by approximately eleven days each year owing to the **lunar Muslim calendar**. A number of secular celebrations coincide with important dates in Turkish history.

### A FESTIVAL CALENDAR

**January 1** New Year's Day (Yilbasi). A one-day holiday similar to that in most countries.

**February/March** Mevlud (Muhammad's Birthday). A one-day break to celebrate the birth of the Prophet.

**April 23** National Sovereignty and Children's Day. A celebration of the opening of the Grand National Assembly of Turkey in Ankara in 1920, an event which marked the establishment of the modern Turkish state. Shared with Turkey.

**May 1** Labour Day. Left-wing celebration of workers, common to many countries around the world.

**May 19** Youth and Sports Day. A commemoration of Ataturk's landing in Samsun, triggering the liberation movement in Turkey. Shared with Turkey.

**July 20** Peace and Freedom Day. Marks the Turkish invasion of Cyprus, which was launched on July 20, 1974.

**August 1** TMT Day. The TMT was a Turkish-Cypriot paramilitary movement established in 1958. Its activities are remembered with folklore festivals in the bigger towns.

**August 30** Victory Day. A commemoration of the battle which ended the Turkish War of Independence in 1922. Shared with Turkey.

**September** Seker Bayrami. End of Ramazan (widely celebrated in Muslim countries as "Eid"), marked by a three-day holiday, with exchange of presents, distribution of sweets (it is sometimes known as the sugar festival) and a funfair in Lefkoşa. Most Turkish Cypriots will make some efforts to mark Ramadan by forsaking alcohol, not eating during daylight hours and praying more often. Nevertheless, disruption is minimal.

**October 29** Turkish National Day. Marks the proclamation of the Turkish Republic in 1923. Actually starts at 1pm on the day before. Shared with Turkey.

**November 15** Independence Day. Festival celebrating the declaration of the Turkish Republic of North Cyprus on this day in 1983.

**November** Kurban Bayrami. Four-day celebration to mark Abraham's willingness to sacrifice his son. Families sacrifice a sheep or chicken according to means (though this practice is beginning to die out among Turkish Cypriots).

**December 25** Christmas Day. Not formally recognized, but increasingly celebrated, especially in tourist areas.

# Sports and outdoor activities

**As in Greece and Turkey, much of the male population of Cyprus is obsessed with football. Otherwise, the most popular activities relate to the island's geography and climate, from paragliding and climbing to sailing and scuba diving, or even, for a few weeks in the year, skiing in the snow-capped Troodos Mountains.**

## Air sports

With its excellent weather and varied terrain and coast, Cyprus is ideal for flying, gliding, parachuting and wingsuiting. For general information contact the Cyprus Airsports Federation (📞 22339771, 🌐 caf. org.cy).

## Birdwatching

Cypriots have the reputation for preferring to eat rather than watch songbirds, but the former is now illegal in the south. Thanks to its position between Africa and Europe, Cyprus is visited by around 250 million birds during their great annual migrations (see page 262). Those interested in **birdwatching** in Cyprus should contact BirdLife Cyprus (📞 22455072, 🌐 birdlifecyprus.org).

## Climbing and hiking

Popular sites for **rock climbing**/bouldering include Eagle Rock and the Chassamboulia rock in Pafos District and Cave Greko near Agia Napa. For detailed information on climbing, contact the Cyprus Mountaineering and Sport Climbing Federation (📞 97770067).

For **hiking** there are numerous marked trails in the Troodos Mountains (see page 150). A section of the European Long Distance Path E4 travels for 539km the length of the island, and there is 322km of good

walking divided into 72 nature trails. An excellent booklet on the E4 Long Distance Path and the nature trails is available in CTO offices in Cyprus and abroad, as are trail guides produced by the Ministry of Agriculture's Department of Forests. The best general walking in the north is in the Kyrenia range and along the Karpaz Peninsula – look out for the tourist office's excellent trail guides *Kyrenia East and West* and *Karpaz East and West*.

## Cycling

**Cycling** has been enjoying a huge boost in popularity in Cyprus, both with amateur hobbyists and professionals. Cycling is a year-round activity, but conditions are best in spring and autumn. Mountain and road bikes can be rented in all main towns and holiday areas (guide rental €10–20/day). For further information look out for *Troodos Cycling Routes* map available in tourist offices, contact the Cyprus Cycling Federation (see page 27) or check out 🌐 bikincyprusadventures.com.

## Fishing

**Fishing**, both in the sea and in freshwater (the latter primarily in reservoirs), is popular in Cyprus. The main source of information regarding angling in the south is the Department of Fisheries and Marine Research (📞 22807807, 🌐 moa.gov.cy/dfmr), who publish a booklet on the subject. In the north look out for sea-fishing trips from the most popular harbours (for example, 🌐 fishingnorthcyprus.com, from Girne). It is possible to get permission to fish in reservoirs, but is probably not worth the effort.

## Football

**Football** is strongly supported across the island. The Cyprus Football Association (🌐 cfa.com.cy) runs a full league of four divisions with fourteen clubs in each, and there are three-cup tournaments. Admission prices are a fraction of what UK league teams charge, and tickets can be bought at the ground, on the day. Despite being relative minnows, Cypriot clubs have reached the group stage of the Champions League a few times in recent years, and in 2012 Lefkosia's Apoel became the first to reach the quarter finals.

## Golf

There are four main **golf courses** in southern Cyprus, three in Pafos District, and one in Lemesos, with another, just outside Larnaka, planned. For a

---

**TOP 5 NATIONAL PARKS**

Cyprus has numerous **national parks** and **nature reserves**, which can range from fairly small semi-urban parks with picnic areas, children's playgrounds and a few paths, to large areas of countryside with extensive marked trails.

**Troodos National Forest Park** Covering 22,600 acres of the Troodos Mountains, this is Cyprus's most visited national park, with four separate nature reserves, nine picnic sites, three campsites and ten nature trails covering over 57km.

**Akamas Peninsula** In Cyprus's northwest corner, the Akamas Peninsula is one of the island's most remote areas, which can be accessed only on foot or via mountain bike, trail bike or 4WD. Once dominated by a British Army firing range, it is now something of a haven for wildlife.

**Petra tou Romiou National Forest Park** Home to one of Cyprus's most photogenic beaches, said to be the birthplace of Aphrodite, the Petra tou Romiou National Forest Park covers 860 acres of woodland and coast 10km outside Pafos.

**Macheras National Forest Park** This is the Troodos Park's little brother, covering 111,000 acres at the eastern end of the Troodos range, and notable for being empty, unspoilt and heavily forested.

**Karpaz Peninsula** North Cyprus has just one national park: the Karpaz Peninsula, the long tapering strip of land that heads northeast towards Asia Minor. Around 80km long but just 20km wide at the base, it has a very low population density (though its roads are manageable), and is famously home to feral donkeys.

---

summary, see Ⓦcyprus-golf-courses.co.uk. In north Cyprus, there are two.

## Horseriding

There are numerous **horseriding** stables in Cyprus, and many offer holiday packages – look out for literature in the CTO office or your hotel. Two of the best are Ride in Cyprus (Ⓦrideincyprus.com), based just outside Pafos, and Drapia Farm in Kalavasos (book through Ⓦcyprusvillages.com).

## Skiing

Though it might seem unlikely, from January to March there's usually enough snow on Cyprus's highest peak, Mount Olympos, to allow **skiing**. The Cyprus Ski Club operates a ski centre on the mountain with four ski lifts serving three slopes: a chairlift on Zeus slope, and T-bar lifts on Hera, Aphrodite and Hermes slopes. For further information, contact the Cyprus Ski Club (Ⓣ22449837, Ⓦcyprusski.com).

## Tennis

There are hundreds of **tennis courts** across Cyprus run by the municipalities as well as many hotel courts. Most have all-weather surfaces and are floodlit. There are numerous local tennis and beach tennis tournaments, and, during the winter, the Cyprus Masters Cup and Aldiana Seniors Open tournament. Cyprus also plays in the Davis Cup. For further information, contact the Cyprus Tennis Federation (Ⓣ22449860, Ⓦcyprustennis.com).

## Water sports and diving

The main coastal holiday areas, in both north and south, all offer the full range of **water sports**, either through centres on or near the beach, or through the big hotels. **Dive schools** in both the south and the north offer accredited courses. Among the numerous recognized dive sites are the wrecks of the *Vera K* and the *Achilleas* off Pafos and the wrecks of HMS *Cricket*, a British army helicopter and, most famously, the *Zenobia* (see page 56) off Larnaka. For scuba diving, contact the Cyprus Federation of Underwater Activities (Ⓣ22754647, Ⓦcfua.org). **Sailing** is widely catered for, either within the island or visiting – there are many ports, marinas and fishing shelters from which to choose. For charters, try Cyprus Yacht Club (Ⓣ70002677, Ⓦcyprusyachtclub.com) in Limassol, Cypus Yacht Charter (Ⓣ24665408, Ⓦcyprusyachts.com) in Larnaka or Cyprus Yacht Charters (Ⓣ26910200, Ⓦcyprusyachtcharters.com) in Pafos.

# Culture and etiquette

**While Greek-Cypriot and Turkish-Cypriot communities shared a long history up to 1974, they are divided by culture, language and, above all, religion. Since 1974 and the de facto division of the island, these differences have become more entrenched, with both sides embittered by the island's history between the**

**1950s and 1970s, and more generally with the south looking back to the heritage of the ancient Greeks and the north to that of Turkey and the Ottoman Empire. Politics aside, a few generalizations can be made about the culture and etiquette that you'll experience across the island.**

After its accession to the EU, Cypriot **standards of living** in the south shot up. At the same time, north Cyprus had the air of a land left behind, compounded after the turn of the millennium by economic problems imported from mainland Turkey. Since the 2008 crash, as in much of the Western world, attitudes in the south to the future have become distinctly gloomy, with a pessimism boosted by dire economic forecasts, lack of progress on the "Cyprus Problem" and the disastrous 2011 Evangelos Florakis Naval Base explosion. However, the Cypriots are nothing if not resilient, and a more optimistic outlook has been noticeable in the last few years.

## Family life

Cypriot society revolves around **family life**, and it is still common for families to eat together, either at home or in a restaurant, especially on Sundays. It is quite common, at the beach or at picnic areas, to see several cars disgorge extended families, including the elderly, teenagers and children, who proceed to set up barbecues, play music on portable sound systems and settle in for the day.

There is widespread respect for the elderly, consideration for pregnant women, and indulgence towards children. Pregnant women are particularly well looked after (partly because of an old wives' tale that if they don't get what they fancy to eat, the child will be birthmarked accordingly). When Cypriots ask about your children or grandchildren, they're not just being polite, they really want to know, so tell them, and ask back.

Although things are changing in the towns, attitudes towards gender in rural villages can still seem relatively unenlightened, with women taking the traditional home-making, child-rearing role and men going to work or sitting in the *kafenío*, drinking coffee, reading the papers or playing *tavli*.

## Social life and etiquette

It is quite common for Cypriots who have only just met strangers to invite them into their homes for a drink (always accompanied by a little something to eat) or even for a full meal. Sometimes this **hospitality** and genuine interest in others can seem a trifle intrusive – expect to be cross-examined about your family relationships, your profession, even the details of your income. Cypriots are also lively conversationalists. What may to an outsider sound like a furious argument might well be a perfectly amicable conversation.

Despite the tribulations of the fight for independence in the 1950s and the perceived involvement of the UK and the US in the events of 1974, Cypriots seem to bear no ill-will towards British or American visitors. Many seem to have a high regard for them and have close friends or family in the UK and the US. However, the 1974 invasion and the whole gamut of problems it has caused are best avoided as a topic of conversation unless raised by Cypriots themselves.

Though young people in Cyprus party as hard as those of any other country, older Cypriots still tend to be socially conservative. Topless sunbathing is frowned upon in any but designated naturist areas, and you are expected to cover up when you come off the beach.

## Religion

In the south, the **Greek Orthodox Church**, its buildings and its clergy, are widely revered, and the church in general and local priests in particular wield considerable political and social clout. Church attendance is high, and Sunday visits to churches and monasteries are a popular day out. In the north, although the population is Muslim, the level of observance is not high – you'll rarely hear a call to prayer, the Western Saturday/Sunday weekend is followed rather than the more usual Friday/Saturday, and there are no problems in getting hold of alcohol.

**Dress codes** in churches, monasteries and mosques are strictly enforced – long trousers and no bare chests for men, covered legs and shoulders for women (and also in mosques, covered heads for women and shoes off for all).

## LGBTQ

Attitudes to **gay people** can display prejudice. Gay clubs do exist in large towns such as Lefkosia, Larnaka, Agia Napa, Lemesos and Pafos, and these are tolerated, but openly gay public behaviour might attract disapproving frowns and the clicking of tongues.

## Racism

Racial stereotyping and racist behaviour, except between Greeks and Turks, have not until recently been a problem, though the huge influx of outsiders, particularly non-EU workers who tend to do unskilled domestic and agricultural labour, has led to anti-immigration rhetoric from far-right groups and isolated outbreaks of violence.

# Travel essentials

## Addresses

**Addresses** in the **south** use the same basic pattern as you'll find in the UK: after the name of the person or business, there's a street number and name (usually in that order but, if in Greek, sometimes reversed). This is followed by a four-digit postcode and a region. The first digit of the postcode tells you the region – 1 or 2: Lefkosia District; 3 or 4: Lemesos District; 5: Ammochostos District (also sometimes called "Free Famagusta" and included in this book with Larnaka District); 6 or 7: Larnaka District; 8: Pafos District and 9: Kyrenia District.

Addresses in the **north** are often given in English as well as Turkish, and therefore are easy to understand. As they are sometimes given only in Turkish, it's useful to know some of the more common words you're likely to come across – Avenue: Caddesi (abbreviated to Cad); Cul-de-Sac: Cikmazi (abbreviated to Cik); Boulevard: Bulvan (abbreviated to Bul); Square: Meydani (abbreviated to Meyd); and Street: Sokak (abbreviated to Sok, or even SK).

## Costs

Many visitors to Cyprus have prepaid for almost everything before they arrive – flights, accommodation, car rental, trips, even, in many cases, meals. For independent travellers, it should be possible to get by on €75 per day (though €100 is more realistic) during high season, less in the winter. It does, of course, depend on what activities you take part in, and how you travel around. Typical costs might include breakfast (continental) €4–6; fixed-menu lunch €12–15; dinner (mezé, inc drink) €22; single bus ticket €1.50; glass of beer €3–5; cinema ticket €7; theatre/concert ticket €25–35.

VAT and local taxes are included though non-EU residents can have VAT refunded on certain goods.

In the north costs are lower for goods imported from Turkey, higher for goods imported from the rest of the world.

When **tipping**, in most situations, a service charge of **ten percent** is already added to the bill, and all that is required is that when paying you round up to the nearest euro. If there is no service charge, than add ten percent yourself.

## Crime and personal safety

Despite a recent spike in the crime rate, Cyprus is still a relatively safe place for visitors. There's not much in the way of burglary or theft, and you're unlikely to see violence on the streets (except, perhaps, that caused by drunken visitors in places like Agia Napa). However, organized crime, especially from Russia in the south and Turkey in the north, has made inroads, and there is now a considerable amount of vice and prostitution. This is confined to bars, clubs and "cabarets" in clearly defined parts of the larger towns, particularly Lemesos, and as long as these areas are avoided there should be no problem. Women on their own can find themselves the subject of unwanted male attention, but Cypriot males are far less persistent than those in some other Mediterranean countries.

A brush with the law rather than criminals is a far more likely scenario. **Speed limits** are strictly enforced, and driving with above the (low) permitted levels of alcohol in blood or breath carries severe penalties. Be cautious around **military areas**. Where access is denied to civilians, stay away and take "No Photography" signs seriously.

## Electricity

**Electricity** supply across the island is 230 volts supplied through 13 amp, three-square-pin plugs. Brits therefore need no adaptors, and can use equipment that they use at home. Others will need adaptors, and though they're readily available, it makes sense to bring your own.

## Entry requirements

All that is needed by most foreign nationals to enter north or south Cyprus is a **valid passport**. There are no restrictions on length of stay for EU nationals in the south; in the north they can stay for up to three months. Nationals of the US, Canada, Australia, New Zealand and Singapore can stay in the south or north for up to three months without a visa. The main complication likely to face visitors is if they want to cross into or out of Turkish-occupied north Cyprus. The republic's position is still that anybody **entering the north** through what they consider illegal ports or airports, or staying in hotels in the north that were

---

### EMERGENCIES

The emergency telephone number for Ambulance, Fire and Police is ☎112.

## ROUGH GUIDES TRAVEL INSURANCE

Rough Guides has teamed up with WorldNomads.com to offer great **travel insurance** deals. Policies are available to residents of over 150 countries, with cover for a wide range of adventure sports, 24hr emergency assistance, high levels of medical and evacuation cover and a stream of travel safety information. Roughguides.com users can take advantage of their policies online 24/7, from anywhere in the world – even if you're already travelling. And since plans often change when you're on the road, you can extend your policy and even claim online. Roughguides.com users who buy travel insurance with WorldNomads.com can also leave a positive footprint and donate to a community development project. For more information, go to ⓦroughguides.com/shop.

owned by Greek Cypriots, might face legal sanctions, though the reality is that this is extremely unlikely. Visitors can cross from south to north Cyprus at any of the (currently seven) official crossing points (see page 27). If using a car rented in the south, a separate insurance policy will be needed for the north (see page 26).

## Health

The main medical inconveniences are likely to be from sunstroke, insect bites, and the odd sting from a jellyfish. All General Hospitals (found in most major towns), and some private ones, have Accident and Emergency Departments, which provide free emergency treatment to all. More routine treatment may have to be paid for so **travel insurance** is recommended. That said, EU citizens may be able to receive free or reduced-cost treatment in the republic on presentation of a European Health Insurance Card. In the north, all visitors are entitled to free emergency medical treatment, but beyond that it must be paid for, so, again, private insurance is strongly recommended. Pharmacies, ubiquitous throughout the island, can help with common minor complaints and ailments. A good source of information is ⓦdh.gov.uk/travellers. Tap **water** in Cyprus is safe to drink, and doesn't have any noticeable chemical taste. Bottled water is cheap.

## Insurance

**Travel insurance** covering medical expenses, personal property, third-party liability and cancellation is recommended. If you intend to try any dangerous or extreme sports, you should check to see whether they're covered, and if not, extend the cover accordingly. Bear in mind that some credit cards carry complimentary insurance. If you have anything stolen, report it to the police in order to get a crime or ID number for inclusion in your claim.

## Internet

In the **south**, free internet access is widely available. Most hotels now offer guests at the very least a dedicated machine, more commonly **wi-fi** in a restricted part of the hotel (bar or foyer), and increasingly wi-fi throughout. Some cafés, restaurants and bars also offer free wi-fi. If you can't find a wi-fi signal you may need to visit an internet café, found in most major towns (and usually packed with teenagers). Though lagging behind the south, wi-fi is becoming more common in tourist areas in **north** Cyprus.

## Laundry

Most large hotels offer **laundry services**, or are happy to arrange them through reception. Dry-cleaners will be found in town centres, with normal turnaround being two days – ask for a fast premium service if that's too long. There are also launderettes (laundromats) in the main towns.

## Mail

The Cypriot **postal system** is relatively reliable. Postcards sent home do arrive, though it can take a week or more. Stamps can be bought at newsagents, which is fine if it's for a standard item like a postcard, but anything more complicated should be paid for at a post office. In the south **district post offices** are open from Monday to Friday 8am–5.30pm; all others are open 8am–2.30pm. Some offices which deal only with parcel post have the same morning hours, but are closed in the afternoons except Wednesday. In the north post offices are open from Monday to Friday 7.30am–2pm and 4–6pm, and Saturday 8.30am–12.30pm, with later opening and earlier closing in winter. When writing to north Cyprus, the destination, significantly, is "Mersin 10 Turkey" not "North Cyprus" – this is to circumvent an international postal union boycott.

## Maps

The CTO produces a range of excellent free **maps** – one of the whole island (*A Visitor's Map of Cyprus*) and separate ones for Agia Napa, Larnaka, Lemesos, Pafos, the Troodos Mountains and Lefkosia which include useful area and town-centre maps. These are in the process of being updated – check the date given in the bottom left-hand corner of the map. There are also special-interest maps such as the *Rother Walking Guide Cyprus – South and North*, and *Cyprus: Car Tours and Walks* in the "Landscapes" series. In the north, the Office of Tourism Promotion and Marketing produces a good general tourist map on which are marked bathing beaches, water sports, sailing, petrol stations and a lot more, together with street maps for all the main towns and some excellent walking maps.

## Measurements

The Republic of Cyprus uses the **metric system**. Distances are in kilometres, areas in square kilometres or hectares, petrol is sold by the litre, weights are in grams and kilos, speed is in kilometres per hour (km/h). In the north the situation is more complicated, with some distance markers in miles and survivals from Ottoman times such as the "okke" (just over a kilo) often used for selling fruit and vegetables.

## Money

In the south, the currency is the **euro** (€), and it is very easy to access your money – there are numerous banks and ATMs, so much so that travellers' cheques are an endangered species. Credit cards are widely accepted. Banking hours are May–Sept Mon–Fri 8.15am–1.30pm; Oct–April Mon 8.30am–1.30pm & 3.15–4.45pm, Tues–Fri 8.30am–1.30pm. There are 24-hour exchange facilities at Larnaka and Pafos airports, and in Lemesos port. In the north, the **Turkish Lira** (₺) is the official currency, though euros, pounds sterling and US dollars are widely accepted. Prices for north Cyprus in this Guide are given in euros for accommodation and Turkish Lira for restaurants, museum admission and other fees.

## Museums, archeological sites and places of worship

Most regional **museums** in the south are open every weekday morning from 8am, with closing times varying from 2.30pm to 5pm. At weekends, many museums are closed, though some open on Saturdays from 9am (usually to 3pm). The most important variation is the Cyprus Museum in Lefkosia, which is open on Sundays from 10am to 1pm, but closed on Mondays. For up-to-date information on opening hours, check ⓦmcw.gov.cy. Museum opening times in the north are similar, though sometimes with additional afternoon hours on Thursdays.

**Archeological sites** usually open daily at 8am, with closing hours varying according to season, from 5pm in winter to 7.30pm in summer. There is an almost universal admission charge for museums and archeological sites of €2.50 (though some of the most popular – the Cyprus Museum, for example, or the Pafos mosaics – are €4.50). In the north, the charge is usually around €7, though more for the more famous sites such as Girne Castle, Bellapais Abbey and Salamis.

**Churches and mosques** tend to be kept locked, with those who wish to visit needing to find the keyholder. However, the more heavily visited sites will often have a custodian hovering around. There are no fixed entrance charges, though all welcome donations. In both churches and mosques, modest dress is insisted upon for both men and women (see page 35).

## Newspapers

Most of the major UK and US **newspapers** can be bought in Cypriot newsagents, at the foreign issue cover price, though a day late. The emphasis tends to be on UK tabloids such as the *Daily Mail* and *Express*. There are two Cypriot newspapers published in English in the south: the *Cyprus Weekly* (online only ⓦin-cyprus.com) and the excellent *Cyprus Mail* (Tues–Sun; ⓦcyprus-mail.com), while in the north *Hurriyet Daily News* (ⓦhurriyetdailynews.com) and the weekly *Cyprus Today* (ⓦcyprustodayonline.com) are in English.

## Opening hours and public holidays

In the south, shop **opening hours** vary depending on season, type of shop and location, but are usually within the range 7am–9pm, with early closing likely to be on Wednesdays and Saturdays. Most shops are closed on Sundays. Closing times are quite late. During the holiday season, and in holiday areas, the types of shops that tourists are most likely to use can be open for enormously long hours. The main **public holidays**, when banks and shops are usually closed, are as listed in the Festivals and Public Holidays section (see page 31). In north Cyprus opening hours are continuous from 8am–5pm in winter, but in summer shops close during the heat of the day, and so are open 8am–2pm and 4–6pm.

## PLACE NAMES IN CYPRUS

Although Cyprus's history of successive occupations by foreign powers and complicated recent political history gives the island a variety of interest and depth of cultural identity, one of the less useful results has been a total confusion as to **place names**. Lusignans, Venetians, Ottomans and British all modified the original Greek names as well as imposing their own, while in the north, the 1974 Turkish occupation was followed by the wholesale replacement of Greek place names by Turkish ones. As a result, if you are visiting the north from the south, you really do need maps which show the post-1974 place names. For this practical reason, in this guide the post-1974 names are used – it does not imply any endorsement of the Turkish occupation or of the new names. Furthermore, the original names are widely used by Turkish Cypriots themselves in the north, and in these cases the original name will be included in brackets when first used, and when referring to pre-1974 events.

As if this weren't complicated enough, in 1994 the south introduced its own changes, with the replacement of place names considered to have been imposed by imperialist rulers with names deemed to have a purer, more Greek, ancestry. In some cases completely new names were introduced ("Lefkosia" for Nicosia, "Lemesos" for Limassol), or spellings were modified ("Larnaca" becoming Larnaka, "Paphos" becoming Pafos). These changes were not without controversy, and many Greek Cypriots in the south persist in using the old names – they even continue to be widely used on road signs. In this guide, the new names (as they appear on official CTO maps) are used, but with the old name in brackets on first use, or when referring to historical events.

## Phones

There are two types of **public phones** – coin operated, and card operated. Cards for the latter are available from banks, post offices, kiosks and some shops. To phone within Cyprus, simply dial the eight-digit number (in the south) or seven-digit number (in the north) used throughout this Guide. In the north, public phones are not common, but can usually be found in or around the local post office; all are card operated, with cards on sale from the post office or some kiosks.

For mobile phones, depending on the provider the codes are 0533 or 0542. If calling a mobile in north Cyprus from outside the island, 0090 needs to be dialled, followed by the mobile number (without the initial 0). If you're already in north Cyprus there's no need to dial 0090.

If you are intending to use your **mobile phone**, consult with your provider as to roaming arrangements and costs. It is often cheaper to buy a local SIM card if you are planning to make calls within Cyprus (though you may need to get your phone "unlocked" at a specialist phone shop – a widely available service in the south, but confined to Girne and Lefkoşa in the north).

## Photography

Photography is prohibited within **military areas** in both the south and the north, and this is strictly enforced. Many monasteries, churches and museums also ban photography, partly because of the intrusive nature of flash, but also because it can harm delicate paintings, artefacts and fabrics.

## Shopping

Serious shopping for Cypriots is dominated by the malls and boutiques of **Lefkosia** (South Nicosia; see page 189), which far outrank anything on offer in Larnaka, Lemesos and Pafos. Nevertheless, you'll find the usual souvenirs – leather goods, especially bags, belts and shoes, ceramics, copper, silver and gold jewellery, woven basketwork, embroidery and lace – in resorts across the island. Wines and spirits, *loukoumi* (aka Turkish Delight), various Cypriot sweets, nuts and olives, also make good-value **gifts**. Non-EU residents can claim VAT back on items carried home in their hand luggage as long as the overall value is €50 or more – shop where there's a **tax-free shopping** sign, ask for a tax-free receipt and get this stamped by customs officials as you leave Cyprus. When crossing the Green Line north to south, you are restricted to 40 cigarettes, 1 litre of alcoholic beverage and no more than €260 worth of other goods. And take this restriction seriously – border staff often carry out spot checks on cars passing through the crossing points.

Cyprus has good open-air and covered markets which are worth visiting for both atmosphere and purchases, and large towns also have American-style shopping malls.

**Haggling** isn't really a part of the Cypriot culture (north or south), and you will usually be expected to pay the marked price. However, it might be worth

## MAKING INTERNATIONAL CALLS

Note that the initial zero is omitted from the area code when dialling the UK, Ireland, Australia and New Zealand from abroad.

**Australia** + 61
**New Zealand** + 64
**UK** + 44
**US and Canada** + 1
**Ireland** + 353
**South Africa** + 27

To call the **Republic of Cyprus** from abroad, dial 00357 followed by the 8-digit number; for **north Cyprus** dial 0090, followed by 392 and the 7-digit local number.

trying to get the price down when chancing on a hotel off the street, or when renting a car. Souvenirs, too, might be subject to haggling if prices are not marked. Even then, reductions are likely to be relatively modest.

## Time

Cyprus is two hours ahead of GMT, seven hours ahead of EST. Daylight Saving Time starts at 1am GMT on the last Sunday of March, when clocks go forward by 1 hour (ie GMT +3), and ends with a return to Standard Time at 1am GMT on the last Sunday in October. Cyprus is therefore usually two hours ahead of the UK.

## Toilets

**Public toilets** are uncommon, though where they exist they are usually free, and are well kept. Otherwise, most convenient are toilets in bars, restaurants, cafés and hotels. If you're not a customer, it's polite to make a small purchase, or to ask permission and leave a tip.

## Tourist information

The major source of information about the Republic of Cyprus is the **Cyprus Tourism Organisation** (CTO; Ⓦvisitcyprus.com). Click on "about us" at the top of the home page for a list of offices in Cyprus and abroad. The CTO produces a variety of extremely useful maps and pamphlets, and the invaluable *Travellers Handbook*. It's also worth checking out the regional tourist board websites, including Ⓦlimassol-tourism.com, Ⓦlarnakaregion.com, Ⓦvisitpafos.org. cy and Ⓦagianapa.org.cy.

For north Cyprus, three publications are particularly useful: *The North Cyprus Tourist Guide*, available from tourist offices and online at Ⓦnorthcyprusonline. com; the *North Cyprus Hotel Guide*; produced by the North Cyprus Hoteliers Association KITOB; and the *Restaurant Guide of Northern Cyprus*, produced by the Cyprus Turkish Restaurateurs Association (Ⓦresbir. net). All are well produced and informative, if rather dominated by adverts and sponsorship. Other useful websites include Ⓦnorthcyprus.net, Ⓦturkishcyprus. com, Ⓦnortherncyprus.com and Ⓦwelcometonorth-cyprus.co.uk.

## Travellers with disabilities

Provision for **disabled visitors** in Cyprus is patchy, though it's better in the south than in the north. The old towns of many resorts have winding, cobbled streets to negotiate and lots of steps. Some ancient sites are also difficult – check the Department of Antiquities website (Ⓦsmcw.gov.cy), which gives detailed accessibility information for all monuments, sites and museums. Otherwise check out expat site Ⓦcyprus.angloinfo.com, which has a useful section for people with disabilities. For a tour company which specializes in disabled access holidays, try Accessible Cyprus (Ⓣ26941528, Ⓦaccessibleholidayscyprus. com).

## Travelling with children

Cyprus is a great destination for **families**, as Cypriot culture is so child-friendly. You'll find your own children smiled at, tickled under the chin and otherwise bathed in approval. You'll even get Cypriot teenagers making a fuss of babies – not something you often see in Anglo-Saxon cultures.

All the paraphernalia of **baby care** – baby food, nappies/diapers, creams, powders and medication – are available in pharmacies and supermarkets, in international as well as local brands. Discreet breast-feeding is accepted. High chairs and books/toys in restaurants are increasingly available. Large hotels usually have a wide range of child-friendly services – kids' clubs, amusement arcades, playgrounds and so on – as well as baby-sitting services.

## TV and radio

The two main **radio stations** with English-language programmes are CyBC Radio 2 (Ⓦcybc.com.cy, on 91.1FM) in the south and Bayrak (Ⓦbrtk.net, on 87.8 and 105FM) in the north, together with numerous commercial stations, all on FM. English-language

## TOP 5 CHILDREN'S ATTRACTIONS

**Aphrodite Water Park, Pafos** Not as much fun as the water park in Agia Napa, but still worth a day out with the kids. See page 121.

**Fig Tree Bay, Protaras** With beautiful sand, safe bathing, shops, showers, cafés, water sports and everything else that Cypriots deem necessary for a day at the beach, you can't beat Fig Tree Bay. See page 68.

**Pafos Zoo** Clean, well laid out, with clear explanations, Pafos Zoo is particularly strong on birds and reptiles, though does also have a range of the bigger beasts. See page 132.

Fasouri Water Mania, Lemesos Accessible from all main hotels via shuttlebus, this park offers enough rides and attractions to fill an entire day. See page 91

**Waterworld Waterpark, Agia Napa** One of Europe's biggest water parks, with delightfully tongue-in-cheek Ancient Greek themes. See page 61.

speakers might also try British Forces Broadcasting Services in Lefkosia (89.7FM), west Cyprus (92.1FM), east Cyprus (99.6FM), the BBC World Service (1323AM), and Voice of America (0100–0130kHz). CyBC also run the principal **TV stations** in the south (1 and 2), and in the north provision is by Kibris TV and BRT2. In the south, people also tune in to Greek TV, as in the north they do to Turkish TV. Most hotels and many apartments and villas have major US and UK digital channels.

# Larnaka
# and around

FIG TREE BAY

# 1 Larnaka and around

Of Cyprus's six districts, the one centred on Larnaka is probably perceived as the least glamorous. Yet it offers one of the best combinations of attractions, beaches, hotels and restaurants. An ideal mix of working town and holiday resort, Larnaka itself has enough day-to-day reality to provide insights into Cypriot life yet enough sights and activities to keep boredom at bay, including an impressive cathedral, a medieval fort and the wonderful Hala Sultan Tekke mosque. It also boasts the island's largest airport and a flourishing marina and therefore attracts a cosmopolitan bunch of expats, entrepreneurs and yachting folk as well as soldiers and diplomats working at the nearby British base at Dhekelia.

To the east of Larnaka is the peninsula upon which stand **Agia Napa**, **Protaras** and **Paralimni**, journey's end for thousands of visitors. Long derided as the haunt of lager louts and marauding squaddies, these settlements have left behind their growing pains and are now largely well-maintained and prosperous towns, devoted to the holiday industry it's true, but none the worse for that. They have plenty of places to stay and to eat, some fine museums, a string of Blue Flag beaches and pretty boat-thronged harbours, plus a scattering of small villages (the **Kokkinochoria**) dotted with the sails of wind pumps.

To the west of Larnaka is an unspoilt rural hinterland of hill villages and small harbours where the pace of life is blissfully slow – driving west from Larnaka on local roads, you'll notice the difference as soon as you pass the airport. This area includes two important **Neolithic sites** at Tenta and Choirokoitia, the world-famous lace-making village of **Pano Lefkara**, and the impressively sited monastery at **Stavrovouni**. It is also where, in 2011, a catastrophic **explosion** ripped apart the Evangelos Florakis naval base (see page 73). The physical damage was repaired with commendable speed, but the effect on political feeling and morale has proved longer-lasting.

## Brief history

The earliest traces of civilization in the Larnaka region are the remains of two Neolithic villages at Tenta and Choirokoitia (see page 74), which date from around 7000 BC. The history of the town itself stretches over 3000 years, having been founded in the late Bronze Age as **Kittim** (aka Cittium). Very early on, it was settled by the **Mycenaeans**, as part of their great outward expansion from mainland Greece. In the tenth century BC it became a ruin, probably as a result of earthquake followed by invasion but, from about 850 BC, the town (now Kition) was developed as a copper-exporting port by the **Phoenicians**. The period of the wars between Greece and Persia was another difficult one for Larnaka – the city initially did very well by supporting the Persians, and in 450 BC successfully held out against the army of the famous general **Kimon**, who had arrived to try to add Cyprus to the Athenian empire. Kimon died during the siege of Larnaka – his marble bust stands on the promenade in the town – but the Greeks finally defeated Persia during the time of **Alexander the Great**, and conquered Cyprus in 323 BC.

During the following 350-plus years' rule by first **Greece** then **Rome** (during which time it became Christian under the first Bishop of Kition, Lazaros), Larnaka became little more than a minor provincial town. This humble status continued under **Byzantine rule**. The last Byzantine king of Cyprus – Komnemos – was defeated in 1191 AD at the Battle of Choirokoitia by Richard the Lionheart,

# Highlights

**❶ Foinikoudes** Larnaka's splendid palm-fringed promenade is a perfect spot to grab an iced coffee or something stronger. See page 49

**❷ Potamos Liopetriou** Two tavernas, a small beach and church, plus dozens of bobbing boats make for an idyllic combination. See page 62

**❸ Fig Tree Bay** Despite the crowds, clutter and noisy jet-skis, this is still an exquisite beach. See page 68

**❹ Cultural Centre of Occupied Famagusta, Deryneia** Food for thought on the division of the island, with views across to the ghost town of Varosha in north Cyprus. See page 70

**❺ Mazotos Camel Park** A classic family day out, plus a great restaurant. See page 72

**❻ Costas Argyrou Museum** Lovely naive artwork with a subtle sense of humour, in a crumbling building designed by the artist. See page 72

**❼ Tenta Neolithic Village** Imaginatively displayed 9000-year-old Neolithic site under a made-to-measure modern canopy – the distant past brought triumphantly to life. See page 74

**❽ Stavrovouni Monastery** Traditional Cypriot monastery which, at almost 700m, offers wonderful views (though it's off limits to women). See page 78

**HIGHLIGHTS ARE MARKED ON THE MAP ON PAGE 46**

## LARNAKA AND AROUND

### HIGHLIGHTS

1. Foinikoudes
2. Potamos Liopetriou
3. Fig Tree Bay
4. Cultural Centre of Occupied Famagusta, Deryneia
5. Mazotos Camel Park
6. Costas Argyrou Museum
7. Tenta Neolithic Village
8. Stavrovouni Monastery

Buffer zone
Limit of full northern control
Limit of full southern control

initiating, in the following year, the period of Frankish Lusignan rule across the island. From 1489 it was part of the **Venetian empire**, and suffered from the preference given by the new rulers to Famagusta and Lemesos. Kition was now called Salina (after the salt lake). From 1571 to 1878 the **Ottomans** ruled Cyprus, and at least one village in the region did very well – Lefkara. Another name-change – the final one – occurred during this time: the town became Larnaka, after the graves ("larnax" is a sarcophagus) that were found outside the town, having accumulated over its long history. Larnaka flourished during the late Ottoman period, with the town, now the main port on the island, attracting foreign consuls and merchants and their families (many of whom are buried at Agios Lazaros). Under the **British** (1878–1960), Larnaka's importance continued until it started to be eclipsed after World War II by Famagusta and Lemesos. Following the Turkish invasion in 1974, however, Larnaka became of primary importance thanks to its airport, which became the main point of entrance for visitors to the island after the closure of Nicosia International.

# Larnaka

For many visitors to Cyprus, all they see of **LARNAKA** (the old spelling "Larnaca" is still commonly used) is its blinding-white salt lake, visible as you come in to land at the airport, or glimpsed from the windows of a coach speeding off to the resorts to the east and west. This is a pity, because the city has a unique character and atmosphere worth sampling for a couple of days. It also makes an excellent base from which to explore the rest of the island, connected as it is by motorway to Pafos and Lemesos in the west, Lefkosia in the north, and Protaras and Agia Napa in the east.

Larnaka is easy to get to know. The road that follows the beach between the marina in the north and the fort in the south – **Leoforos Athinon** – has a host of hotels and restaurants along the landward side and a sunbed-and-parasol-packed beach to the seaward, lined by the stately palm trees that give the pedestrianized seashore its name – **Foinikoudes (Palm Tree) Promenade**. Many of the main sights, including the **Municipal Cultural Centre**, the ancient church of **Agios Lazaros** and the old **fort**, are a few steps away from this axis. Further west are the town's **archeological** and **natural history museums**, the site of **Ancient Kition**, the **Municipal Theatre** and the impressive old **Kamares Turkish aqueduct**. South of the fort, along **Piyale Pasa** which continues to skirt the sea, are **Skala**, the old Turkish area now dominated by craft shops, the distinct holiday area of **McKenzie Beach**, and the huge **salt lake** with its haunting, palm-shaded **Hala Sultan Tekke**.

## LARNAKA FESTIVALS

As with towns and villages across Cyprus, Larnaka loves its festivals, and the major religious festivals (see page 31) are celebrated in the town with unrivalled enthusiasm. In addition, there are several celebrations that are unique to the town.

**Procession of St Lazaros** (April) Celebration of the feast day of the town's patron saint, which involves a procession through the streets headed by the icon of the saint normally kept in the church.

**Anthestiria** (May) With pagan roots going back to ancient Greece, Anthestiria celebrates the arrival of spring with parades of floats where the emphasis is on fresh flowers, which are carried down to the seafront.

**Larnaka Summer Festival** (July) A great celebration of the arts – drama, music, dance, film and poetry – at venues across the town.

**August Village Festivals** (August) Look out for village festivals throughout the region – live music, traditional Greek dancing and lots of food and wine.

1

# LARNAKA

Ancient Kition

DHIMITRIOU DHIANELLOU
LEOFOROS ARCHIEPISKOPOU KYPRIANOU
KIKIS
DIMITRAS
LEOFOROS ARCHIEPISKOPOU MAKARIOU III

EVAGORA PALLIKARIDHI
TEFKROU
PANAGIAS CHRYSOPOLITISSAS
AGIOU SPURIDONOS
ANDREA STELIOU
EINAR GJERSTAD
KIMONOS
KOSTI PALAMA

Bus station

NIKODHIMOU MYLONA
MARKOU DHRAKOU
KYRIAKOU MATSI
KOURIOU
SOFRONIOU CHRISTODOULOU
FILIOU
TSIGARIDI

Bamboula Hill

KILKIS
Archeological Museum
KALOGRAION

Theatro Skala

KONSTANTINOU ZACHARIADI
LOUKI AKRITA
KIMONOS

DOUKAI
QUILLAM DOUKAI
LEOFOROS GRIGORI AFXENTIOU
GLADSTONOS
LORDOU VYRONOS
STASINOU
LEOFOROS GRIGORI AFXENTIOU

Municipal Cultural Centre

Larnaka Marina

Natural History Museum
NIKOU ANTONIADI
PLATEIA EVROPIS
VASILEOS PAVLOU

Municipal Gardens
LOUKI PIERIDI
STYLIANOU LENA
PARASKEVIS IOANNINA
VIKTOROS OUGKO
KONSTANTINOU KALOGERA
GALILEOU
FANOU

Pierides Museum

LEOFOROS GEORGIOU GRIVA DIGENI
VASILEOS GEORGIOU
Municipal Theatre

ASKLIPIOU
AGIAS ELENIS
STYLIANOU APOSTOLIDI

House of Arts and Literature

Armenian Monument

F. ZANNETOU
ARMENIKIS EKKLISIAS

STADIOU
KOSTAKI PANTELIDI

LEOFOROS ATHINON
ERMOU
ZINONOS KITIEOS

Foinikoudes (Palm Tree) Promenade

VASILEOS OTHONOS
DIOGENOUS
STADIOU
Kyriazis Medical Museum
AGIOU LAZAROU
LEONTIOU
NIKOLAOU LANITI
KOSMA LYSIOTI
KREMTIN KALOGERA

LEOFOROS ARTEMIDOS
AGNONIDOS
AKROLITIS

DEINARCHOU

Kamares Aqueduct & K Cineplex

LEOFOROS FANEROMENIS
Agios Lazaros & Byzantine Museum
LEOFOROS FANEROMENIS
LAIKI GEITONIA
P. VALSAMAKI

RIMINI
STALINGRAD
EL ALAMEIN
Grand Mosque
Fort & Museum

ANNIVA FRANCIS
PASTER
ONISILOU KITIEOS
APOLLONIOU KITIEOS
MEHMET ALI
HALOMER

Larnaka Bay

CHALKIDOS
IPEIROU
OKKULAR
NIKOLAOU DIMITRIOU
NIKOLAOU DIMITRIOU
PREVEZIS
ISTANBUL
OKKULAR
MENZIL
ZENKA
PITALE PASA
ERTUTUTLUS

LEOFOROS ARTEMIDOS

Patticheon Amphitheatre
KOCA TEPE
KOCA TEPE
SKALA
AK NTENIZ
TUZHANE
BOZ DAG

Salt Lake Park

OZET ALI
SAKARYA

N

0 — 200
metres

UMM HARAM
MEHMET NIYAZI
TUZHANE

## Foinikoudes (Palm Tree) promenade

Lined with hotels, cafés, restaurants and its titular palm trees, **Foinikoudes** probably shouldn't work, yet it does. Thronged with pedestrians, joggers, cyclists and mothers wheeling buggies, it radiates relaxation for both residents and holiday-makers. Try it on a Sunday evening, when it is thronged with Cypriots of all ages – family groups, children chasing after each other, flirting teenagers, old folk taking the air, as well as a fair contingent of visitors.

## Municipal Cultural Centre

Plateia Evropis • Mon–Fri 10am–1pm & 4–7pm, Sat 10am–1pm • Free • ☎ 24658848

In a row of five handsome British-era buildings – the old Customs Houses – that line the western edge of the square, the **Municipal Cultural Centre** consists of an art gallery devoted largely to Cypriot art (though it does have numerous visiting exhibitions), and the Municipal Archives (Mon–Fri 9am–2.30pm; free; ☎ 24657745), which, although likely to appeal more to local residents than visitors, does include a range of fascinating photographs of old Larnaka. The Pierides Municipal Museum of Paleontology, which used to occupy part of the building, has now been disbanded and its collections dispersed.

## Larnaka Marina

To the northeast of the square is **Larnaka Marina**, one of the largest on the island and an official port of entry to Cyprus with berths for 450 yachts. It is popular with sailors not least because of the huge choice of cafés and restaurants on its doorstep. Though the hoi polloi are not allowed in, you can still get a glimpse of how the other half live from the nearby beach, or from the substantial pier, lined with boats-for-hire, that juts out to sea beside it.

## Armenian Monument

Right next to the marina entrance is the **Armenian Monument** which commemorates the landing of Armenian refugees in Larnaka in 1915, fleeing the genocide being perpetrated by the Ottomans during World War I. Larnaka is of course no stranger to refugees – an influx followed the Turkish invasion of the island in 1974, and over a hundred Syrian refugees landed at the British Akrotiri base in 2015.

## House of Arts and Literature

Vasileos Pavlou Square • ☎ 99565184, ⓦ cornaroart.com

West of Plateia Evropis, in the old Ottoman Bank building between the Municipal Cultural Centre and the Tourist Information office, is the recently established **House of Arts and Literature**. It offers a wide range of talks, courses, shows and exhibitions in the general areas of the arts and literature – get details from the centre, or from the tourist office across the road.

## Pierides Museum

4 Zenonos Kiteos • Mon–Thurs 9am–4pm, Fri & Sat 9am–1pm • €3 • ☎ 24145375

The **Pierides Museum** (or, to give it its full, post-sponsorship title, "The Pierides Museum Bank of Cyprus Cultural Foundation") occupies the home of the eponymous Pierides family, about five minutes' walk from the Municipal Cultural Centre. Built up over five generations, the collection started with the efforts of Demetrios Pierides (1811–95) to prevent the export to Europe and America of priceless Cypriot antiquities. With its shuttered windows, veranda and upstairs gallery, flagpole,

1

elegant columns and balustrades, it looks like a Mississippi riverboat sailing down Zenonos Kiteos. Inside its shady interior, with its high ceilings, polished wood and tile floors and stately staircase (upstairs, incidentally, is out of bounds), is a wonderful collection of treasures from all over Cyprus. As you enter, the **Medieval room** on the right is succeeded by one full of **Roman glass** and then a collection of **ancient maps** of Cyprus. Taking up the whole of the left-hand side of the building, a long room covers **Greek antiquities** from Neolithic to Classical times – statues, busts, bowls, vases. So used does one become to seeing copies in tourist shops that it's hard to realize that what you can see here are the genuine article. Look out particularly for the famous "**howling man**", an amusing figure sitting on a stool, elbows on knees, head thrown back and mouth wide open – water poured into his mouth would come out of the truncated appendage between his legs. Schoolboy humour perhaps, but over 7000 years old and exquisitely executed.

## Archeological Museum

Plateia Kalograion • Mon–Fri 8am–4pm, Sat 9am–4pm • €2.50 • ☎ 24304169

Despite some key pieces being nabbed by Lefkosia's Cyprus Museum, Larnaka's **Archeological Museum** makes a fair fist of outlining the history (and prehistory) of the district through its four galleries of well-displayed, comprehensively labelled artefacts.

The **entrance hall** includes two large limestone sarcophagi with carved male and female lids, and copies of important items, which have now fetched up abroad, such as the *stele* (gravestone) of Sargon II (the original now in Berlin) and the statue of Artemis (now in Vienna). Among the highlights in the galleries are pieces taken from Choirokoitia and Tenta, including a rebuilt Neolithic tomb, numerous pieces of Mycaenean pottery, archaic terracotta figures (of a horse and rider, for example, and a man and woman in a chariot), a ceramic torch and foot warmer, and a variety of plaques and figurines from Ancient Kition (see below).

In the yard behind the museum is a collection of large **monumental sculptures** and *stellae*, a fascinating reconstructed olive press from the second century BC (they were still using the same design in the twentieth century), views over the perimeter fence across the southern part of the Kition site, and information boards about things that you can't actually see: particularly exciting have been recent finds relating to the Phoenician harbour and boat sheds dating from the fifth century BC, and the Sanctuary of Astarte from a hundred years later.

## Ancient Kition

Area II excavation, Archbishop Kyprianos Avenue • Mid-April to mid-Sept Mon–Fri 9.30am–5pm; mid-Sept to mid-April Mon–Fri 8.30am–4pm • €2.50 • ☎ 24304115

The excavation of **Ancient Kition**, as Larnaka was once known, has thrown much light on the history of the town. A great deal of the remains lie beneath the modern town, and therefore cannot be explored by archeologists. However, the acropolis (Bamboula Hill) lies immediately behind the archeological museum, and has been excavated, as have two further sites (Areas I and III), which lie just north near the church of Panagia Chrysopolitissa.

The best place to see part of Ancient Kition, though, is the **Area II excavation** just off Leontiou Machaira, about fifteen minutes' walk north of the archeological museum. Though to the untutored eye the site at first looks little more than a jumble of stones, use of the wooden access walkways to get above the ruins and careful reading of the badly sun-damaged information boards provides an emerging picture of the ancient city from its late Bronze Age origins through its development by the Phoenicians as a city and port from the ninth century BC. Identifiable ruins include five consecutive temples (culminating in the Phoenician Sanctuary of Astarte) and copper-smelting

**ZENO AND THE BIRTH OF STOICISM**

Just outside the Municipal Gardens stands a bust of the philosopher **Zeno**. Born in Larnaka around 336 BC, he became hooked on philosophy on a visit to Athens where he listened to the locals debating in the colonnaded arcade (the stoa) surrounding the market (agora). He stayed, studied and eventually taught, founding the **Stoic (from stoa) school**, which taught that the virtuous life should be lived in accordance with nature, conferring goodness and peace of mind, and that the best indication of a person's virtue was not what he said but how he lived. Stoicism's biggest cheerleaders were not Greek but Roman, in particular the emperor Marcus Aurelius and the historian Seneca who perhaps summed up the approach with "the happy life is to have a mind that is free, lofty, fearless and steadfast – a mind that is placed beyond the reach of fear, beyond the reach of desire". Zeno died in around 264 BC allegedly by the novel method of holding his breath.

works perhaps connected to the four earlier temples, dating from the thirteenth to the eleventh centuries BC.

## Cyprus Museum of Natural History

Leoforos Grigoriou Afxentiou • Mon–Fri 8.30am–1pm, free • €0.50 • ☎ 22585834, Ⓦ natmuseum.org.cy

Due west of the northern end of the promenade lie Larnaka's **Municipal Gardens**, well worth a detour not for the gardens themselves, though they're pleasant enough, but for the **Natural History Museum**. Small scale and understated, it nevertheless offers a good introduction to the flora and fauna of the region, with displays of stuffed animals and birds, and collections of insects, fossils, plants and minerals. Outside cages of live peacocks, geese and chickens provide a good distraction for kids. The dinosaur replicas are a lot of fun to look at.

Elsewhere in the park are the **Municipal Library** and **Theatre**, several small statues – look out for the bust of Zeno (see page 51) just outside the gardens – and a comprehensive children's playground.

## The fort

Leoforos Athinon • Mid-April to mid-Sept Mon–Fri 8am–5pm, Sat & Sun 9.30am–5pm; mid-Sept to mid-April Mon–Fri 8am–5pm, Sat & Sun 9.30am–5pm • €2.50 • ☎ 24304576

Once little more than a tumbledown ruin, Larnaka's **fort**, at the southern end of the promenade and separating it from Piyale Pasa and the old Turkish quarter, now provides a fine ending to the long promenade and beach. The fort was built during the reign of the Lusignan King of Cyprus, James I (1382–98 AD); it then fell into disrepair, was rebuilt by the Ottomans in the early seventeenth century, and was used as a prison by the British. Once through the Ottoman two-storey building which blocks off the end of the promenade, and past a row of medieval cannons, you'll see to the immediate right a wooden staircase leading to the fort **museum**. Though it's all a bit jumbled, broadly Room I contains displays of early Christian artefacts, Room II photographs relating to the Byzantine period, and Room III an excellent collection of fourteenth- to sixteenth-century Byzantine and Islamic glazed pottery – the greens and browns of the sgraffito ware are truly stunning. There's also a reconstructed "divan room" – the sort of place where you'd lie around puffing dubious substances in your hookah. When you go back downstairs, you'll find that the lush **gardens** (which host summer evening concerts) are worth lingering in. In the far right-hand corner a flight of steps gives access to the battlements, with fine views across the city.

For a taste of the darker side of the fort's history, take a look in the room on the left of the main gate as you leave. Here is a massive wooden beam with a pit beneath it, discovered during renovation work – the gallows used by the British for executions.

Relatives of the condemned were allowed to watch from the gardens, from where they wouldn't be able to hear the thump of the trapdoor opening. The last execution was carried out in 1945, shortly after which the police station was transferred to its current building at the north end of the promenade.

## Grand Mosque (Buyuk Camii)

Kamil Kenan Street (next to the fort) • Open at all times for worship; casual visitors are welcome outside prayer times • Free

Larnaka's **Grand Mosque** was built in the sixteenth century (though it could be argued that it stems from the 13th century when it used to be a catholic church of Santa Katerina) and has been much restored since, both during the nineteenth century and in the last few years. It's a handsome building which serves the few Muslims left in the area. Though visitors are not admitted during prayers, you might be able to get in at other times, and even climb the minaret. The grave of Seyit Elhac Mehmet Aga, who restored the mosque in 1835, lies behind the building, and those of a number of other officials are at the front.

## Agios Lazaros

Agiou Lazarou • **Church** Mon-Sat March–Oct 8am–6.30pm, Sun 6.30am-12.3pm & 3.30-6.30pm; Nov–Feb Mon-Sat 8am–12.30pm & 2.30–5.30pm, Sun 6.30am-12.30pm & 3.30-5.30pm • Donations requested • **Museum** Mon–Sat 8.15am–12.30pm & 3–5.30pm (closed Wed & Sat afternoons) • €1 • ☎ 24652498 • ⓦ en.agioslazaros.org.cy

Larnaka's cathedral, **Agios Lazaros** is just around the corner from the Grand Mosque – between them they marked the border between the Greek and Turkish Cypriot parts of town. Lazaros was one of the earliest Christians, having, famously, died and been brought back to life by Christ (see page 52) Dating from the ninth century AD when it was built to house the remains of the saint, the church has been through many changes. The southern portico was added in the eighteenth century, as was much of the internal woodwork – the iconostasis, the altar and the bishop's throne. Finally, in 1857 the belfry completed the building as it now stands.

The inside of the church has the usual Greek Orthodox sumptuousness, all carvings and gold leaf and brass – if a little muted by a fire in the 1970s. Look out in particular for the twelfth-century icon of St Lazaros, and, down some steps to the right after you've entered, the (empty) coffin of the saint himself.

In the arcade to the left of the church are a religious bookshop, an icon gallery and, in the far corner, a recently renovated and now rather splendid **Byzantine Museum**. Beautifully displayed Byzantine icons, vestments, manuscripts, books and holy

---

### LAZAROS: A MUCH-TRAVELLED CORPSE

**Lazaros** (or Lazarus in the Latinized form) was an early Christian in the Holy Land, who died, was buried (at Bethany), and, according to the Bible, was brought back to life by Christ. Orthodox tradition then suggests he fled to Cyprus (in fear for his life), where he became the first Bishop of Kition (Larnaka). Despite his holiness, Lazaros had a reputation as being something of a curmudgeon – it's said that, after his **resurrection**, he never smiled, the result presumably of the horrors he'd seen during his four days in the underworld. Local tradition also has it that he was responsible for creating **Larnaka's salt lake**, having cursed a local vineyard owner for not providing him with water. Lazaros is said to have lived for another thirty years after his resurrection before dying (this time for good). Centuries later, in 890 AD, his sarcophagus was found, marked "Lazaros the four day dead and friend of Christ". The Byzantine Emperor, Leo VI, had the holy remains transported to Constantinople, and in return had a splendid church built on the spot where they were found (now Agios Lazaros cathedral). From Constantinople, the Crusaders took the remains to Marseilles where they promptly disappeared, never to be seen again.

objects occupy five attractive old stone-floored, timber-roofed rooms on two floors – atmospheric, and what's more, air-conditioned. The illustrated guide is, at €5, well worth the money. To the right is a fascinating, and rather poignant, small **cemetery** where British and Dutch colonial administrators, merchants, missionaries and their families are buried – among them are Mary Palmer, the wife of Levant Company employee Samuel, buried with her infant daughter in 1720, and Helena Augusta Jane, daughter of the British Consul Niven Kerr, who died shortly before her first birthday in 1847. You'll also find the grave of Lorenzo Warriner Pease, an American missionary who lasted less than five years, and died at the age of 30 in 1839 – the diaries he kept between 1834 and 1839 provide a vivid picture of Cyprus and the Middle East at that time (see page 263).

## Kyriazis Medical Museum

Karaoli Demetriou • Wed & Sat 9am–noon • Free (but donations welcome) • ☎ 24626302

Occupying a beautiful old house (balcony, blue shutters, tiled hallway) in a backstreet near the cathedral, the **Kyriazis Medical Museum** offers insights into the always interesting, sometimes harrowing, medical practices of the past. Topics covered range from a tubal insufflator designed to establish whether a woman's fallopian tubes were blocked to the gynaecological operating table upon which half of the original residents (some 10,000 babies) of Larnaka were born, from the wood-shaving-filled dish used to catch amputated limbs to numerous anatomical drawings and depictions of primitive operations carried out without anaesthetic. Worth an hour's browsing, but not for the faint-hearted.

## Skala

The winding alleys and lanes of **Skala**, thahe old Turkish part of Larnaka, lie south of the fort and west of Piyale Pasa, the road (named for the Ottoman admiral who landed his army here during the invasion of 1570) that follows the shore southwards. The area retains its Turkish architecture and street names, though the Turkish Cypriot residents moved out in 1974, to be replaced by Greek-Cypriot refugees from Famagusta and the Karpaz Peninsula.

## McKenzie Beach

South of Skala, still following the coast, you come to an area which has a distinctive character – **McKenzie Beach** (sometimes Mackenzie or Makenzie). Dotted with restaurants serving traditional Cypriot food, several apartment blocks and a couple of hotels, it is also the ice-cream capital of the region, with numerous *gelato* establishments which attract hordes of locals. A particularly agreeable section is the short stretch which starts at the Fishing Shelter and runs along a serpentine wooden walkway past the *Psarolimano Restaurant* to the lifeguard tower and the golden, Blue Flag beach. A short distance beyond this a spur, left off Piyale Pasa, runs right up to the perimeter fence of the airport: close enough to smell the kerosene vapour and the tang of tortured rubber from the landing wheels. The road out to McKenzie Beach, and the beach itself, have been recently smartened up by the addition of pedestrian and cycle tracks, glass barriers between them and the beach, and newly laid car parks.

## Larnaka's salt lake

If you come in to land at Larnaka Airport during daylight hours you can't help but be aware of the huge **salt lake** around which the town is built. Consisting of extremely brackish water during the winter and blinding-white dry salt during the summer, it is actually a complex of three interconnected lakes. Until quite recently salt was harvested here by donkey during the summer months, but today the lake is valued more as a habitat for around 85 species of bird, including its famous flamingos. Tradition has it that the salt lake was created in a fit of pique by St Lazaros (see page 52).

## Hala Sultan Tekke Mosque

Mid-April to mid-Sept 8.30am–7.30pm; mid-Sept to mid-April 8.30am–5pm • Donations requested

Approaching **from Larnaka**, as you get to the airport keep straight on at the first roundabout, and when you get to the next (signposted "Control Tower"), instead of going "through the roundabout" as the sign tells you to, double back as if returning to Larnaka; the turn-off to Hala Sultan Tekke is on the left, clearly signposted. There's a car park immediately after the turning which you can use if you want to walk the footpath; otherwise there's ample parking next to the mosque itself.

On the shore at the far end of the salt lake from Larnaka is one of Cyprus's most important Muslim sites, the **Hala Sultan Tekke Mosque**. With its elegant domes and minaret peeping out from a grove of palm and cypress trees on the shimmering edge of the lake (if you're lucky, the lake will be full of pink flamingos) the mosque is extremely atmospheric, only slightly marred by the distracting wind turbines located on the hillside behind.

The reason for the mosque's veneration is the presence of the tomb of **Umm Haram**, variously described as the friend or wet nurse of Mohammed. One of the earliest followers of the Prophet, the story goes that she accompanied an invading Arab force in 649 AD, was immediately thrown by her mule and was killed. A mosque was built on the site of her burial beneath, legend has it, stones from a prehistoric dolmen that stood on the spot.

There's a public footpath (the Kyprida Afroditi) along the edge of the lake to the mosque, with periodic benches (you'll need them if it's a hot day). Entry to the mosque's environs is through a couple of elegant gateways, and past a sign directing you to recently discovered prehistoric remains. A hexagonal kiosk (*sadirvan*) outside the mosque's entrance allows the faithful to wash their feet before prayer – non-believers simply have to remove their shoes.

Inside, the mosque is attractively human in scale, the floor lined with decorative prayer mats. The tomb of Umm Haram, guarded by a golden gate and lush green curtains, takes pride of place, while five other tombs, including that of the grandmother of King Hussein of Jordan – erected around 1930, it's a big, white two-storey affair – can be seen in a separate alcove off to the left. Yet another legend attached to the mosque is that the three stones of the dolmen that stands over the graves flew here from Mecca on the day of Umm Haram's death, and that the fifteen-tonne crosspiece was once suspended in midair, before coming to rest on the pillars. Incidentally, the current mosque is not particularly ancient, having been built in the early nineteenth century. But the whole scenic set piece reminds you that Cyprus lies on the very border of Western Europe and the Middle East.

## Kamares Aqueduct

At the opposite end of the salt lake from the airport, and best approached from the main Larnaka to Lemesos road (you can also get to it on a dirt road from the Hala Sultan Tekke mosque, however, the road may be inaccessible if it's been raining), is the remarkable **Kamares Aqueduct**. Built in 1745 by Abu Bekir Pasa, the then Ottoman governor of Cyprus, and designed to bring water into the town from 10km away, it was only replaced by modern pipes just before World War II. Nowadays its sinuous route across a shallow valley makes an impressive sight, especially when lit up at night.

## PYLA: GATEWAY TO THE NORTH

**PYLA** is worth visiting for two reasons. One is that it is the **only mixed Greek/Turkish village** remaining on the island. It lies in the Buffer Zone between the Turkish Occupied Zone, the Cypriot Republic and the British Sovereign Base of Dhekelia, and has a population whose Greek-Cypriot/Turkish-Cypriot breakdown is roughly 2:1. Superficially at least, they seem to rub along fairly successfully, though schools and even cafés are segregated, and it may be that it's only the presence of a UN watchtower that keeps the peace.

The other reason is that it lies on one of the **seven crossing points** into north Cyprus – it's the main crossing point to the north from Larnaka. This one's for vehicles, and it takes just a matter of minutes to get through the two checkpoints (though if you don't have motor insurance valid in the north, you'll need to take a policy out at the border – there's a kiosk). Make sure that you've got a good map – neither side goes out of its way to signpost the crossing – and that, if you're renting a car, you've cleared it with the rental company.

### ARRIVAL AND DEPARTURE
### LARNAKA

**By air** Larnaka Airport (☎ 25123022, ⓦ hermesairports. com), through which the majority of visitors to Cyprus pass, is well organized and has ATMs, car rental booths, a tourist information point, taxi stands and bus stops. There are frequent buses from the airport into Larnaka (€1.50; 30min) and also shuttles to Lefkosia and Lemesos. A number of routes link the airport to the town – #407/#417/#418/#419/#425/#429 during the day,

#446/#456 at night. A taxi into Larnaka should cost around €15.

**By bus** The main intercity bus stop is at Finikoudes promenade just south of Plateia Evropis.
Destinations Agia Napa/Paralimni (Mon–Fri 10 daily, Sat & Sun 8 daily; 1hr); Lefkosia (Mon–Fri 12 daily, Sat & Sun 8 daily; 1hr); Lemesos (Mon–Fri 10 daily, Sat & Sun 8 daily; 1hr 30min). For timetables visit ⓦ intercity-buses.com.

### GETTING AROUND

**By bus** Bus transport in Larnaka is efficient, provided by the blue buses of Zinonas Buses Ltd (☎ 80007744). Their own website (ⓦ zinonasbuses.com) isn't up to much – far better is ⓦ cyprusbybus.com. The central bus station is just north of Finikoudes, behind the police station – ask for details at the tourist office, where their excellent free map has the

main stops and which routes they serve marked on it.
**By taxi** Taxis are plentiful and uniformly metered. Within the town centre, though, it's probably wise to consider walking rather than taking a cab – the one-way system is so labyrinthine that you could end up travelling several times further than the direct route.

### INFORMATION AND TOURS

**Tourist office** The main office is at the British Colonial building on Plateia Vasileos Pavlou, backing onto the Municipal Cultural Centre. (Apr–Oct Mon–Sat 8.15am–2.30 Mon, Tue, Thur & Fri also 3–6pm, Nov–March Mon–Fri 8am–2.30pm, Mon, Tue, Thurs & Fri also 3–5pm, Sat 8am–1pm; ☎ 24654322, ⓦ larnakaregion.com).

**Tours** Larnaka is easily explored on foot, otherwise try one of the VeloBikes (☎ 96784065), a kind of space-age two-seater rickshaw, ridden by a professional guide. There's a choice of three routes ("charming town", "cultural sights and city centre" and "McKenzie Beach and Salt Lake"); they take 45–50min, and cost €6/person.

### ACTIVITIES

Despite being less overtly touristy than other island resort's there are a fair number of things to do dotted around Larnaka, many involving the sea.
**Diving and fishing** For divers Larnaka has one major advantage: the wreck of the *Zenobia*, one of the finest in the Mediterranean (see page 56). Dive-In (☎ 24627469, ⓦ dive-In.com.cy) and Alpha Divers Dive Centre (☎ 99866383, ⓦ alpha-divers.com) both arrange dives to the *Zenobia*, as do Dive Zenobia (ⓦ divezenobia.com), who also put on a range of cruises and fishing trips.
**Quad biking** For a land-based adrenaline rush try Quad Bike Safari (☎ 24647729, ⓦ quadbikingsafari.com) on the

Dekelia road.
**Ten-pin bowling** There's ten-pin bowling at K-Max Bowling Centre (Mon–Fri 4.30pm–midnight, Sat & Sun 3pm–midnight; ☎ 77778383, ⓦ kcineplex.com) in the same complex as the K Cineplex (see page 58).
**Water sports** For beach-based activities try Central Water Sports (☎ 99465855, ⓦ centralwatersports.com), in the hotel complex north of town on the Larnaka–Dhekelia road, which offers the full range of parasailing, windsurfing, waterskiing, wakeboarding, speedboat/pedalo/canoe and dinghy rental, as well as banana-boat rides.

**1**

## THE SINKING OF THE ZENOBIA

The wreck of the **Zenobia** lies in 43m of water some 1.5km off Larnaka. The story of its sinking remains something of a mystery. A brand-new roll-on/roll-off ferry, launched in Sweden in 1979, the *Zenobia* embarked on its maiden voyage to Syria in 1980, sailing from Malmö and through the Strait of Gibraltar. As it approached Greece, steering problems started to develop, and the ship began listing to port. It became clear that a computer malfunction was causing excess water to be pumped into the ballast tanks. The problem apparently solved, the ship continued to Cyprus. While in Larnaka harbour, however, the listing recurred and got worse. Eventually the captain was ordered to take her out of the harbour, in case she sank and became a hazard to other ships. Anchored offshore, the situation got worse, so much so that the captain ordered the crew to abandon ship. In the early hours of June 7, 1980 she turned turtle and sank. Compared to most shipwrecks, the whole drama was played out relatively slowly, and as a result there was no loss of life (though several divers have been drowned in the wreck since). Apart from the catastrophic failure of a state-of-the-art ferry, the mystery is that, despite her intrinsic value and the €200 million cargo she carried (including over 100 lorries), no investigation was ever carried out, and the owners never tried to collect the insurance. However, all is not lost; the wreck of the *Zenobia* is now considered to be one of the best **dive sites** in the world.

## ACCOMMODATION

Larnaka's big resort hotels are grouped up the coast to the northeast of the town, beyond the Nautical Club and the oil refineries. Within Larnaka itself are numerous smaller hotels and self-catering apartments. McKenzie Beach makes for a tempting alternative, though it is subject to aircraft noise from the airport.

★**Eleonora Hotel Apartments** 55 Ermou ☎24624400, ⓦeleonorahotelapts.com; map p.48. Right in the centre, overlooking Ermou (Hermes) Square, these apartments are clean, functional and fully equipped, providing a good, low-cost base for exploring the town. **€60**

**Flamingo Beach Hotel** 152 Pyiale Pasa ☎24646022, ⓦflamingohotelcyprus.com; map p.48. The *Flamingo* benefits from its location overlooking the sea and the new promenade, yet within walking distance of the town and numerous bars and restaurants. It has modern rooms, a patio area overlooking the beach, excellent wi-fi, regular buffet dinners and Greek music and dancing displays that are popular with residents and non-residents alike. That said, some rooms are a little tired or noisy if near the lifts (check first), and breakfasts can seem a bit perfunctory. **€100**

**Hotel Opera** Saint Lazaros Square, 11 Faneromenis Street ☎24400210, ⓦhoteloperalarnaca.com; map p.48. Overlooking Larnaka's cathedral, boutique *Hotel Opera* is in the heart of the town yet a 5min walk from the main beach. Excellent friendly staff, nice ambience, but room facilities (balcony, tea-making facilities etc) vary, so check when booking. **€72**

**Livadhiotis City Hotel** 50 Nikolaou Rossou ☎24626222, ⓦlivadhiotis.com; map p.48. *Livadhiotis* is right at the heart of things: on a corner a few meters from Agios Lazaros church, and just around the corner from the promenade and Larnaka's main pub and restaurant area. The hotel has 58 simple rooms, all the in-room facilities you're likely to need, and a stylish café (*Café Blu*) and bar. **€120**

**Lokal** 98 Agiou Lazarou ☎24023102, ⓦlokalcyprus. com; map p.48. Classy, beautifully renovated seventeen-room boutique hotel in a former listed mansion located near the Agios Lazaros church. **€225**

**Lordos Beach Hotel** Larnaka–Dekeleia road ☎24647444, ⓦlordosbeach.com.cy; map p.48. Outside of town and not quite as large as the *Palm Beach* (see below), and with a slightly less contemporary feel, the *Lordos Beach* offers a similar experience, though with a more limited range of facilities. It's always busy, though – and tends to be popualr with Russian tourists. **€126**

★**Palm Beach Hotel and Bungalows** Larnaka–Dekeleia road ☎24846600, ⓦpalmbeachhotel.com; map p.48. The hotel has everything you need, which is just as well since it's 7km out of the town. The on-site facilities are extensive: two restaurants, tavern, coffee shop, four bars, three swimming pools, water-sports centre, tennis and squash courts, and for children the paddling pool, playground and kids' club. Also, there's a bus stop just outside, a taxi rank in the car park, and the hotel is a 5min drive from the motorway, giving fast access to the whole of Cyprus. Accommodation is comfortable and well proportioned, with a wide choice of rooms, suites and bungalows. **€146**

**Sun Hall Hotel** 6 Leoforos Athinon ☎24653341, ⓦsunhallhotelcyprus.com; map p.48. Well located on the promenade right next to the Municipal Cultural Centre, the *Sun Hall* combines the benefits of a town-centre business hotel with those of a holiday resort. It's just across the promenade from the beach, it has a swimming pool, gym, sauna, fitness room, restaurant and cocktail bar, and 24hr service. Rooms are tastefully smart after refurbishment (all have a fridge). Don't get it confused with the *Sun Hall Beach Hotel Apartments* – they're different. **€144**

## EATING

Larnaka offers a good range of places to eat. There are some fine Greek-Cypriot tavernas and fish restaurants strung along beside the sea on Piyale Pasa and McKenzie Beach. There's also a concentration of bars and restaurants in the Laiki Geitonia district, clearly signposted off the promenade down near the fort.

★ **1900 Art Café** 6 Stasinou ☎ 24653027, ⓦ artcafe 1900.com.cy; map p.48. By now something of an institution in Larnaka, the atmospheric *1900 Art Café* – all paintings and photographs on the walls, wooden floors and fires in winter in a mansion built in – yes – 1900 – offers good Cypriot food in convivial surroundings. Main courses include *stifado*, meatballs, stuffed vegetables and various chicken dishes, from around €10. If you get the chance, sit out on the balcony. Mon, Wed & Sun 6pm–2am, Thu & Sat 6pm–1am.

**Alasia Café-Restaurant** 38 Piale Pasa ☎ 24655868; map p.48. Next door to *Militzis*, you might easily miss the understated *Alasia*. Yet for fresh ingredients, few places can equal it. In particular, go for the *koupez* (basically, minced pork cooked in a shell of cracked bulgar wheat) at €4.40/ person, followed by traditional Cypriot sweets *pourekia* and *stamisi* (at €2.20 each). A real taste of Cyprus without breaking the bank. Daily: April–Oct 9am–midnight; Nov–March 10.30am–11pm.

**Feng's House** 103 Leoforos Athinon ☎ 24657176; map p.48. Well placed for people-watching on the promenade at the entrance to Laiki Geitonia district, and fronted by a cheery Buddha figure, *Feng's House* offers good-quality Chinese food at reasonable prices, with main courses starting at around €10. Reservations recommended. Daily 12.30–3pm & 6.30–11.30pm, Sun 6.30–11.30pm.

**Hobos** 14 Leoforos Athinon ☎ 24652584, ⓦ hobos steakhouse.com; map p.48. A popular café/restaurant providing a wide range of not particularly Cypriot snacks – burgers at less than €10, or Italian dishes between €5 and €10, as well as cocktails around the €5 mark. It's a good choice for breakfast, and to bring kids – there's a small funfair on the pavement right next door. The steak house upstairs offers a range of quality beef and lamb dishes (€15–26), as well as a more varied menu (stuffed chicken breast, for example). Café daily 9am–midnight; steak house Mon–Sat 4pm–midnight, Sun noon–midnight.

**Lush** McKenzie Beach ☎ 70008089, ⓦ lushbeachbar. com; map p.48. The latest of a scrum of establishments on the sand at the far end of McKenzie Beach, *Lush* is a kind of one-stop shop: beach café, swanky restaurant, cocktail bar, nightclub. The focus is on international cuisine with good meat and pasta dishes (€16–24). Claims to be always open, but core hours are 10am–midnight.

★ **Militzis** 42 Piyale Pasa ☎ 24655867; map p.48. A hugely popular (with Cypriots as well as visitors) traditional Greek-Cypriot restaurant just beyond the fort on busy sea-lapped Piyale Pasa, *Militzis* is hard to miss – there's a big wind-pump wreathed in climbing plants at the front, and an industrial-scale clay oven at the back. Its roasted and grilled meats are out of this world, the service is excellent, and the prices are very reasonable. Arrive early if you want to sit out on the terrace. Mains €7–13.50. Daily 11am–11pm (kitchen closes slightly earlier).

★ **Psarolimano** 118 Piyale Pasa ☎ 24655408, ⓦ psarolimano.com; map p.48. You couldn't ask for a better-sited fish restaurant – it's on the dock at Larnaka's fishing harbour. Surrounded by potted greenery, it sticks largely to what it does best – fresh fish. Main dishes start at around €12 though a lot of the prices are by weight ("Fish B", for example, is €56/kg). Highly recommended. Daily noon–midnight.

**Stou Rousha Tavern** 26 Nicolau Laniti ☎ 96509590; map p.48. Good-quality traditional tavern in a renovated house tucked into the narrow streets behind the Town Hall, with a standard Greek-Cypriot menu of beautifully cooked (largely meat-based) food. Mains €7–12, *sheftalia* €8.50, *souvlakia* in pitta (pork or chicken) from €7. Mon–Sat noon–4pm & 7–11pm, Sun noon–4pm.

**To Kazani** 28th October ☎ 99313236, ⓦ facebook. com/ParadosiakiTavernaToKazani; map p.48. A traditional place with a friendly family atmosphere and live music every Friday and Saturday from 8pm. Their meze counts among the best on the island - and there's a vegan option as well. The dishes are almost too much to eat, you have no chance of leaving *To Kazani* hungry. It's slightly off the main tourist paths but well worth the trip. Main courses between €11 and €19. Mon–Sat 6pm–2am.

## DRINKING AND NIGHTLIFE

For a relatively small town without the reputation for nightlife of an Agia Napa or Lemesos, Larnaka in fact does very well. It's sometimes difficult to differentiate between bars, pubs, restaurants and clubs – indeed, what is a café/bar during the day can become a lively venue during the evening and a nightclub into the small hours. For bar hopping the best bet is the small Laiki Geitonia area off the promenade down towards the fort.

### BARS

**Jungle Gardens Music Bar** Laiki Geitonia ☎ 99122458; map p.48. The *Jungle Gardens Music Bar* specializes in exotic cocktails (€4.50–5.50) and varied musical tastes and appeals to a younger crowd. Daily 6pm–2am.

★ **Savino Rock Bar** 9 Watkins ☎ 24620861; map p.48. Bar with loud music, a wide range of beers, ciders and cocktails and the odd game of pool. Daily 2pm–

2.30am, Fri–Sun till 3.30am.

**Seagull Bar** Piale Pasha ☎24654434; map p.48. Well-established family-run bar with a wide range of beers and spirits at knock-down prices – for example, €3 for spirit doubles, draught beer at €3–4. Doesn't let great sporting events or festive dates (St Patrick's Day, New Year's Eve etc) go uncelebrated. Daily 10am–2am.

## CLUBS

**Club Deep** 73 Leoforos Athinon ☎70007950, ⓦclub deepcyprus.com; map p.48. Club Deep was once divided into three but is now a single large venue offering a wide range of garage, old school, RnB and house, together with Greek hits. It's not easy to find, squashed between

*McDonald's* and (at the time of writing) a building site. Fri & Sat 11.55pm–5am.

**Geometry** 8 Karaoli & Demetriou ☎70009440; map p.48. Offers contemporary dance, and earns its name from the hundreds of crystals in its ceiling. Fri & Sat 9pm–4am.

**Secrets Freedom** 67 Leoforos Artemidos ☎99557433, ⓦsecretsfreedomclub.com; map p.48. *Secrets Freedom* is a little out of the centre, on the main dual carriageway out to the airport (on the left just after Elomas Supermarket). One of the biggest and best of Cyprus's gay clubs, it welcomes straight as well as gay customers and puts on a wide range of special events and parties. Wed, Thurs & Sun 10pm–3am, Fri & Sat 11am–4pm.

## ENTERTAINMENT

**Cinema** ☎24819022 ⓦkcineplex.com. The six-screen K Cineplex is at the intersection of Potamou Indou and Peloponisou west of the town centre near the Kamares Aqueduct. The complex also includes a bowling alley and a pub.

**Theatres** Larnaka is justly proud of the range and quality of the dance, drama and music that it provides. Its four

venues – the Municipal Theatre in the Municipal Gardens (☎24665795), the Pattichion Amphitheatre at the northern end of the Salt Lake (☎24629300) and the Theatro Skala at 15 Kyriakou Matsi (☎24652800), together with the gardens in the old fort, mount a series of plays, concerts and performances of dance, especially during the summer.

## SHOPPING

Given fast motorway links with the capital, most locals head to Lefkosia for serious shopping. That said, Larnaka offers a fair range of shops, especially ones that are likely to appeal to visitors. The main shopping streets are Zinonos Kitieos, which runs parallel to the promenade one block west, Ermou which strikes northwest from Zinonos Kitieos's southern end, and the streets and alleys in between.

**Beauty Line** 51 Ermou ☎24650181; map p.48. One of a Cypriot chain of shops selling top-end beauty products and perfume. Mon–Sat 9am–8pm.

**Dodici** 173 Ermou ☎24823950; map p.48. Classy men's and women's shoes from Greece. April–Oct Mon, Tues & Thurs 9am–7pm, Wed 9am–2pm, Sat 9am–3pm; Nov–March Mon, Tues & Thurs 9am–6pm, Wed

9am–2pm, Sat 9am–3pm.

**Kalopedis Jewellery** 38 Zinonos Kitieos ☎24655501, ⓦkalopedis.com; map p.48. A long-established family firm where the jewellery – much of it with a Greek theme – is designed and made on the premises. Look out for worry beads, evil eye and Greek key pattern jewellery for example, and a wide range of both ancient and modern designs. Mon–Fri 9am–7pm, Sat 9am–2pm.

**Tofarides** 45–47 Zinonos Kitieos ☎24654912; map p.48. A newsagent, stationers and bookshop selling English-language as well as Greek titles. April–Oct Mon, Tues, Thurs & Fri 9am–7pm, Wed 9am–2pm, Sat 9am–3pm; Nov–March Mon, Tues & Thurs 9am–1.30pm & 3–5pm, Wed 9am–1.30pm, Sat 9am–3pm.

# Agia Napa

**AGIA NAPA** (often appearing as Ayia Napa), 35km east of Larnaka, is not everybody's cup of tea. If you want peace and quiet, or to commune with nature, or to get to grips with traditional Cypriot life, go somewhere else. But if you're young and want the company of people of your own age and lots of stuff to do, or if you're a family with teenagers who are easily bored, or if you find bars and restaurants flamboyantly advertising their presence with giant cows, or elephants, or huge cocktail glasses mounted on their roofs funny rather than tacky, this is one of the best holiday regions in Europe. The area is certainly overdeveloped, but no more so than any other typical Mediterranean package-holiday destination.

Though much of the resort's appeal is down to its nightlife, there's now a lot more to it than that. Its remarkably compact centre sits behind a surprisingly charming small harbour (Limanaki) with some fine stretches of sand, notably **Nissi beach**, running

International Sculpture Park & Cactus Park

Love Bridge

● **EATING**
| | |
|---|---|
| Fiji | 6 |
| Garden of Eden | 7 |
| Hokkaido | 3 |
| Limelight | 4 |
| Los Bandidos | 2 |
| Sage Restaurant and Liquid Wine Bar | 5 |
| Stamna | 1 |

■ **DRINKING & NIGHTLIFE**
| | |
|---|---|
| Car Wash | 3 |
| Castle Club | 2 |
| Club Black'n'White | 1 |
| Makronissos Beach Club | 4 |
| Pepper Bar Lounge | 5 |

■ **ACCOMMODATION**
| | |
|---|---|
| Alion Beach Hotel | 5 |
| Atlantica Aeneas Hotel | 1 |
| Florence Hotel Apartments | 3 |
| Grecian Sands Hotel | 6 |
| Limanaki Beach Hotel | 7 |
| Napa Mermaid Hotel | 4 |
| Nissi Beach Hotel | 2 |

- - - - European Long Distance Path E4
- - - - Cycling path

N

KAVO GKREKO

E306
E306
E306

MELISSI
MELISSI
MELISSI

LEOFOROS KRYOU NEROU
LEOFOROS KRYOU NEROU

Limanaki Beach

Thalassa Museum

OKTOVRIOU 1

Bus station

MISIAOULI & KAVAZOGLIOU

DHIONYSIOU SOLOMOU

LEOFOROS ARCH. MAKARIOU III

LEOFOROS ARCH. MAKARIOU III

Limanaki

TEFKROU ANTHIA

D'IPERTI

PLATEIA SEFERI

Agia Napa Monastery

Panagia

Eman Travel and Tours

GRIGORI AFXENTIOU
LOUKA LOUKA
ABI VELOUCHIOTI

Parko Paliatso Luna Park

LEOFOROS NISSI

AGIAS MAVRIS

KATALYMATON

E309

ODYSSEA ELYTI

DHIMOKRATIAS

GIOUNY GKAGKARIN
GIOUNY GKAGKARIN

LEOFOROS NISSI

**AGIA NAPA**

0          200
metres

## GUNS, GANGS AND GARAGE

Much of **Agia Napa**'s toxic reputation stems from the early 2000s when turf wars between different UK garage "crews" broke out, during which several people (including a young Dizzee Rascal) were stabbed. Violence broke out again with the mafia-style shooting of three Cypriots and two Romanians on the streets of the town in June 2012 and the murder of a young British soldier in a bar-room brawl in November 2012. Then there's been the 2016 shooting in which 4 died and 2 were injured, and finally, in 2017, a Russian businessman was killed by gunfire. With all the tumultuous nightlife it seems hard to believe how sedate and family friendly the town is in the daytime.

west from here. Look out too for **Agia Napa Monastery** and the excellent **Thalassa Museum**, the fine **amusement park** in the centre of town, and the colossal **Waterworld Waterpark** to the west. In addition to larger-scale projects like the Sculpture Park and the Love Bridge, Agia Napa municipality has invested time and money in a range of street art, from the "Mermaid and the Fisherman" in the harbour area through pictures dotted around the area to the rather naff "I Love Ayia Napa" sculpture in the centre of the town.

## Agia Napa Monastery

Plateia Seferi • Daily: summer 9am–9pm; winter 9am–3pm • Free • ☎ 23722584

Amid the bars and traffic of Agia Napa, it's something of a shock to find a beautifully renovated **monastery** (originally a convent) – looking like a stern elderly relative from a bygone age frowning at all the nonsense going on around her. As with many religious sites in Cyprus, it comes with a complicated and confused story. A hunter, out with his dog, discovered a cave and spring in the woods. Not only did his mangy dog develop a new healthy-looking coat after bathing in the spring water, but the hunter also found an icon of the Virgin Mary in the cave, hidden there during iconoclastic attacks on such pictures in the eighth and ninth centuries. This story led to widespread belief in the miraculous powers of the water and the icon. In around 1500, a convent was built on the site as a refuge for a Venetian noblewoman whose father had refused her permission to marry a commoner. After the Ottoman conquest of 1571 the Roman Catholic Venetians were replaced by Greek Orthodox nuns, and in 1668 they in turn were replaced by monks. Today an Ecumenical Conference Centre, its courtyard and octagonal fountain are a haven of tranquillity at the heart of Agia Napa's frenzy. The courtyard and church (partly underground – this was the cave in which the icon was found) are open to the public, though there seems to be no sign of the icon.

## Thalassa Museum

14 Krynou Nerou • June–Sept Mon 9am–1pm, Tues–Sat 9am–5pm, Sun 3–7pm Oct–May Mon 9am–1pm, Tues–Sat 9am–5pm • €4 • ☎ 23816366, ⓦ thalassamuseum.org.cy

Situated next to the tourist office, the **Thalassa Museum** ("Sea Museum"), which opened in 2006, emphasizes Agia Napa's determination to be known for more than drunken revelry. The undoubted star of the show is the **Kyrenia II**, an exact replica of a fourth-century BC Greek merchant ship discovered off the coast of Kyrenia in the mid-1980s (the original is on show in Girne castle). There's also a reconstruction of a **papyrus vessel** from much earlier times (9200 BC), though this is based on far less evidence than the *Kyrenia II*. Downstairs in the semi-basement is the **Tornaritis-Pierides Marine Life Museum**, a collection of stuffed birds, fish, mammals and sea turtles together with shells, corals, sponges and lobsters.

## Parko Paliatso Luna Park

Off Leoforos Nissi • Daily 6pm–12.30am • Cost of rides varies, paid for by token or 3 types of wristbands starting from €25 • ☎ 23724744,
Ⓦ parkopaliatsocy.com

Close to the town centre is the **Parko Paliatso Luna Park**, which offers more than 25 rides, from gentle, such as the sedate Ferris wheel, to white-knuckle. A large indoor play area (including bumper boats, teacups and trampolines) caters for small children, while the fearsome "Blizzard", "Slingshot" and others ring to the screams of terrified teens and adults.

## Waterworld Waterpark

18 Agia Thekla • Daily: May–Sept 10am–6pm; April & Oct 10am–5pm • Under-2s free, 3–12-year-olds €24, over-13s €38 • ☎ 23724444,
Ⓦ waterworldwaterpark.com

One of the largest waterparks in Europe, **Waterworld Waterpark** is a cracker. Establishing its ethos as soon as you arrive (the car park is dotted with plaster copies of classical statues and buildings), the park is organized into a wonderful array of ancient-Greek-themed attractions – from the "Fall of Icarus" (a huge open slide topped by the figure of the sun) to the "Drop to Atlantis" (a massive ride with three-person cars, light and sound effects). The theme is carried on into its restaurants and shops – *Minotaur's Pizza, Homer's Burger Palace, Dionysos Temple Self-service Restaurant*. Totally over the top, but who knows, it might inspire the odd child to take up Homer.

## Limanaki

Agia Napa's **Limanaki** or "little harbour" is an unexpected delight. It has convenient paved walkways, modern street lighting, a fish market, restaurants and cafés, all set around a vibrant jostling harbour of leisure, charter, tourist and fishing boats (guided into port by little conical lights). There's also a small beach and ample car parking.

## Agia Napa International Sculpture Park and Cactus Park

Leoforos Protara-Kavo Gkreko • Always open • Free • ☎ 23816300, Ⓦ ayianapaopenmuseum.com

The **International Sculpture Park**, and the **Cactus Park** next to it (directly opposite the *Marina Hotel*), represent an imaginative addition to Agia Napa's charms. Opened in 2014, a host of modern sculptures are fetchingly dotted around among cacti and succulents on a rocky headland overlooking the sea – an interesting and thoughtful alternative to some of Agia Napa's more raucous attractions.

## Love Bridge

Perhaps with an eye to the increasing number of foreigners who choose to get married on Aphrodite's island, and the spreading fashion around the world for weighing down any available bridges with padlocks (presumably to represent the permanence of relationships rather than their restrictiveness), a "**Love Bridge**" was inaugurated on the road to Limnara west of Agia Napa in 2014. Made of concrete but with wooden handrails, it spans a dry gully in a rather arid stretch of countryside. Nice views of the sea, though.

## Agia Napa's beaches

The most central of Agia Napa's **beaches** is right next to Limanaki harbour. Though the sand's good, it's a fairly thin strip, and, as you might expect, it is often absolutely heaving. You're usually better off heading west to **Nissi Beach**, notable particularly for the small island ("Nissi" is the Greek for "island") in the bay to which you can swim or wade. The sand here is particularly fine, there are plenty of water sports on offer, and the water, compared to the deep blue depths beyond the island, is a pale, shimmering ultramarine. Further west still, **Makronissos Beach** offers the usual mix of beach facilities, plus a bit of archeological interest. Three kilometres past here is **Agia Thekla**, a series of tiny bays dominated by a rather fine modern church of that name. On Saturdays a market springs up around the church, flogging everything from fresh fruit to jewellery, toys and DVDs, all to the accompaniment of loud recorded Greek music.

## Makronissos archeological site
Daily dawn–dusk • Free

Beyond Makronissos beach, and well signposted at the end of a paved road, is the **Makronissos archeological site**, a collection of nineteen rock-cut tombs that date from the years straddling the birth of Christ. It's like an underground village, with flights of steps running down to tombs where bodies were placed in sarcophagi (one is on show at the Thalassa Museum).

## The cave church at Agia Thekla

At Agia Thekla look out for the tiny **cave church** or tomb (nobody's quite sure which), let into a small rock face below the modern church – there are concrete steps down to it. The little church, marked by a cross on the rock above the entrance, has a number of icons on the rock walls, and a table bearing offerings of oil and candles. Legend has it that this is where Pyiele Pasa landed during the Ottoman invasion of Cyprus in 1571.

# Potamos Liopetriou

Three kilometres west of Agia Thekla (and a minute off the motorway – it's clearly signposted) is **Potamos Liopetriou**, a long sinuous estuary of a small river, lined on both sides with traditional Cypriot fishing boats. Two tavernas overlook the river – the *Potamos* about halfway down the crowded river bank, and the *Demetrion* next to where the river disgorges into the bay beside a small sandy beach and a pretty little church. Even if you don't read Greek, the picture of the killing of the dragon on the slate marker as you enter the churchyard leaves you in no doubt that the church is dedicated to St George. Potamos is a rare treat – there's nothing quite like it anywhere else on the island. Incidentally, the French poet Arthur Rimbaud worked here in the late 1870s as a quarry foreman, before having to return to France with suspected typhoid.

## ARRIVAL AND INFORMATION
AGIA NAPA

**By bus** Agia Napa's main bus station is on Leoforos Arch. Makariou III, just north of the harbour.

Destinations Larnaka (Mon–Fri 8 daily, Sat & Sun 6 daily; 1hr); Paralimni (Mon–Fri half-hourly, Sat & Sun hourly; 1hr).

**Tourist office** The main office is at 12 Leoforos Kryou Nerou (Mon–Fri 8.15am–2.30pm, plus odd hours and some Saturdays as advertised outside the office; ☎23721796),

next to the Thalassa Museum. Be sure to pick up free copies of the two excellent maps of the area, Agia Napa and Paralimni/Protaras.

**Travel agents** There are numerous travel agencies in Agia Napa which offer coach trips, jeep safaris, boat cruises and the like. Try Eman Travel and Tours at 32 Arch. Makariou III (☎23721321, ⓦemantravel.com).

---

### AGIA NAPA FESTIVALS

**Agia Napa Festival** (Sept) Held annually since 1985, the town's main festival is a feast of music, drama and dance, taking place largely in the town square and monastery.

**Cultural Winter** (Nov–April) Concerts and recitals put on by the municipality in the town (☎23816307 for details).

**Folk singing and dancing** (April–Oct) Every Sunday in Seferis Square.

**Youth Festival** (Aug) Free three-day event held in the square next to Limanaki harbour, with music of all sorts but mainly rock and metal.

## GETTING AROUND

**By bus** Buses in the Agia Napa region are run by OSEA (☎23819090, ⓦosea.com.cy). The most popular routes include the #101 and #102 to Paralimni, Protaras, Cape Greco and the Waterpark, the #201 and #301 circular routes around the Agia Napa area, and the #501 and #502 to Deryneia. Intercity buses to Larnaka and Lefkosia run every 1–2hr (less frequently at weekends). The area also has tourist buses which are a good way of finding your bearings (Red Bus Tour ☎96423602, ⓦtheoriginalredbus.com).

**By taxi** As you'd expect in an area famous for its nightlife, the Agia Napa/Protaras/Paralimni area has numerous taxi companies, many of which publish a fixed price list

for popular journeys (try East Coast Taxis ☎23724353, ⓦeastcoasttaxiscyprus.com). Consider also the shared taxi service (see page 26).

**By car and motorbike** All the major car rental agents are represented with prices starting from around €20/day. One of the most popular ways of getting around the area is to rent a motorbike, buggy or quad bike. Prices can be quite steep – anything between €20 and €35/day (often with a two-day minimum) for a small motorbike to between €300 and €400/week for a large buggy (have a look, for example, at Easy Riders, based in Agia Napa's main square (☎23722438, ⓦeasyriders.com.cy).

## ACTIVITIES

**Boat trips** Numerous boat trips run from Limanaki harbour. Try the glass-bottomed Yellow Submarine (☎99596280, ⓦyellowsubmarinecy.com), which employs divers to attract fish to the viewing window, or the Dolphin Boat Safari (☎99607181, ⓦdolphinboatsafari.com), which runs trips to Famagusta and snorkelling trips. Fares start at around €20 for a 2hr trip and rise to €80 for a 4hr tuna-fishing trip.

**Bungee jumping** Bungee Downunder (☎99404208; May–Oct 3pm–1am) operate a scarily high crane at Nissi

Beach. There's usually a barbecue and loud music as well.

**Karting** The best of several karting tracks is EMW Go Cars next to Waterworld. Prices are €12/6min, €16/10min. (☎23723111).

**Water sports** Your best bet is Nissi Beach, which offers everything from banana-boat rides to jet-skis, wakeboarding, waterskiing and paragliding. For scuba diving try Sunfish Divers at 26 Arch. Makariou III (☎23721300, ⓦsunfishdivers.com).

## ACCOMMODATION

Agia Napa's main hotel areas are along Kryou Nerou, the road in from the east, and Leoforos Nissi (Nissi Avenue), the road that comes in from the west. For a degree of peace and quiet, go for the east; for busy beaches with lots of water sports, go for the west. There are also a few options in the heart of town close to the action. Most of the large hotels have a minimum stay of a week during high season.

★ **Alion Beach Hotel** Kryou Nerou ☎23722900, ⓦalion.com; map p.59. Set amid lush gardens on a sweeping beach, rooms have unfussy decor, there's a choice of five restaurant/bars, a health spa and fitness centre, indoor, outdoor and kids' pools, a range of entertainment and sports activities, though with more emphasis on adults than children. Open all year. €180

**Atlantica Aeneas Hotel** 100 Leoforos Nissi ☎23724000, ⓦaeneas.com.cy; map p.59. Notable for its position a short walk from popular Nissi Beach and its huge labyrinthine swimming pool with bridges, fountains, whirlpools, and three bars dotted among the foliage, the *Aeneas* is one of Agia Napa's flagship hotels. The range of facilities includes all you'd expect (spa, health club, hairdressing salon, souvenir shop, kids' club and lots more), and the service is effortlessly smooth and efficient. €257

**Florence Hotel Apartments** 74 Leoforos Nissi ☎23722088, ⓦflorencehotelapts.com; map p.59. Just west of the Agia Napa's centre, the *Florence* offers good basic accommodation away from the bustle of the town at budget rates. Few frills, though there is a swimming pool. €80

**Grecian Sands Hotel** 44 Kryou Nero ☎23721616, ⓦgreciansands.com; map p.59. Built after the Turkish invasion of 1974 during the first moves to re-establish Cyprus as a tourist destination, the *Grecian Sands* is in some ways rather old-fashioned. However, a rolling programme of refurbishment, a management that is on the ball (making a big play, for example, for the growing wedding trade) and an enviable position on a bay east of the town centre keep it competitive. €200

**Limanaki Beach Hotel** Limanaki ☎23721600, ⓦlimanakibeach.com; map p.59. Right in the heart of things, virtually on the bustling harbour, the *Limanaki Beach* doesn't have the range of facilities that the big resort hotels offer but it manages a pool, sauna (extra charge), fitness room, bars and restaurant and a café. €200

★ **Napa Mermaid Hotel** 45 Kryou Nerou ☎23721606, ⓦnapamermaidhotel.com.cy; map p.59. Elegant and immaculate, the *Napa Mermaid* is a triumph of style, comfort and cleanliness. There are two restaurants offering everything from snacks to fine dining, two bars, and facilities include the full range of swimming pools, health and fitness equipment, beauty treatments and sports, and thoughtful service. If the hotel has a downside it is the lack of beachfront. €177

**Nissi Beach Hotel** Leoforos Nissi ☎23721021, ⓦnissi-beach.com; map p.59. The unique selling point here is the hotel's position on one of the most popular beaches in Cyprus. With a range of restaurants and bars, health and

1

beauty facilities, entertainment and sports opportunities, the *Nissi Beach* is ideal for adults, while its kids' club (with everything from face painting to mini discos), children's pool and two playgrounds keep the little ones happy. **€177**

## EATING

**Fiji** 21 Archiepiscopou Makariou ☎23725925, ⓦtinyurl.com/FijiPolynesian; map p.59. Opposite Agia Napa monastery, this restaurant couldn't be more central. Don't be put off by the over-the-top Polynesian theme – the food is delicious. Pacific chicken curry, coriander pork and Mongolian lamb (mains around the €20 mark) are particularly good, washed down with some of the restaurant's exotic cocktails. Daily 5.30–11pm.

**Garden of Eden** 144 Leoforos Nissi ☎23724810, ⓦthegardenofedencyprus.com; map p.59. Good range of Greek and international dishes (you'll find shepherd's pie under "exotic and ethnic"), efficient and friendly service, with main courses from around €10. Good indoor and alfresco dining, with children's playground to keep the kids occupied. April–Oct lunch & dinner.

**Hokkaido** 35 Agias Mavris ☎23721505, ⓦhokkaido japaneserestaurant.business.site/; map p.59. Fine Japanese restaurant with accomplished cooks offering what amounts to a floor show, with food thrown in: sashimi and sushi, with most items on the menu between €4.80 and €13.50. Daily 4–11.30pm.

★ **Limelight** Dimetri Liperti ☎23721650, ⓦlimelight taverna.com; map p.59. Greek-Cypriot taverna offering massive choice and portions of traditional food; for example,

charcoal-grilled steak, lobster, suckling pig and much more, with prices mostly in the €10–30 range. The *keftedes* and *koupepia* are delicious. Apr–Nov Daily 1–11pm

**Los Bandidos** 2 Ari Velouchioti ☎23723528, ⓦfacebook. com/losbandidosmexican/; map p.59. Near the main square, *Los Bandidos* is claimed by some to be the best Mexican restaurant in Cyprus (though how many there are is another question). The food is good, though service can be slow, especially at busy times. "Not just a restaurant, it's an experience" is its tagline – and the experience includes wearing sombreros or six-guns at the table. Main courses from €7, though you'll pay more for something exotic – over €20 for a crocodile fajita, for example. Daily 5.15–11.15pm.

**Sage Restaurant and Liquid Wine Bar** 10 Kryou Nero ☎23816110, ⓦsagerest.com; map p.59. Modern Mediterranean-type menu of well-cooked food in a restaurant with stylish ambience, friendly (or, if you're a curmudgeon, intrusive) service, extensive opening hours and prices that range from €25. May–Oct daily 5–11pm.

**Stamna** Dimokratias ☎23721386, ⓦstamnatavern. com; map p.59. Family taverna in what it claims is Agia Napa's oldest house. Authentic Greek-Cypriot food, together with more international dishes, at affordable prices (from under €10). Mid-April to mid-Oct 5pm–midnight.

## DRINKING AND NIGHTLIFE

While the wilder extremes of partying that gave Agia Napa an unenviable reputation throughout Europe have now been reined in, there is still a very lively scene. Clubs come and go, but some have become fixtures, in many cases by reinventing themselves every year or two. Most of the action centres on the main square in the town centre and roads leading off, with the scene really getting going in the small hours.

**Car Wash** Agias Mavris ☎99420976, ⓦcarwashcyprus. com; map p.59. Another stayer (established 1996). Emphasis on 1970s and 1980s disco, with unparalleled sound system and lighting. Daily 1.30am–5.30am.

**Castle Club** Grigori Afxentiou ☎97775550, ⓦthecastle club.com; map p.59. Large venue with three main rooms, fourteen bars, VIP and chill-out lounges, and updated TV, sound and light systems, the *Castle Club* (yes, the building looks like a castle) offers a mixture of RnB, house, trance, chart and disco. Daily 10pm–5am.

★ **Club Black n'White** 6 Louka Louka ☎99611126, ⓦnapasound.com; map p.59. Established way back in 1985, the small and underground *Club Black n'White* is right in the centre of Agia Napa. With a mix of hip-hop, RnB and old-skool garage, it also maintains links with Choice FM, BBC 1XTRA and Kiss100. And when you're knackered, enjoy the chill-out lounge. March–Oct daily 1.30–4am, Nov–Feb Fri & Sat 1.30–4am.

**Makronissos Beach Club** Makronissos Beach ⓦlove ayianapa.com/makronissos-beach-club; map p.59. Bar/restaurant during the day, packed club at night. Wide range of top artists and DJs in a lovely setting on the beach opposite Waterworld. Mon & Sat 8am–1am, Tues 8am–3am, Wed & Thurs 8am–6pm, Fri 8am–11pm, Sun 8am–10pm.

**Pepper Bar Lounge** Makarios Avenue ☎99595515; map p.59. Popular (and large) cocktail bar meets sushi restaurant on Napa Plaza, with lively atmosphere and eclectic music. April–Oct daily 5pm–2am.

# Around Agia Napa

A few kilometres northeast of Agia Napa are the fine beaches of **Protaras**, as well as rugged **Cape Greko**, perfect for exploring on foot or racing around in a dune buggy.

Inland are the so-called "red villages" or **Kokkinochorio**, set among fields of red soil (hence the name) dotted with wind pumps and within spitting distance of the Turkish-occupied north. **Deryneia**, on a north slope facing Famagusta and with views across the modern part of that city, flourished until 1974, but is now a derelict ghost town.

This easternmost part of south Cyprus is easily accessible – the national motorway links it to the rest of the island, while other excellent main roads (the E306, 307 and 327) make moving around within it a doddle. It also boasts a good bus service and even well-marked footpaths. Incidentally, the Agia Napa/Protaras area is technically part of Famagusta District, but since a large chunk of that is now occupied by the Turkish Army (and covered in Chapter 6), it has been included in this chapter.

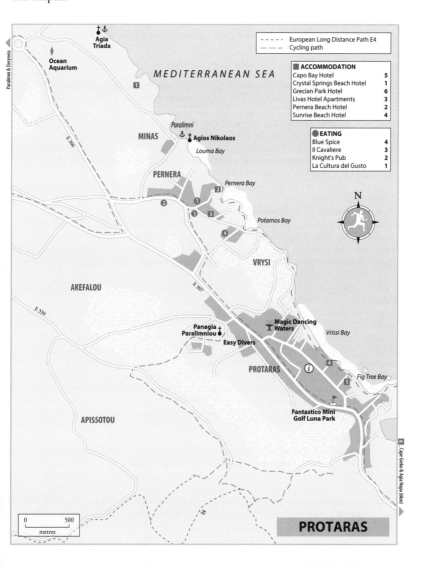

1

# Cape Greko

Separating the beaches of Agia Napa and Protaras, **Cape Greko** is a bare, rocky headland dotted with sea caves. Though protected as a nature reserve, it gets busy with locals hurtling around on motorbikes and dune buggies. The road to the actual cape is cut off by a fence and a stout gate – it's a British military installation, and access is denied. However, a left turn before the gate will bring you to a natural rock bridge (much photographed, but you're not allowed to actually walk across it) and, a bit further on, the church of Agii Anargyrii. There's often an ice-cream van in the car park, and beyond the church there are steps down to a "sacred" sea cave and a signpost to others some 4km away. Elsewhere on the Cape there are picnic sites, walking trails (the Agioi Anargyroi and Aphrodite paths) and a new Environmental Centre. Along this stretch of the coast you are likely to come across cruise boats anchored offshore for people to have a swim, and youngsters testing their mettle by jumping or diving off the cliffs. If you're tempted yourself, be careful – there are dangerous currents.

# Protaras

Beyond Cape Greko, and facing east, **PROTARAS** is a family-friendly version of its big brother, Agia Napa, along the coast. A long, linear strip from Agia Trias in the north to Fig Tree Bay in the south, Protaras largely fills in the space between the E306 Paralimni to Agia Napa road and the sea. In particular, it spreads along a one-way main street that loops down then rejoins the E306, with spurs heading east to the beaches. Its attractions are particularly human in scale and child-orientated – the **Ocean Aquarium**, the **Magical Dancing Waters**, the **mini-golf courses** and **amusement arcades**. Like Agia Napa, Protaras also has its share of intimate Blue Flag **beaches**.

### Ocean Aquarium

5318 Paralimni • Daily: April–Oct 10am–6pm; Nov–March 9am–4pm • €13 • ☎ 23741111, ⓦ protarasaquarium.com

Housed in a purpose-built yellow structure on the main road from Protaras to Paralimni, the **Ocean Aquarium** is an eclectic mix of penguins, crocodiles, exotic birds, coral reefs and over four hundred species of fish and turtles, few actually native to the region. It's not up there with the world's greatest aquariums, but it might be worth a visit, especially with younger children.

### Magic Dancing Waters

Protaras Avenue • Apr–Nov daily 9–10pm (restaurant open from 7.30pm) • €23 adults, €15 children • ☎ 99623143, ⓦ magicdancing. szm.com

Imagine first of all a curtain of pulsing, churning water tinted by coloured lights, throbbing to highly amplified music. Progressively throw in a flashing laser show, and end with a crescendo of simulated volcanic eruptions, fire spilling out of the crater and smoke billowing everywhere, all to the sound of Europe's "The Final Countdown". This all happens at the **Magic Dancing Waters**, in front of a terrace upon which the customers sit at tables, eating and drinking. The display takes about an hour, and you'll either love it or hate it. What is indisputable is that it's not cheap.

### Protaras beaches

Protaras more than outdoes Agia Napa in the range and quality of its **beaches**. At the far north of the town there's the fishing shelter of **Agia Triada** (just past the aquarium), there's a little harbour with a modern church, locals fishing off the rocks, and the ever-present *Helen Snacks* van providing sustenance. Just a couple of kilometres south, at **Paralimni**, a paved terrace overlooks a harbour full of fishing boats. There's a taverna (with no name) with a terrace offering fine views of the harbour, and the photogenic church of **Agios Nikolaos** on the end of the promontory to the right.

**1**

## SUN, SAND AND BARBED WIRE

The area **around Agia Napa** is one of the regions of the south most affected by the Turkish invasion of 1974 – in much of it you cannot but be aware of the **Green Line**, of the UN troops manning it, and of Turkish-occupied north Cyprus in many places within clear view beyond. The area, too, has a continued UK presence in the British base at Dhekelia. If you stay within Agia Napa itself, then the only indication you're likely to have of this is the possible presence of British soldiers (though the town is supposedly out of bounds to them). But the short trip to Deryneia will give you a good view of ruined Varosha, left high and dry by the invasion (see page 257), and you can visit Gazimağusa (Famagusta) in the North by using either of the crossing points in the area (see page 27).

Beyond the church, palm trees sweep down to the sandy beach of **Louma Bay** and its clutch of hotels. Further south a number of other beaches have equally good sand and numerous hotels and restaurants – **Pernera Bay**, **Potamos Bay**, **Vrissi Bay** and, the jewel in Protaras's crown, **Fig Tree Bay**, known for its beauty across the island. In some ways Fig Tree Bay (also known as Protaras Bay) is a victim of its own celebrity – the natural allure of its pellucid water, fine sand and, yes, even a few fig trees, has been tempered by wooden boardwalks, concrete steps, showers, and the roar of speedboats and jet-skis (try ⑩figtreebaywatersports.com or ⑩stavroswatersports.com for water sports) – but its setting is still hard to beat. A new paved walkway meanders northwards along the coast from Fig Tree Bay to Pernera.

### ARRIVAL AND INFORMATION                                    PROTARAS

**By bus** There is no main bus station in Protaras, since the town is on the main Agia Napa to Paralimni route but there are regular stops along the two main roads.
Destinations There are frequent buses linking Protaras with Paralimni (15min), Larnaka (1hr) and Lefkosia (2hr).

**Tourist office** Cavo Greko, off Lefkolla Square (first and third week of the month Mon–Fri 9am–3.30pm; second and fourth week of the month 9am–3.30pm & Sat 9am–2pm; ☎ 23832865).

### TOURS AND ACTIVITIES

A variety of cruises up the coast (most with swimming stops and barbecues), fishing trips and scuba-diving expeditions are on offer in the boat harbours around Protaras. Prices range from €10 to €45. For diving try Easy Divers Cyprus at 352 Kavo Grecko Ave (☎ 23833662, ⑩ ezdivers.com).

### ACCOMMODATION

**Capo Bay Hotel** 2 Iasonos ☎ 23831101, ⑩ capobay. com; map p.65. An attractively designed and luxurious hotel in prime position on the beach in the centre of town, with a terrific range of rooms and suites, classy restaurants and bars, a large pool, gym, spa, diving centre, sports facilities, and a kids' club. April–Oct. **€171**

**Crystal Springs Beach Hotel** 95 Vrysoudion ☎ 23826900, ⑩ crystalspringsbeachhotel.com; map p.65. The elegant and luxurious *Crystal Springs* offers access to a sandy beach, its own scuba-diving centre, and a wide range of sporting and entertainment activities. If the hotel has a drawback it's the location, well away from the town centre, so to get anywhere else you need to drive, get a cab, or catch the bus outside the hotel. This might explain, of course, the wide range of in-house activities and also what is, for this grade of hotel, a very reasonable tariff. High-season minimum stay of five nights. April–Oct. **€136**

**Grecian Park Hotel** 81 Konnos ☎ 23844000, ⑩ grecian park.com; map p.65. As regards location, it doesn't get any better than the *Grecian Park*, perched on its cliff above Konnos Bay, with views across to Cape Greko. From the same stable as the *Grecian Sands* in Agia Napa, the hotel boasts a cool elegance of design, a health club, spa and wellness centre, top-class restaurants (and its own nightclub and sushi bar) and in its *Cliff Bar* one of the best views on the island. There's a nature trail down onto Konnos Beach, and a kiosk there for drinks and snacks. April–Nov. **€208**

**Livas Hotel Apartments** 1 Thaleias ☎ 23831756, ⑩ livashotelapts.com; map p.65. At rates below what you'll pay at the big hotels, the *Livas* offers clean rooms with kitchenette (useful for saving a few pennies if you don't wish to eat at the hotel's restaurant), two pools (one for kids), tennis court, pool table and video games. The studios and apartments are fairly spartan, but then you'd not expect to be spending much time indoors. With friendly staff, a nearby beach and lots going on in the vicinity, it's a good budget choice. April–Oct. **€60**

**Pernera Beach Hotel** Pernera ☎ 23831011, ⓦ pernera. com.cy; map p.65. Terrific location right on Pernera Bay, with a wraparound restaurant overlooking the beach. The hotel has a full entertainment package for kids and friendly, committed staff. It's also the base for the excellent Taba Diving School which operates right off the beach. Minimum stay high season five nights. **€160**

★ **Sunrise Beach Hotel** Vrissi Bay ☎ 23831501, ⓦ sunrise.com.cy; map p.65. Near the centre of Protaras on Vrissi Bay, a very popular beach with tourists and Cypriots alike, the *Sunrise Beach* has a beachside pool (with whirlpool), three restaurants, four bars, scuba-diving school, health club, a fitness centre and courts for tennis and squash. It is also a good choice for families – there's a kids' club, children's pool and playground, and children's menus and high chairs in the restaurants. April–Oct. **€230**

## EATING

**Blue Spice** Paralimni ☎ 23832088, ⓦ bluespice restaurant.com; map p.65. A restaurant overlooking the sea which is a nice place to spend a Friday night if you want to enjoy some entertainment, Within the restaurant area there's a small but interesting gallery and if something catches your eye, you can buy one of the paintings. Daily 9am–midnight.

**Il Cavaliere** 6 Pernera ☎ 23831022; map p.65. Fairly standard Italian restaurant – pasta, pizza – but with regional dishes as well. It's particularly welcoming if you've got kids – there's a children's menu and play area. Main

courses from around €10–15. Daily 1–11pm.

**Knight's Pub** 56 Pernera Avenue ☎ 23831497, ⓦ knightspub.com; map p.65. A good pub with a wider then usual food selection on the menu. A lot of people come here for the cocktails but return to sample more of the dishes. Daily 10.30am–2am.

**La Cultura del Gusto** 9 Ifestou (on way down to Pernera beach) ☎ 23833860; map p.65. Excellent choice of modern Italian and Mediterranean staples as well as game and suckling pig. Main courses from around €10. Daily 6–11pm.

# Paralimni

**PARALIMNI**, which took over the role of regional capital when Famagusta was cut off by the Turkish invasion of 1974, is easier on the eye than a lot of people give it credit for. Though not exactly worth a special trip, it can be a welcome respite from the frenetic coastal strip. A big open town square boasts no fewer than **three churches**, all in a row – the big, brash new Agios Georgios, the mellow arcaded old Agios Georgios, and the appealing Panagia. Also around the square are a statue and **memorial** to local EOKA leader and regional commander-in-chief Tasos Markou (who disappeared during the 1974 invasion); a wind pump typical of those that dot this region's landscape; and a rather good **children's playground**. Around the corner from the square is an open-air theatre, and the town hall, frequently the scene of local weddings. Paralimni offers a range of shops and numerous bars, cafés and restaurants.

### The Traditional House

Agias Marinas 5 • Mon–Fri 7am–2.45pm • Free • ☎ 23819300, ⓦ paralimni.org.cy

Just south of Paralimni's main square is the **Traditional House**, located inside a beautiful early nineteenth-century cottage. The collection on show includes a wide variety of household furniture, textiles, crockery, utensils and equipment which provides older locals with a nostalgic trip down memory lane, and younger ones, and visitors, with a window on the town's past. Many villages have their own folklore museums, but few are as beautifully presented as this one.

# The Kokkinochoria

The area around Paralimni is dotted with villages known collectively as the **KOKKINOCHORIA** (singular *Kokkinochorio*), or "red villages", which get their name from the rich red soil which surrounds them. This is market gardening country and is sprinkled with plastic greenhouses and the tall shapes of wind pumps which traditionally raised water from underground to irrigate the fields. There's not an awful lot to see, though you'll come across the odd museum – the **Avgorou Ethnographical**

1

**Museum** (Mon–Fri 8.30am–1.30pm, Tues, Thurs & Fri also 4–6pm, Sat 9am–1pm; €1.71; ☎23923340), for example, well signposted from the A3 motorway, which offers an interesting if patchy picture of the past life of the village. Other notable villages in the area include Sotira, Frenaros and Xilofagou, all pleasant enough but lacking the present-day political interest of Deryneia.

## Deryneia

A few kilometres north of Paralimni, **DERYNEIA** has a dinky square containing the usual war memorial, a small church, a village museum and a *kafenío*. So far so typical of many Cypriot villages. The unique thing about Deryneia, though, is its position on a hillside overlooking the Green Line, which offers impressive views over Gazimağusa in north Cyprus (the town is still defiantly known as Famagusta here). Nowhere are the effects of the 1974 invasion clearer or more affecting. At the bottom of the slope the Turkish flags, military buildings and barbed wire begin, and beyond them stretches the suburb of Varosha, once a vibrant coastal resort, now a sorry expanse of empty and increasingly dilapidated buildings (see page 236).

### The Cultural Centre of Occupied Famagusta
35 Evangorou • Mon–Fri 7.30am–4.30pm, Sat 9.30am–4.30pm • Free • ☎ 23740860

The best place from which to view Varosha is the **Cultural Centre of Occupied Famagusta**, clearly signposted from the centre of the village. There's a short video to watch, a diorama of Famagusta, and you can borrow binoculars or a telescope (free of charge) and climb up to the rooftop viewing area. The highly committed curator is happy to answer any questions, and will pick you up on your terminology if you refer to "the border" – borders are between countries, and north Cyprus is an occupied zone, not a country. You might also be told about the murders of two young Greek-Cypriot men in 1996, during demonstrations against the Turkish occupation. This makes for a sad, thought-provoking visit which emphasizes just what a disaster the events of 1974 were for both Greek- and Turkish-Cypriot communities on the island.

### Folk Art Museum
2 Demetri Liperti • Winter Mon–Sat 9am–1pm & 3–5pm; summer 9am–1pm & 3–6pm • €2 (includes admission to the Open Air Museum of Traditional Crafts) • ☎ 2374 0353

Clearly signposted from the main road through the village, the **Folk Art Museum** (sometimes known as the Folkloric Museum) occupies an attractive traditional house, with rooms kitted out with the furniture, tools, utensils, crockery and textiles which would have been typical of such a house in the past. In the small front garden are a dome-shaped wood-burning stove and a well.

### Open Air Museum of Traditional Crafts
3 Demetri Liperti • Museum: Winter Mon–Sat 9am–5pm, summer 9am–8pm; coffee lounge: 10am–late • €2 (includes admission to the Folk Art Museum) • ☎ 23102771

Directly across the road from the Folk Art Museum, and amounting to a modern extension to it (and therefore easily found if you follow signs to the latter), the **Open Air Museum of Traditional Crafts** is arranged around a courtyard in a series of what look like lock-up garages. Opened in 2014, each "garage" contains a display illustrating the work of a particular village craft – the fisherman, the carpenter, the stonemason, the blacksmith, the cobbler, the tailor and so on. Perhaps as a result of a dawning realization of how male-orientated all this was, there's also a display on the "Women of Derynea". The garden/courtyard is dotted with pieces of arcane equipment, and there's a really nice coffee lounge. Indeed, the museum coffee shop has become something of a meeting place for local people, who gather to drink coffee, eat ice cream, and watch football on a flat-screen TV.

# West of Larnaka

The area to the **west of Larnaka** is an almost polar opposite to the in-your-face tourism and the ever-present political division to the east. Instead you'll find a rural hinterland of farmland and small villages, with Venetian towers, churches, monasteries and convents, little ports like Zygi, and Troodos foothill villages. In particular, look out for **Neolithic settlements** at Tenta and Choirokoitia, the eccentric **museum** of naive artist **Costas Argyrou** at Mazotos, a **camel park** in the same village, and a **museum of embroidery and silver** (and lots of lace and silverware shops) in Lefkara.

## Kiti and Pervolia

West of Larnaka, just beyond the airport, is the odd, slightly windblown area around the villages of **KITI** and **PERIVOLIA**. Though increasingly dominated by the spread of apartment blocks and villas, it has several sights which offer a vivid introduction to different aspects of Cyprus's history. Principal among these is the famous church of Angeloktisti ("built by angels") in Kiti village – it's well signposted, and lies just off the main road into the village from Larnaka. Incidentally, be aware that there's another church right in the centre of the village at the intersection of several streets. It's attractive, but it's not the one.

### Angeloktisti

Kiti • June–Aug Mon–Sat 6am–6.30pm; Sept–May Mon–Sat 6am–4.35pm • Free

Built in the eleventh century on the ruins of a much earlier church, the exquisite church of **Angeloktisti** is famous partly for its architecture, but mainly for a very early (probably sixth century) **mosaic** which decorates the apse on the right after you've entered. Considered to be one of the, if not *the*, best mosaic in Cyprus, it is of the Virgin Mary and the baby Jesus, flanked by two archangels with peacock wings. Although damaged, this survivor from one and a half thousand years ago still has beauty enough to take your breath away. Outside is a massive terebinth tree with benches around its base, a small café and a children's playground.

---

**DEATH ON THE GREEN LINE**

Ever since the Turkish invasion in 1974, incidents have flared up along the **Green Line**. Two of the worst happened in 1996. That year was the 22nd anniversary of the Turkish invasion of Cyprus, and to mark the occasion over two hundred bikers left Berlin to ride to Lefkosia in order to demonstrate against the occupation. Under pressure from the UN the bikers were persuaded not to cross into north Cyprus. However, on August 11, a group of **Greek-Cypriot demonstrators** ignored this and entered the **Buffer Zone near Deryneia**. Facing them were several hundred members of the Grey Wolves, a Turkish far-right group, as well as military personnel armed with batons. During the confusion, a young Greek Cypriot called Tassos Isaac was surrounded by a mob and beaten to death. Three days later, on August 14, during further demonstrations sparked by Isaac's funeral, Solomos Solomou, a relative of Isaac, climbed a flagpole in the Buffer Zone to pull down a Turkish flag. He was shot three times and died at the scene.

The two murders had several consequences. They represented a spectacular public relations own goal for Turkey and the north, having occurred in front of a scrum of journalists and photographers there to cover the demonstrations. The killers of both young Greek Cypriots were easily identified from numerous photographs and videos taken at the scene: Isaac was killed by a combination of Turkish settlers and Turkish Cypriots, Solomou by none other than the minister of agriculture of north Cyprus. Isaac and Solomou have since became martyrs to both Greek Cypriots and to citizens of Greece, and the whole tragedy drew further attention to the bitter division of the island.

**1**

### Venetian Tower

To the southwest of Larnaka, just southeast of Perivolia (signposted "Pyrgos Rigenas"), stands an immaculate (though much restored) **Venetian Tower**, built in the years before 1500 as part of an early warning system to try to prevent an Ottoman invasion of the island. It might even have worked for a while – Venetian rule struggled on till 1571. Some 6m square at the base, there is no way to get into it (the door is about 3m off the ground), but despite its slightly forlorn air (it sits in scrub surrounded by a chain-link fence, though the gate is open) it's certainly atmospheric.

### Ottoman Lighthouse

Guarding the southern approaches to Larnaka's port, on the first promontory south – Cape Kiti – is the dinky little **lighthouse** built to warn ships of the danger represented by the cape. It dates from 1864, during the dying years of the Ottoman occupation, it has a 9m octagonal tower and is attached to the lighthouse-keeper's cottage. Apartment and villa building has in the last four years turned this previously rather charming area into a building site not really worth visiting – at least until its development is complete.

## Mazotos Camel Park

Mazotos • Daily: March–Oct 9am–7pm, Nov–April 9am–5pm • €3; camel ride (15min) is an additional €6 • ☎ 99416968, ⓦ camel-park.com

Some 10km west of Kiti, by the sleepy village of **Mazotos**, and well signposted (look out for little silhouettes of camels), is the **Mazotos Camel Park**, a sure-fire hit with families. In addition to over fifty haughty, lugubrious camels, there are ponies, donkeys, goats, ostriches, loads of amusements (a flight simulator, table tennis, bumper cars, mini-motorbikes, trampoline, bouncy castle) and, oddly, reconstructions of a Cypriot farmhouse and a Bedouin tent. There's also a souvenir shop, an ice-cream kiosk, a swimming pool and a surprisingly good restaurant.

## Costas Argyrou Museum

Mazotos • closed for renovation • ☎ 24432277

On the edge of Mazotos village is the excellent **Costas Argyrou Museum**. Costas Argyrou was a local man, born in 1917. During his fifties he visited Larnaka's archeological museum, which inspired him to devote the rest of his life to art. Untrained and working in the naive tradition, he started producing the range of paintings, sculptures, mosaics and woodcarvings now on show here. The themes are religion, mythology and the history of Cyprus, all created with an understated sense of humour and an eclectic use of materials. Next to the museum is a small **church** in which the artist had wanted to be buried along with his wife (he died in 2001). The authorities refused permission and he was buried in the local cemetery, so now two empty tombs take up the central floor space. There's a final footnote to this remarkable story. Argyrou designed the museum building himself, but, being as untrained in architecture as he was in art, it experienced all sorts of structural problems, which became the bane of its administrators.

## Golden Donkeys Farm

7731 Memila–Skarinou • Daily: April–Oct 9am–7pm; Nov–March 9am–5pm • €3 • ☎ 9962073, ⓦ goldendonkeys.com

The new kid on the block in the Skarinou area (and replacing the previous Dipotamos Donkey Farm and Fatsa Wax Museum, both still advertised by the tourist board and in many guidebooks) is the **Golden Donkey Farm**. It lies about 3km west of the village, accessible via narrow country roads, the last kilometre of which is dirt track. Though tortuous, the route is extremely well signposted, with life-size models of

1

golden donkeys pointing the way. Home to some two hundred donkeys, the farm offers a slightly odd bundle of attractions which somehow works. In addition to donkey rides, there's a shop selling a range of cosmetics made from donkey milk (a wonder product that the farm all but claims is the key to life eternal), a spacious restaurant and small outdoor café, a building kitted out as a church ("Mother Mary of Memila" – probably not consecrated), and a wax museum which has recycled some of the material from the defunct Fatsa Wax Museum, stripped of the more bloodthirsty tableaux to illustrate normal rural life and crafts instead. There's a large paved outdoor area surrounding an olive tree claimed to be 1,500 years old, labelled aromatic herb beds, and, dotted around, pieces of photogenic farm machinery. The whole establishment has a pristine cleanliness that reflects its newness and the care taken in its construction. It's worth a half-day visit, though its rural location makes for slow driving.

## Zygi

**ZYGI** is a small fishing port about halfway between Larnaka and Lemesos. Though somewhat lacking in atmosphere (its harbour being so obviously new and raw), Zygi's pleasant position and good seafood restaurants have made it a popular day-trip from Larnaka, Lemesos and Lefkosia. Developed originally as a point of export for carob (sometimes known as locust) beans and boasting some attractive old carob warehouses, the village went into a brief decline as demand fell, but then received a population boost as refugees flooded in from the north after 1974. In July 2011 the massive explosion at the Evangelos Florakis Naval Base, just along the coast, caused widespread damage in the village. In case you're wondering, the tall antennae to the west belong to the British East Mediterranean Relay Station.

## Kalavasos

The village of **KALAVASOS** lies about 4km inland from Zygi, on the other side of the A1 motorway. It is nicely sited astride the valley of the Vasilikos River, and has a growing reputation as a centre for walking in the surrounding hills. The area around Kalavasos was once the centre of a flourishing copper and gypsum mining industry, the output of which flowed down a narrow-gauge railway to the port of Vasiliko for export. The industry is now defunct, but you can still see traces of the railway line – indeed, there's a surviving locomotive and wagons on a bridge over the river near the village, kept as a memorial and lit up at night. Since it lost its livelihood, the village has become a major agrotourism village, with many of its houses renovated and let to visitors.

---

**THE BIG BANG: JANUARY 11, 2011**

In the early hours of January 11, 2011, thousands of people in Larnaka district were awoken by a huge **explosion** at the **Evangelos Florakis Naval Base** just outside Zygi. A hundred containers of gunpowder and other explosives being stored at the base (confiscated from a Cyprus-registered ship taking them from Iran to the Gaza Strip in 2009) had ignited, either spontaneously or by the spread of a bush fire. Thirteen people died in the blast, among them the commander-in-chief of the navy, and damage was caused throughout the area. Cars on the Lemesos to Larnaka motorway were showered with debris, almost all the windows in Zygi were smashed, schools in both British Sovereign bases had to be closed and the BBC transmitters broadcasting to the Middle East went off the air. The power station at nearby Vassilikou, which produced around half of the country's electricity, was destroyed. As a result, a rolling programme of power cuts had to be introduced, and generators brought in from Greece and Israel. Disputes as to who was to blame started immediately and continue to this day.

# Tochni

In the next valley east from Kalavasos is **TOCHNI**, a peaceful village with a quaint, if slightly dishevelled, look. Climbing up the steep sides of a ravine, with steep walls and houses perched above substantial drops, you'll often see local people sitting out on tiny balconies or small terraces to catch the breeze and enjoy the view. Legend has it that St Helena – mother of the Emperor Constantine and famous religious relic hunter (see page 78) – on arrival in Cyprus from Jerusalem in 325, built a bridge in Tochni bearing a church in which to deposit a fragment of the True Cross. That church was destroyed by fire, but a new one was built in the nineteenth century, also straddling a bridge. The combination of bridge, cloister and church tower makes a picturesque group at the heart of the village. The history of Tochni has, alas, in more recent times been a bloody one. In 1974 an EOKA-B contingent massacred 85 Turkish Cypriots from the village and surrounding area.

# Neolithic settlements

The three valleys that run north from the main Larnaka–Lemesos road (to Kalavasos, Tochni and Choirokoitia) contain two extremely important **Neolothic sites**, both well signposted from both the A1 and the B1.

## Tenta Neolithic Village

Daily mid-April to mid-Sept 9.30am–5pm; mid-Sept to mid-April 8.30am–4pm • €2.50 • ⓦ tinyurl.com/tentasite

You can't miss the **Tenta Neolithic Village** – it's protected by a sort of modern wigwam, erected in 1995, that can be seen for many kilometres around (including from the A1 motorway that passes nearby). Discovered in 1947 and further excavated between 1976 and 1984, the site was probably originally settled about 9000 years ago. It consists of the remains of clusters of circular huts made of limestone, sun-dried mud bricks and probably timber. Around 150 Neolithic people lived here, with their sheep, goats and pigs (but not cattle, for some reason). The dead were buried under the floor or just outside the huts; there were no grave goods, but numerous utensils and ornaments (now in museums in Lefkosia and Larnaka) were found. Access to the site is via wooden steps and walkways, and huts are clearly numbered and explained on information boards. Look out particularly for Structure 35, where red ochre was worked (it contained a large stone basin with lumps of partially worked ochre and the stone tools used to grind it), and Structure 11, which had ochre wall paintings of two human figures with arms raised. Entry to the site includes a pamphlet which outlines its history and the finds associated with it – just enough detail to contextualize what you see, but not enough to be tedious. Tenta really is a must-visit – all archeological sites should be this imaginatively displayed and clearly and comprehensively explained.

## Choirokoitia archeological site

Daily: mid-April to mid-Sept 8.30am–7.30pm; mid-Sept to mid-April 8.30am–5pm • €2.50 • ☎ 24322710, ⓦ tinyurl.com/choirokoitia

The **Choirokoitia archeological site**, originating about 9,000 years ago, is of similar age and type to the Tenta one, but is much more extensive, and contains modern reconstructions of what the circular huts might have looked like. Discovered in 1934, and excavated from 1936 to 1946, with additional work having been done since 1976, Choirokoitia became a UNESCO World Heritage Site in 1998.

The site lies on a steep hillside, accessed via a lung-busting flight of steps. Uniquely, this Neolithic village had a massive **defensive wall** (of which a stretch of around nearly 200m still stands to a height of 4m or more on the side not protected by the river), and there's a vast entrance structure consisting of three flights of steps designed not only to allow those entering the village to climb up from the lower, external level, but also to act as a first line of defence against enemies. The huts vary in size, though are usually around 10m external diameter, 5m internally, and, as at Tenta, are built of stone and sun-dried mud bricks, with a probable timber superstructure. Interestingly, huts are clustered together around common courtyards, presumably according to function or family size, with this open area being used for activities such as grinding corn. The **reconstructed huts** at the bottom of the actual site were made as far as possible using only materials, techniques and skills available to the people of that time, so the mud bricks were made without moulds, and only pine timber was used. In addition to four complete reconstructed huts, a couple of "cut-away" reconstructions house excellent information boards.

After the exertions of the site, especially if you've climbed right to the top, you could do worse than stop for drinks and a snack at the *Chrismarie Bakery* at the entrance to the car park.

## Choirokoitia

Beyond the Neolithic site on the F112, at the top of a long hill, stands **CHOIROKOITIA** itself, a village that occupies a long ridge with splendid views. It is reputedly the site of two influential medieval battles. The first was between **Richard the Lionheart** and **Isaac Komnemos** (see page 85), the then ruler of Cyprus, in 1191 – it is said that the final capture of Komnenos took place at Choirokoitia. The other battle took place in 1426 during the latter part of Lusignan rule. **King Janus of Cyprus** lost to a Mamluk/Egyptian army (partly because he couldn't give his troops the wine they wanted before battle), was captured, and spent ten months being humiliated before he was ransomed and returned to Cyprus. There's not much left to see of this "Battle of Choirokoitia" – just a small church where Janus was captured, and the remains of a Knights Templar tower where the crucial lack of wine became apparent. They're a few hundred metres up a dirt track west of the village, signposted respectively "Panayia tou Campou" (the church) and "Vasilicos Ekos" (the tower).

## Vavla

In the hills north of the main Lemesos to Lefkosia/Larnaka motorway is **VAVLA**. Located at 500m above sea level, the village remains fresh and cool even during the summer. Suffering severely from depopulation yet with lots of gorgeous traditional architecture, it has become a good illustration of the benefits of agrotourism (see page 30) – renovated houses provide accommodation for visitors who want to enjoy peaceful countryside dotted with carob, olive and almond trees, and fields of cereal, herbs and wild flowers.

## Agios Minas Convent

Mon–Sat: May–Sept 9.30–11.30am & 3–4.30pm; Oct–April 9.30–11.30am & 2–4pm • Free • ☎ 24342952

Between Vavla and Lefkara stands the **Agios Minas Convent**. Once through the entrance arch you pass a series of vivid modern mosaics/icons – the first is of Agios Minas himself – on the right before arriving at the convent itself. The buildings originate from the fifteenth century, though they were extensively renovated in around 1740. With its high buttressed walls and shuttered windows, it looks a little forbidding, though when you have gone through the entrance you walk out into a lovely shady courtyard decorated with a riot of potted plants. The nuns make a living by painting and selling icons and producing and selling honey.

## Kato Drys

Just south of the lace settlement of Lefkara, the village of **KATO DRYS** is tightly packed with atmospheric and beautifully restored old houses. Though the village has traditionally survived by livestock farming and beekeeping, more recently viniculture

**1**

has come to the area with the opening of the Ktima Christoudia winery (6 Agiou Mina Rd, ☎99034828, ⊕ktimachristoudia.com; April–Oct Mon–Sat 9am–5pm, Nov–March daily 9am–6pm) in 1991.Remarkably for such a small place, Kato Drys is the birthplace of two famous Cypriots. **St Neophytos** founded a famous monastery in the Pafos district, and Reo Stakis founded the Stakis chain of hotels. The village also boasts not one but two museums: the Bee and Embroidery Museum (April–Oct daily 10am–1pm and 4–7pm, Nov–March daily Mon–Wed & Fri–Sun 10am–4pm; €2; ☎99892677), on the right as you enter the village, lies at the end of a path through a lush garden; and the **Rural Museum** (daily 9am–3pm, though can vary; ☎24342648), which is in a mellow old house full of agricultural equipment and odds and ends. The views from parts of the village are spectacular.

## Pano Lefkara

The best-known hill village in this region is **PANO (UPPER) LEFKARA** (there's also Kato – Lower – Lefkara just down the hill, but there's not a lot there), which stands at almost 700m above sea level, at the end of the excellent E105 that climbs up to it from the Larnaka to Lemesos road. (Parking is not allowed on the streets – they're too narrow – but there's a new two-storey car park at the top of the village, near the post office.)

Though pretty enough, Pano Lefkara's main claim to fame, attracting numerous tour coaches to the village, is its **lace**, **embroidery** and **silverware**. A local, probably apocryphal, legend suggests that **Leonardo da Vinci** was so impressed with the lace that he bought some for the altar cloth for Milan Cathedral. Today the village exports goods all over the world. Women in the village (seen patiently working their needles outside) are said to pass on their skills to their daughters when they get to the age of ten, while the men ply their trade making silver ornaments and jewellery. It is difficult to fathom how true this is today, and a lot of the stuff you'll see on sale is manufactured elsewhere, but there is still a good proportion of top-quality lace and embroidery for sale here. Be prepared, however, for ferociously hard sells and cunning subterfuges to get you into shops. Try D & A Lefkara Handicraft centre (☎24342686) on the left before you enter the village, or Harry and Maria Loizou (☎24342204).

### Patsalos Museum

House of Patsalos • Daily: mid-April to mid-Sept 9.30am–5pm; mid-Sept to mid-April 8.30am–4pm • €2.50 • ☎24342326

Clearly signposted in the village centre, the **Patsalos Museum of Traditional Embroidery and Silversmithwork** (to give it its full, rather long-winded, title) is located in a magnificent old house with blue doors and shutters (it belonged to one of the richest families in the village). A visit to the museum gives you a feel for what real Lefkara lace and embroidery looks like, and also displays furniture, textiles and pottery in a series of elegant, high-ceilinged rooms.

## Kornos

If Lefkara is famous for its lace, **KORNOS**, some 16km to the northeast along an excellent mountain road (and just west of the A1 Lemesos to Lefkosia motorway), is known for its **pottery**. As you approach the area you can see why – you will be surrounded by a strange moonscape of granite hills whose weathering has bequeathed the area with a layer of good-quality clay. In the past the village specialized in the huge geometrically decorated jars known as *pitharia* and used for transporting water, wine, olive oil and even grain (and these days much used by householders to decorate their entrances or gardens), but the village's potters, adapting to circumstances, now produce items – jars, jugs, ceramics – more likely to appeal to visitors at the mercy of airline weight restrictions. The village is also trying to diversify into tobacco production.

# 1 Chapelle Royal

Pyrga • mid-Apr to mid-Sept Mon–Fri 9.30am–5pm; mid-Sept to mid-Apr Mon–Fri 8.30am–4pm • €2.50 • ☏ 96603664, ⓦ bit.ly/ChapelleRoyal

Just east of the main B1 Lemesos to Lefkosia road (signposted "Medieval Chapel"), on the right just as you come into the village of Pyrga, is the **Chapelle Royal**, a building whose fame is on first view hard to credit – a tiny (7m by 4m) oblong structure squashed between a much larger modern church and a children's playground. The reason so much is made of it is that it is the only complete survival from the last of the Lusignan rulers of Cyprus, King Janus. Beautifully restored, it was built in 1421 as the chapel of a royal manor (since destroyed), and is decorated internally with **frescoes** in a mishmash of Byzantine and Italian styles, but with **inscriptions** in medieval French. Since the French seems to have been written phonetically, it is thought that the frescoes may have been the work of a native Greek Cypriot. In a crucifixion scene, two figures kneeling at the foot of the cross are thought to be those of the king and his (second) wife Charlotte de Bourbon. Their piety, alas, did them little good. Within five years she was dead and he was riding backwards on a donkey in Cairo, being jeered at by the populace.

## Stavrovouni Monastery

Stavrovouni Mountain, south of Pyrga off the B1 • Daily: April–Aug 8am–noon & 3–6pm; Sept–March 8am–noon & 3–5pm • Free • ☏ 22533630

The **Stavrovouni Monastery** ("Hill of the Cross") – the oldest in Cyprus – tops an impressive 690m hill that rises steeply from the surrounding plain. According to legend, the original monastery was established by **St Helena** in 327 AD to house some of the numerous **relics** she brought back from Jerusalem – a piece of the True Cross, the whole of that of the penitent thief, and pieces of rope and nails used in the Crucifixion. The monastery buildings were destroyed in 1426 after the battle of Choirokoitia, again in 1570 during the Ottoman conquest, and yet again by fire in 1888 – so the current buildings date from the late nineteenth century.

With strong historical links with the monasteries of **Mount Athos** in northeastern Greece, the monks follow a similar regimen, setting aside a third of their day for prayer, a third for physical labour, and a third for rest. For the same reason Stavrovouni is the only Cypriot monastery that follows the Mount Athos practice of **banning females** – even baby girls are not allowed within its precinct: ironic, really, given that the monastery was allegedly established by a woman. Photography is also banned – the whole mountain sits in the middle of a military zone. This might also explain the severe (and surreal) signs prohibiting "Drones and other flying objects". Men who visit the monastery must not wear short trousers, and must leave their cameras and their female companions at the entrance. Women are allowed into the church ("All Saints of Cyprus") at the opposite side of the car park, though this may be scant recompense.

---

### ST HELENA, RELIC-FINDER GENERAL

**Saint Helena** (Agia Eleni) is a figure shrouded in mystery. The mother of the Emperor Constantine, nobody's sure where or when she was born, where she spent her early years, or even whether she was married to Constantine's father Constinius or was just his mistress. However, she burst into history when her son, by then emperor, asked her to visit the Holy Land to find and recover Judeo-Christian relics. Her trip took place during the years 326–328 AD – by which time she was in her seventies. While there, she investigated the scenes of Christ's birth, crucifixion and ascension, and had built the **Church of the Nativity** in Bethlehem and the Church of the Mount of Olives over the first and last of these. During the excavations, she is said to have discovered parts of Christ's tunic, ropes and nails used to bind him to the Cross, the cross of the penitent thief, and the **True Cross** itself (identified by its power to cure the sick). On her way back to Rome, the story goes, she came to Cyprus and built more churches, leaving relics in Tochni (see page 74) and Stavrovouni (see page 78). She died around 330 AD, and her tomb can today be seen in the Italian capital.

Once through the entrance building, steep steps and a paved path lead up onto the summit, where the monastery buildings surround a courtyard. Visitors are allowed to enter the **church**, but not the area beyond the courtyard, which is reserved for monks. The church is small, and the only thing of note is a silver-encased wooden cross to the right of the iconostasis, perhaps representing St Helena's penitent thief's cross, and sometimes though not always present, a gilt reliquary containing, it's claimed, a few splinters of the True Cross.

## GETTING AROUND · WEST OF LARNAKA

**By bus** By far the best way of exploring the area to the west of Larnaka is to rent a car, though it is also relatively well served by buses. Routes #401 to #410 all serve one or more of the villages described above: the #401, for example, links Larnaka to Kalavasos, Tochni, Choirokoitia and Kofinou. There are usually three buses a day (two on Sundays). The #417, which runs to Kiti and Perivolia, is more frequent (12/day, 9 at weekends), and there are also night buses (routes #448, #452 and #455).

**By car** Access to the area west of Larnaka is easiest on local roads beyond the airport for the nearer villages, otherwise via the A5/A1 motorway.

## ACCOMMODATION

Unlike Larnaka itself and the tourist hotspots of Agia Napa and Protaras, there are not many big resorts in the area to the west. However, the coast is seeing hotels and villas popping up, and agrotourism is making headway, especially in the Troodos foothills.

**Aunt Maria's** Lefkara ☎ 99356652, ⓦ auntmarias.com. Typical of the best of agrotourist accommodation, *Aunt Maria's* offers three one-bedroom and one three-bedroom self-catering apartments on the hillside near the village square, with a full range of facilities. Rooms are clean and simple. The house was renovated using traditional materials in 2008 and stands in well-designed gardens. **€55**

**e-hotel** Pervolia ☎ 24747000, ⓦ hotel-e.com. Hotel perched on the tip of Cape Kiti, right behind the lighthouse, with bang up-to-the-minute spa, gym, luxuriously appointed rooms, studios, suites and villas, excellent restaurant, two bars (a beach bar and one on the roof) and two pools – one indoor, one outdoor (small, but surrounded by four-poster beds). Take its claim that it overlooks pristine white sands with a pinch of salt, though – the beach isn't up to much. **€168**

**Lefkara Village Hotel** 42 Timiou Stavrou, Lefkara ☎ 24342154, ⓦ cyprus-hotels.com/lefkara-hotel. Ten comfortable en suite rooms and a cracking restaurant housed in an arcaded building which, at different times in its past, has been a pilgrims' hostel, a coffee shop and even a cinema. Despite its age, the hotel has a good array of mod cons, with satellite TV, a/c, heating and wi-fi in all rooms, and is, of course, in one of the prettiest villages of the region. **€60**

**Library Hotel** Kalavassos ☎ 24817071, ⓦ libraryhotel cyprus.com. Nineteenth-century stone building housing eight rooms and three suites opening onto a courtyard. True to its name, it has a lounge which is also a library; what you might not expect is that it also has an air of pampered luxury, with a wellness suite, fine restaurant and outdoor Jacuzzi. Adults only. **€82**

## EATING

The region west of Larnaka has a wealth of restaurants which Cypriots are prepared to drive considerable distances to reach. Thus the clientele at tavernas and restaurants is a good mix of locals and discerning types from Lemesos and Lefkosia.

**Archontiko Papadopoulo** 67 Makariou III Avenue, Kornos ☎ 24531000. An elegant old balconied house – all stone floors and gorgeous high ceilings – knocking out delicious Greek-Cypriot food and drink at surprisingly reasonable prices: main courses around €11–22. You can eat inside, in the courtyard or on a balcony. Look out for the village's trademark product *pitharia* (large clay jars). Tues–Sun 9.30am–3pm, 6–11.30pm.

★**Captain's Table** 48 Grigoris Afxentiou, Zygi ☎ 24333737. One of the best of Zygi's numerous fish restaurants, the *Captain's Table* is in an unbeatable location right on the new boat-crowded harbour. On two floors, it offers main courses that start at €22 (try the love plate at €87 for two) and is known for its lobster dishes (priced per kilo, so it's difficult to judge the value). It also provides a choice of "Meat Dishes for the Non Fish Lover" (€18–32). Not a cheap night out, but wonderful food in a dockside setting. Daily 10am–11pm.

**Platanos Taverna** Kato Drys ☎ 24342160. Just outside Kato Drys, the *Platanos* is a typical Cypriot taverna with tables and chairs spread out beneath a large plane tree. Main courses start at €9, with mezé at €15/person. Tues–Sun 9am–midnight.

**Santa Elena** 4 Apostolou Varnava, Zygi ☎ 24332203. Another of Zygi's numerous fish restaurants, *Santa Elena* is housed in an old Turkish carob warehouse opposite the church, and has clean lines and cheerful tablecloths. Healthy portions at reasonable prices, with main courses costing €8–20. Daily 11am–11pm.

★**Tochni Taverna** Tochni ☎ 24332998. Run by Cyprus Villages (their office reception is in the same building), the *Tochni Taverna* specializes in traditional Cypriot food – souvlakia, *stifado*, *koupepia* et al – even the humble *fasolia* (bean stew). Expect to pay around €15/person. Nice views across the village. Daily 7.30am–11pm; closed March 7–April 7.

# Lemesos
# and around

TIMIOU STAVROU MONASTERY, OMODOS

# Lemesos and around

Lemesos (Limassol) is the republic's second city and premier port, with a reputation for fast living, frenetic (and occasionally sleazy) nightlife, fine hotels and sophisticated restaurants. The rest of the region boasts numerous traditional villages, the outstanding archeological sites of Amathus and Kourion, two of the greatest Crusader castles in Lemesos and Kolossi, and, in the Troodos foothills, a wealth of pretty hill villages and vineyards, the latter linked by well-marked wine routes.

The coast east of Lemesos has its fair share of vast hotel complexes attached to mediocre beaches, though there are enough amusement parks (including the island's largest water park) to keep children and young adults entertained. If you're seeking something quieter, head south and west towards, and beyond, the British Sovereign Base at **Akrotiri**, which has blocked development in those directions. With good motorway links with Pafos, Lefkosia, Larnaka and Ayia Napa, and good links by ordinary road with the Troodos Mountains, Lemesos is one of the most convenient places to stay on the island.

## Lemesos

**LEMESOS** (still widely known as "Limassol") is a teeming multicultural city of just over 184,000 inhabitants, which grew substantially after 1974, when Greek Cypriots flooded in from the north. Since then, it has welcomed migrants from Lebanon, Iraq and other Middle Eastern trouble spots. Russians, too, are very much in evidence – you'll see Cyrillic script in menus and shop signs across town.

The city centre is remarkably compact. It stretches about 1km from the castle and old harbour to the Municipal Gardens in the west. Near the castle are a cathedral and mosque as well as the cool cafés, bars and restaurants of the **Carob Mill Complex**. Inland is the old **Turkish quarter**, ideal for aimless wanderings. Along the seafront a 16km pedestrian and cycle path links the old town with sandy beaches further east.

After a lengthy period of remodelling which started in 2007, Lemesos city centre has emerged transformed. Extensive pedestrianization, and development of the palm-fringed seafront, **Old Port** and **marina** have changed what was a hot, dusty, traffic-dominated hell into a peaceful, people-friendly place in which to potter about, with lots of shops, cafés, bars and restaurants and enough museum-type attractions to be getting on with.

### Brief history

Once a nondescript fishing village overshadowed by its eminent neighbours Kourion to the west and Amathus to the east, Lemesos became a little more high-profile when its competitors were destroyed in seventh-century Saracen raids. However, it was Richard the Lionheart who really put it on the map when he landed to rescue his sister Joan and his fiancée Berengaria from the ruler of Cyprus Isaac Komnenos (see page 85).

The city received another boost to its fortunes a century later when, with the fall of Acre, the two great Crusader organizations, the Knights Templar and the Knights Hospitallers, fell back to Cyprus and made Lemesos their headquarters. When the Templars were purged and outlawed in 1307, the Hospitallers adopted their lands and their influence. Lemesos's story during the following two centuries was one of prosperity interspersed with earthquakes and attacks from the sea. During the Ottoman occupation from the sixteenth century onwards, it settled back into obscurity, stymied by a swingeing harbour duty designed to concentrate trade in Larnaka. This trend was

KOLOSSI CASTLE

# Highlights

**❶ Carob Mill Complex, Lemesos** A lively area of museums, bars and restaurants in Lemesos old town, particularly vibrant at night when everything's lit up. See page 85

**❷ Lemesos Marina** Thronged with young people and families enjoying the cafés, restaurants and shops, Lemesos's new marina has changed the atmosphere of the city centre. See page 88

**❸ Lemesos Wine Festival** Whether you're an earnest oenophile or a jolly boozer, the Lemesos Wine Festival offers good value and the chance to try wine from all over Cyprus in convivial surroundings. See page 90

**❹ Kolossi Castle** Literally a massive reminder of Cyprus's links with the world of medieval knights. See page 98

**❺ Cyprus Wine Museum** All you need to know about Cypriot wine and its place in the island's history, nicely packaged in a traditional house. See page 98

**❻ Ancient Kourion** Perched on a promontory high above the Mediterranean, Kourion is one of the island's most spectacular ancient sites. See page 100

**❼ Omodos** A village rightly proud of both its history and its wine, with cobbled square, monastery, winery and lots of stalls and shops. See page 105

**HIGHLIGHTS ARE MARKED ON THE MAP ON PAGE 84**

## LEMESOS AND AROUND

### HIGHLIGHTS

1. Carob Mill Complex, Lemesos
2. Lemesos Marina
3. Lemesos Wine Festival
4. Kolossi Castle
5. Cyprus Wine Museum
6. Ancient Kourion
7. Omodos

Akrotiri British Sovereign Base Area

MEDITERRANEAN SEA

TROODOS

PISILIA

KOUMANDARIA REGION

KRASSOCHORIA

Lythrodontas
Pano Lefkara
Skarinou
Maroni
Vavatsinia
Lageia
Ora
Kampi
Akapnou
Parekklisia
Moni
Kyperounta
Agros
Dierona
Arakapas
Akrounta
Finikaria
Ancient Amathus
Germasogeia
Agios Pavlos
Agios Konstantinos
Kalo Chorio
Louvaras
Gerasa
Germasogeia Dam
Zoopigi
Lemesos (Limassol)
Lemesos Marina
Agios Mamas
Trimiklini
Laneia
Alassa
Kouris Dam
Harbour
Akrotiri Bay
Doros
Monagri
Agios Georgios
Silikou
Pano Kividhes
Kolossi
Erimi
Kalokonati
Salt Lake
Lady's Mile Beach
Mandria
Pera Pedi
Agia Mavri
Koilani
Vouni
Potamiou
Agios Amvrosios
Sanctuary of Apollon Ylatis
Ancient Kourion
Akrotiri
Agios Nikolaos ton Gaton
Arminou
Omodos
Vasa
Arsos
Malia
Kissousa
Pachna
Paramali
Episkopi Bay
Akrotiri Peninsula
Cape Zevgari
Cape Gata
Agios Ioannis
Gerovasa
Dora
Anoyira
Avdimou
Kolineia
Pentalia
Agia Marina
Kelokedara
Prastio
Chapotami
Alektora
Pissouri Bay
Cape Aspro
Falea
Stavrokonnou
Souskiou
Mamonia
Pissouri
Diarizos

Governor's Beach
Kalymnos

N

0                    10
kilometres

**RICHARD THE LIONHEART**

In April 1191 **Richard the Lionheart** of England was sailing from Messina to Acre on the Third Crusade when his fleet was dispersed by a storm. A number of ships were wrecked on the Cypriot coast, one carrying treasure destined to finance the campaign, another his sister Joan and his fiancée Berengaria. At the start of May, Richard landed in **Lemesos** and demanded that the ruler of Cyprus, one Isaac Komnenos, return the two women and the treasure (which loomed largest in his mind, it is difficult to say). Komnenos, who had a reputation as a violent bully, refused, so Richard promptly sacked the city and went on to conquer the rest of the island. This was done under the leadership of Guy de Lusignan, one of Richard's Crusader generals and at the time nominal king of the Crusader state of Jerusalem. Komnenos was captured and put in silver chains (since, so the story goes, he'd been promised that he would never be put in irons). While this was going on, Richard and Berengaria were married in Lemesos, he becoming **king of Cyprus**, she becoming queen of both Cyprus and England. Richard then proceeded to pick up the reins of his main priority – the Crusade. To raise money for this expensive endeavour, he **sold Cyprus** to the Knights Templar, who, when they found it more bother than it was worth, passed it on to **Guy de Lusignan**, who became first in a long line of Lusignan rulers of the island.

**2**

partially reversed under British rule, with road building and harbour improvements, and in particular by the huge growth in British Empire demand for the region's wine. By the end of the nineteenth century Lemesos was established as a major port. Its importance has since been enhanced by the Turkish invasion, which not only denied the republic access to the port of Famagusta, but also created an influx of refugees from the north which more than tripled its population.

## Lemesos Castle

Castle & Museum: Mon–Sat 8am–5pm, Sun 10am–1pm • €4.50 • ☏ 25305419

Built by the Lusignans in the fourteenth century on the site of an earlier Byzantine fortification (supposedly the venue for Richard the Lionheart's marriage to Berengaria in 1191), **Lemesos Castle** has been destroyed numerous times. A Genoese assault in 1373 was followed by a partial collapse during an earthquake of 1525. The castle was demolished and rebuilt, only to be destroyed again by the Venetians towards the end of the 1560s. After the Turkish conquest it was rebuilt yet again, later becoming a military HQ and jail under the British. Further restored in the 1950s, the building is in good order, and since 1987 has contained the **Cyprus Medieval Museum**.

Seemingly under siege by the restaurants and bars of the old town, the castle is an impressively vast maze of rooms, staircases and vaulted ceilings, but its numerous restorations rob it of any claim to classic medieval military architecture. The contents of the **museum** are also something of a hotchpotch, with pistols, rifles and cannons from various eras, a fine-looking suit of armour (a copy, alas), helmets, stirrups, pottery, coins, silver plate, tankards, candlesticks and lamps all jostling for attention. There are tombstones rescued from an Augustinian establishment in Lefkosia, an interesting photo display illustrating the development of Byzantine ecclesiastical architecture, some classic sgraffito pottery, a seventh-century bronze lamp from Amathus, and the relief tombstone of a priest dating from 1558, looking stark and strangely modern. Perhaps the best thing about a visit here is the views from the castle battlements.

## Carob Mill Complex

Vasilissis Street • Open daily, though times vary according to season • Free • ☏ 25820430

Immediately behind the castle lies the **Carob Mill Complex**, a great example of a tasteful urban regeneration project. This L-shaped group of pristine early twentieth-century

2

Lemesos General Hospital

# LEMESOS (LIMASSOL)

| ACCOMMODATION | |
|---|---|
| Curium Palace | 1 |
| Four Seasons Hotel | 5 |
| Londa | 6 |
| Mediterranean Beach | 4 |
| Park Lane Resort & Spa Limassol | 3 |
| Pier Beach Hotel Apartments | 2 |

Rialto Theatre

Folk Art Museum

Municipal Market

Seafront Promenade Sculpture Park

Cathedral of Agia Napa

Cami Kabir (Grand Mosque)

Castle & Medieval Museum

Carob Mill Museum

Carob Museum

Carob Mill Complex

Wooden Pier

Old Port

Marina

Pissouri (30km), Fasouri Water Mania, Water Museum, Archimedes & Cyprus Historic and Classical Motor Museum

N

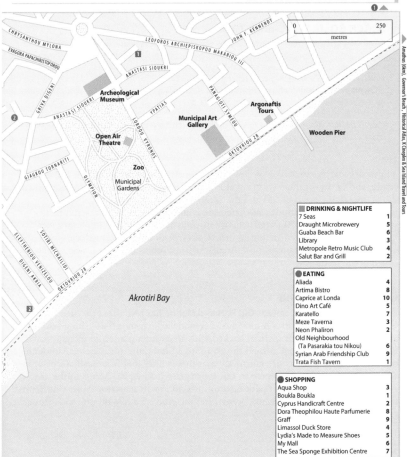

Amathus (6km), Governor's Beach, Historical Atlas, K Cineplex & Sea Island Travel and Tours

**2**

| ■ DRINKING & NIGHTLIFE | |
|---|---|
| 7 Seas | 1 |
| Draught Microbrewery | 5 |
| Guaba Beach Bar | 6 |
| Library | 3 |
| Metropole Retro Music Club | 4 |
| Salut Bar and Grill | 2 |

| ● EATING | |
|---|---|
| Aliada | 4 |
| Artima Bistro | 8 |
| Caprice at Londa | 10 |
| Dino Art Café | 5 |
| Karatello | 7 |
| Meze Taverna | 3 |
| Neon Phaliron | 2 |
| Old Neighbourhood (Ta Pasarakia tou Nikou) | 6 |
| Syrian Arab Friendship Club | 9 |
| Trata Fish Tavern | 1 |

| ● SHOPPING | |
|---|---|
| Aqua Shop | 3 |
| Boukla Boukla | 1 |
| Cyprus Handicraft Centre | 2 |
| Dora Theophilou Haute Parfumerie | 8 |
| Graff | 9 |
| Limassol Duck Store | 4 |
| Lydia's Made to Measure Shoes | 5 |
| My Mall | 6 |
| The Sea Sponge Exhibition Centre | 7 |

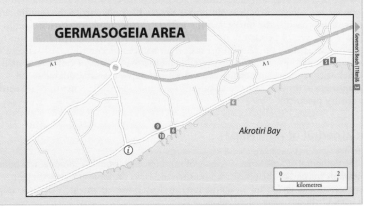

**2**

---

**BLACK GOLD: THE CAROB TREE**

Found across the Mediterranean region, the **carob tree** (*Ceratonia siliqua*) grows up to 10m tall, and produces broad-bean-like pods which, when ripe, turn black and fall to the ground. The pods are then eaten by animals and birds (or become stuck to the soles of your shoes), which helps to distribute the seeds far and wide.

   **Carob production** has a long history in Cyprus. It was an important source of sugar before cane and beet (carob syrup was known as "black gold"). It is still widely used as a substitute for chocolate in baking and in health foods, and has been an ingredient in the production of everything from film stock to medicine. You'll see carob warehouses in many of the island's coastal towns, such as Zygi (see page 73) and Lakki (see page 139).

---

industrial buildings in mellow yellow stone consists of the **Carob Museum** and cultural centre, and to the southwest a string of hip modern restaurants and bars, among them the *Artima Bistro* (see page 94) and the *Draught Microbrewery* (see page 95). The museum houses some impressively large and complete carob-crushing equipment, still in use up to the 1970s, together with displays centring on this important local industry. The exhibition area hosts a variety of events, many concerned with food – Greek cooking, for example, or molecular cuisine; others involve musical recitals, concerts and lectures.

## Old Port and Marina

The redevelopment of Lemesos **Old Port and Marina** has revitalized the area just to the south of the city centre. A new pier, a remodelled haven full of fishing boats, and an extensive modern marina, packed with chain restaurants and interspersed with high-end shops, have turned the area into a focal point for the city. Although of burgeoning popularity, it's fair to say that there's little that is typically Cypriot in all this – you could be anywhere in Europe or indeed America. Access to the area is good, with a new surface car park next to the Old Port, a new two-storey one behind the marina and even a "Nextbike" rental station. And it's a five-minute walk from the city centre.

## Cami Kabir

Genethliou Mitela • Visitors welcome if gate open, but avoid prayer times • Free

East of the castle is the **Cami Kabir (Grand Mosque)**. Surrounded by a medieval tangle of alleys and snickets, coming across it is always a surprise. If the gate's open, have a look, though avoid prayer times. The only part of the building visible as you approach is the rather stumpy minaret, standing above the surrounding roofs. A haven of peace, the mosque is fronted by a small courtyard containing fountains used by the faithful to wash their feet before entering. The sixteenth-century building itself, with its striking alternating courses of yellow and ochre brickwork, is more interesting as a working mosque than for any historical importance, though recent excavations have uncovered the remains of its tenth-century precursor.

## Cathedral of Agia Napa

68 Agiou Andreou St • Visitors welcome when services not in progress • Free

The **Cathedral of Agia Napa**, a couple of minutes' walk from the mosque, was built towards the end of the nineteenth century and lacks the atmospheric setting or architecture of its Islamic rival. The interior does, however, provide a classic example of Greek Orthodox (over)-decoration.

## Municipal Fruit and Vegetable Market

Georgiou Gennadiou • under renovation at the time of writing, to be opened in 2019

Housed in a spacious and airy building off Saripolou dating from 1917, the **Municipal Fruit and Vegetable Market** is worth a quick visit. Entering through its imposing arch-topped doorway, you're soon enveloped by a bustling atmosphere with stalls lit by large fanlights and rows of small windows. On sale is a wide selection of foodstuffs – fruit, vegetables, nuts, honey, nougat and much else, together with attractive basketwork and ornamental gourds. The building has been nicely renovated, as has the square on which it stands, which has shops and restaurants around the edge. It's a great meeting place for visitors, and is much favoured by twenty-something locals.

2

## The promenade

Lemesos **promenade**, which is made up of a paved walkway interspersed with boardwalks, runs 16km east along the coast from the Old Port to the hotel complex at Germasogeia. It passes through an attractive **sculpture park** dating from the start of the millennium, and offers views of the shipping lanes that lead into Lemesos harbour. Watch out, though, for earnest joggers and speeding cyclists. Beside the walkway runs a passable beach, dotted with loungers and sun umbrellas, and with the occasional café and restaurant.

## Municipal Gardens

Oktovriou 28 • Daily: April–Oct 7am–8.30pm, Nov–March 7am–7.30pm • Free

About 1.5km east from the Old Port, facing the coast road, the **Municipal Gardens** mark the edge of Lemesos's extended city centre. Wooded with pine, palm and eucalyptus trees, the gardens, though relatively small, are a good place to wander around, have picnics and let the children loose.

Within the park are three attractions: the renovated **zoo**, which specializes in smaller animals and birds (pony rides also available), a small, rather forgettable **Museum of Natural History**, and an **Open Air Theatre** which puts on regular summer concerts (look out for details at the tourist office). The gardens also play host to the greatest **wine festival** on the island (see page 90), well worth timing your visit for.

### Limassol Zoo

Daily: March & Oct 9am–5pm; April, May & Sept 9am–6pm; June –Aug 9am–7pm; Nov & Feb 9am–4.30pm; Dec & Jan 9am–4pm • €5 • 📞 25588345, 🌐 limassolzoo.com

Tucked away in a corner of the Municipal Gardens, **Limassol Zoo** is clean and well organized, with plenty of shade from its numerous trees and shrubs. Though it has none of the big beasts associated with zoos – no elephants, giraffes, lions, tigers or rhinos – it's ideal for small children, with hosts of mammals, birds and snakes endemic to the island, all fully named and explained in English as well as Greek – cattle, goats, ponies, pigs, flamingos, pelicans, ducks, meerkats, bats, rats and many others, all in a naturalistic environment fully remodelled between 2012 and 2014. There's a café, picnic area and children's playground.

## Folk Art Museum

253 St Andrews St • Mon–Fri 7.45am–2.45pm • €2 • 📞 25362303, 🌐 bit.ly/FolkArtLemesos

Lemesos' **Folk Art Museum** occupies a grand stone building, which opened as a museum in 1985. It consists of a collection of folk art and craft from the nineteenth and twentieth centuries – jewellery, lace, urban and rural costume, domestic equipment, furniture and agricultural tools, colourful national costume, tapestries, woodcarving and a loom with all its associated equipment. Don't neglect, either, to look down at your feet – the museum has a variety of handsome tiled floors.

**2**

**LEMESOS WINE FESTIVAL**

Over two weekends in the middle of September the Municipal Gardens are transformed into a tent city as the **Lemesos Wine Festival** (ⓦ limassolmunicipal.com.cy/wine/en/wine-festival) hits town. The festival offers, in the words of the organizers, "a revival of ancient festive manifestations of worship of Dionysus and Aphrodite", or, to the more cynical, a chance to get very drunk. Dozens of Cypriot wine producers offer tastings and talks, and there's plenty of information on the island's wine routes. It's an inclusive, fun affair – giant figures dressed in traditional Cypriot costume wander around the park holding bunches of grapes in one hand and wine bottles in the other. Free buses run to the festival from all over Cyprus, and entry fees (adults €5; children 6–18 €3, additional payment for a wine bottle or glass on entry) are modest.

## Municipal Art Gallery

Oktovriou 28 • Mon–Fri 7.45am–2.30pm • €2• ☎ 25586212, ⓦ bit.ly/MunicipalArtGallery

On the seafront, the **Municipal Art Gallery** offers the chance to cast an eye over the work of noted Cypriot artists from the city's permanent collection, as well as enjoying works from further afield in a series of temporary exhibitions. The paintings illustrate the fact that Cypriot art is clearly part of the European mainstream, with a mixture of naturalistic figurative and abstract art, expressed through painting, sculpture and ceramics, as well as some mixed-media work. A further reason to visit the museum is the building itself, classic Art Deco architecture dating from just before World War II.

## Archeological Museum

Vyronos/Siokri Street • Mon–Fri 8am–4pm • €2.50 • ☎ 25305157, ⓦ bit.ly/ArcheologicalMuseum

Now rather dated-looking, the **Archeological Museum** opened in 1975, an impressive achievement considering that this was immediately after the Turkish invasion of 1974.

Organized into **prehistoric** (8000–1050 BC) and **historic** (1050 BC–400 AD) eras, exhibits are well displayed and labelled in English as well as Greek (though the information is a little basic). As in most archeological museums, there are hundreds of pots (clay is one of the great survivors), including some very large urns, many of them from Sotira and Erini, and other domestic items which really bring the past alive, such as mirrors, spoons, tweezers, glassware and items in ivory. In addition, there are numerous **Greek and Roman statues**, many, it has now been discovered, carved in workshops at Fasoula, 9km north of the city. Look out particularly for the statue of the Egyptian God Bes, from second-third-century AD Amathus. It consists of a torso and head, below which, on a separate fragment, are his feet. But it's the face that draws the eye – it is notable for its extreme ugliness. Even more affecting is the fragment of a statue, also from Amathus and dating from 324–150 BC, of the lower part of a man's anatomy, from the hem of his toga to just above the feet. Not much there to get excited about, you may think. But it's the pose that is so touching – the legs are crossed at the calf, as if he's leaning on a lamppost, waiting for a bus.

## Historical Atlas

12 Andokidu St • Daily 8.30am–8pm • €14; children under 12 €8 • ☎ 97846367

**Historical Atlas** is as odd an attraction as you're ever likely to come across. Housed in a huge air-conditioned marquee, in the heart of the Geroskipou tourist area just off the main drag, it consists of a gigantic relief map/model of the whole of Cyprus as it was during the Middle Ages, complete with castles, churches, monasteries, towns, villages and ports. Given an audioguide as you enter, you circulate around the map/model, stand in numbered designated places and listen to the commentary in your own language. That's the core of the experience (it takes about 45min), though you can add overviews from four castle viewpoints, your kids can take part in treasure hunts, you can experience medieval swordsmanship, make models and much more. The concept is the brainchild of Russian architect Svetlana Petrachkova, and seems to be a Russian/Cypriot co-production, with a team of modellers, craftsmen and computer whizzes who between them created the whole extraordinary edifice. Interestingly, the model buildings were produced, not by traditional modelling methods, but by a 3-D printer. Distinctly odd, then, not cheap and rather fact-heavy, yet certainly worth a look, especially if you're interested in Cyprus's medieval history, so often overshadowed by the classical period at the one end and the modern at the other.

## Fasouri Water Mania

Franklinou Roosevelt Ave • May–Oct; May, Sept & Oct daily 10am–5pm; June & Aug daily 10am–6pm • Adults €30; children 3–12 €17 • ☎ 25714235, ⓦ fasouri-watermania.com

Just west of the city centre, **Fasouri Water Mania** bills itself as the "No. 1 waterpark in Cyprus". It certainly has a wide range of slides, pools, paddle boats and swings and together with the usual fast-food joints and souvenir shops. Look out in particular for the giant mushroom-like "Wet Bubble" and the vertiginous "Kamikaze" slide which reaches speeds of 50km/h. A shuttle bus runs to the park from all the main hotels along the seafront between *Le Meridien* and the *Pier Beach Hotel Apartments*. Not cheap but perfect on a hot day (arrive early to make the most of it).

## Water Museum

Franklin Roosevelt 66 • Mon–Fri 10am–1pm • €1 • ☎ 25830000

Housed in the Old Pumping Station built in 1925 to supply Limassol with water, and located next to the modern Water Board headquarters, the **Water Museum** contains the original pump plus a variety of exhibits related to water purification and distribution – pumps, filters, testing equipment. Though it might seem odd to have a whole museum devoted to water, it must be remembered that water supply has always been, and still is, a highly charged issue on what is a very dry island: the building of a water pipeline under the Mediterranean to occupied north Cyprus is viewed with considerable suspicion in the south.

## Bread Museum

Grigori Afxentiou 9 • Mon, Tue, Thurs, Fri 9.30am–12.30pm, 4–7pm, Wed & Sat 9.30am–12.30pm •free • ☎ 25340347

**Ploumisto Psomi** is a museum which shows how artful the act of bread making can be. There are traditional plumed breads (or rather replicas) on display and others, ranging from the simple to the ornamental, each with its own cultural significance. You'll learn about the different types of breads baked for different occasions - wedding, funerals, Sunday masses. Surprisingly, there's even a recipe for something eaten during a fasting period! The museum organises workshops for children in the afternoons. The entrance is free but you may choose to attend a guided tour with the cost ranging from €2 to €15.

## Cyprus Historic and Classical Motor Museum

Epimitheos Street • April–Oct Mon–Fri 9am–5pm, Sat & Sun 10am–6pm, Nov–March Mon–Sun 10am–5pm • €11 • ☎ 70009000, ⓦ cyprusmotormuseum.com.cy

The **Cyprus Motor Museum** is an attraction to gladden the hearts not only of petrol heads but also of all those in whose lives cars have played any part whatsoever. In addition to a wide range of standard production cars – from the 1912 Model T Ford to a 2004 Piaggio pickup, and including a variety of motorcycles and scooters – the museum also contains what you might call "celebrity models" – Makarios's bullet-proof Cadillac, Mr Bean's green mini, a car used by Margaret Thatcher, and the yellow Baywatch lifeguard pickup, complete with surfboards. Of particular interest to Brits are a British armoured car, a classic City of Nottingham fire engine and caravan, and a London double-decker bus.

## ARRIVAL AND DEPARTURE
LEMESOS

**By plane** Lemesos is roughly equidistant between the republic's two main airports at Larnaka and Pafos and is linked to both by fast motorways. There's a shuttle bus between Larnaka Airport and Lemesos (Lemesos Airport Express ☎ 77777075, ⊛ limassolairportexpress.eu). It costs €9 one-way, with the drop-off point on Christofi Ergatoudi, in front of Agios Georgios Havouzas Church northeast of the centre. From Pafos Airport you'll need to head into Pafos itself then take one of the Intercity Buses (€4 one-way; ☎ 24643493, ⊛ intercity-buses.com).

**By bus** Lemesos's links to other parts of Cyprus by bus are good. Buses can be caught at both the old and the new ports. They depart every 1–2hr: Larnaka (1hr 30min); Lefkosia (1hr 45min); Pafos (1hr).

## GETTING AROUND

**By bus** Lemesos has a well-organized bus system covering all parts of the city centre, outlying suburbs, and villages throughout Lemesos District. All routes are run by EMEL (☎ 77778121, ⊛ en.limassolbuses.com). The main bus station is on Leontiou, beyond its intersection with Gladstonos. The most useful route for tourists is the #30, which runs from the city centre along the seafront, from My Mall to *Le Meridien Hotel*.

**By taxi** As in all Cyprus's main towns, taxis operate 24hr, and all have compulsory meters (see page 26). If you have any issues regarding taxis or taxi drivers, contact the Road Transport Department (Korivou-Kampos Polemidion ☎ 25870452).

**Car rental** All the main international car rental companies have offices in Lemesos. There are also numerous local companies; try Chris Car Hire (1178, Makariou III ☎ 70006770, ⊛ chriscarhire.com) or St Georges Car Hire (62 Makariou III ☎ 25563027, ⊛ stgeorges-carhire.com).

## INFORMATION AND TOURS

**Tourist office** Lemesos's tourist office (Mon, Tues, Thurs & Fri 8.15am–2.30pm & 3–6pm, Wed 8.15am–2.30pm, Sat 8.15am–1.15pm; ☎ 25362756) is at the Old Port Roundabout. There's also a branch office at Dasoudi, in Germasogeia (same opening hours). The office runs occasional guided walks around Lemesos (usually Mon 10am).

**Tour operators** Recommended operators include Argonaftis Tours (☎ 25586333, ⊛ argonaftis.com) and Sea Island Travel and Tours (☎ 25583728, ⊛ seaislandtravel. com), both of whom run sightseeing tours to Kykkos Monastery, Pafos and the Troodos Mountains.

## ACTIVITIES

There is no shortage of activities in Lemesos. Most hotels and beaches offer water sports, while the main focus for splashing about is the Fasouri Water Mania park (see page 91).

**Go-karting** The Need 4 Speed, Erimi Village (☎ 99462269, ⊛ limassolcity.com/go-karts). Closed Mon.

**Golf** Vikla Golf and Country Club Vikla Village, Kellaki, northeast of Lemesos (☎ 99674218, ⊛ vikla4golf.com). Green fees July & Aug €20 (for 18 holes); club hire available.

**Horseriding** Try Amathus Park Riding School in Parekklisia Village (☎ 99604109) or Curium Equestrian in Parekklisia Village (☎ 99564232).

**Tennis** Most large hotels have their own tennis facilities for guests; otherwise, try the Lemesos Sporting Club at 4 Zachariadou (☎ 99383864).

**Ten-pin bowling** Space Bowling 1, Erakleous, Mouttagiaka Tourist area (☎ 25310000); Galaktika 53 Makariou III (☎ 25750666).

## ACCOMMODATION

Most accommodation in Lemesos is strung out along the coast road east from the city centre. In particular, there are two main concentrations – the big package holiday and resort hotels in Germasogeia, east of the city centre, and smaller, more traditional and cheaper hotels dotted around the Municipal Gardens. In villages north of the city, an increasing number of traditional houses, vacated by depopulation, are being converted in agrotourism schemes (see page 30).

### LEMESOS

**Curium Palace** 11 Vyronos ☎ 25891100, ⊛ curium palacehotel.com.cy; map p.86. Well placed in the Municipal Gardens area of the city, the Curium Palace is likely to appeal to those who favour a more quirky, non-chain-hotel atmosphere. It's a little dated but it provides as much peace and quiet as you're likely to get in a Cypriot city-centre establishment. March–Oct. **€110**

**Pier Beach Hotel Apartments** 261a Oktovriou 28

## LEMESOS FESTIVALS

### FEBRUARY & MARCH

**Carnival** (10 days before Lent – usually Feb/March). All the usual components of a carnival are held in various parts of the city; there are masked balls, parties, parades of floats, fancy dress, singing, dancing, eating and drinking.

### MAY

**Flower Festival** (early May). This festival includes traditional singing and dancing, and a craft market, as well as the flower parade along the seafront. Held in the Potamos Yermasoyia district, 3km east of the old town.

**European Dance Festival** (mid-May; ⓦ rialto.com.cy). Performances take place by European and Cypriot dance groups in the Rialto Theatre.

### JUNE

**Kataklysmos** (fifty days after Easter). As in other Cypriot seaside towns, Kataklysmos is celebrated with a variety of water-based events – boat races, swimming competitions, water fights – as well as singing, dancing and feasting.

**Russian–Cypriot Festival** (early June). A sign of the growing influence of Russia on Cyprus. Dance, music, clowns, fireworks and a lot of commercial displays.

**Shakespeare Festival** (second half of June). Plays by the bard are mounted in the spectacular ancient theatre at Kourion (€20 admission).

### JULY

**Amathusia Festival** (late June/early July) Performance by a variety of contemporary dance groups, music groups and choirs. Only of interest to those who want to get an insight into Cyprus's serious music scene, though the setting, in the ruins of Ancient Amathous, is wonderful.

**Ethnic World Music Festival** (throughout July; ⓦ rialto.com.cy). World music performed at the Rialto Theatre.

**Lemesos Beer Festival** (late July or early August) Free entrance, live music, and lots of local and imported beer. Held, like the wine festival, in the Municipal Gardens.

### AUGUST, SEPTEMBER & OCTOBER

**Lemesos Wine Festival** (see page 90).

**International Documentary Festival** (early Aug) and **Short Film Festival of Cyprus** (mid-Oct; ⓦ isffc.com.cy). Held at the Rialto Theatre, with workshops and lectures as well as the film screenings.

---

☎ 25749000, ⓦ pier-beach.com; map p.86. On the coast road before you get to the Municipal Gardens (near St Catherine's Church), the *Pier Beach* is more like a hotel than an apartment block – with its own restaurant, roof terrace and bar. Accommodation is clean and simple, staff are welcoming, and some rooms have fine sea views – an excellent, inexpensive alternative to the usual Lemesos accommodation. Expect a fair amount of traffic noise, though. Breakfast not included. **€80**

### GERMASOGEIA (TOURIST AREA)

★ **Four Seasons Hotel** ☎ 25858000, ⓦ fourseasons. com.cy; map p.86. One of the best-known hotels on Cyprus, the *Four Seasons* is a large, popular five-star located on the beach in Germasogeia. Recently extensively renovated, it is set in luxurious grounds with a great pool, and has all the bells and whistles you might expect – a PADI dive centre, a wide range of room types, places to

eat, drink and shop, a Shiseido Spa – together with helpful staff. It can get very crowded in high season, especially with conventions or weddings going on. Those without kids might want to look out for the adult-only pool: it's marginally more relaxing. More peaceful too are the sea-facing rooms: the others face a busy four-lane highway. **€380**

★ **Londa** 72 Georgiou tou Protou ☎ 25865555, ⓦ londahotel.com; map p.86. Approximately halfway along the coast road between the city centre and tourist area of Germasogeia, the *Londa* bills itself as "Cyprus's first boutique hotel". Completely renovated in 2005, the rooms are stylishly designed with expensive-looking furniture and beautiful bed linen, while the restaurant and bar could be described as "futuristic minimalist". A classy pool area, spa and gym complete the picture, though the beach is nothing to write home about. Best for couples or those with babies. Feb–Oct. **€275**

**2**

**Mediterranean Beach** ☎25559999, ⊕medbeach. com; map p.86. Close to the Amathus archeological site – and therefore about 9km from the city centre – the *Mediterranean* has a pool, health spa, five restaurants, and numerous bars and is dotted with attractive terraces throughout. There's lots to do, with water and other sports on offer and live music and folk nights. The accommodation itself, however, despite a cheerful Mediterranean colour scheme, feels rather regimented, organized in vast honeycomb blocks. March–Oct. €180

**Parklane Resort & Spa Limassol** 11 Giannou Kranidioti St ☎25862000, ⊕marriott.co.uk; map p.86. Located beyond ancient Amathus, just after the marina, *Parklane* is even bigger than the *Four Seasons*. Already boasting terrific facilities and a personal level of service which belied its size – with its own Blue Flag beach, a wide range of water sports, comprehensive children's activities, three outdoor and one indoor swimming pools (one seawater and one adults-only), as well as a state-of-the-art spa and health club. €320

## EATING

Lemesos is unquestionably the best place to eat out in Cyprus, with the widest range and highest quality of restaurants. This is partly because it is both a year-round city and a multicultural one with an eclectic range of cuisines on offer. As elsewhere in the world, restaurants come and go, and while those recommended below have demonstrated a certain staying power, this shouldn't deter you from seeking out exciting new ones. A new concentration of places to eat and drink – bars, chain restaurants and fast-food outlets – particularly patronized by younger locals, has been provided by the redeveloped Marina, which is located just south of the city centre.

### LEMESOS

**Aliada** 117 Eirinis ☎25340758; map p.86. The *Aliada* is best known for its sumptuous, table-groaning cold buffets of traditional Greek/Cypriot food. It's located in a period mansion set in the heart of the old town, with fine tiled floors and an atmospheric walled garden. There's a set menu (at €26/person) consisting of a soup to start, followed by the cold buffet, a main course (the chicken kebabs and home-made burgers are recommended) and a choice of sweets from a trolley, often eaten to the accompaniment of a tinkling piano. Mon–Thurs & Sun 11am–11pm, Fri & Sat 11am–midnight. Reservations essential Fri & Sat.

**Artima Bistro** Carob Mill Complex ☎25820466; map p.86. One of the cluster of restaurants and bars in the atmospheric Carob Mill Complex behind the castle. Stylish Italian/Mediterranean food in spacious bistro surroundings, with additional tables outside and on an internal balcony. Try the Wagyu beef fillet, or any of the pasta dishes. Expect to pay around €40/person. Daily noon–11pm.

★ **Dino Art Café** 62–66 Eirinis ☎25762030; map p.86. Centrally located near the castle and the port, the welcoming *Dino Art Café* is more of an experience than just somewhere to eat. A range of colossal sandwiches, and inventive salads, sushi, savouries and desserts created by owner Dino Kosti starts around €8, and often art and photographic exhibitions are included. Mon–Sat 10am–11pm, Sun 4pm–midnight.

**Karatello** Carob Mill Complex ☎25820464; map p.86. Extensive mezé choices or à la carte (the *kléftiko*'s good) in a

cool well-lit room with bare brick walls. Outdoor seating at the base of the castle walls (with patio heaters for cooler evenings), live Cypriot music Fridays and Saturdays during autumn and winter. Grill from around €10.25–22. Mon–Thurs 6–11pm, Fri 6–11.30pm, Sat noon–11.30pm, Sun noon–11pm.

**Meze Taverna** 209 St Andrews St ☎25367333, ⊕facebook.com/pm.mezetaverna/; map p.86. Good old-fashioned Greek taverna (complete with cod-Greek script menus) with main courses coming in at between €10 and €18. Great family atmosphere – it could be the model for all those tavernas exported all around the world. Mon–Sat noon–3pm & 6–10pm.

**Neon Phaliron** 135 Gladstonos ☎25365768, ⊕neon phaliron.com; map p.86. Posh-nosh restaurant yet with large portions, plucking its recipes from Greece, Turkey, Italy, the Caribbean and elsewhere, with particular emphasis on seafood and steak. Cool brown and cream interior, extensive wine list – there's also a separate wine lounge. Main courses start at around €15. Restaurant: Mon–Sat noon–4pm & 6.30pm–midnight, Sun noon–4pm; wine lounge: Mon–Sat 10am–midnight, Sun 10am–4pm.

★ **Old Neighbourhood (Ta Psarakia tou Nikou)** 14 Angkyras ☎25376082; map p.86. Noted for the freshness of its ingredients, the *Old Neighbourhood* looks a bit dowdy yet attracts a lot of locals after good traditional Greek-Cypriot food. It can get very busy, especially at weekends, when there is often live music. Mains from around €20. Mon–Sat 7pm–midnight.

**Trata Fish Tavern** 1 Iakovou Tompazi ☎25586600; map p.86. Located among the hotels east of Lemesos, this specialist fish restaurant is known for its seafood mezé (from around €20). Simple decor, popular with locals, very busy at weekends. Mon–Sat 5–11.45pm, Sun 11.45am–4.30pm.

### GERMASOGEIA (TOURIST AREA)

★ **Caprice at Londa** Londa Hotel, 72 Georgiou tou Protou ☎25865555, ⊕londahotel.com; map p.86. Fine-dining hotel restaurant with a choice of Italian-influenced à la carte or bistro menus. Main courses on the à la carte menu start at €17, with most falling between €22.50 and €32.50, while the bistro menu offers a range of cheaper snacks, sandwiches, salads and main courses from around €12.50. Daily 7am–11am, 1–11pm.

**Syrian Arab Friendship Club** 3 Iliados ☎ 25328838; map p.86. Out towards the Germasogeia hotel complex (it's off the main drag, roughly opposite the *Apollonia Beach Hotel* so not easy to find), the *Syrian Arab Friendship Club* provides its customers with Middle Eastern food (all pulses, herbs, spices, grilled meats and sticky puddings) in distinctly Middle Eastern surroundings – hookahs and belly dancers abound. Authenticity is attested to by the number of expat Arabs who use the place. Main courses from €10, mezé from €16. Daily noon–11.30pm.

## DRINKING AND NIGHTLIFE

Lemesos has a vibrant nightlife, fuelled not only by holiday-makers but also by young locals. As a rule of thumb, clubs in Germasogeia, an eastern suburb of the city, tend to be mainly for tourists, while city-centre clubs attract both locals and visitors. Like many other port cities, it also has a seedy side, with a range of "gentlemen's clubs" with names like *Mirage Topless* and *Silk and Velvet* spread along the seafront.

### LEMESOS

**7 Seas** Columbia Plaza ☎ 25258000, ☜ 7seaslive.com; map p.86. In the old town but close to the beach, *7 Seas* boasts most of Cyprus's best DJs as well as live music. There's a dress code, so don't turn up in your beach gear. Daily 10.30pm–late (closed Sun, Mon & Thurs off season).

★ **Draught Microbrewery** Carob Mill Complex ☎ 25820470, ☜ carobmill-restaurants.com; map p.86. Another highlight of the Carob Mill Complex, the *Draught Microbrewery* (Cyprus's first) has a stylish long bar backed by vast copper vats brewing its signature ale. Top-notch bar food – nachos, chicken wings and mixed grill (€39.90 for two) – soaks up the booze, while in the evening DJs take to the decks. Daily 11am–2am.

**Library** 1 Themidos ☎ 25361361, ☜ librarybar.com.cy; map p.86. A wide selection of cocktails. During the summer their Gin Garden opposite offers a pleasant place to grab a bite and something to drink. Mon–Thurs & Sun 5pm–1am, Fri & Sat 5pm–2am.

**Metropole Retro Music Club** 6 Ifigeneias St ☎ 97755554; map p.86. It does exactly what it says on the tin – it's in the *Metropole Hotel* (just off the main coast road, just past the tourist information centre), and it concentrates on retro music from the 1970s, 1980s and 1990s. A big club spread over two floors, it has three bars and a large dancefloor. A good night out, but bouncers can be less than polite. Fri & Sat 11.30pm–5am.

**Salut Bar and Grill** 71-73 Saripolou ☎ 97692091, ☜ salutbar.com; map p.86. Situated in an old building, *Salut Bar and Grill* offers an atmospheric place to relax in and have fun; it can get very busy at weekends. Mon–Thurs & Sun 10am–1am, Fri & Sat 10–2am, Food service: daily 11am–11pm.

### GERMASOGEIA (TOURIST AREA)

**Guaba Beach Bar** 7 Amathuntos ☎ 96340000, ☜ guaba beachbar.com; map p.86. Next to the *Aquarius Hotel* out towards Germasogeia, the *Guaba Beach Bar* is right on the beach. A young, energetic crowd head here for the house, dance and electro music and relatively cheap cocktails. Frequent guest DJs. Dress code is jeans and T-shirt at the formal end, barely covered at the more relaxed. Mon–Sat 10pm–3am, Sun 10pm–midnight.

## ENTERTAINMENT

**K-Cineplex** 8 Ariadnis ☜ kcineplex.com. One of a chain, with cinemas also in Lefkosia and Larnaka, Lemesos's K-Cineplex is certainly the best, and certainly accessible in the tourist area east of the city. It shows up-to-the-minute English-language films on five screens, and there's a cafeteria, juice bar and a/c throughout.

**Rialto Theatre** 19 Andrea Drousioti ☜ rialto.com.cy. A striking old theatre which hosts concerts, gigs and plays, as well as several festivals (see page 93).

## SHOPPING

Most of Lemesos's shops are concentrated broadly in the area between Leoforos Archiepiskopou Makariou III, which arches around the city centre to the north of the Old Town, and the main road along the seafront (called, as it travels east, Syntagmos, Spyrou Araouzou, Christodoulou Chatzipavlou and finally Oktovriou 28). Makariou III has numerous international stores selling all the top clothing labels, and other streets to look out for are Kolonakiou (sportswear, more clothes and household goods), and Anexartisias and Agiou Andreou (clothes, jewellery, shoes, leather goods), which cross just off the seafront road. An additional focus for shopping has been provided by the redeveloped marina, which offers a number of top-end shops such as Dora Theophilou Haute Parfumerie and Graff jewellers.

### BEAUTY PRODUCTS

**Dora Theophilou Haute Parfumerie** 2/7 Limassol Marina ☎ 25051212, ☜ doratheophilou.com; map p.86. Wide range of perfumes and other beauty products in the cool setting of the new marina. It's also a pharmacy (with different hours). April–Oct Mon–Sat 11am–9pm; Nov–March Mon–Sat 11am–7.30pm.

**2**

**The Sea Sponge Exhibition Centre** Old Port Roundabout ☎ 25871656, ⓦ apacy.com; map p.86. Unashamedly kitsch but nevertheless great fun, The Sea Sponge Centre sells sponges and loofahs of all shapes and sizes, and has diversified into other products such as natural soaps, olive oil and spa products. Displays are interspersed with jolly nautical artefacts such as a diver's helmet, ship's wheels, lifebuoys, even a life-sized model of Jacques Cousteau, together with shells and fish: a good source of small portable gifts for people back home. Mon–Fri 9am–7pm, Sat 9am–3pm.

### ANTIQUES, ARTS AND CRAFTS

**Cyprus Handicraft Centre** 25 Themidos; map p.86. Guaranteed quality Cypriot gifts and souvenirs – handicrafts, jewellery, pottery, all made locally using traditional methods. May–Sept Mon, Tues, Thurs & Fri 8am–1pm & 4–7pm, Wed & Sat 8am–1pm; Oct–April Mon, Tues, Thurs & Fri 7.30am–5.30pm, Wed & Sat 8am–1pm.

### CLOTHES, SHOES AND ACCESSORIES

**Aqua Shop** 16 Georgiou. ⓦ aquamaritime.hr; map p.86. A charming little boutique offering mostly blue-tinged beach clothing and items for the whole family. Daily 10am–2pm & 4–8pm.

**Boukla Boukla** 252 Agiou Andreou, ⓦ bouklaboukla. com; map p.86. Boutique selling top-end women's fashion by Greek designers. Mon, Tues, Thurs & Fri 11.30am–7.30pm, Wed & Sat 10.30am–3pm.

**Graff** E7 Limassol Marina ☎ 25354040, ⓦ graff diamonds.com; map p.86. Luxury jewellery from a company that manufactures as well as sells top-end products. Also sells watches. Daily 24 hr.

**Limassol Duck Store** 29 Ankara. ⓦ limassolduckstore. com; map p.86. Ever wanted a rubber ducky with a little panache to it? Why not bring one home from Cyprus. Mon–Sat 11am–8pm, Sun 11am–5pm.

**Lydia's Made to Measure Shoes** 14 Tzami (Jami) St. ☎ 25372898, ⓦ lydias-shoes.com; map p.86. Shoes, boots, sandals, and specialist riding, golf and orthopaedic shoes made to measure. Orders can be completed within two to three days so there's usually time to fly home with your purchase rather than ship it. Mon–Fri 8am–8pm.

### DEPARTMENT STORES AND MALLS

**My Mall** 285 Franklin Roosevelt, Zakaki ☎ 25343777, ⓦ ssmymall.com.cy; map p.86. The largest mall in Cyprus with a range of big-name shops including Apple, M&S, Lacoste, Monsoon, Ralph Lauren, Zara and many more, over three floors. There are fifteen restaurants and coffee shops, a bowling alley, ice rink, children's play area and video arcade. Ample parking. The mall is located southwest of the city centre off the Akrotiri road (#30 bus). Shops daily: 10am–8pm; dining & entertainment daily: noon–11pm; cafes daily: 8.30am–10pm.

### DIRECTORY

**Hospital** Lemesos General, Nikaias, Pano Polemidia ☎ 25801100.

**Medical** Doctors on call ☎ 90901435.

**Pharmacies** Near the Municipal Market there is Agathocles Kyriazis at 13 Andrea Themistokleous Street ☎ 25364451.

**Police** Lemesos Divisional HQ ☎ 25805050. North of the city on Leontiou, near where it intersects with Gladstonos.

**Post office** The Central Post Office at the western end of Gladstonos is a fair distance from the centre. The most convenient is the branch at 2 Saripolou Street (☎ 25305143).

# East of Lemesos

Between Lemesos and the border with Larnaka district, and equally accessible (and well signposted) from the A1 motorway and B1 coast road, is one of Cyprus's best known beaches, **Governor's Beach**, and one of its greatest archeological sites at **Ancient Amathus.**

## Governor's Beach

A pretty group of coves, notable for its dark sand and bright white cliffs, **Governor's Beach** lies just off the A1, and gets very busy, especially at weekends. It has all the facilities you need for a civilized day at the seaside – tavernas, showers, beach umbrellas and loungers – with easy access via a clifftop path and a number of flights of steps down to the sand.

The eastward view from the beach, once merely unedifyingly industrial, now takes in the dramatic aftermath of the island's worst peacetime disaster, the Evangelos Florakis Naval Base explosion of January, 2011 (see page 73). The remains of the Vasilikou power station squat next to the base's red and white chimneys, with the radio masts of the BBC relay station at Zygi in the background.

## Ancient Amathus

Daily: Mid-April to mid-Sept 8.15am–7.45pm; mid-Sept to mid-April 8.15am–5.15pm • €2.50 • ⓦ tinyurl.com/amathus

Nine kilometres or so east of Lemesos centre and clearly visible right next to the B1 coast road, **Ancient Amathus (Amathous)** is of enormous significance in the history of Cyprus, with origins that can be traced back over three thousand years. Unfortunately, its present-day remains don't quite live up to its historical importance, and it's difficult to get, from the jumble of masonry, columns and drums, a mental picture of what the city must have been like during its heyday. It is, however, certainly accessible to thousands of holiday-makers: it's right next to one of the biggest hotel complexes on the island.

The city was probably first established by Greek islanders fleeing from the eastward spread of the Dorian invasion around 1000 BC, though myth has it that a pregnant Ariadne, eloping with Theseus from Minoan Crete, died in childbirth at Amathus and was buried nearby. By around 800 BC the city had been settled and developed by the Phoenicians, and a new harbour built. During this time **temples to Aphrodite** and Hercules were established (Amathus was one of Hercules's sons). The city supported the Persians during the Greco-Persian wars, and was subsequently ruled by the heirs of Alexander the Great and the Ptolemies. During the Roman occupation it became one of four prosperous regional capitals, but subsequently suffered Arab raids in the seventh century AD, and attack by Richard the Lionheart in 1191. History then passed it by, with much looting of treasures and stealing of stone, and it became largely forgotten until it was identified in the late nineteenth century by British archeologists A.H. Smith and J.L. Myers, and excavated from the 1970s onwards by the French School of Athens.

Today the broad areas of ancient Amathus can, with effort, be discerned, with the open agora, or market place, backed by the acropolis hill behind. The outline of houses can be seen, together with sections of wall, the rills and pipes of a water distribution system, a temple and several later Byzantine basilicas. Many of the finds from the site can be seen in Lemesos's Archeological Museum (see page 90) and Lefkosia's Cyprus Museum (see page 179); others have been plundered during Cyprus's periods of occupation – a 2m-high, 14-tonne stone jar is now in the Louvre in Paris, for example, while other treasures are lodged in the British Museum and New York's Metropolitan Museum of Art.

### ACCOMMODATION                                    EAST OF LEMESOS

**Art by Praxis** 13 Petraki Kiprianou, Governor's Beach ⓣ 25632375, ⓦ artbypraxis.com. Minimalist in design and decor, environmentally friendly in construction, and looking more art gallery than apartment block, *Art by Praxis* offers not only simple comfort, yoga and access to a gym, but a great location near the famous cliffs of ever-popular Governor's Beach, all white cliffs and black sand. There's also a fair bit of modern art. Two-night minimum stay. €50

**Villa Retreat** Akrounta ⓣ 99696483, ⓦ villaretreat cyprus.com. In the hills above Lemesos, just beyond the Germasogeia Reservoir, *Villa Retreat* is a one-off: peaceful, intimate, beautifully decorated, with lots of sequestered nooks and crannies yet also a swimming pool, lovely gardens and terraces. Two-night minimum stay. €80

### EATING

★**Sofroniou Beach Restaurant** Governor's Beach ⓣ 25633150. One of a number of tavernas along the cliffs at Governor's Beach, the *Sofroniou Beach* is a reliable option for Greek-Cypriot food. You can eat inside or out, and the views across to what remains of the Evangelos Florakis naval base are quite attractive after dark – the chimneys and gantries are dotted with red lights. Food is traditional taverna fare, and is very reasonable – a mixed grill and kalamari particularly so. It's wise to book, especially at weekends. Mon–Sat noon–10pm & Sun noon–4.30pm.

# West of Lemesos

To the west of Lemesos city centre lie three fine attractions – the greatest Greco-Roman site on the island at **Kourion**, the best-preserved Crusader castle at **Kolossi**, and a fine private **Wine Museum** at Erimi. All are a short drive from each other and from the centre of Lemesos. Beyond them are meandering lanes and some surprisingly uncrowded beaches – the British base at Akrotiri stopped the westward spread of the city – and the stylish resort of Pissouri Bay.

## Kolossi Castle

Daily: mid-April to mid-Sept 8.15am–7.45pm; mid-Sept to mid-April 8.15am–5.15pm • €2.50 • ☎ 25934907, ⓦ tinyurl.com/kolossi

Eleven kilometres west of Lemesos, at the southern edge of the village of the same name, is **Kolossi Castle**, a great brutalist lump of Crusader military architecture, impressive in both its dimensions and its state of preservation. Originally built by the Knights Hospitaller in 1210 AD on land granted to them by the Lusignans, it became far more important after 1291 when, following their retreat from the Holy Land, the Hospitallers made Kolossi their military headquarters. It fell into the hands of their rivals the Knights Templar in 1306, but was returned to the Hospitallers six years later when the Templar order was dissolved. Although the Hospitallers subsequently moved their main operation to Rhodes, Kolossi Castle remained their command centre in Cyprus, controlling more than forty villages in the region (still called "the Koumandaria"). In 1426 the castle was destroyed in a Mameluke attack, then rebuilt in its present form by Louis de Magnac in around 1454 – his coat of arms can be seen, together with those of Jerusalem, Cyprus and Armenia, in a recessed cross on the eastern external wall of the castle.

The castle follows the classic medieval design of a square keep. The sides are 16m long on the outside, 13.5m on the inside, and 21m tall. Accommodation inside is on three floors, and the views from the crenelated roof are worth the climb up the steep spiral steps.

As interesting as the castle itself are the ruins in its grounds. The main building, which looks for all the world like a church, is actually a sugar factory, and although there is no access for visitors, the aqueduct which brought water to the cane-crushing mill can clearly be seen. The millstone is still *in situ*. In 1488 the sugar factory was transferred from the Hospitallers to the Venetians, following their takeover of the island, and production continued into the seventeenth century, when competition with the West Indies finally brought Cypriot sugar production to an end.

## Cyprus Wine Museum

42 Paphou St, Erimi • Daily 9am–5pm • €5 including wine tasting and nibbles; €4 entry only; under-12s free • ☎ 99907636, ⓦ cypruswinemuseum.com

Based in an attractive traditional house in the village of Erini, some 10km west of Lemesos centre, the excellent **Cyprus Wine Museum** provides the lowdown on over five thousand years of wine production on the island, as well as, of course, the opportunity to sample a few vintages. With almost divine appropriateness, shortly after the museum was opened in 2004 wine flasks were discovered close to Erini village and dated to around 3500 BC, among the earliest evidence of wine production in Europe. Divided broadly into the past (upstairs) and present (downstairs), you'll find lots of information on these discoveries and the evolution of the famous Commandaria sweet white wine under the Knights Templar. There is a range of good-quality wine-related merchandise for sale, effective use is made of quotations from ancient writers and depictions in ancient mosaics, there are photographs and tableaux, an interesting audiovisual presentation and a useful pictorial wall map of the vineyards of Lemesos and Pafos districts. A recent development – the Commandaria Orchestra (and friends) – is based at the museum, which plays a variety of classical, Greek and Cypriot music all over the region. It's worth noting that the museum might open a few minutes late on a Sunday morning – it depends on the length of the service at the local church, at which the museum curator (and son of the owner) is a chanter.

TEMPLE OF APOLLON YLATIS, ANCIENT KOURION

## Ancient Kourion

Northwest corner of the Akrotiri Peninsula • Daily: mid-April to mid-Sept 8.15am–7.45pm; mid-Sept to mid-April 8.15am–5.15pm • €4.50 • 🕿 25934250, 🖰 bit.ly/KourionMuseum

The **Kourion** complex of archeological sites (including the Sanctuary of Apollo) is blessed with both archeological significance and a spectacular location. Sitting high on a hill overlooking the deep blue of the Mediterranean, its tumble of ochre columns and walls, its theatre set like a fossilized shell into the hillside, its paved roads and mosaic floors are both spectacular and well preserved, offering a portal through which we can glimpse life as it was lived two thousand years ago. Settlement in the area goes back to Neolithic times, with the city of Kourion itself being established during the Mycenaean and Dorian invasions of Cyprus from about 1200 BC. Nearly all of what you can see today, though, is of Roman origin, revealed by excavations from the 1930s onwards by a series of American teams, and from 1964 by the Cypriot Department of Antiquities.

After passing through the main entrance, visit the pavilion area which houses a relief model of the whole site as well as a small cafeteria and toilets. Immediately in front of the pavilion are two of the gems of the site. The **House of Estolios**, sitting under its elegant timber protective roof, gives a good idea of the sort of luxury enjoyed by a rich Roman of the fourth or fifth century AD, with its numerous rooms, courtyards, bath complex and intricate mosaic floors of fish, birds, and one of a young woman holding a measuring rod, with the word "Ktisis" ("Creation") above it. Inscriptions tell us not only the house-owner's name, but also the fact that he was a Christian. One inscription, at the entrance, charmingly welcomes the visitor: "Enter to thy good fortune and may thy coming bless this house". Next to the house sits Kourion's famous **theatre**, first erected in the second century BC, but rebuilt by the Romans in the second century AD. Seating 3500 spectators, it is still used today for cultural events.

A short walk to the northwest lies the **Roman Agora** (marketplace) and public baths, and beyond them the **House of the Gladiators**, a third-century AD structure so-called because of its vivid mosaics of gladiatorial combat, and the **House of Achilles**, a fourth-century AD Roman villa named, again, for a mosaic showing the revealing of Achilles' true identity by Odysseus in the court of the king Lycomedes at Skyros. These are the highlights of the site, though in among them are subsequent remains of early Christian origin. There are also fine views of the forbidding eroded terrain to the north and across fields and stables to the beach and the sea to the south.

## GEORGE H. MCFADDEN

Something of a real-life Indiana Jones, **George H. McFadden** was a graduate of Princeton University (class of 1930) who became the leading light in the excavation of the **Kourion archeological site**. In charge of a University of Pennsylvania excavation team, he was working on the site off and on for nearly twenty years from 1933, wintering on site and returning to America for the summer. Work stopped when the US entered World War II in 1941, and resumed in 1948. Though some doubts have been cast on the rigour of his methodology, his work certainly drew attention to the importance of the site, and paved the way for further work by the Cypriot Department of Antiquities from 1964. McFadden is still revered in the area, and his death by drowning at the age of 46 in a sailing accident in April 1953 is regarded as a great tragedy. As the framed eulogy in the Kourion Museum rather floridly put it, "It was fitting that he should find his end in the Greek and briny sea whence came the goddess of beauty herself to his beloved island – Cyprus".

**2**

### Sanctuary of Apollon Ylatis

Daily: mid-April to mid-Sept 8.15am–7.45pm; mid-Sept to mid-April 8.15am–5.15pm • €4.50 • ⓦ tinyurl.com/kourionsite

Two kilometres west of the main Kourion site is the **Sanctuary of Apollon Ylatis** (sometimes Apollo Hylates), originating from as early as the eighth century BC, and dedicated to "Apollo of the Woods". Much modified over the twelve hundred years up to the fourth century AD, with most of what is now visible dating from the first century AD, it is as impressive and as enlightening as the remains of Kourion itself, and in some ways even easier to get your head around, the only drawback for the visitor being that the information boards that stand in direct sunlight have faded and cracked so badly as to be virtually illegible.

On entering the site, the first building of note is the **palaestra** or gymnasium, a succession of rooms lining the edges of an open space where athletes could be seen exercising or taking part in wrestling bouts. Across the entrance where once stood the **Kourion Gate** lie the remains of the **baths**. West of this cluster of buildings, the remains of a colonnade mark a large building along the south side of the sanctuary, presumed to have been **dormitories** for pilgrims. At its western end are the remains of the **Pafos Gate**, to the north of which is a further building whose function is not clear – perhaps a **display hall** for votive offerings. Directly east across from this, and next to the baths, is the **Priest's House**, probably incorporating the temple kitchens and treasury. Beside it is a **pit** into which votive offerings would be thrown.

Striking north from this cluster of buildings the paved "**Sacred Way**" climbs up past a circular structure, thought to have been a **sacred garden**, to the heart of the Sanctuary, the **Temple of Apollo** itself. Standing at the end of twelve steps, it is flanked by the remains of an ancient **altar**, at which votive offerings were perhaps dedicated to the god. Touching this altar was, according to ancient sources, a sacrilege which would earn the unfortunate culprit a plunge from nearby cliffs into the sea.

### Kourion Museum

10 Kouriou, Episkopi (it's well signposted to the right off the main road to Kourion as you approach from Lemesos) • Mon–Fri 8am–3.30pm • €2.50 • ☏ 25932453

Best visited after the site itself, the **Kourion Museum** is lodged in a colonial-style house, which was built for George H. McFadden, the American archeologist who started excavations here in 1933. Bronze Age artefacts and tomb goods are displayed in the first room, while the main exhibition hall features finds from Kourion and the Sanctuary of Apollon Ylatis. These include votive figures, a bronze *strigil* or body scraper, arrowheads, a miner's terracotta lamp, and a good selection of different types of pottery and statues, among them a boy riding on a dolphin and a head of Aphrodite. One of the most affecting finds is a family group of male, female and child skeletons, victims of a major fourth-century earthquake, discovered in the remains of a Roman house.

## Pissouri and Pissouri Bay

Along the coast beyond Erimi and the Kourion/Kolossi sites, several beaches remain relatively unspoiled, protected from development by the fact that they are within the boundaries of the British Sovereign Base. **Paramali** and **Evdimou** beaches, each with a taverna, are worth braving the dirt tracks to get to. Beyond them, **PISSOURI** is the first village and beach outside British control. A large settlement equidistant from Lemesos and Pafos, it consists of the village itself some 3km inland, and its beach **Pissouri Bay.** Pissouri is developing into a stylish holiday resort in its own right, which makes for a pleasant alternative to both Lemesos and Pafos. Popular with families from the base and with expats, the village has a range of accommodation and places to eat, while the beach resort, some 3km south, has windsurfing facilities and is quiet and unhurried. The beach itself is long (2km) and scenic, sweeping up to Cape Aspro, named for its supposedly white cliffs (they're more a pale brown).

## Anoyira

From Pissouri village, a short diversion inland brings you to **ANOYIRA**, a tangle of lanes and alleys and old houses perched on an escarpment. Unspoilt, the village is beginning to realize its tourist potential, not least by being the only place on the island where *pasteli*, a traditional sweet made from carob juice, is made. You can find out all about it at the **Pasteli Museum** (daily: April–Oct 9am–7pm, Nov–March 9am–5pm; free; ☎25222679); the sweet itself is something of an acquired taste. Other attractions include: the ruins of **Timios Stavros monastery** (open access; free), slowly being renovated; **Oleastro** (daily 10am–6pm; €3; ☎99565768, ⓦoleastro.com.cy), an olive mill/museum/coffee shop, which does for olives what the Pasteli Museum does for carob juice; and **Nicolaidi's Winery** (☎25221709).

**ACCOMMODATION**                                                    **WEST OF LEMESOS**

### PISSOURI AND PISSOURI BAY

**Bunch of Grapes Inn** 9 Loannou Erotokritou St ☎25221275, ⓦthebunchofgrapesinn.com. Housed in an old mansion high above the coastal plain near the centre of the village, the *Bunch of Grapes* is bursting with character. Known more as a restaurant than as a place to stay, it has eleven simple, reasonably priced rooms accessed via wooden external galleries and stairs, and fabulous views down to the sea. €50

**Columbia Beach Resort & Columbia Beach Hotel** Ampelonon, Pissouri Bay ☎25833000, ⓦcolumbia resort.com. Dominating the beach at Pissouri, the *Columbia*

*Beach Resort* and *Columbia Beach Hotel* (the latter a cheaper version of the former) have comprehensive facilities, including a vast pool, spa and health club, restaurants, bars and sports facilities. They even have their own rather luridly painted chapel. Beach Resort €319, Beach Hotel €300

**Hill View Hotel Apartments** 60 Stadiou ☎25221972, ⓦhillview.com.cy. A cracking little hotel perched above Pissouri, the *Hill View* has spacious studios and apartments a super bar and restaurant, a small swimming pool, terrific views across the town towards the sea or back towards the mountains, and staff who couldn't be more helpful, all at bargain prices. Studio €82, one-bed apartment €88

# The Akrotiri Peninsula

The **AKROTIRI PENINSULA** lies southwest of Lemesos, the bulk of it occupied by the British Sovereign Base, one of two retained by the UK when Cyprus became independent in 1960. Driving through it can be a disorienting experience, since it looks and feels like a chunk of suburban England, out of place in the climate of Cyprus's southernmost point. However much one feels that this remnant of Britain's imperial past is somehow inappropriate to the twenty-first century, it has had the collateral benefit of stopping the westward spread of Lemesos's unattractive sprawl.

There's not a lot to draw the visitor out onto the peninsula itself, but three attractions are well worth the drive.

**WILDLIFE IN THE AKROTIRI**

The Akrotiri Peninsula is of **great environmental significance**, having been designated a wetland of international importance in 2003 under the Ramsar Convention. It is also interesting **geologically**, having once been a separate island now joined to the rest of Cyprus. At its centre is a salt lake similar to the one in Larnaka, which fills with water in winter and dries out in summer. The peninsula boasts **27 natural habitats** hosting a wide diversity of plants, animals and birds – the famous greater flamingo, but also the glossy ibis, the demoiselle crane and a variety of other waders, ducks and gulls.

**2**

## The Akrotiri Environmental Centre

4640 Akrotiri Village • Mon–Sun 8am–3pm • Free • ☎ 25826562, ⊕ akrotirienvironment.com

The **Akrotiri Environmental Education Centre** was set up in July 2004, and is financed partly by the British government. It's on the junction where the road to Lady's Mile branches off. If you miss it, you can't go too far wrong – a few hundred metres beyond it the road comes to an end at the gates of the British Akrotiri Base. In 2015 the Centre moved from its previous rather ramshackle home to a handsome, purpose-built and fittingly eco-friendly structure across the road. It covers the same ground as the old Centre, but more comprehensively and professionally. Outside there are labelled plants, and, inside, a large aerial photograph of the Akrotiri Peninsula dominated by its huge salt marsh to give perspective, then displays devoted to its local crafts such as basket weaving, prehistoric inhabitants from men to pygmy hippos, seabirds and bird migration routes, and seals and turtles. This room opens out onto a terrace with recognition pictures of birds, some powerful binoculars, and spectacular views of the salt marsh itself.

## Agios Nikolaos ton Gaton (St Nicholas of the Cats)

Akrotiri • Daily 8am–5pm • Donation expected • ☎ 25952621

In the middle of the flatlands to the south of the Akrotiri Peninsula's salt lake lies the monastery of **Agios Nikolaos ton Gaton**. Originally established in 325 AD, the present buildings date from the thirteenth to the fifteenth centuries. Surrounded by citrus groves, and altogether rather unprepossessing, the monastery owes its celebrity to the presence of the **cats** that give it its name. They were introduced, it is said, by St Helena (see page 78), to keep the monastery clear of snakes or, as another version has it, to replace young boys as companions for the monks. The monastery was abandoned after the sixteenth-century Ottoman invasion, but has since been taken in hand by an order of nuns who are bringing it back to life (and who look at visitors rather as if they expect them to make off with the silver). There's a small one-room shop run by the nuns. Part of the appeal of the monastery is that its practice of keeping cats around ecclesiastical buildings spread to other parts of Cyprus and beyond – though today you'll see far more cats in Larnaka's Hala Sultan Tekke than in St Nicholas of the Cats.

## Lady's Mile Beach

Occupying most of the east coast of the Akrotiri Peninsula lies a vast area of hard-packed sand crisscrossed with tyre tracks and, at the sea's edge, the 7km **Lady's Mile Beach**, which sounds nicer than it is. Dotted with several tavernas and lifeguard towers, the beach does have a strip of good-quality sand, but it's rather narrow and the views across the bay to the industrial port of Lemesos add little to its allure. The beach, incidentally, is not named after the Virgin Mary or even Aphrodite, as might seem likely in Cyprus, but after a horse called Lady whose polo-playing military owner used the beach for a gallop every morning.

# The Troodos foothills

Spreading in an arc north of Lemesos, the **Troodos foothills** offer an opportunity to get away from the brashness and heat of the city and the coast. This is open countryside that rises in a series of ridges towards the heights of the Troodos massif, dotted with hill villages that have supported themselves over the centuries by cultivating citrus fruits, olives and above all **wine**. The southward-facing slopes provide the perfect terroir for growing grapes (particularly indigenous Mavro and Xynisteri, as well as imported Grenache and Cabernet Sauvignon varieties), something they've been doing in this area for over five thousand years.

It's not easy to explore the foothills of Lemesos District in any systematic way. One approach would be to follow the **wine routes** (see page 105) organized by the Cyprus Tourism Organization and contained in a useful free guidebook available from tourist centres and participating wineries.

Another approach might be to cluster the villages to be visited into geographical groups – the ones sometimes called the "**Krassochoria**" (wine villages) to the west, the group in the centre, once ruled by the Hospitallers in Kolossi and known collectively as the **Koumandaria**, and the villages to the east marketed, rather hopefully, by the tourist authorities as "the Cypriot Tuscany". Or you can, of course, simply meander through the region, going where the spirit takes you. Do, though, stick to the main roads, even though this can mean a lot of doubling back – what on the map may look like a tempting short cut between villages could turn out to be a rutted dirt road for which you'll need a 4WD.

## The Krassochoria (wine villages)

The **Krassochoria** (sometimes Krasochoria) are best approached, appropriately enough, through **Erimi**, home of the Cyprus Wine Museum. Driving away from Lemesos through the village with the museum on your left, cross the bridge then turn right onto the E601. This is Wine Route 4, which visits a total of twenty villages, the best of which are covered below.

### Vouni

In the middle of the Krassochoria area, **VOUNI** is a delightful hill village built on a ridge at the confluence of two rivers. With its mountain architecture protected by law, its winding lanes, numerous balconied houses, lush gardens of fig, pomegranate, apricot, orange, lemon and almond trees, and views across the gorge, it gives some idea of what these hill villages must have been like during their heyday. Though now in something of a decline caused by rural depopulation – it once had 2500 residents, compared to its current hundred or so – there is still a lot of renovation going on, and families which have left often maintain the ancestral home as a summer residence. Sadly, the Vouni donkey sanctuary, once a highlight of the region, has now closed.

### Koilani

On the northeastern edge of the Krassochoria region, **KOILANI** is very much a wine village, though it did make a brief appearance in Cypriot history when Richard the Lionheart destroyed a camp here set up by Isaac Komnenos. The village today has the usual narrow winding streets and alleys as well as great views of the surrounding mountains. A winery to look out for is **Vlassides Winery** (daily 11am–4pm; ☎97789560, ⊕vlassideswinery.com), halfway between Vouni and Koilani, which runs free tastings, has English-speaking guides and ample parking. Elsewhere in the village, there's a small **ecclesiastical museum** (open by appointment; free; ☎99213682) containing mainly icons, woodcarving and ornate metalwork covering seven hundred years of the village's history (star attraction: the skull of Agia Mavri, the village patron),

**THE WINE ROUTES**

The Cyprus Tourist Organization's excellent guide to **wine routes** in Pafos and Lemesos Districts is a must for any oenophiles visiting Cyprus. **Six routes** are described, three in Pafos District, three in Lemesos District. The routes are also clearly signposted on the ground with signs that are, appropriately, a Burgundy colour. Each route includes a summary of the climate, terrain, vineyards and grape varieties to be experienced, a detailed description of the roads to be travelled and the villages to be visited, and a list of wineries and tavernas to be found along the way, together with a lot of advice on the storage and drinking of wine. The Lemesos District is covered by Route 4 (the Krassochoria), Route 5 (Koumandaria) and Route 6 (Pitsilia).

2

and an even smaller **Museum of Viticulture** (to arrange access, phone ☎25471008). About 1km east of the village is the pitched-roof church of **Agia Mavri**, strikingly set in a river gorge. The legend of the saint is that she was a virgin whose father was insisting that, for financial or dynastic reasons, she must marry a man she loathed. On the wedding night she fled, but was cornered by her father and her suitor at the stream where the church stands today. Calling on the Virgin Mary to save her, the cliff behind swallowed her up, and she was never seen again. The church was established to commemorate the event.

## Malia

One of a cluster of three villages on the northwestern edge of the Krassochoria, **MALIA** was notable until 1974 for its large Turkish-Cypriot minority, attested to by the minaret which is still visible in the village. The main reason for visiting the village today is the large winery, **Malia (Keo) Ltd** (Mon–Fri 8am–2pm; ☎25942131), which, though built in 1930, was fully modernized in 1996. Known as one of the few Cypriot wineries to produce Riesling, it has free tastings, a shop, ample parking, audiovisual presentations, a restaurant and vineyard tours.

## Vasa

The village of **VASA** is dotted with *pitharia*, the huge earthenware wine containers – they can be seen in gardens, courtyards and inside houses themselves – a reminder that, in days gone by, each household made its own wine. At the northern edge of the village is the **Argyrides Vasa Winery** (Sat 10am–1pm; ☎25945999, ⓦvasawinery.com), which offers tours of the vineyard (only for large groups; appointment only).

## Omodos

**OMODOS** is the epitome of the Troodos foothills wine village. That's why it attracts so many visitors and that's why it's lambasted for being too touristy. Don't listen to the critics – if you've only got time for one village, make it this one. Surrounded by vineyards, Omodos is laid out around a large pedestrianized cobbled square which slopes gently down to **Timiou Stavrou (Holy Cross) Monastery**. Around the square is a bunch of souvenir shops, together with a good range of tavernas/café-bars: check out the *Village Inn*, for example. There's a massive old wine press near the square, dating from the Lusignan period, while 1km north is the **Ktima Gerolemo winery**, which offers winery tours and wine tasting (Mon–Sat 10am–5pm, Sun 11am–5pm; ☎25422122, ⓦktimagerolemo.com), as well as a gift shop. In addition to wine, Omodos also makes *zivania*, an explosive spirit, together with a number of sweets made from wine must.

### Timiou Stavrou (Holy Cross) Monastery

Monastery and museums: Mon, Tues & Thurs–Sun 9.30am–1pm & 2–7pm; Wed 9.30am–12.30pm • Free • ☎ 25222679

Outside the entrance to **Timiou Stavrou (Holy Cross) Monastery** a statue commemorates a past abbot, Dositheos, who was one of 486 Greek Cypriots beheaded or hanged in Nicosia by the Turkish authorities on July 10, 1821 during the Greek War of

Independence. Inside, what was the monastery church now acts as the parish church, while several of the rooms and outbuildings have been colonized by the **Struggle Museum**, which has lots of memorabilia of the EOKA campaign against the British (see page 256). Other areas of the monastery host an **Icon Museum**, which not only includes icons, but also decorative woodcarving (look up at the ceiling for a wonderful example), and an **Ecclesiastical Museum**. The museums give an interesting taste of how the village sees itself.

## The Koumandaria

The group of villages in the central foothills above Lemesos is collectively known as the **KOUMANDARIA**. While of great importance to those who know about wine – "Commandaria" is one of the oldest wines in the world – they lack the character of the villages to the west, though the pleasantly cool climate offers respite from the heat of the coast. The most direct route to these villages is up the B8, from Junction 28 on the A1 as it curves around the north of Lemesos; for a more interesting return trip, use the E110.

The first group of villages of passing interest lies off to the west of the B8, starting with **Monagri**. The fact that it was once one of the Linovamvakoi villages is illustrated by the fact that, in the church of the **Archangelos monastery** in the village, there's a *mihrab*, a semicircular niche in the wall, indicating the direction of Mecca. There's a Roman olive mill (the only one on the island) in the outbuildings. Beyond Monagri, the villages of **Agios Georgios** and **Silikou** are worth a brief stop and stroll. If you return to Monagri, a left turn brings you to **DOROS**, yet another vineyard-surrounded village, this time with a winery with visitor facilities. Next to the sixteenth-century church of Agios Epifanios, the **Karseras Winery** (daily 10am–5pm; ☎99319646, ⓦkarseraswinery.com) provides ample parking and free tasting, and, if you phone to prearrange the visit, commentaries in English.

Back on the B8, a short detour north of Doros and east of the main road takes you to the nicely preserved village of **LANEIA**, one of the prettiest in the Kommandaria. Spreading across several small hills, it offers a number of cafés, tavernas and shops, a supermarket and post office. It's also home to a lot of expats, many of them artists who sell their work here. For example, visit Michael Owen Galleries (☎25432404, ⓦmichaelowengallery.com), or take a look at the work of Anne Pays (ⓦannepays.com).

Continuing north on the B8, a right turn onto the F812 after **TRIMIKLINI** brings you to the village of **Agios Mamas** and then, just east of the E110, the substantial village of **Kalo Chorio, Zoopigi** to the north, and, beyond **Kalo Chorio**, **Agios Pavlos** and **Agios Constantinos**. The air here (at around 700m) is beautifully cool and fragrant with the scent of citrus orchards, while the villages have lots of colourful gardens to appreciate. In Kalo Chorio, the **Co-operative Company of Viniculture** (☎25542266) offers free wine tastings.

---

### THE LINOVAMVAKOI

The **Linovamvakoi** (singular Linovamvakos) were descendants of the Venetians and Greek Cypriots who, for pragmatic reasons, **superficially converted to Islam** while remaining Christian in belief (being a Muslim was initially safer, and later carried considerable benefits and tax breaks under the Ottomans). The first wave of converts tended to be Roman Catholic, later ones Greek Orthodox. The name comes from a type of two-ply cloth which was cotton on the outside, linen on the inside, that is "Muslim on the outside, Christian on the inside". When the British took over Cyprus, many Linovamakoi reverted to Christianity, but others remained Muslim, either because mixed marriages had muddied the waters (many were spurned by the local Orthodox communities), or because of rumours that Britain might hand Cyprus back to Turkish rule. It is also true that the British authorities did not make reversion easy. Many of those who remained Muslim became, in due course, integrated into what is today thought of as the Turkish-Cypriot community.

The return to Lemesos down the E110 can, with diversions, take in the village of **Louvaras**, whose timeless centre is unspoilt, and whose painted chapel of Agios Mamas is well worth seeking out.

## The eastern foothills

The villages of the **eastern foothills** of the Lemesos region have less of specific interest to the visitor than those of the centre and west. However, a drive through the empty countryside that rises steadily towards the mountains from the coast can be exhilarating, and helps to emphasize that, despite the overcrowding caused by the influx of migrants from the north in 1974, there are still empty parts of the island, even close to the main conurbations.

The best route to take is the F128, from Junction 24 on the A1. Within minutes the lake of **Germasogeia** appears on the right, often thronged with determined canoeists and rowers out practising, the shore dotted with their cars and those of supporters. For energetic visitors there's a nature trail (clearly signposted), and for hungry ones there's a café/snack bar in the nearby village of **Finikaria**.

From the reservoir, the road winds upwards above the Germasogeia River through the heart of the **Lemesos Forest**, a hilly wilderness of brush, cypress and olive trees. Despite the proximity of Lemesos, there's a real feeling of isolation here – between the dam and the sizeable settlement of **Arakapas**, there's only one village: **Dierona**, sprawling on its hillside. From Arakapas, the road west gives access to the Koumandaria villages.

2

# Pafos and around

AKAMAS PENINSULA

# Pafos and around

Pafos district, which takes up the whole of the western end of Cyprus, is probably the single most varied and most attractive region on the island. Wild and remote in parts, it was long regarded in the rest of Cyprus as something of a rural backwater, its inhabitants frequently lampooned as clueless country folk. This situation changed substantially in the 1980s with the opening of Pafos Airport and the development of motorway links with the rest of the island. Suddenly the Pafos area became a magnet for developers keen to exploit its natural riches.

For a start, the area has the longest **coastline** of any district, swinging around from **Aphrodite's birthplace** in the south to **Aphrodite's Baths** in the north and beyond, with beaches facing south, west and north along its length. It has, in the **Akamas Peninsula** and the forests of **Tilliria**, two of the island's great wilderness areas, crisscrossed with trails and dotted with picnic sites. And inland stretch beautiful sunny uplands, carpeted in vineyards and dotted with wineries, monasteries and pretty villages. **Pafos town** itself might at first appear to be the archetypal beach-and-booze resort – no different, you might think, from hundreds of others across the Mediterranean. Yet look more closely and, laced through the maze of bars and restaurants and hotels, are a number of fascinating historical remains, some of which have been granted UNESCO World Heritage status. And in **Polis** on the north coast, with its beach, little fishing port and hinterland villages and unspoilt stretch of coast, it has a relaxed, away-from-it-all feel.

# Pafos

**PAFOS** (locals still often use the old spelling, "Paphos") has two parts, each with a distinct character. **Kato (Lower) Pafos** is the area around the harbour and castle, from which it also runs east and south along and behind a palm-studded promenade (Poseidonos). This is the main tourist area, packed with hotels, cafés, bars, restaurants, souvenir shops, amusement arcades, boat-cruise touts and a couple of indifferent beaches. However, leavening this unrelenting holiday heaven/hell are some truly excellent historical and archeological sites which are conveniently close at hand. As well as the **castle** there are the magnificent **Roman mosaics** immediately behind the harbour, a group of **Byzantine remains** linked with Saint Paul directly across the road, and the eerie **Tombs of the Kings** to the north.

**Ktima Pafos** (perhaps best translated as "the lands of Pafos") lies 3km north, on a steep hillside overlooking the lower town. Its narrow winding streets provide a contrast with Kato Pafos and there are several worthwhile sites including an **art gallery**, a medieval **mosque** and **hammam**, and a couple of diverting **museums**. In general, Ktima Pafos offers a less hurried experience than the rather brash lower town – it even seems cooler, though the 65m elevation is hardly enough to account for it.

### Brief history

The original town, **Palaipafos**, lies some 22km to the southeast of the present one, on the edge of the modern village of Kouklia (see page 125). It was established during the late Hellenistic period, and was one of two city kingdoms in the west – the other being Marion, near modern-day Polis. When **Alexander the Great** died in 323 BC, the Pafiot king **Nicocles** was faced with the same dilemma as all the other towns in Cyprus – which of Alexander's warring successors to support. He chose the Egyptian **Ptolemy**

ROMAN MOSAICS, PAFOS

# Highlights

**❶ Roman mosaics, Pafos** Some of the most perfectly preserved Roman mosaics in the world. See page 113

**❷ Shopping in Ktima Pafos** All the fun of the bazaar, in a warren of roofed narrow streets in Pafos old town. See page 118

**❸ Geroskipou Folk Art Museum** One of the best folk museums on the island – a terrific glimpse into the past of ordinary Cypriots. See page 124

**❹ Aphrodite's birthplace** A fine beach, so photogenic it appears widely on tourist literature, which has a rich crop of mythical associations. See page 125

**❺ Agios Neofytos Monastery** Not only an excellent example of a Greek Orthodox monastery, but with a fascinating back story and a museum to boot. See page 128

**❻ Grivas Museum** An illuminating if one-sided introduction to the EOKA leader and his campaign against the British. See page 131

**❼ The Akamas Peninsula** Empty, unspoilt hills and beaches, coastal vistas and numerous marked hiking trails. See page 133

**❽ Polis** With its pretty fishing port, Lakki, Polis is a reminder of how Pafos district used to be, before the motorway and the airport arrived. See page 136

**HIGHLIGHTS ARE MARKED ON THE MAP ON PAGE 112**

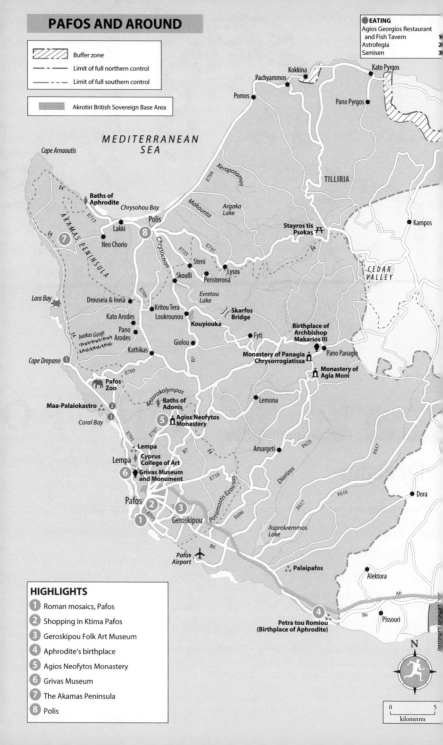

dynasty, which indeed eventually won. This did Nicocles little good, however. Deciding to rule Cyprus directly rather than through a proxy, the Ptolemies used a false charge of treason to get rid of him (Nicocles avoided execution by committing suicide). The new rulers of Cyprus decided to move the administrative capital from Salamis in the east to the fine new city of **Nea Pafos** in the west: apart from being closer to their home base of Alexandria, it was convenient for patrolling the western approaches to the island, and, through the thick forests inland it was able to meet the almost insatiable demand for timber of the Egyptian navy.

The transition to **Roman rule** in 58 BC did Pafos no harm at all, and it continued as the capital of the island. This period was the high point of Pafos's fortunes, and the origin of its wonderful Roman mosaics and plentiful early Christian ruins. The New Testament (Acts 13, verses 4 to 13) relates how **St Paul** visited Pafos and converted the Roman ruler of the island, Sergius Paulus, to the new faith, though not before the evangelist was tied to a post (the so-called St Paul's Pillar) and lashed "forty times less one" for spreading the gospel.

In 365 AD the city was destroyed by an **earthquake**, and in 653 AD by a Saracen raid. It never recovered. Most of the inhabitants moved away from the coast, onto the hill of what today is Ktima Pafos, and the status of capital was moved back to Salamis. The harbour silted up, the land around it became marshy, and for centuries visitors to what remained of Pafos had little good to say about it. In the fourteenth century the **Lusignans** built a castle to protect Christians in transit to the Holy Lands; in the sixteenth century the Ottomans built a fort on its remains. But Pafos continued as a quiet backwater until the building of the airport and the motorway in the late twentieth century brought about a surge in tourism.

## Kato Pafos

The heart of **Kato Pafos** is the **harbour area**, a south-facing hooked finger that seems to beckon in boats from the sea. The harbour combines workaday buildings – the Customs House, Department of Fisheries and the Port Authority – with important historic sites including the **castle**, the wave-washed remains of an ancient breakwater, and the memorial to St Paul's visit during his first missionary journey. Close by is the entrance to the **archeological park** that contains the town's world-famous **mosaics**.

### The castle

Daily mid-Sept to mid-April 8.30am–5pm; mid-April to mid-Sept 8.30am–7.30pm • €2.50

**Pafos Castle**, sitting at the edge of the harbour and reflected in the water that surrounds it, presents a scene worthy of any romantic watercolourist. Unsurprisingly, it is frequently used as a backdrop for concerts, plays and operas (it has been known for incoming jets to be diverted out to sea so as not to disrupt performances during the Paphos Festival). As with many Cypriot castles, it has a complex back story: built by the Lusignans around 1391, it was destroyed by an earthquake towards the end of the fifteenth century, and what was left was levelled by the Venetians to prevent it falling into the hands of the Turks. Despite this, the castle was rebuilt and garrisoned by the Ottomans in 1592. After the British takeover of Cyprus, the castle was relegated to a salt store. The main attraction of a visit is to climb up to the battlements where once twelve cannons stood guard. The clear field of fire they required now offers excellent views across the harbour to the distant low hills to the north.

### The Roman mosaics

Leoforos Apostolou Pavlou (behind the harbour) • Daily mid-Sept to mid-April 8.30am–5pm; mid-April to mid-Sept 8.30am–7.30pm • €4.50 • ☎ 26306217

Housed in an archeological park northwest of the harbour (you can't miss the large entrance gates just behind the quay, fronted by a modern clock tower), Pafos's

Pafos International Airport

**PAFOS**

0    500
metres

**Roman mosaics** are one of the glories of Cyprus and are simply unmissable. The mosaics were first revealed in 1942 when British soldiers digging trenches for air-raid shelters uncovered a representation of Hercules and the Lion. The ancient artwork was swiftly covered up to protect it from German bombs and its location, and even existence, in due course forgotten. In the 1960s, more mosaics were revealed during building work, and the Department of Antiquities stepped in to excavate the site.

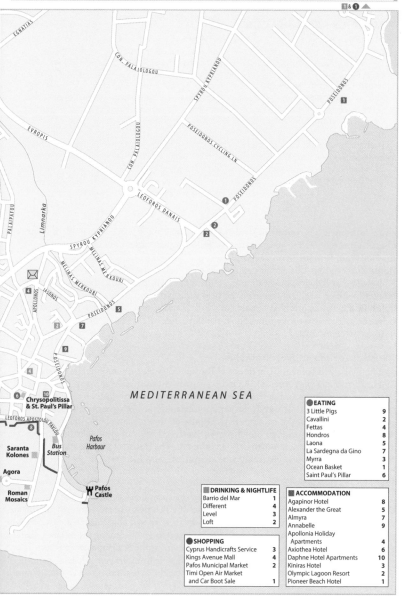

MEDITERRANEAN SEA

Chrysopolitissa
& St. Paul's Pillar

Saranta
Kolones

Bus
Station

Pafos
Harbour

Agora

Roman
Mosaics

Pafos
Castle

| ● EATING | |
|---|---|
| 3 Little Pigs | 9 |
| Cavallini | 2 |
| Fettas | 4 |
| Hondros | 8 |
| Laona | 5 |
| La Sardegna da Gino | 7 |
| Myrra | 3 |
| Ocean Basket | 1 |
| Saint Paul's Pillar | 6 |

| ■ DRINKING & NIGHTLIFE | |
|---|---|
| Barrio del Mar | 1 |
| Different | 4 |
| Level | 3 |
| Loft | 2 |

| ● SHOPPING | |
|---|---|
| Cyprus Handicrafts Service | 3 |
| Kings Avenue Mall | 4 |
| Pafos Municipal Market | 2 |
| Timi Open Air Market and Car Boot Sale | 1 |

| ■ ACCOMMODATION | |
|---|---|
| Agapinor Hotel | 8 |
| Alexander the Great | 5 |
| Almyra | 7 |
| Annabelle | 9 |
| Apollonia Holiday Apartments | 4 |
| Axiothea Hotel | 6 |
| Daphne Hotel Apartments | 10 |
| Kiniras Hotel | 3 |
| Olympic Lagoon Resort | 2 |
| Pioneer Beach Hotel | 1 |

So far, four villas have been unearthed, each named after one of the more notable mosaics it contains.

### Planning your visit

Set aside at least half a day to see the mosaics. Once through the incongruous modern entrance gates, you'll see the barn-like stone **visitors' centre**, a good starting point. It's

## MOSAICS – A ROUGH GUIDE

**Mosaics** such as those found in Pafos were expensive to make, and therefore were confined to public buildings and the houses of the rich. Even in the great villas of important men, mosaics were installed only in the public rooms where they could be seen and admired (and envied) by visitors. In bedrooms floors were far more likely to be of simple pebbles set in mortar, while kitchens and workshops would have to manage with beaten earth floors. Most mosaic customers choose from a library of set patterns while the super-rich commissioned their own designs.

The artworks were painstakingly created by dozens of men using small cubes of pottery or glass called **tesserae**. First, relatively unskilled apprentices hacked out and levelled the ground before filling it with crushed stone, gravel and/or pottery shards mixed with lime mortar. After this a layer of fine plaster was laid, into which the tesserae were set. More skilled workmen created geometric patterns, while compositions involving figurative representations of humans and animals would be left to the master craftsman. Finally, marble dust, sand and lime were rubbed over the finished surface to fill in the joints and any cracks, and a drainage hole was created so that the mosaic could be periodically washed with water.

**3**

also worth buying the excellent guide to the mosaics published by the Bank of Cyprus Foundation (€5.50). However, instead of following the order contained in it, visit the **Houses of Theseus**, **Aion** and **Orpheus** first, then take on the biggest and best, the **House of Dionysos**. This allows you to better appreciate the scale of the site.

Elsewhere in the archeological park are the remains of the **agora**, the reconstructed **odeion** in which concerts and plays are held during the summer, a pretty little **lighthouse**, and the jumbled remains of a Lusignan fortress, **Saranda Kolones** ("forty columns"). They're worth a quick look, perhaps, but only if you've already paid to get in to view the mosaics.

### The Houses of Theseus, Aion and Orpheus

The first villa you come to, **The House of Theseus**, contains the mosaic discovered in 1941: *Theseus and the Minotaur*. A circular artwork, it positively glows in its uncovered setting of ochre floors and what remains of dried mud-brick walls. Note the maze-like geometric design that surrounds the central medallion – this represents the Labyrinth in which Theseus slew the Minotaur. The **House of Aion** is named after the pagan god Aion depicted inside (though only his head survives). You can also make out Apollo and Hermes among these fourth-century mosaics. The **House of Orpheus** further west features the god of music charming various animals with his lyre.

### The House of Dionysos

There is no doubt that the jewel in the crown of the Pafos mosaics is the **House of Dionysos**. This represents the central public area of a rich man's home, clustered around an atrium. The mosaics here are stunning and all the more remarkable considering that the complex suffered a direct hit during a Turkish air raid in 1974. Among the mosaics, there are some particularly striking works. First, as you enter, is the **Scylla mosaic** in Room 1, which is rather drab and incomplete, but is the only one from the early Hellenic period (late fourth/early third century BC), making it by far the oldest mosaic on Cyprus. Found at a lower level, it was lifted and re-laid here, and depicts the girl/monster Scylla (of Scylla and Charybdis fame), bewitched by Circe, who attacked all ships that ventured between Sicily and the Italian mainland. She is portrayed holding a trident in one hand and the mast of a ship in the other, and she has a body which ends in a serpent's tail and crab's claws. Beyond this, look out for the figure of Ganymede being carried off by Zeus in the form of an eagle (Room 8), and the hunting scenes in the porticoes that surrounded the atrium: a leopard with the head of a donkey in its mouth, pouring blood and with the decapitated body lying nearby (Room 10), a hunter attacking a leopard with a spear (Room 11), a running tiger, a hunter attacking a bull and another attacking a lion (Room

12). A particularly graphic and interesting group of mosaics adorns the westernmost portico (Room 16). One, showing the story of **Icarios and the god Dionysos**, depicts a mythic booze-up. Icarios, the first maker of wine, is surrounded by inebriated shepherds intent on murdering him. Icarios's right hand points to the figures of Dionysos, the god of wine (who taught Icarios how to make it), and Akme, the personification of perfection. They too are drinking, but with decorum and restraint. Standing at the entrance to the "tablinum" or dining room, it appears to be a polite warning to guests not to overindulge.

## Chrysopolitissa and St Paul's Pillar
St Paul's Pillar Street

East of Leoforos Apostolou Paulou (and signposted from it) are **Chrysopolitissa** and **St Paul's Pillar**, the first of several survivals from the period after the end of the Roman Empire. Despite being just a few hundred metres from the busy road linking Kato Pafos to Ktima Pafos, and not far from the crowded promenade, the sense of peace and history is palpable. The ruins of the huge Christian basilica of **Panagia Chrysopolitissa** (the earliest parts of which date from the fourth century AD), with its seven aisles, surround the sixteenth-century church of **Agia Kyriaki**, the whole creating a harmonious and picturesque scene of jumbled columns, mosaic fragments (interesting, though not a patch on the ones across the road) and low stone walls. Here it was, tradition has it, that **St Paul** was chained to a column and scourged 39 times (one of five times he received this punishment from the Jews according to 2 Corinthians 11:24–29). A further memorial is dedicated to **Eric Ejegod**, King of Denmark (1095–1103), who died in Pafos on his way to the Holy Land. An extensive network of walkways gives excellent access to the highly photogenic ruins and church.

## The catacombs of Agia Solomani
Leoforou Apostolou Pavlou (opposite Ploutarchou) • Open access • Free (but donations welcome)

The **catacombs of Agia Solomani** – dank in atmosphere, obscure in origin – show the stubborn will of the early faithful to worship. On busy Leoforou Apostolou Pavlou, the well-signposted entrance is overlooked by a large terebinth tree covered in twists of cloth and paper – votive prayer offerings common on holy sites (both Christian and Muslim) throughout the Middle East. In its shade a flight of steps takes you down into hollowed-out rock chambers. The first has several icons, a gate covered in more prayer offerings, the odd plastic bottle of oil and a sign asking you not to light candles. Steps then take you down into a further chamber, perhaps a holy well. It may be that the catacombs were once a pagan shrine which was later used as a synagogue in Roman times, before becoming a shrine dedicated to Agia Solomoni, the Jewish mother of the seven **Maccabee brothers**.

## Fabrica Hill

On the east side of Leoforos Apostolou Pavlou, where it intersects with Agion Anargyron, diagonally across from the new Kings Avenue Mall, stands the rocky outcrop of **Fabrica Hill**, scored with excavations about a fourth-century AD stone quarry. In many places its tunnels and nooks were recycled as burial places. Some of the tombs, dotted with icons and votive offerings, can be seen from Agia Kyriaki, the side street which skirts the hill on its eastern side. Visible too are the remains of a recently excavated **classical theatre**, set like a fossil shell into the hillside and created, not by building, but by digging out the living rock. Archeological exploration continues on the northern face of the hill, much of which is now fenced off, though there's still access in places. Be careful if you do visit – the ground is very uneven and caves abound.

## Tombs of the Kings
Tafon ton Vasileon • Daily: mid-Sept to mid-April 8.30am–5pm; mid-April to mid-Sept 8.30am–7.30pm • €2.50 • ☎ 26306217

Off the main road from Paphos to Coral Bay lies one of the strangest, most atmospheric ancient sites you're likely to come across – the so-called **Tombs of the**

**Kings**. This is an extensive necropolis used from the third century BC to the fourth century AD for the burial, not of kings, but of high-up administrators, civil servants and their families. There is evidence that early Christians also used it to bury their dead, while in the Middle Ages people even lived in the tombs.

In the nineteenth century, the indefatigable **Luigi Palma di Cesnola** plundered the tombs. More considered excavations continued in the early twentieth century, but systematic archeological exploration by the Cyprus Department of Antiquities didn't start until 1977. Since then, eight large tomb complexes have been identified. Each follows a similar plan, with an underground atrium surrounded by Doric columns and a portico, with the tombs dug into the walls behind – imagine a Greek temple, but built in a deep pit. The actual burial chambers and niches would have had plastered walls covered in frescoes, but apart from suggestions of colour here and there, these have now disappeared. Mind where you tread (especially if you have children in tow) – the unfenced drops into the tombs are sometimes quite considerable. The whole necropolis is scattered across an arid, rocky promontory with views of the sea and passing ships, and although sources of water are provided, take a hat, sunscreen and plenty of water (an ice-cream van is usually on site during the summer months).

## Ktima Pafos

A short bus ride up the hill from Kato Pafos stands **KTIMA PAFOS**, the more sedate administrative centre of the town. Its most atmospheric part is the old **Turkish Quarter**, or Mouttalos. This teeming area of narrow lanes has been turned into a covered market by the addition of glass and timber roofs. In these labyrinthine streets you can buy anything from souvenirs and sunglasses to slippers and tablecloths. Along the southern edge of the Turkish Quarter, on Pafiasafroditis Street, a series of cafés and restaurants offers fine views south towards the harbour.

### Mehmet Bey Ebubekir Hammam

Located opposite the covered market, next to a large car park • Opening hours vary • Free

Built in 1592 by the Ottoman Governor of Pafos **Mehmet Bey Ebubekir** (who also built the nearby Cami Kebir, or Grand Mosque), and sporting the usual domes, this **hammam** served the Muslim community for three hundred years before being turned into a museum by the British. Now part of a rather up-market bar, customers can wander through the interconnected rooms – the tepid room, the hot room, the stoke pit, the changing room and so on – and read about how they were used. Some areas are fitted out as they would be in a working hammam, and in places transparent panels

---

**TOMB RAIDER: LUIGI PALMA DI CESNOLA**

In the literature surrounding a lot of Cypriot archeological sites, the name of **Luigi Palma di Cesnola** (1832–1904) has attracted a fair amount of infamy. An Italian soldier of fortune, he fought on the Union side in the American Civil War, eventually winning the Congressional Medal of Honor. When the war ended, he was rewarded with an appointment as US consul in Larnaka, where he served from 1865 to 1877. A keen amateur archeologist, he spent his twelve years in Cyprus digging up antiquities all over the island – especially from Kition in Larnaka, Idalion in Lefkosia, Amathus and Kurion in Lemesos and the Tombs of the Kings in Pafos – discovering, so he claimed, 35,000 items. Most of these he sold abroad, in particular to the Metropolitan Museum of Art in New York (whose first director he became in 1879). Di Cesnola's methods were unorthodox to say the least – leaving the bulk of the work to assistants, he often invented discovery locations, rarely photographed finds, and exaggerated their significance. And the accusations didn't stop there – during his time at the Met he was accused of carrying out "deceptive restorations", and of being insufferable to his staff. He died in New York in 1904, and is buried in nearby Valhalla.

## HAMMAMS

The "Turkish Bath" or **hammam** was the Ottoman take on the Greek and Roman Bath, and can be widely found in the areas of Western Europe and North Africa that once formed a part of their respective empires. Though they differed in detail (the Romans, for example, favoured full immersion in cold water, the Ottomans preferred to splash themselves), the principles – communal bathing, cleansing in rooms of different temperatures, relaxation and the taking of refreshment – were the same. In Cyprus hammams can vary from the opulent to the workaday, from the ruined to the bustlingly contemporary. They can always be recognized by their cluster of domes, one of which – the one that covers the hot room – is dotted with tiny windows made of what looks like bottle glass, designed to create an attractive half-light within. Modern hammams, like hotel spas, offer a range of pick-and-mix or packaged treatments, together with refreshments.

have been built into the floor so that you can see the hypocaust (underfloor heating system) below.

**3**

### Municipal Gardens

**Municipal Gardens** Open access • Free • **Municipal Art Gallery** April–Oct Mon–Fri 10am–1pm & 3–8pm, Sat & Sun 10am–1pm; Nov–March Mon–Fri 10am–1pm & 3–5pm, Sat & Sun 10am–1pm • Free • ☎ 26930653

In the space between Gladstonos (the extension of Leoforos Apostolou Pavlou) and the east-bound Leoforos Georgiou Griva Digeni lie the extensive **Municipal Gardens**. Here you'll find the town hall, the Pafos Bishopric, the **Municipal Art Gallery** and, in the streets just south of it, two museums worth visiting: the Byzantine Museum and the Cultural Heritage Museum. At the bottom of the gardens is **Kostis Palamas Square**, centred on a Neoclassical rotunda, and across from this a memorial to Kostis Palamas (1859–1943), the Greek poet who composed the words to the Olympic Hymn.

### Byzantine Museum

5 Andrea Ioannou • Mon–Fri 9am–2pm, Sat 9am–1pm • €2 • ☎ 06231393

In an imposing building next to, and run by, the Holy Bishopric of Pafos, the **Byzantine Museum** houses a collection of icons and other religious paraphernalia. Though its collection is undeniably beautiful and intrinsically interesting to ecclesiastical historians, committed Christians and Russian Orthodox visitors, it is perhaps less so to the casual sightseer. Among the icons on show is one claimed to be the oldest in Cyprus – that of Saint Marina flanked by scenes from her martyrdom, which dates from the seventh or eighth century – together with many more from the twelfth to nineteenth centuries. Other rooms contain frescoes rescued from derelict churches, wood and metal artwork, vestments and other embroidered cloth, manuscripts and old printed books.

### Cultural Heritage Museum

1 Exo Vrisis • Mon–Sat 9am–6pm, Sun 9am–1pm • €2 • ☎ 26932010

Generally called the "Ethnographical Museum" on tourist maps, but signposted as the **Cultural Heritage Museum**, this is a private assortment of finds collected by George S. Eliades, a local secondary-school teacher and amateur archeologist. Laid out on two floors plus the garden at the rear, the museum's charm lies in the sheer beauty of the building and the variety of exhibits within it (though the labelling is a little patchy). Of particular interest are architectural details such as decorative lintels, and the tools associated with particular trades – spinning and weaving, winemaking, grinding corn, and so on. In the grounds are a wagon, traditional stone-built ovens, and even a pre-Christian tomb.

## Pafos Archeological Museum

Leoforos Georgiou Griva Digeni • Mon–Fri 8am–4pm • €2.50 • ☎ 26955801

The **Pafos Archeological Museum** (also called the "District Museum") is a useful adjunct to visits to the sights of Kato Pafos. There are five rooms in all, housing, respectively, Chalcolithic remains (Room I), Archaic and Classical artefacts (Room II), objects from Hellenic and Roman times (Room III), and Roman and early Christian finds from Kato Pafos (Rooms IV and V). All are worthy of unhurried viewing, but if you're short of time, concentrate on the last two. Highlights include a second-century AD statue of Asklepios from the House of Theseus, an exquisite pair of gold earrings dating from the third century BC, a medieval sword and helmet, a couple of bathtubs made of clay (eighth century BC) and limestone (eleventh century BC), and a series of glazed ceramic vessels in the shape of different parts of the human anatomy – these were filled with hot or cold water to bring relief from injury or disease. Look out, too, for an amusing carving of a monster's face and a group of four women ("angel statues from Gothic temple") holding up a roof, both in the final room.

**3**

### ARRIVAL AND DEPARTURE

PAFOS

**By plane** Pafos Airport is 16km east of the town, connected by both a main road (B6) and a motorway (A6), and has all the facilities you'd expect in an international airport – bank and cashpoint, tourist information, car rental and taxi ranks (agree a fare before getting in – expect to pay around €30). Two bus routes run from the airport into town: the #612 to the Harbour Bus Station in Kato Pafos (April–Nov every 1hr 10min 7am–12.30am; Dec–March 10am–8.30pm), and

the #613 to the Karavella terminus in Ktima Pafos (4/day 8am–7pm). The flat rate fare is €1.50.

**By bus** Intercity buses (⟨w⟩ intercity-buses.com) throughout the republic leave and arrive at the Karavella terminus in Ktima Pafos.

Destinations Lemesos (Mon–Fri 11/day, Sat & Sun 6/day); Lefkosia (Mon–Fri 8/day, Sat & Sun 5/day).

### GETTING AROUND

The two halves of Pafos are small enough to be explored on foot. Getting from one to the other is a long walk (3km) so a bus is preferable.

**By bus** Local buses in Pafos are run by OSYPA (⟨w⟩ pafosbuses.com). There are two bus stations serving the two parts of the town: the Harbour Bus Station in Kato Pafos, and the Karavella Bus Station in Ktima Pafos, linked to each other by routes #603 and #618. For Coral Bay take the #615 from the harbour. From Karavella Bus Station, useful routes include Polis (#641, #645),

Episkopi (#609), Agios Neofytos (#604) and Geroskipou (#601).

**By taxi** As in the other main towns, you can either pre-book taxis or hail a taxi on the street. All taxis have metres and the charges are standard across Cyprus.

**By car** Pafos is fairly car friendly in that there are large free car parks (in Kato Pafos just behind the harbour, in Ktima Pafos south of the hammam). Elsewhere, there are numerous pay-and-display car parks, and, particularly in Ktima Pafos, a fair amount of on-street parking.

### INFORMATION

**Tourist office** The main tourist office is in the centre of Ktima Pafos, in the heart of the covered market area at Agoras 8 (Mon, Tues, Thurs & Fri 8.30am–2.30pm & 3–6.30pm, Wed & Sat 8.30am–2.30pm; ☎ 26932841,

⟨w⟩ visitpafos.org.cy). Another office serves Kato Pafos at 63a Poseidonos (hours as for the Agoras office; ☎ 26930521) and at there's also an office at Pafos Airport (daily 9.30am–11pm; ☎ 26007368).

### ACTIVITIES

**Bowling** Cosmic Ten Pin Bowling on Leoforos Apostolou Pavlou (☎ 26220033, ⟨w⟩ cosmicbowlingclub.com; €5.50/game) has eighteen lanes. For lawn/crown green bowls try the *Athena Beach Hotel* (☎ 26884300, ⟨w⟩ athena-cbh.com; €8, €5 for hotel guests) on Poseidonos.

**Go-karting** Coral Bay Karting Centre (☎ 70001314; €20 for 20min) has one- and two-seater karts. Daily 11am–8pm.

**Golf** Elea Golf Club in Geroskipou (☎ 26202004, ⟨w⟩ eleaestate.com) was designed by Nick Faldo and is the newest and most exclusive of Cyprus's eighteen-hole courses. It's a 10min drive

from Pafos and is close to the airport. Green fees are €107 in the high season (Sept–Nov & Feb–May), and €79 in the low season. Aphrodite Hills Golf Club in Koulia (☎ 26828200, ⟨w⟩ aphroditehills.com/golf) charges from €101 (including one buggy) per round of its eighteen-hole course. For those who don't want to splash out on the big prestigious eighteen-hole courses, Marios Gold Park (☎ 26271555, ⟨w⟩ mariosgolfpark.com) might be the answer. On the E701 between Pafos and Coral Bay (opposite the *Azia Hotel*), it has a mini golf course and a driving range, and offers footgolf (€12 for 9 holes).

## PAFOS REGION FESTIVALS

### MAY
**Anthestiria Flower Festival** (early May) Celebrates spring's arrival, with floats covered in flowers parading down the seafront.
**Pafos Guitar Festival** (mid-May) Classical guitar festival with concerts and classes.

### JUNE
**Choir Festival** (late June) International choir festival held in the Ancient Odeion.

### JULY
**Koumandaria Festival** (mid-July) Celebrations of the famous wine in a number of Koumandaria villages.
**Ancient Greek Drama** (late July/early Aug) Part of an island-wide festival, with a performance in the Ancient Odeion on Fabrica Hill in Kato Pafos.

### AUGUST
**Arkadia Festival** (mid- to late Aug) A village festival in Kallepeia, with food, drink and music.
**Dionysia Festival** (late Aug) Three-day wine festival with a wide range of displays, food and dance, held in the village of Stroumbi.

### SEPTEMBER
**Aphrodite Festival** (early Sept; ⓦ pafc.com.cy). An opera company is invited each year to mount a production in front of the castle.

**3**

**Water slides** Aphrodite Water Park off Poseidonos (daily: Apr–June 10.30am–5.50pm, July–Aug 10am–6pm, Sept–Oct 10am–5pm; ☏ 26913638, ⓦ aphroditewaterpark.com; adult €30, child €17) offers a wide range of water slides (including the white-knuckle "zero gravity"), plus one of the largest wave pools in Europe. Take bus #611 from the harbour.

## ACCOMMODATION

The bulk of the big resort hotels are clustered along the beach road (Poseidonos) that stretches to the southeast of Kato Pafos and along the coast road to the north (Tafon ton Vasileon) which runs past the Tombs of the Kings. For something smaller and with a little more atmosphere, try staying in Ktima Pafos.

### KATO PAFOS AND POSEIDONOS
**Alexander the Great** Poseidonos ☏ 26965000, ⓦ kanikahotels.com; map p.114. The highly popular *Alexander the Great* is well placed within walking distance (about 600m) from the centre of Kato Pafos. Staff are friendly, and thought goes into removing perpetual irritants like nabbing a sunbed – you're allocated one for the whole of your stay. **€218**

**Almyra** 12 Poseidonos ☏ 26888700, ⓦ almyra.com; map p.114. Just on the edge of Kato Pafos centre, the *Almyra* combines proximity to everything with an expansive site and facilities. Cool, clean look, elegant terrace overlooking the sea, spectacular pools indoors and out, plus a huge range of activities, including those for children. **€236**

**Annabelle** 10 Poseidonos ☏ 26885000, ⓦ annabelle. com.cy; map p.114. Luxurious, beachfront hotel with excellent facilities and staff. Its six acres of palm-fringed gardens are set around meandering free-form pools –

almost over-the-top but not quite. Remarkably quiet for a hotel so close to the centre of Kato Pafos. Activities on offer include yoga, tennis, scuba diving and kitesurfing. **€242**

**★ Apollonia Holiday Apartments** 20 Ikarou ☏ 26221787, ⓦ apolloniacy.com; map p.114. In the heart of Kato Pafos, near the post office, the *Apollonia* is a welcome contrast with the all-bells-and-whistles beach hotels, giving the greater freedom and lower prices that self-catering apartments offer. Good range of apartment types, a swimming pool, a "trust the drinker" bar, and perfectly adequate furniture and fittings. Communal areas are fine, if florid. **€73**

**Daphne Hotel Apartments** 3 Alkminis ☏ 26933500, ⓦ hoteldaphneapartments.com; map p.114. Good basic accommodation just behind the Kato Pafos seafront, with clean simple apartments, a small pool and a bar/restaurant on site. Not luxurious, but a place to lay your head. It's in the absolute centre of the pub and bar area of Pafos, so be prepared for bustle and noise. **€85**

**★ Olympic Lagoon Resort** Poseidonos ☏ 26883300, ⓦ kanikahotels.com/Olympic-Lagoon-Resort-Paphos; map p.114. Top-end luxury holiday resort hotel at the far end of Poseidonos. Originally the *Amathus Hotel*, the place has been re-badged as the *Olympic Lagoon Resort*, following full renovation under the management of Kanika Hotels. It continues to have every facility you can imagine, including a fabulous spa and pool area, as well as hugely attentive staff (iced face towels available on request, tea brought out to you on a silver platter). You might never want to go out. Minimum stay five nights. **€327**

**Pioneer Beach Hotel** Poseidonos ☎ 26964500, ⊛ pioneer-cbh.com; map p.114. At the furthest end of Poseidonos, and therefore 3km southeast of the centre of Kato Pafos, the *Pioneer Beach* is too far from the centre to walk in, but equally clear of the town-centre noise. Terrific setting, good beach, and close to public swimming pool, playing fields, bowling green and the Aphrodite Water Park. Well-appointed rooms and full range of services as you'd expect (though wi-fi, surprisingly, is not free). Four-night minimum stay. **€182**

### KTIMA PAFOS

**Agapinor Hotel** 24–30 Nikodimou Mylona ☎ 26933926, ⊛ agapinorhotel.com.cy; map p.114. Conveniently located in Ktima Pafos, the *Agapinor* is a good base for those who are more inclined towards shopping and sightseeing

than lazing on the beach. It has a smallish pool and separate children's pool, café, bar and restaurant, but it is the location (and budget price) rather than facilities that is its USP. Minimum two-night stay. **€90**

**Axiothea Hotel** 2 Ivis Malioti ☎ 26932866, ⊛ axiothea hotel.com; map p.114. Budget hotel just south of the Municipal Gardens in Ktima Pafos, and therefore within easy reach of the museums and the shops of the Turkish quarter. Five storeys high and set on a hillside, the views are wonderful. Rooms are basic but clean, services limited, and the restaurant only serves breakfast, but you're in the heart of things so it doesn't matter. **€55**

**Kiniras Hotel** 91 Makarios ☎ 26941604, ⊛ kinirashotel. com; map p.114. A boutique hotel in a fifteenth-century Venetian mansion in the centre of Ktima Pafos, the family-run *Kiniras* has bright colourful modern rooms, a gorgeous, plant-decked restaurant offering traditional Cypriot dishes and paintings by the owner throughout. Award-winning service and a relaxed atmosphere. **€107**

## EATING

### KATO PAFOS AND POSEIDONOS

**3 Little Pigs** 14 Tombs of the Kings ☎ 70003233; map p.114. An unpretentious traditional grill restaurant offering large portions for quite a moderate price. The interior may be modern in style but the cuisine is much more old-fashioned and of a high standard. This is also a place for football fans - there's always a match on for you to watch as you munch on your "Big Bad Wolf Special". Mon–Sat noon–11pm.

**Cavallini** 65 Poseidonos ☎ 26964164; map p.114. Near the *Lagoon Resort*, this quality Italian restaurant marries an excellent (child-friendly) atmosphere with authentic reasonably priced food – allow €50 for two people, with a bottle of wine. The pasta dishes – spaghetti with prawns and mussels, for example – are good, as are the steak, chicken and fish. Parking can be difficult in high season. Mon–Sat 6.30–11.30pm.

★ **Hondros** 96 Apostolos Pavlos ☎ 26934256, ⊛ facebook.com/HondrosTaverna; map p.114. Established 1953, Hondros claims to be the oldest traditional taverna in Pafos. Excellent Greek-Cypriot food, plenty of seating inside and out and a traditional wood-fired oven and charcoal grill outside. Main courses €10–20, mezé from around €20. Right on the main road, though, so there can be a lot of traffic noise. Daily 11am–midnight.

**La Sardegna da Gino** 70 Apostolos Pavlos ☎ 26933399; map p.114. About 200m past the Begonia Garden Centre crossroads, on the way to Ktima Pafos. Owned and run by a Sardinian, this place specializes in delicious wood-fired pizzas, with a huge variety of toppings. Prices (€12–16) seem steep until you see the size of the pizzas. Mon–Sat 6–11pm, Sun 12.30–3pm & 6–11pm.

**Ocean Basket** Avanti Holiday Village Piazza

☎ 26961379, ⊛ oceanbasket.com; map p.114. A couple of kilometres along Poseidonos in the Avanti Holiday Village (and therefore well placed for all the hotels in that area), the *Ocean Basket* is one of a large South African chain of seafood restaurants. Fast-food atmosphere, good fresh fish, great value for money. Mains €8–16. Mon–Sun noon–10.30pm.

**Saint Paul's Pillar** 7 St Paul's Pillar St ☎ 99450423; map p.114. Endearingly ramshackle little restaurant on the approach to the ruins that include St Paul's Pillar – the clue's in the name and address. The menu relies mainly on Cypriot staples (moussaka €9, *kléftico* and *stifado* €12), fish (€9–15) and grills (*souvlaki* in pitta €5.50, otherwise €8–20). They do a Sunday lunch for €9. Good value and amazingly quiet considering it's next to a busy road. Tues–Sun 9am–10.45pm.

### KTIMA PAFOS

**Fettas** 33 Ioanni Agroti ☎ 26937822; map p.114. Good-value Greek food at a small taverna which is patronised mainly by local Greek Cypriots. Copious meat mezé, with a menu that varies with the seasons. Most main courses fall into the €10–20 range. Live music on Fridays and Saturdays. It gets busy so it's wise to book in advance. Mon–Sat 6.30–11pm.

**Laona** 6 Votsis ☎ 26937121, ⊛ laonarestaurant. blogspot.com; map p.114. In a backstreet near the covered market in Ktima Pafos, the *Laona* isn't easy to find; if you get lost then you can phone and the owner will come to get you. A gem of an old-fashioned Greek restaurant which doesn't overdo the choices – the menu is on the blackboard, and staff will advise if you're not sure what to have. Mains €8–10, mezé €13.50–17. Mon, Wed, Thurs & Sat 11am–3.30pm, Tues & Fri 10am–10pm.

**Myrra** 37 Neopoleos St ☎ 26938381; map p.114. At the corner with Lambrou Sepi in Ktima Pafos, the friendly, family-run *Myrra* occupies a slightly dishevelled house with occasionally naff decor. Good grills and mezé, own-label wine, and organic, seasonal vegetables grown by the owners. Allow €20/head with wine. Reservations recommended at weekends. Mon–Sat 6–11pm.

### CORAL BAY AND BEYOND

★ **Agios Georgios Restaurant and Fish Tavern** 224 Agios Georgios ☎ 26621306; map p.112. Overlooking the little harbour on Cape Drepano, this is a popular restaurant with locals and visitors – don't be put off by the garish Keo adverts above the entrance. Great views, and the fish on offer is freshly caught. Expect to pay €14–17 for individual dishes, or €19.50 for fish mezé. Daily: April–Oct 9am–11pm; Nov–March 8.30am–6pm.

★ **Astrofegia** Coral Bay ☎ 26622500; map p.112. Although it has a small seating area in a conservatory, *Astrofegia*'s great strength is as a takeaway. It offers a range of traditional Greek food, and not just the sort of kebabs you'd get back home – pick from a daily changing menu of stews and hot-plate dishes, plus a wide range of vegetarian mains featuring cracked wheat, ladies' fingers, sweet potato and lentils. A godsend if you're staying in the Coral Bay area. Dishes of the day €5–10. Daily 9am–10pm.

**Samisen** 57 Coral Bay Avenue ☎ 26622243, ⓦ samisenjapanese.com; map p.112. Highly rated Japanese restaurant in the centre of Coral Bay, where the culinary theatricals are as entertaining as the food itself. First-class cuisine – order a set menu (€25–45/person) if you don't know your way around Japanese food, or pick and mix if you do (sushi €2.50–3.50/item). Kids' portions half size and half price. Daily 12.30–11pm.

### DRINKING AND NIGHTLIFE

**Barrio del Mar** Geroskipou; map p.114. Vast (2000 capacity) beach club with six bars and a thumping sound system. Mainstream Greek and international music, resident DJs. Entry €12. May–Sept Mon–Sat 11pm–3.30am, Sun 3–9.30pm.

**Different** Agias Napas ☎ 99453716, ⓦ differentbar.com; map p.114. In the pedestrianized heart of Kato Pafos, just behind the seafront, *Different* prides itself on its wide range of musical tastes, on a huge selection of cocktails and on being LGBTQ-friendly. Daily 6pm–3am.

**Level** Apostolou Pavlou, Kato Pafos; map p.114. About halfway between Kato and Ktima Pafos, and beginning to look its age, the *Level Club* caters for a late-twenties upwards age group. Moving feast of special events Fridays, standard mainstream DJ sets Saturdays. Fri & Sat 11pm–4am.

**Loft** 1 Archemidous ☎ 77777742; map p.114. On the east side of Kato Pafos centre. Outside dancing in summer to Greek, pop, RnB and electronica; inside in winter. All-age clientele and dramatic special acts featuring flames. Wed, Fri & Sat 11pm–5am.

### ENTERTAINMENT

**Cinemas** K-Cineplex at the Kings Avenue Mall (☎ 26222848); Othellos Cinema, 41 Evagora Pallikaridi, Ktima Pafos (☎ 26946256); Revekka Cinema, 1 Vasili Michailidi, Geroskipou (☎ 26962984).

**Theatres** Summer productions are mounted at The Odion on Fabrica Hill and Castle Square.

### SHOPPING

**Cyprus Handicrafts Service** 64 Leoforos Apostolou Pavlou, Kato Pafos ☎ 26306243; map p.114. One of the government-run chains selling good-quality art copies and crafts. Mon–Fri 9am–4.30pm.

**Kings Avenue Mall** corner Leoforos Apostolou Pavlou and Tomb of the Kings ☎ 70007777, ⓦ kingsavenuemall.com; map p.114. Opened in 2013 and claiming to be the largest and most modern mall in Cyprus, the Kings Avenue Mall has just about everything – well over a hundred shops and boutiques, a Carrefour supermarket, a multiplex cinema, restaurants, cafés, children's indoor and outdoor play areas, underground car park and a variety of services. Its air-conditioned comfort and convenience can't be beaten – something that myriad local shops, cafés and restaurants bitterly regret. Mon–Sat 10am–8pm, Sun 11am–7pm.

**Pafos Municipal Market** Agora St, old town; map p.114. Buzzing fruit and vegetable market surrounded by covered pedestrianized streets. Mon–Sat 9am–2pm.

**Timi Open Air Market and Car Boot Sale** Timi Village (near the airport); map p.114. Worth a look for fruit and vegetables, clothes and toys. Sun 8am–2pm.

### DIRECTORY

**Medical** Pafos General Hospital Anavargos, Ktima Pafos ☎ 26803100, Polis Hospital Thessalonikis ☎ 26821800; private doctors available at weekends/holidays ☎ 90901436; pharmacies after hours ☎ 90901416.

**Police** Central Police Station, Griva Digeni and Gregori Afxentiou ☎ 26806060; Port and Marine Police ☎ 26811390; Traffic Police ☎ 26806060.

**Post office** There are two post offices serving the two main areas of the town – the Old Post Office on Nicodemou Milona (Ktima Pafos) and one on Ikarou (Kato Pafos).

# Day-trips from Pafos

Pafos is blessed with numerous day-trip destinations. To the southeast is **Geroskipou** with its fine church and first-rate folk museum and, beyond it on the outskirts of the village of Kouklia, the remains of **Palaipafos** (the original town of Pafos) with, on the coast, the pretty cove of **Petra tou Romiou**, legendary **birthplace of Aphrodite**. Driving east and northeast involves a climb to a plateau dotted with villages and vineyards, the **Monastery of Agios Neofytos** and the large village of **Pano Panagia**, birthplace of Archbishop Makarios III. Driving along the coast road north from Pafos takes you through a resort area with good **beaches** and some interesting small museums.

## Geroskipou

**GEROSKIPOU**, although a separate municipality southeast of Pafos, is now virtually a suburb of the larger town. Yet its handsome square, dominated by the church of Agia Paraskevi, and its fame as a centre of *loukoumia* production, give it a character all of its own. The name Geroskipou derives from the Greek for "Holy Garden", a reference to the nearby temple of Aphrodite in Palaipafos.

### Folk Art Museum

Leontiou Street (clearly signposted from main street) • Daily: Mid-Sept to mid-April 8.30am–4pm; mid-April to mid-Sept 8.30am–5pm • €2.50 • ☎ 26306216, 🖥 bit.ly/Geroskipou

Geroskipou's **Folk Art Museum** is one of the best of the many on the island. Its location, the "House of Hadjismith", is a listed building once owned by one Andreas Zoumboulakis, the British Vice Consul from 1800 to 1864. In fact, much of the enjoyment of this museum lies in its setting – shady paved courtyards, wooden shutters and balconies, flagged rooms and rustic stone walls. The eclectic collection features everything from ceremonial "wedding breads" (*glistarkes*) of stunning intricacy and traditional waistcoats and scarves to musical instruments and even children's swimming floats made from gourds. Look out too for the *tapatsia*, a basket which was slung from the ceiling on a rope to keep bread out of the reach of vermin. Everything is clearly labelled in Greek and English, with occasional sketches showing how things worked.

### Agia Paraskevi

Agia Paraskevi Square • ☎ 26821000 • Daily Mon–Sat 8.30am–1pm & 2–4.30pm • Free

The church of **Agia Paraskevi** is an important and rare Byzantine structure originating in the ninth century AD. It has five domes over a nave and two aisles, with an additional small dome over an odd little annexe attached below the belfry, used as a reliquary. Inside is a range of frescoes, some of which are "aniconic" (that is, using crosses and abstract patterns rather than representations of human figures), dating from the period when the iconoclasts held sway in the Byzantine Empire. Later representational wall paintings date from the twelfth to the fifteenth centuries.

---

### LOUKOUMIA – CYPRIOT DELIGHT

Geroskipou is famous for its "**loukoumia**", or what the rest of the world calls Turkish Delight. Indeed, it has Protected Geographical Indication, like champagne or Cornish pasties. Many shops along the main road and in the square sell the sweet, and it's far more versatile than you might imagine. You can buy *loukoumia* flavoured with chocolate, nuts, vanilla, lemon, orange, mint or banana as well as the more traditional rose-petal flavour. Try Aphrodite Delights (🖥 aphroditedelights.com), which has a slick showroom and visitor centre a couple of minutes' walk from the main square.

## Palaipafos

Daily: mid-Sept to mid-April 8.30am–5pm; mid-April to mid-Sept 8.30am–7.30pm • €4.50 • ☎ 26432155

Sixteen kilometres southeast of Pafos is the site of Nea Pafos's ancient predecessor, **Palaipafos**. The entrance is right in the heart of **KOUKLIA** village, which is remarkably unspoilt given its proximity to a major attraction. Among the ruins is the **Sanctuary to Aphrodite**, dedicated to the goddess, a range of Roman remains, and a number of Lusignan buildings. While the whole site is of inestimable archeological importance, having been continuously occupied from 2800 BC, it's difficult to grasp on the ground. For example, the sanctuary itself, divided into Late Bronze Age Sanctuary 1 and Roman Sanctuary 2, amounts to little more than some massive blocks of dressed stone. Perhaps of more interest is the House of Leda, built by a wealthy Roman and named for the magnificent mosaic of Leda and the Swan found in it (the mosaic is now in the museum – the one on site is a modern copy).

The most visible structure on the site is the so-called Lusignan manor house of **La Cavocle**, actually built in the thirteenth century AD to administer local sugar production. It was adapted after the Ottoman Conquest to become the residence of a local Turkish *chiflik* (landowner). Now the **Kouklia Local Museum** (daily mid-April to mid-Sept 8.30am–7.30pm, mid-Sept to mid-April 8.30am–5pm; entry covered by site admission charge), it contains a conical black stone thought to represent Aphrodite, and a massive bath carved out of chalk from around 1000 BC. The downstairs Gothic rib-vaulted banqueting room is often used for music recitals.

Outside the limits of the archeological site is the church of **Panagia Katholiki** (free), a twelfth- or thirteenth-century church, extended in the sixteenth century and worth a look for its fifteenth-century wall paintings.

Before leaving Kouklia, try to have a look at the fascinating remains of Palaipafos's **northeast gate** on the Marchellos Hill – it's about 700m through the village on the road (F612) to Archimandrita. This complicated and formidable fortification shows in detail the effects of the **Persian siege of 498 BC**. The Persians had thrown up a huge siege ramp against the city walls. In response, the defenders laboriously dug four tunnels under the walls, eventually managing to set fire to the ramp with burning oil. One of the tunnels (Tunnel 1) is still intact, and the paraphernalia used by the diggers – oil lamps, water jugs and even the bronze cauldrons that carried the oil – have been recovered. Whether the ruse succeeded or not, it would only have caused a temporary setback, since we know that the Persians breached the gate and the city fell. During the century following the siege, the Paphians, while renovating the defences, found it easier to incorporate the remains of the ramp into the new defences rather than try to remove them.

## Petra tou Romiou (the birthplace of Aphrodite)

An attractive pebble beach, 9km or so west of Kouklia (and technically in Lemesos district), **Petra tou Romiou**, is where, according to legend, Aphrodite rose from the sea and came ashore (which may explain the sanctuary nearby). The Greek name refers to a different myth: Digenes Akritas, also known as Romios (or, more disappointingly, Basil), was the Byzantine hero of an epic song. He killed bears, lions and dragons with his bare hands, and leapt from Cyprus to Asia Minor, gaining purchase by grabbing the Five Finger Mountain near Kyrenia. He once vanquished some foes by throwing huge rocks at them, one of which is the biggest of those on the western tip of Petra tou Romiou. Whatever its origins, Petra tou Romiou is an iconic vision of limpid sea and picturesque rocks. The beach is best accessed from the B6 – park next to the café opposite, then use the underpass beneath the road. Though you sometimes wouldn't think so, climbing on the rocks is not allowed, but their shade is highly prized by visitors. As befits the birthplace of Aphrodite, love-hearts marked out with pebbles dot the beach and the surrounding low cliffs.

## THE CULT OF APHRODITE

You don't need to spend long in Cyprus to become aware of the island's proud association with **Aphrodite**, whether it's the dozens of hotels and restaurants named in her honour or everything from tea towels to T-shirts bearing her image. A brief primer is therefore worthwhile.

In the beginning there were only two beings – **Ge**, goddess of earth, and **Uranus**, god of the sky. Their children became known as the **Titans**. **Cronus**, their leader, on his mother's orders cut off the genitals of his father, and threw them into the sea. From the resulting maelstrom of foam ("aphros"), the comely Aphrodite arose, and floated ashore on a scallop shell. She became the goddess of love – to be more specific, of beauty, pleasure and procreation – and created havoc with her power to bewitch both mortals and gods. The stories about her are copious. The most important in the Cypriot tradition involves **Kinyras**, king of Cyprus. He became Aphrodite's adoring acolyte and favourite but was tricked into sleeping with his daughter, Myrrha, by a jealous Aphrodite. Kinyras almost killed Myrrha before the gods intervened, turning her into a fragrant myrrh tree. From the trunk of this tree **Adonis**, the ideal male, was born. Aphrodite soon fell in love with him, as did Persephone, queen of the Underworld. The pair fought over him until he is killed by a wild boar, and died in Aphrodite's arms.

The **cult of Aphrodite**, practised at temple sites across the island, seems to have degenerated from a celebration of love and fertility to temple rites that included orgies and prostitution. Fifth-century BC Greek historian Herodotus describes how all women were expected to attend the temple and give themselves to any passing stranger. Attractive women, he comments wryly, could expect to complete their duty on the first night, while it might take ugly ones three or four years.

Aphrodite has, of course, been the subject of innumerable **sculptures and paintings**, from the demure Aphrodite of Cnidus and Botticelli's golden-haired Birth of Venus to various soft-porn representations by Victorian artists. A number of seashells are associated with her too – scallops, because that was what she rode ashore on – and the suggestively shaped cowrie, which is named Cypraeidae in her honour.

# Lempa

The village of **LEMPA**, 5km north from the centre of Pafos just off the road to Kissonerga, has largely been swallowed up by suburbia. It does, however, have a quite separate history, being one of the oldest villages in Cyprus, dating from the Chalcolithic era. It was also almost entirely Turkish Cypriot until 1974. In their place came a tide of students: the Cyprus College of Art, forced to leave Famagusta during the conflict, has resettled here.

## Prehistoric Lempa

Open access • Free

A Chalcolithic village dating from about 3500 to 2500 BC, **Prehistoric Lempa** consists of a cluster of round houses made of stone and mud similar to those at Tenta and Choirokoitia. There are several modern reconstructions, each with low circular mud-brick foundations, mud-and-straw walls and timber joists upon which is laid a stone-and-earth roof. One of the huts, much larger than the others, has walls which are decorated inside and out with patterns in ochre paint, and has a central hearth surrounded by massive tree-trunk pillars holding up the roof. Though now having something of an abandoned air, the site is still interesting and well served by its excellent information boards.

## Cyprus College of Art

6 Stas Paraskou • Free • ☎ 99225331, ⊕ artcyprus.co

The **Cyprus College of Art** was formed in 1969 by Cypriot artist Stass Paraskos (see page 128). Very much focused on art rather than academia, the college has the feel of a cooperative, reflecting its origins in the British art school ethos of the late

**3**

## THE UNLIKELY BIRTH OF THE CYPRUS COLLEGE OF ART

The **Cyprus College of Art** has somewhat eccentric origins. Greek Cypriot **Stass Paraskos** (born 1933 near Larnaka) travelled to Leeds in 1953 to become a chef in his brother's restaurant. The restaurant was popular with local art students, and when Paraskos not only showed an interest but also considerable ability in art, they encouraged him to apply to enter Leeds College of Art. Despite a lack of formal qualifications, he was accepted and flourished, later going on to teach at the college. In 1966 some of Paraskos's paintings – nudes – were judged to be "lewd and obscene" by the authorities. He became something of a cause célèbre, garnering support from Roy Jenkins and punk music giant and fellow artist Ian Dury, who became a friend. Paraskos lost his case however, and was fined £5. In 1969, during tutorials conducted in a local pub, it was suggested that Paraskos use his Cypriot connections to arrange summer art schools on the island. This he did, and as it became an annual event, interest was expressed by numerous other art colleges. These informal arrangements grew into the Cyprus College of Art, based at first in Famagusta, moving to Pafos after the 1974 invasion, and settling finally in Lempa. In 2007 a second branch of the college, now known as the Cornaro Institute, was opened in Larnaka. Paraskos died in 2014, and as a tribute the street on which the college stands has been renamed "Stas Paraskou".

1960s. For the visitor, the main attraction is its famous, or infamous, "**Artistic Wall of Lempa**", made up of hundreds of pieces and contributions by its students. Variously hailed as inspirational or damned as an eyesore, it's difficult not to smile at its sheer, unadulterated exuberance.

## Agios Neofytos Monastery

**Monastery and museum** Daily Apr–Oct 9am–1pm & 2–6pm; Nov–Mar 9am–4pm • €2 • ☎ 26652481

Such is the ubiquity and range of monasteries in Cyprus that visiting them can begin to feel like a chore, at least for the non-believer. Not so in the case of **Agios Neofytos**, about 17km north of the centre of Pafos (best accessed by climbing up the steep hills through Emba and Tala, at which, incidentally, it's worth a refreshment stop in its very pleasant village square). It boasts a fascinating back story (see page 129), and a spectacular setting worth a visit in itself. For a full appreciation of the monastery, do buy the guidebook published by the church authorities (€5).

The monastery itself, through the main gate, past the gift shop and café, consists of a residential block, church and cloisters surrounding a lush garden; beyond here there's a spacious terrace dotted with benches overlooking the valley. At the far end of the terrace, accessed by a stone bridge, is the reason for all the fuss – the **Enkleistra**, the caves dug out by St Neofytos himself.

The Enkleistra consists of three rooms – the first two are the nave and sanctuary of a chapel (the Church of the Holy Cross), the third is Neofytos's cell. The walls of the **nave** are covered in **frescoes**, the upper ones sixteenth century, the lower ones earlier works which might have been painted by the saint's own hand. In the **sanctuary** are more frescoes, this time twelfth century. Look out in particular for the one at the western end of the roof, of Neofytos (the bearded figure with wings) being escorted to the Day of Judgement by two angels. The saint's pious expression seems to suggest that he's taking nothing for granted and the inscription reads "I fervently pray that this image should come to pass". Beyond the sanctuary, through a low doorway, is the saint's **cell**, also frescoed, and containing a bed, table, desk, chair, bookshelf, even a quill niche, all carved out of the rock. It also houses his tomb – he expressed a wish that, when he died, his body be interred in it, and the cave sealed off. However, in 1756 the sarcophagus was opened and his bones transferred to the **monastery church**, where, once your eyes have adjusted to the gloom, you can see (and, if you wish, kiss) his silver-encased skull, and inspect his sarcophagus – it's on the left, under the pulpit.

Across from the church is a **museum**, housing the monastery's many treasures – crosses, chalices, censers, sacred texts, bibles, vestments, icons and much else. Some of these objects are unbelievably exquisite: the 1560 Venetian bible, for example, and an illuminated manuscript from the late eleventh century. Sign of the times – all signs are in Russian as well as Greek and English.

# The Baths of Adonis

Daily: summer 9am–8pm, winter 9am–6pm • €9 • ☎ 26965652, Ⓦ adonisbathswaterfalls.com

The waterfalls and pools of **The Baths of Adonis**, north of Pafos, are widely touted as one of the district's premier attractions. While their location on the Mavrokolympos River is undeniably appealing, be prepared for a heavy dose of tourist kitsch. The infrastructure surrounding the waterfalls was built by flamboyant actor Pambos Theodorou, who has a penchant for comically bad statues of Greek gods and mythical creatures. These include a plaster figure of Aphrodite which, at 10m high, is claimed to be the world's tallest, and one of Adonis where women who wish to become pregnant are enjoined to touch his "appendage". A further explicit statue, of "Priabos" in a state of high excitement, is claimed to be effective for women "even if they are sixty years old". On the positive side, plunging into the pools is certainly refreshing – it is not unknown for bathers to strip off completely in the upper of the two pools, though the water can be very cold, even in summer. The on-site museum is a tribute to the life of the owner, including memorabilia from his family's past and his long and illustrious theatrical career. The display includes photographs of the owner as a (devilishly handsome) serving soldier, and books on a variety of topics written by him (€6 each). Another word of warning: signs which direct you from all nearby roads ("Adonis Baths Mavrokolympos. The road is good for all cars") are optimistic to say the least – despite Mr Theodorou's protestations to the contrary, the road is absolutely awful.

# Amargeti

About 24km northeast of Pafos (8km on the A6 motorway and a further 16km up into the hills on the E606), **AMARGETI** is a village whose air of tranquillity belies its (possibly apocryphal) racy past as the centre of a druggy cult. A rudimentary mud-brick temple was unearthed here stuffed with clay and rough-hewn votive figures dedicated to "Melanthios Apollonas" – perhaps "Apollo of the opium poppy". It's not

---

## AGIOS NEOFYTOS – THE HERMIT SAINT

**Agios Neofytos** (1134–1219) was born near the village of Lefkara. As a boy he had a strong yearning towards the spiritual life, especially when his family arranged a marriage for him to which he took exception. He fled to the monastery of Chrystomos, near Buffavento Castle in the north, became a monk, and finally occupied a **cave** north of Pafos which had been vacated by a previous ascetic. Neofytos expanded it, and settled into a life of quiet contemplation. God clearly had other plans. Neofytos's reputation for piety had spread, and acolytes from far and wide converged on the cave, bringing food and other gifts. So raucous did this informal encampment become that Neofytos had to retreat further (in 1197) by moving into the cave above, accessible only by a ladder which he pulled up behind him. The new cave he called, with touching optimism, "New Zion". Here he wrote a variety of commentaries, meditations, hymns and prayers, as well as a chronicle about the catastrophe that was overcoming Cyprus at the time – conquest by Richard the Lionheart and the start of Lusignan rule of the island. Not bad considering that he only learned to read aged 18. Neofytos communicated with his followers through a hole in the floor and the site became the basis of an official monastery, the forerunner of the current one, established in 1170 AD. Neofytos died in around 1219, aged over eighty.

too big a leap to believe that there may have been a cult of Apollo in which smoking opium played a part. It would certainly explain why the temple and the votive offerings were so half-hearted. Today the centrepiece of the village is the church of **Zoodochos Pigi** ("Life-giving spring"), which has a handsome terrace on which stand monuments to local heroes. Opposite is the **Folk Art Museum**, opened in 2009 in a building that was, until 1974, the Turkish-Cypriot school. The museum also boasts a terrace which includes several presses and an olive mill – the views aren't half bad either. Fifty metres beyond the museum (and continuing the village's dedication to mind-altering substances) is the **Kalamos Winery** (☎26723224, ⊛kalamoswinery.com) – it does wine tastings for groups, and English is spoken. Its *zivania* is particularly highly thought of.

## Monastery of Agia Moni

The monastery of **Agia Moni**, on the E606 between Amargeti and Pano Panagia, is worth a brief stop, both for the peacefulness of the monastery itself (visitors are welcome as long as they are dressed appropriately, which usually means no shorts or bare shoulders), and for the wonderful views across vineyards towards the sea in one direction and Kannaviou Reservoir in the other. Although dating originally from the sixth century AD and apparently built over a pagan temple dedicated to Hera (it might even have used some of the masonry from the temple building), the current monastery is largely seventeenth and eighteenth century.

## Monastery of Panagia Chrysorrogiatissa

Daily: May–Aug 9.30am–12.30pm & 1.30–6.30pm; Sept–April 10am–12.30pm & 1.30–4pm • Free but donations accepted • ☎ 26722457

Just north of Agia Moni on the left of the main road is the **Monastery of Panagia Chrysorrogiatissa**. It was established in 1152 (though the current buildings date from 1770) by a certain Ignatios who, it was said, found an icon near Pafos which had been thrown into the sea in Asia Minor during the iconoclastic period and miraculously found its way to Cyprus. Popular for its frescoes, icons and various treasures, in many ways the monastery's chief claim to fame is its peculiar name, translated as "Our Lady of the Golden Pomegranate". The monastery sells its own wine, and outside is a stall selling nuts and preserves. The huge tree near the monastery – a *Pinus Brutia* (or, whisper it, Turkish Pine) – is 130 years old.

## Pano Panagia

One of Cyprus's more remote villages, **PANO PANAGIA** lies 800m up at the edge of civilization, with the wilds of Tilliria stretching to the north and the rugged mountains of the Troodos range to the east. It would probably attract little attention if it weren't for its connection with one of Cyprus's greatest sons – **Archbishop Makarios III** (see page 161) – architect of independence and first president of the republic.

### Makarios III Historical and Cultural Centre

Main Street • Daily: April–Oct 9am–1pm & 3–5pm, Nov–March 9am–1pm & 2–4pm • €0.50 • ☎ 26722473

On the main village street stands a small square dominated by a statue of the distinctive figure of the archbishop, his hand raised in blessing. The low building behind it is the **Makarios III Historical and Cultural Centre**. Any fears that this will be an earnest trawl through the career of Makarios are soon dispelled – the centre is chock-a-block with touchingly personal memorabilia: his books, desk ornaments, photographs of the great man alongside world leaders (Indira Gandhi, Nehru, Nasser), his religious vestments, even his fountain pen, fork and dressing gown. It all has the unmistakeable stamp of the pride of a family, and of a village, in the achievements of one of its own.

### Birthplace of Archbishop Makarios III
Daily: April–Oct 9am–1pm & 3–5pm, Nov–March 9am–1pm & 2–4pm • Free

Off Panagia's main street, signposted down a narrow lane, is the **birthplace of the archbishop** (key available from the Makarios III Historical and Cultural Centre). Born Michail Christodolou Mouskos, son of a shepherd, he was raised in the village and tended his father's sheep in the surrounding hills. The house in which he lived as a child has now been turned into a **museum**. A simple double door in a stone wall (with a number "4" above) opens into a small garden from where a paved path leads up to the single-storey dwelling. It is simple and affecting – whitewashed walls, ornaments on shelves, sparse wall hangings, a ladder up to a sleeping platform, a cast-iron bed. There are only two rooms – one for the family, the other for the animals.

## Fyti

Of the villages that dot the upland vineyards west and south of Pano Panagia, the one most worth visiting is **FYTI**. High on a hill (680m) and overlooking the neighbouring villages of Kritou Marottou, Milia and Lasa, it is cool even in summer. Indeed, surrounded by cornfields, vineyards and woodland, it's hard to believe you're on the edge of the Middle East. In the central square is a small church, and surrounding it are trees offering shade, a bust and memorial fountain dedicated to local dignitaries, and a couple of tavernas – in short, a perfect place to while away an afternoon. A couple of sights are devoted to the local weaving industry – a **factory shop** houses exhibitions of "Fytiotika", the local tapestry, and the **Fyti Museum of Weaving and Folkloric Art** (May–Oct Mon–Sat 8am–noon & 2–5pm, Nov–Apr Mon–Sat 9am–noon & 1–4pm; free, but donations appreciated) contains a chaotic array of spinning and weaving machinery, and a wealth of old photographs, labelled in Greek and English. Though the village depends fairly heavily on tourism, it retains a very authentic feel, with locals stopping in their battered pick-ups for coffee or a snack.

## Grivas Museum and Monument
Daily 9am–6pm • Free

On the Chlorakas coast 4km north of Kato Pafos, clearly signposted from the main road (bear left at the *St George Hotel*, then follow the road around to the right), a monument and statue mark the spot where **General George Grivas** (see page 165) landed on November 10, 1954 to spark off the **EOKA uprising**. Next to the memorial is a small museum housing the caïque *Agios Georgios* which ran guns and EOKA fighters during the struggle for independence before being intercepted by the British. The boat was bought by order of Archbishop Makarios to become a symbol of the resistance. Other (inevitably nationalistic) exhibits include weapons, documents and photographs relating to the gun-running activities along this coast, plus a visitors' book which makes enlightening reading – somebody who'd served in the British Army in Cyprus, for example, commented that the museum was "biased", which makes one wonder what they expected.

## Coral Bay

**CORAL BAY** is a relatively quiet but rather characterless extension of the Pafos resort area, 12km north of the harbour. Its *raison d'être* is its several good beaches in contiguous bays, separated by a peninsula, with free access and parking, clear water and convenient beach bars and hotels. There's also a campsite, a decent supermarket, and an excellent takeaway. What really sets it apart is the Bronze Age **Maa-Palaiokastro prehistoric site**, which occupies the peninsula between the two bays (if driving, park at the *Thalassa Hotel* then walk down the paved path to the site entrance).

**3**

### Maa-Palaiokastro

Daily: winter 8.30am–4pm, summer Mon–Fri 9.30am–5pm • €2.50 (same ticket for site and museum) • ⓦ tinyurl.com/paliokastro

**Maa-Palaiokastro** dates from the first wave of Greeks to colonize Cyprus. These were Mycenaeans from the Aegean who came to the island around 1200 BC, starting the process of Hellenization. Excavations here have revealed imposing protective walls and some public buildings whose features show their Aegean heritage. Also discovered were the remains of earlier Chalcolithic inhabitants who lived in caves covered with timber constructions. There's not much for the non-specialist to see, though you can still follow the course of the two walls and some of the buildings.

In 1996 a modern **museum** was built on the site. Designed by Italian Andrea Bruno, its architecture is certainly innovative: the building looks as if a flying saucer had landed heavily and buried itself in the ground. The museum, accessed down a flight of steps, contains no original artefacts, but rather a restrained collection of copies and explanatory photographs and notes relating to the Maa-Palaiokastro site.

## Pafos Zoo

St George, Peyia • Daily: Jan–March & Nov–Dec 9am–5pm, April–July & Sept–Oct 9am–6pm, Aug 9am–7pm • €15.50, children aged 2 to 12 €8.50 • ☎ 26813852, ⓦ pafoszoo.com • Bus #616 from Coral Bay (linked to the #615 from Kato Pafos); if driving to the zoo, the route to it from the main road is complicated, but extremely well signposted

Educational and well organized, **Pafos Zoo** is well worth a visit. The whole park is attractively set on a gently sloping site laid around a water feature, with none of the feeling of claustrophobic exploitation you get at some zoos. There's a fair range of larger animals – lions, tigers, elephants, giraffes, camels, zebras – but, given its origins (it was until recently Pafos Bird Park), it is particularly strong on birds, with a good selection of hornbills, toucans, flamingos, owls, eagles, doves, cockatoos, parakeets, cranes, storks and much more. The snake and reptile house is also particularly good. Despite its relative isolation, 15km from Pafos and 6km north of Coral Bay, the zoo is well signposted and runs transfers from hotels. So if the kids want to visit, you have little excuse. For a large family, though, it can be quite expensive.

## Cape Drepano

Driving north from Pafos through banana plantations, you finally get to **Cape Drepano**, which marks the end of the main Pafos resort area and of the E701, and the beginning of the wild Akamas Peninsula. The cape, long a destination for pilgrimages, is marked by the village of **Agios Georgios** where everything is named after the titular saint, including the modern church sitting in the midst of a large car park (which often hosts market stalls), and the small medieval chapel beyond. Further on are the remains of a huge **sixth-century basilica complex** (daily: mid-Sept to mid-April 8.30am–4pm, mid-April to mid-Sept 9.30am–5pm; €2.50; ☎ 26812301) discovered in the 1950s. Here you can distinguish the ground plans of three separate basilicas, extensive mosaics, a necropolis and pilgrims' lodgings, together with survivals from an earlier Roman settlement. Below the archeological site are some rock-cut tombs in the cliff which can be approached from the top but are most clearly visible from the beach below.

But it's not just for the past that Agios Georgios is worth visiting – the splendidly sited **fish restaurant** *Agios Georgios* (see page 123) overlooks the flat-topped offshore **island of Geronisos** (upon which, incidentally, further archeological remains have been found) and a small modern harbour with a beach next to it, useable when it's not knee-deep in seaweed. There has been a long history of boats using this tiny haven, as it was directly on the route from Alexandria to Constantinople, and it is still thronged with fishing vessels.

# The Akamas Peninsula

The **AKAMAS PENINSULA** makes up the northwest tip of Cyprus and is one of the least inhabited places on the island. It is an area of great beauty – especially the rugged coast – and attracts **walkers**, **mountain bikers** and **off-road drivers** (there are no main roads – just dirt tracks and footpaths). As with most peninsulas, where it begins is debatable. For the purposes of this Guide, it is broadly defined as the area north of Pegeia and west of Polis.

Once used as a **firing range** by the British Army – which kept away even the most determined hotel developers – the peninsula has an extraordinary range of **wildlife**, and contains virtually every type of habitat to be found on the island, from the dense forests of the south to arid pine scrub at the tip. Among the flora and fauna are 39 of Cyprus's endemic plants, 160 or more varieties of bird, twelve types of mammal, twenty reptile species and sixteen types of butterfly. Top billing, however, goes to the **sea turtles** (both green and loggerhead) which lay their eggs on the peninsula's beaches. Though not a national park, the peninsula does have some measure of **protection** – the Pegeia and Akamas Forests are the responsibility of the government, and other bits are controlled in various ways – but there seems to be no overarching plan to protect it. This is a worry, as powerful forces (not only the usual developers, but also the Cypriot Orthodox church authorities are keen to exploit the glorious beaches out here).

Driving on the Akamas means either **renting a 4WD** or signing up for a **jeep safari** (try ⓦfreetimetours.com who do an Akamas jeep safari at €37/person), and only experienced walkers, properly dressed and equipped, should attempt it on foot. Given its military past, if you find anything that looks like a live shell or other **ordnance**, leave well alone. For the faint of heart, the best way to see the peninsula is from the comfort of a boat – excursions run from Pafos and Lakki (Alkion run cruises in glass-bottomed boats along the Akamas coast; see ⓦlatchiboatcruises.com).

**3**

## Akamas from the south

Around 19km from Pafos, just before getting to Agios Georgios on the E701, a signpost points off to the right – "Akamas Peninsula 18km". Following this, the surfaced road continues for about 1km, until you come to a large brown Forest Department sign announcing that "You are entering into the south coast of the Akamas Peninsula", with warning about litter, fires and camping, all of which are prohibited. Beyond it the road curves down into a valley where the **Aspros (White) River** disgorges into the sea. A beach sits at the foot of some white cliffs, and upstream there's a taverna, the *White River Fish Tavern and Snack Bar*. Beyond this the road becomes a dirt track. After just over 1km of bouncing from rut to rut, you arrive at **Toxeftra Beach**, which is where the next river – the Avgas – runs out into the sea. Following a Forestry Department sign to the right, the river valley, full of citrus and banana plantations, splits into two gorges. This is as far as you'll get on wheels. Park, and follow the path up the right-hand **Avakas Gorge**, which becomes increasingly spectacular the further you walk. After about fifteen to twenty minutes the going gets tough enough for casual walkers to turn back.

Back on the coast, the road continues north for 5km or so, hugging the shore, until it reaches Lara Bay.

### Lara Bay

One of the most beautiful and most isolated beaches in Cyprus, **Lara Bay** is a haven for loggerhead and green turtles. During the turtle laying season (May–Aug) volunteers monitor the beach for female turtles and relocate their eggs to a fenced hatchery, protecting them from predators. These measures, as well as the lack of light pollution,

**3**

## AKAMAS WALKING TRAILS

Walking trails through the Akamas are well marked, and in summer can be quite crowded. However, despite their relative user-friendliness, don't be lulled into a false sense of security – it's very remote, and all the usual precautions should be taken, so wear a hat, use plenty of sunscreen and carry bottles of water. Maps of the walks (and the excellent "Nature Trails of the Akamas" booklet which covers the routes below) are available from tourist offices in Polis and Paphos, and copies are posted in several locations. If you get into difficulties, phone the local police station (☏ 26806280), tell them what trail you're on and the number on the last sign you passed. If you haven't got a phone, or there's no signal, you're on your own.

### TRAILS FROM LOUTRA TIS AFRODITIS (BATHS OF APHRODITE)

**The Trail to Fontana Amoroza** is the easiest walk from the Baths of Aphrodite, a 6km stroll which follows the coast to a small spring. The Fontana Amoroza ("Fountain of Love") was named by Italian poet-traveller Ludovico Ariosto, who probably mistook it for the Baths of Aphrodite (the contrast between the grandiloquent name and the actual tiny spring is amusing). The route is hugely popular, and if you do this walk in summer try to set off very early or late in the day, not only to avoid the heat, but also the noise of speedboats, quad bikes and 4WDs. If you don't want to do the full 12km return walk, catch a boat from Lakki to Fontana Amorozo and walk back.

**The Aphrodite Trail** starts off along the same route as the one to Fontana Amoroza, but then swings west and climbs up to Muti tis Sotiras (370m), down to Pyrgos tis Rigainas (the indistinct ruins of either a Lusignan fortification or a Byzantine monastery), then back to the Baths of Aphrodite. Being a circular route (it's around 7.5km), it can be done in either direction.

**The Adonis Trail** is also a circular route, again about 7.5km long, which loops south of the Baths of Aphrodite, then strikes north to Pyrgos tis Rigainas, where it joins the Aphrodite Trail for the return to the Baths.

Both the Aphrodite and Adonis trails involve a fair bit of ascent and are therefore quite strenuous.

### TRAILS FROM NEO CHORIO/SMIGIES

**The Smigies Trail** is a circular route to the north of the Smigies picnic site and it has two variations – a short trail of 2.5km, and a longer one of 5km. The route offers terrific views both north across Chrysohou Bay and west towards Lara Bay, and includes some walking through dense forest. The route is classed as average difficulty, and does include a number of fairly steep climbs. The long trail links up with the Adonis Trail.

**The Pissouromouttis Trail** is a 3km circular route to the south of the Smigies picnic site, offering similar views and level of difficulty.

---

mean thousands of baby turtles make it to the lapping waves of the Mediterranean. So far, Lara Bay has escaped development; it is a protected area under a law passed in 1971 and also lies within the Akamas State Forest. However, there's no room for complacency – a distressing amount of rubbish accumulates on the sand, despite the efforts of the volunteers. Contact with the Lara Bay Hatchery is in no way formalized, but those who run it welcome genuine interest and offers of help. Otherwise most people visit on a boat cruise or a 4WD safari (note that private vehicles are banned from approaching the beach during the laying season).

From Lara Bay you can either go back the way you came, take the **dirt road inland** to Ineia and Drouseia, or continue up the coast and strike **east** up to the Smigies picnic grounds, from where you can head east to Neo Chorio or south to Drouseia. Though these dirt roads are relatively well signposted, you're a long way from help if anything goes wrong.

## Akamas from the north

Apart from Agios Georgios, the most popular way of getting onto the Akamas Peninsula, and by far the most convenient for the more remote northern part, is via

Loutra tis Afroditis – the Baths of Aphrodite – (see page 139) on the north coast. A good main road – the E713 – leads west from the outskirts of Polis to the baths, where it peters out at a car park and drinks kiosk. A poster with a map of the area provided by the Forestry Department shows the main trails that start here. You can either go through the baths, or skirt them by following the "Fontana Amoroza 6km" sign. Beyond the baths, further signs welcome you ("You are entering into the North Side of the Akamas Peninsula"), warn you that this is a wildlife conservation area, and give details (with map) of the cycling routes that crisscross the peninsula.

## Akamas from the east

The Akamas Peninsula is also accessible along its eastern edge from several of the villages of the **Laona Plateau** – from north to south **Neo Chorio**, **Drouseia**, **Ineia** and **Arodes** (Kato and Pano) and **Kathikas**. A number of these villages are worth visiting in their own right, and offer interesting **agrotourism accommodation** (see page 30) as a result of the work of the **Laona Foundation** (🐦laona.org).

**3**

### Neo Chorio

**NEO CHORIO**, a pretty and nicely kept village high on a hill south of the coast road, is a burgeoning agrotourism centre, with lots of traditional balconied houses being adapted for tourists to rent (and, it has to be said, new villa developments on the outskirts). There's also a stone church (Agiou Mina), and a memorial to three villagers who were members of EOKA and who died on the same day in 1956. There are superb views across Chrysohou Bay from here, too. Neo Chorio is the nearest easily accessible village to the **Smigies picnic site**, which is about 2.5km west of the village and the starting point of two marked trails. These are less popular, and therefore less crowded, than the ones that start at the Baths of Aphrodite.

### Drouseia and Ineia

Hilltop **DROUSEIA** is set around an attractive eighteenth-century church. There's a small **Weaving Museum** (Mon–Fri 8.30am–noon & 2–4pm, Sat 8.30am–noon), a good selection of places to eat, and access to the southern part of the Akamas Peninsula on dirt roads – to Smigies and the Akamas Forest by driving northwest, and to the Pegeia Forest area to the south and west via Ineia.

Virtually part of Drouseia, **INEIA** has its own small **Basket Weaving Museum** (June–Sept Mon–Fri 11am–1pm & 4–7pm; Oct–May Mon–Fri 11am–1pm & 3–6pm; Sat 11am–1pm all year) with displays of one of Cyprus's oldest crafts. The museum is in the yard outside the village church (the large church just up from the main road, not the small one on the main street).

### Kathikas

**KATHIKAS** is a large village packed with traditional houses (stone walls, shuttered windows, balconies) and narrow paved streets. It has become popular with visitors, particularly those who want to stay in the houses, and teeters on the edge of commercialism. It has a useful visitor centre, a donkey sanctuary (which is unfortunately not open to the public anymore), and some excellent places to eat. The village is surrounded by vineyards and has two wineries (Sterna and Vasilikon) just outside, and it is another gateway to the Akamas – a dirt road heads west towards Agios Georgios, roughly parallel to the main E709/E701 which covers the same ground, but a lot more quickly. There is also a short marked trail, the **Agiasmatos Trail**, which starts about 1km from the village on the road to Pegeia, ends in Kathikos, and is an easy 2km (45min) walk.

# Polis

The north coast of Pafos district is dominated by the small town of **POLIS** (or Polis Chrysochous, to give it its full title) which sits on the banks of the Chrysochou River where it empties into wide **Chrysochou Bay**. A small, appealing and unpretentious market town which was attacked by the Turkish air force during the Kokkina Incident (see page 137), Polis licked its wounds, repaired the damage, and became a favourite with backpackers in the 1980s. Since then, reservations about its rate of development have been expressed but appear a little premature – while the town centre is full of restaurants and bars, it's still a delightful place at which to fetch up, has an interesting and varied hinterland, and represents an important counterweight to brash and breezy Pafos.

There's not a huge amount to see in town – a venerable old church, a neat little archeological museum and a rather old olive tree (supposedly aged 700) – yet just to the north is a good sandy **beach** with a campsite and views of the Akamas Peninsula.

### Brief history

According to tradition, the Mycenaean Akamas, son of Theseus, first established a city here, having landed nearby on his way back from the Trojan War. Whatever the truth of this, it is likely that the Chrysochou Bay was indeed first settled by the Mycenaeans more than a thousand years before the birth of Christ. By around 750 BC it was one

POLIS — Chrysochou Bay

Polis Beach ①

CHRISTODOULOU PAPANIKOLAOU-LOU

② Loutra tis Afroditi & Lakki (1km)

**EATING**
| | |
|---|---|
| Arsinoe Fish Tavern | 4 |
| Chix Chox | 2 |
| Finikas | 3 |
| The Old Town | 5 |
| Polis Camping Site | 1 |

DIOS POLIEOS

MEGALOU ALEXANDROU

SOPHOKLI DE METRIOU

VERGINAS

THESSALONIKIS

APOSTOLOU ANDREA

SELINOUS

LEOFOROS MARIOU

Polis & Kato Pyrgos

**Marion-Arsinoe Archaeological Site**

Municipal Park

LEOFOROS MARIOU

KYPAOLEONTOS

② ③

**Church of Agios Andronicos**

**Archeological Museum of Marion-Arsinoe**

ⓘ ⑤ **Bus Station**

N

MARIOU

LEOFOROS VASILEOS STASIOIKAOU

EFESOU

KONSTANTINOUPOLEOS

SMYRNIS

TIMOCHARI

**ACCOMMODATION**
| | |
|---|---|
| Bougainvillea Hotel Apartments | 3 |
| Chrysafinia Hotel Apartments | 5 |
| Mariela Hotel Apartments | 4 |
| Natura Beach | 1 |
| Nicki Holiday Resort | 2 |

0 — 250
metres

▼ ⑤

**THE KOKKINA INCIDENT**

The events of 1964 surrounding the village of **Kokkina** on the north Cypriot coast were in many ways a rehearsal for the Turkish invasion ten years later. This part of Cyprus had a high proportion of Turkish Cypriots, and after independence in 1960, the village of Kokkina, 27km west of Polis, became in effect an armed Turkish-Cypriot enclave where TMT paramilitaries landed arms and goods from Turkey. EOKA, unsurprisingly, took exception to this and – despite being warned not to by President Makarios – attacked the town on August 6, 1964. On August 10, with the Turkish Cypriots facing defeat, Turkey intervened by sending jets over to strafe and napalm villages and towns, including Polis, causing heavy casualties. All-out war was avoided only by UN intervention. From then on, Kokkina became a **Turkish military area** – all Turkish-Cypriot civilians were relocated elsewhere. After the full Turkish invasion of 1974 effectively divided the island, the Green Line between the two armies was established just east of Kato Pyrgos. This left the **Kokkina Enclave** separate from the rest of north Cyprus, a situation which continues to this day.

**3**

of Cyprus's great city-kingdoms, called **Marion**. It flourished because of its copper and gold mines and traded closely with the Aegean islands, Corinth and Athens. The city fell to the Persians but was freed by Kimon in 449 BC. Following the death of Alexander the Great, it backed the wrong horse during the struggle between his successors, and in 312 BC the victor, Ptolemy I, destroyed the city and resettled its inhabitants in Pafos. A new city was built near or over the ruins of Marion by Ptolemy II and named in honour of his wife (who also happened to be his sister) **Arsinoe**. As far as we know, the city continued to be inhabited, though it suffered from Muslim coastal raids during the seventh century. Now called Polis (simply the Greek word for "town"), it continued as a small rural settlement, a remote part of a remote district, and didn't hit the headlines again until the explosive "Kokkina Incident" in 1964.

## Church of Agios Andronicos

Kouliou • Sun 9am–4pm • Free

West of the town centre, and in a small park that's ideal for a picnic, stands the tiny, sixteenth-century **Church of Agios Andronicos** (not to be confused with the more modern church in the town centre). The church was used as a mosque during the Ottoman period, and continued to be attended by local Turkish Cypriots during the British occupation. It has a rather odd look from the outside, its simple traditional architecture compromised by a lean-to addition as big as the original church, used as an anteroom by Muslim worshippers. Abandoned in 1963 as Turkish Cypriots moved away, it has since 1974 been renovated, revealing important **Venetian frescoes** that had been hidden by whitewash. Officially open only to organized groups, arrangements seem to be very flexible, and you might find the church not only open but unattended. If in doubt, phone the archeological museum.

## Archeological Museum of Marion-Arsinoe

Archiepiskopou Markariou III Avenue • Mon–Fri 8am–4pm, Sat 9am–3pm • €2.50 • ☏ 26322955, ⓦ bit.ly/MarionArsinoe

On the road that heads east from the town centre (opposite a Lukoil filling station) is the **Archeological Museum of Marion-Arsinoe**. Founded in 1998, this is the place to see artefacts from the ancient city-states that once flourished here. The museum is housed in a Neoclassical building, and has two galleries that lead off a central atrium: Room I covers the history of the area from its early Neolithic roots right up to medieval times, while Room II concentrates on the rich haul of artefacts that were taken from the necropolis at Marion. Some of the amphorae and statuettes are of stunning quality, and the ceramics are painted with scenes from daily life. There's also lots of gold and some stylish ancient Greek and Roman jewellery which wouldn't look out of place on the catwalk today. Look out for the female terracotta funeral statuettes, and the pieces of a huge male statue, reassembled against an outline figure and looking like some sort of modernist sculpture.

## The beach

Polis's expansive **beach** is about 1km north of the town, down a tarmac road which winds through eucalyptus groves and becomes increasingly rutted as you approach the sea. The sand quality is good, there's a lifeguard tower, and a **campsite** with attached restaurant. The site has that backpacker-friendly feel that's rare in Cyprus (though camping on the sand itself is prohibited). The sea is clear and safe, and there are views westward towards the Akamas Peninsula. If there is a criticism, it's that there's not much shade.

### ARRIVAL AND INFORMATION                                                        POLIS

**By bus** The main bus route between Polis and Pafos is the #645 (Mon–Fri hourly, Sat & Sun less frequent; 1hr). Buses start from Kyproleontos, southeast of the main square in Polis (running from the Karavella Station in Ktima Paphos).
**By car** For motorists, there is ample parking in the town – either in pay-and-display car parks or on the streets.

**Tourist office** The tourist office is on Vasileos Stasioikou, opposite the bus terminal (Mon–Fri 8.30am–4pm; first week of each month Mon–Fri 9am–3.30pm, Sat 9am–2pm; ☎ 26322468).

### ACCOMMODATION

**Bougainvillea Hotel Apartments** Veryinas ☎ 26812250, ⓦ bougainvillea.com.cy; map p.136. A 5min walk north of the centre of Polis on the road to the beach, the *Bougainvillea* has six studios and 26 apartments which sleep up to four people. Staff are friendly and helpful, accommodation is adequate if a little Spartan, and there's a bar, pool, and a reception desk open from 9am to 2am. Look out for extra charges, especially for breakfast and a/c. **€65**
★ **Chrysafinia Hotel Apartments** Prodromi ☎ 26321180, ⓦ chrysafinia.com; map p.136. Set in well-tended gardens, in quiet Prodromi on the outskirts of Polis about a 15min walk from the centre. Apartments are clean and serviceable, all have balconies, and communal facilities include a bar and pool. Portable air-conditioners on request. **€48**
**Mariela Hotel Apartments** 3 Arsinoe St ☎ 26322310, ⓦ marielahotel.com; map p.136. A substantial block on the southeast edge of Polis, the *Mariela* has a pool, and

all apartments have a balcony. Family-owned and very friendly. Breakfast and a/c extra. **€85**
**Natura Beach** Christodoulou Papanikopoulou St ☎ 26323111, ⓦ natura.com.cy; map p.136. Just behind the beach east of Polis amid olive and citrus groves (and goats), the *Natura Beach* was renovated in 2011 and offers a choice of rooms or villas, all with balconies or verandas. The hotel has a bar and restaurant, a gift shop and swimming pool, mini-gym and sauna. Villas have their own swimming pools. **€105**
**Nicki Holiday Resort** Leoforos Akamantos ☎ 26322226, ⓦ nickiresort.com; map p.136. Lying conveniently halfway between Polis and Lakki, and 2km from each, *Nicki Holiday Resort* has two restaurants and bars, a floodlit tennis court, fitness centre and gym and two pools. Accommodation ranges from studios through a variety of different-sized apartments, all with the usual TV, balcony and kitchenette. **€85**

### EATING

None of Polis's restaurants can claim to be outstanding, and your experience can vary according to how busy they are, but all are agreeably set, either in the cheerfully crowded central square or looking across the sea or the harbour in Lakki, a couple of kilometres west.
**Arsinoe Fish Tavern** Grigoriou Digeni ☎ 26321590, ⓦ arsinoe-fishtavern.com; map p.136. Just south of the central square, and inconspicuously located next to a large estate agent, *Arsinoe Fish Tavern* is popular with locals as well as tourists. The fish is fresh (the menu depends on what

has been caught that day) and the service friendly. Main courses around €10–16. April–Nov Mon–Sat 6–11pm.
**Chix Chox** Central Square ☎ 26322366; map p.136. Right at the heart of things, *Chix Chox* offers Cypriot specialities, grilled meat and fish, mezé and, not always present in Cypriot restaurants, a few vegetarian dishes. Seating is under canopies in the village square, facing a lion fountain – a great spot to watch the world go by. Mains €10–18. Mon–Sat 9.30am–11pm (or later, depending on number of customers).

★ **Finikas** Central Square ☎ 26323403, ⓦ finikas restaurant.net; map p.136. Housed in a fine old building right on the central square, *Finikas* has the air of being a cut above the usual tourist joint. It does a complete range of meals – fish, meat, charcoal grills, steak, Cypriot dishes, pasta, salads – and has kids' and vegetarian menus. House specials (from €12.50) include a delicious chicken dish topped with mushrooms and cheese, and kebabs using beef rather than the more usual pork or lamb. Dinner only.

**The Old Town** 9 Georgiades Kyproleontas ☎ 99632781,

ⓦ theoldtownrestaurant.com; map p.136. Not the cheapest option in Polis (mains around €20–25), but good locally sourced Greek-Cypriot food in a classy setting. Its courtyard is shaded and cool, even on hot days, and tables are well spaced out. Nicely understated service too. Mon, Tues & Thurs–Sun 6–11pm.

**Polis Camping Site** Polis Beach ☎ 26815080; map p.136. Cheap and cheerful beach taverna knocking out burgers, omelettes, pizzas, pastas and grills (€5.50–10). March–Oct daily 8am–midnight.

# West of Polis

West of Polis are two of the region's biggest tourist magnets – the harbour, beaches, water sports and restaurants of Lakki, and the renowned Baths of Aphrodite, which attracts not only visitors to the rather underwhelming spring, but also those wishing to explore the Akamas Peninsula.

**3**

## Lakki

A couple of kilometres west of Polis, **LAKKI** (widely called "Latchi" or "Latsi" by the locals) is one of the most picturesque little villages in Cyprus. It's clustered around a small fishing harbour, and the quayside is a mass of restaurants, cafés, bars and kiosks offering cruises in glass-bottomed boats, water sports and diving trips. On either approach to the village there are wide sandy beaches surrounded by villa developments. Despite its popularity and accusations of overdevelopment, it hasn't lost its charm, and is still a laidback place to stop for a coffee or a meal and watch the boats coming and going.

## Loutra tis Afroditi (The Baths of Aphrodite)

The main road west from Polis (the E713) ends at **Loutra tis Afroditi** or "**The Baths of Aphrodite**", natural pools where supposedly the goddess bathed and splashed about with Adonis. Despite its romantic name, it's all rather underwhelming. That said, if you want some easy walking along cleanly paved paths, through shady trees to a pool ringing to the sound of running water, then you might just enjoy its understated appeal. This is also the start of several walks onto the Akamas Peninsula (see page 134), and beyond the baths you might be greeted by the welcome sight of an ice-cream van. Back at the car park, on the opposite side of the road, the *Baths of Aphrodite Restaurant*, run by the Cyprus Tourist Organization, offers great views of the cove below.

**EATING**                                                                                          **WEST OF POLIS**

★ **Baths of Aphrodite Restaurant** ☎ 26321457. With killer views across the bay below the Baths of Aphrodite and well-priced food, this CTO-run restaurant is frankly more interesting than the baths themselves. Mains from €10–17, fish mezé €17.50. Daily: April–Sept 11am–11pm; Oct–March 11am–8pm.

**Porto Latchi** Lakki ☎ 26322530, ⓦ portolatchi.com. Housed in a centuries-old carob warehouse (renovated after a 2004 fire), the Porto Latchi specializes in fish, though it does offer meat dishes as well. Main courses are €8.50–

45. The fish mezé is particularly good (€18.50/person, minimum two people), as is the house wine. Service can be slow. Daily 10am–10pm.

★ **Yiangos and Peter Taverna** Akamantos Avenue, Lakki ☎ 26321411. Another great seafood option in Lakki, well patronized by locals, the *Yiangos and Peter Taverna* does excellent battered fish dishes, and good salads. Main courses range widely in price (€10– €40) depending on type of fish (and you need to order fries etc separately). Daily 8am–midnight.

# East of Polis

East of Polis is a sweeping bay along which runs the E704 through the villages of **Pommos** and **Pachyammos**. The road leaves the coast to get around the Turkish-Cypriot **Kokkina Enclave**, then returns to it just before the small seaside town of **Kato Pyrgos**. Isolated from the rest of Cyprus by the Turkish invasion of 1974, Kato Pyrgos became a border town in 2010 with the opening of a new crossing point on the Green Line (see page 27), making it possible to drive directly to Lefkosia and the east of Cyprus without having to take the long diversion through Pafos or drive across the tortuous mountain roads of Tilliria.

## Pomos

The first village of any size, 20km east from Polis, is **POMOS**. It straggles along the main road around an attractively rocky bay, and although there's a tiny boat haven, several restaurants, and a small **natural history museum** (in the Municipal Hall), you're only likely to stop here if staying in one of the local villas.

## Pachyammos

About 5km beyond Pomos is the village of **PACHYAMMOS**, hard up against the fortifications of the Kokkina Enclave. Its main claim to fame, which attracts coachloads of Cypriots, is the large modern church of **Saints Rafael, Nikolaos and Eirini**, and within it the shrine of St Raphael, who is reputed to be able to heal the sick and disabled. The church stands on a wide terrace which overlooks the dunes and the beach, and contains several war memorials, including one to members of the National Guard and civilians killed during the Kokkina Incident in 1964 (see page 137). If several coaches arrive simultaneously, the whole terrace and church can become very busy.

## Kato Pyrgos

The final Republic of Cyprus village on this stretch of the north coast is **KATO PYRGOS**, in some ways a place that time forgot, and certainly one with a unique atmosphere. To reach it you need to drive inland from Pachyammos (effectively the end of the coast road), around the Kokkina Enclave's fences, guard towers and Turkish and UN troops; what should be a short hop is now a 23km drive along serpentine mountain roads. When you return to the coast, it's another 6km into the unexpectedly large village, which occupies a wide hill-girt bay. Squeezed between the Kokkina Enclave to the west, north Cyrprus to the east, and to the south Tilliria, the largest wilderness area in Cyprus, Kato Pyrgos has been pretty well isolated since the mid-twentieth century.

---

### CROSSING INTO THE NORTH FROM KATO PYRGOS

The Kato Prygos **crossing point**, scenically sited among low hills 4km to the east, is the most convenient for those staying around Pafos district. The roads are good, and this venture into the north can make for an interesting cross-cultural experience. Unlike some of the other crossings, it is easy to find on both sides of the border – the road has nowhere else to go. Once over the Green Line (the actual crossing takes 5–10min), the road, although marked on the maps as a very minor one, is in fact of good quality and makes for an **exhilarating drive**. The first Turkish-Cypriot village you get to is Yesilirnak/Limnitis, and beyond this are the two ancient sites at Vouni and Soli, on the left and right of the road respectively, followed by Xeros where you join the main road to Güzelyurt. From there you can bear left for Kamlibel and Girne, or continue straight towards Lefkoşa. For the return to the south, you can either retrace your steps to Kato Pyrgos, or cross back through the Astomeritis/Zodhia or the Agios Dometios/Metehan crossing just outside Lefkosia (see page 27).

However, the opening of the new crossing point just east of the village in October 2010 has gone some way to ending this, since there is now a direct route to Lefkosia through the Turkish-occupied North. Kato Pyrgos has a few hotels, the westernmost of which, the *Tylos Beach*, overlooks the modern harbour, home to a small fishing fleet. Either side of the harbour is a rocky shore, often waist-deep in dried seaweed. Incidentally, it was in Kato Pyrgos that Makarios was based when he made desperate and ultimately futile attempts to stop Grivas and the National Guard attacking the Kokkina Enclave.

# South of Polis

South of Polis is an upland area dotted with villages and vineyards, easily accessible from the main B7 Polis to Pafos road and from the F723. Though its numerous villages might not be worth a specific visit, they certainly merit looking out for, or making a short detour to.

**3**

## Steni

The first thing you notice in **STENI**, 7km south of Polis on the F723, is the war memorial, which stretches along the main street. Rather than the usual statues representing the fallen, to be found in most Cypriot villages, it consists of a simple wall with parts dedicated in turn to the two World Wars, the campaign against the British, and the Turkish invasion of 1974. Directly across the road is the **Museum of Local Life** (daily 10am–4pm: free, though donations welcome), heaving with artefacts that cover virtually every aspect of existence – rural life, local crafts, domestic equipment, musical instruments, coins – from 1800 to the end of World War II. Many Cypriot villages have such rural museums, but this one's an absolute cracker. Outside a wide piazza is a row of picnic tables and a small children's playground. Elsewhere in the village is a good restaurant, the *Steni* (☎26322506), and the *Neromylos* coffee shop (☎26352059, ⊕neromyloscafe.com). Many of the villagers emigrated to South Africa after the Turkish invasion, and some are now returning to do up their ancestral homes. Surrounding the village is attractively hilly and unspoilt countryside, through which run several walking paths.

## Peristerona

On the F723 10km from Polis lies **PERISTERONA** whose traditional, and in many cases renovated, houses lie on a hill which is dominated by the buildings of the Bishopric of Arsinoe. This diocese was subsumed into that of Pafos in the thirteenth century, but re-established in 1996 after centuries of ecumenical wrangling. The church buildings, set in a courtyard that has an old olive mill and press (and with modern mosaics of goats set into the crazy paving), contain a **Byzantine Museum** (☎26325515, April–Aug Mon–Fri 10am–1pm & 3–6pm; Sept–Mar 10am–4pm; €2.00) which has more than sixty icons and a good range of woodcarvings, vestments and manuscripts dating back to the sixteenth century. If the museum's locked, try looking for the custodian in the church. Just down the hill and on the same side of the road, a lane branches off to the right. This leads to the attractive **Aetofolies Gorge**, haunt of eagles according to the name and pigeons according to the evidence of one's own eyes (in fact, the village name derives from "*peristeri*", meaning pigeon).

## Lysos

Some 12km from Polis, on the F733, lies **LYSOS**, one of the largest villages in this part of Pafos district. On a terrace just below the centre stands the fifteenth-century church of **Panagia Chryselousa** (main square; open to visitors when no service is in progress), dominated by its rather incongruous freestanding campanile. The church is interesting in that its architecture is largely Lusignan rather than the more usual Byzantine, with coats of arms of the local Lusignan overlords above both the north and south doors. Elsewhere in the village, a concerted effort is being made to develop the local tourist trade – through the building or renovation of a number of villas, but especially through the *Paradisos Hills Hotel* (see below), which offers guided hikes, cooking classes and wedding packages. Horseriding (including overnight treks) is available from Ride in Cyprus (☎ 99777624, ⊛ rideincyprus.com). A track near the hotel leads to the abandoned Turkish-Cypriot village of Melandra, largely destroyed by shelling in 1974.

| ACCOMMODATION | LYSOS |
|---|---|

**Paradisos Hills Hotel** Leoforos Tassou Papadopoulou ☎ 26322287, ⊛ paradisoshills.com. Peaceful, smallish (fifteen-room) hotel in a picturesque village on top of a hill with extensive views over land and sea. The *Paradisos Hills* boasts attentive staff, spotless rooms, good food – and cookery classes if you fancy learning Greek cuisine. **€105**

## Kritou Terra

Directly south of Polis, between the E709 and the B7 and accessible from both, lies the village of **KRITOU TERRA**. It's a warren of narrow streets (best park on the outskirts and explore the village on foot – there's a useful street plan next to the bus stop at the bottom of the village) that contains a number of unique attractions, the most startling of which is an early **casino**, which opened in the 1870s and closed in the early 1900s. Featuring belly dancers from Syria and Lebanon, it catered largely for Turkish Cypriots and visitors from the Middle East. The whitewashed building, now maintained by the Department of Antiquities, contains murals dedicated to a hero of the Greek War of Independence, Athanasios ("Diakos") Massavetas, who was executed by impalement in 1821. Also of interest is the variety of ways in which the four streams which flow through the village have been harnessed – look out for the **washing holes** down a turning just before the Co-op bank (local women didn't use soap, but a mixture of ash and water called *alusiva*). There's also a **restored watermill**, one of seventeen that once operated in the area.

## Loukrounou

East of Kritou Terra is what's left of the village of **LOUKROUNOU**, which briefly held out as a Turkish-Cypriot enclave after the 1974 invasion. The last remaining forty or so villagers were finally escorted into the occupied north by UN troops in 1975. Today buildings damaged in the fighting, roofless and windowless, are slowly crumbling and returning to nature.

## Skarfos Bridge

Worth a detour off the B7 and then the E712, and well signposted, is the elegant little single-spanned medieval **Skarfos Bridge**. Carrying the main Lusignan Pafos to Polis road across the Stavros tis Psokas stream, the bridge is in an isolated valley full of almond trees and loud with the sound of running water (in spring, at least), and is easily accessed via a path and steps. The remains of the road up to the bridge can be clearly seen, and on the north bank, some distance away, is a ruined watermill.

## Kouyiouka Watermill

Museum and coffee shop: Mon, Tues, Thurs & Fri 7.30am–2.30pm, Wed 7.30am–5pm (although hours can be dependent on staff numbers); restaurant by appointment • museum entrance €1 • ☎ 26632847, ⊛ kouyiouka.com/19409964

On the B7 Polis to Pafos road, a couple of kilometres from the village of **GIOLOU**, is the **Kouyiouka Watermill**, which is a lot more interesting than it sounds. The complicated multilevel mill is a listed building which has been thoroughly renovated – once a dilapidated ruin, it is now in excellent shape. The mill contains a fascinating museum displaying all the bits and pieces used in the production of bread, oil and wine (labelling is only in Greek). There's also a delightful coffee shop and a shop selling bread freshly baked on the premises.

# Tilliria

The forest wilderness of **TILLIRIA** lies south of the coast between Polis and Kato Pyrgos and northwest of the Troodos Massif. The region makes for a great drive with endless forest vistas. Drive with caution, though – look out for bends, and for rocks that have fallen from cliff faces above. Despite what it says on older maps, which show it crisscrossed only by 4WD tracks, there is now a well-surfaced road (the **F740**) that cuts right through the forest from the road around the Kokkina Enclave. Apart from Stavros tis Psokas there are no settlements (or petrol stations), and only the very occasional picnic site (though there's a beautiful one deep in the forest at Livadi). During the summer you're likely to come across a fair amount of traffic – especially coaches, jeeps on safari and forest wardens' vehicles – but outside the main holiday season you might not see another vehicle for hours.

**3**

## Stavros tis Psokas Forest Station

Though a working forest station, **Stavros tis Psokas** is also a popular destination for walkers and tour groups. It lies in a beautiful setting 3km off the road to Kykkos, along a side road which drops down through a wooded valley. A collection of buildings lies scattered under the trees – wooden cabins, the Chapel of the Holy Cross ("Stavros" means "cross"), a large **hostel** (☎26991858) and a picnic site with children's playground and a café/restaurant. There is also a large, hilly and wooded **mouflon enclosure**, where, if you're lucky, you may see these iconic wild mountain sheep, the emblem of Cyprus. You can't go into the pen (in 2011, a man who climbed the fence and goaded the animals was gored), but a path up some steps from the road runs around the perimeter fence. Elsewhere in the forest station a fairly rudimentary campsite nestles under the trees. From Stavros tis Psokas there are several **forest walks** from 3–5km (the station is a stopping point on the E4 European Long Distance Path). Beyond the forest station a road (marked "earthen road", so you've been warned) eventually leads to Polis.

## Cedar Valley

**Cedar Valley** is one of Cyprus's best-known beauty spots. It takes its name from the cedar trees (*Cedrus brevifolia*), a native species, closely related to the better-known Cedar of Lebanon, that grows here in abundance, and attracts hordes of visitors during the summer months. It's 21km east of Stavros tis Psokas and 18km west of the Kykkos Monastery. If you don't know your cedar from your silver birch, then after a long drive through impenetrable forest the unique nature of Cedar Valley might be lost on you, but it's certainly pretty to look at. Facilities are, though, a little threadbare – a drinking fountain, a few paths and a row of wooden benches plonked next to the road. Like Stavros tis Psokas, Cedar Valley is on the E4 Long Distance Path.

# The Troodos Mountains

PEDOULAS MOUNTAIN VILLAGE

# The Troodos Mountains

If you look at a satellite image of Cyprus, you'll see a large block of green stretching across the southern half of the island, speckled with white. This is the Troodos Massif, a massive plug of igneous rock, now carpeted with forest which, millions of years ago, rose like Aphrodite from the sea. Here, even at the height of summer, you will find cool, pine-scented air, quiet mountain villages and lonely monasteries, sometimes with a bird of prey circling above. This is Cyprus, but not entirely as we know it.

Rich in minerals, especially copper, the mountains have been extensively **mined**, though otherwise they were for centuries synonymous with isolation and poverty. Conversely, it was this very rugged seclusion that saved the area from the worst excesses of marauding invaders experienced elsewhere on the island. The Troodos became a haven for dissidents and rebels and a stronghold for the Orthodox Church, as evidenced by its wealth of **monasteries** and **painted medieval churches**. Of all the various rulers of Cyprus, the British made the biggest inroads here, mainly in search of summer retreats in which to escape the relentless heat of the coast.

Today, with villages losing their young people to the coastal towns or even abroad, the Troodos region is relying more and more heavily on **tourism**. Roads have been greatly improved, and many traditional homes have been adapted into small hotels, restaurants and agrotourism endeavours. And there's plenty to reward a few days' stay here – the south-facing foothills are draped in vineyards, with the higher mountains dotted with hiking and skiing trails, and picnic areas in spectacular settings. Declared a **national park** in 1992, and containing four specified nature reserves, the Troodos National Forest Park contains 750 species of plant, of which twelve are endemic; among its birds and animals are the rare Bonelli's eagle and the iconic Cypriot mouflon (a species of wild sheep).

Within the park are five distinct **areas**: the village/resort of **Troodos** itself which surrounds **Mount Olympos** (2000m), the island's highest peak; **Marathasa** to the northwest, home to the village of **Pedoulas** and Cyprus's greatest monastery **Kykkos**; **Solea** to the northeast, with **Kakopetria** and other villages lining the main road to Lefkosia; largely treeless **Pitsilia** whose main villages are **Agros** and **Palaichori** to the east, and **Machairas** further east still, notable for the **Machairas Monastery** and the charming village of **Fikardou**. For the greatest concentration of frescoed churches, walks and picnic areas, hotels and restaurants, go for the first three; for a more laidback taste of the mountains, the last two are best.

## ARRIVAL AND GETTING AROUND                    THE TROODOS MOUNTAINS

If you just want to get a flavour of the mountains, a day-trip from your base in Agia Napa, Larnaka, Lemesos, Pafos or Lefkosia will probably be enough. Tours are available from all these places. If, however, you'd like to explore the region in more depth, renting a car is the best option.

**By car or motorcycle** Given the lack of public transport (a few local taxis serve the villages), your best bet is to rent a car or motorbike. Bear in mind that the roads are convoluted and in some cases of poor quality, so journeys could take longer than you might expect from the distances marked on the map.

**By bike** Road cycling is a popular way to get around the

Troodos Mountains, though given the terrain, you need to be fit. Mountain biking too is gaining in popularity, and the CTO has developed the "Troodos Cycling Route", a comprehensively marked and signed 57km trail that circles the National Park. You can pick up a copy of "Cyprus Cycling Routes" from tourist offices; it covers routes all over the Republic, including two starting from Troodos Square. Or just explore as the spirit takes you – the mountains contain hundreds of kilometres of side roads and dirt tracks.

**On foot** The Troodos range is an ideal place to enjoy walking on the many signed routes, the best of which are in the area around Troodos village.

KYKKOS MONASTERY

# Highlights

**① Geopark Visitor Centre** The Troodos Mountains' new geological museum explains why the area's unique geology attracts experts and students from around the world. See page 149

**② Walking** A good range of hiking trails traverses the mountains, often visiting waterfalls or circling the peaks themselves – for a start try the Artemis trail. See page 150

**③ Pedoulas** A particularly scenic mountain village, also hosting a fine museum and a famous church. See page 155

**④ Painted churches** Ten churches in the region have been declared UNESCO World Heritage Sites, owing to the stunning medieval frescoes they contain. See page 156

**⑤ Kykkos Monastery** A fine example of a modern Greek-Cypriot monastery, with the added interest of its links with Archbishop Makarios III. It's also a great place to pick up souvenirs. See page 157

**⑥ Fikardou** This mountain village, meticulously preserved by the Department of Antiquities, provides a snapshot of the past. See page 166

**HIGHLIGHTS ARE MARKED ON THE MAP ON PAGE 148**

# THE TROODOS MOUNTAINS

## HIGHLIGHTS

1 Geopark Centre
2 Walking
3 Pedoulas
4 Painted churches
5 Kykkos Monastery
6 Fikardou

**Buffer zone**

Limit of full northern control

Limit of full southern control

N

0 — 5 kilometres

LEFKOSIA

LARNACA

NORTH CYPRUS

TILLIRIA

PAFOS

MARATHASA

SOLEA

TROODOS

PITSILIA

MACHAIRAS

LEMESOS

KOUMANDARIA REGION

Akaki

E903

Potami

Anoglemi

Agios

Lefka

Karavostasi

Frodsia

Tsakistra

Vyzakia

Mitsero

Linou

Evrychou

Galata

Kalopanagiotis
Gerakies

Motoullas

Kampi

Palaichori

Agridia
Agros

Zoopigi

Arakapas

Ora

Vavalsinia

Fikardou
Lazaniás
Goumi

Panayia tou
Machaira Monastery

Kionia
Picnic Site

Kampi

Panagia tis
Asinou Church
Asinou

Spilia

E909

Kakopetria

B9

Agios Nikolaos
tis Stegis

Monastery of
Agios Ioannis
Lampadistis

Pedoulas

Panagia tou
Moutoulla

Xystarouda
Picnic Site

EOKA
Hideouts

Kykkos
Monastery

Tomb of
Archbishop
Makarios III

Myllkou

Prodromos

Foini

Mandria

Plátres

Olympus
(1950m)

Troodos
Botanical
Gardens

Geopark
Centre

Monuments
of Heroes

Kyperounta

Pelendri

FOR DETAIL SEE
MT OLYMPUS AND AROUND MAP

E908

E912

Xeros

Diarizos

## ● EATING

Argentina Tzeillari            1
Cyprus Restaurant              1
Linos Inn                      1
Mylos Restaurant               1
Zoumos Restaurant              1

## ■ ACCOMMODATION

Linos Inn                      1
Marjay Inn                     2
The Mill Hotel                 1
Rodon Hotel                    3

# Troodos village and around

At 1750m **TROODOS** village is only 250m below Mount Olympus, the island's highest point. It has the longest history of catering for visitors (during the winter it doubles as a ski resort), and therefore has the best infrastructure, with numerous hotels and restaurants, extensive hiking and cycling trails, and a tourist office serving the whole region. It's not particularly attractive – basically a clutch of tourist services housed around a central square – but if you want to get a taste of the mountains without roughing it too much, this is the place for you.

## Troodos Square

The focal point of the village is **Troodos Square**, best described as functional rather than aesthetic. There's ample parking for cars and buses (but even this becomes strained at the height of the season) next to the large *Troodos* hotel (see page 152), a good choice of restaurants, plus a shopping area – a series of unlovely hexagonal brick buildings selling everything from ice cream and preserved fruit to wind chimes and postcards. Across the road, horse rides are on offer.

## Forestry Department Visitor Centre

200m west of Troodos Square • Mon–Fri 9am–2.30pm • €1 • ☎ 25420145, ⓦ moa.gov.cy/forest

In an appropriately rustic stone-and-timber building, the **Forestry Department Visitor Centre** provides an indispensable introduction to the Troodos National Forest Park. A scale model of the mountains is useful for orientation, while other displays fill you in on geology, a variety of other local topics from mushrooms to bats, and the impact of humans. Presentations on various aspects of the park are given in the film and lecture theatre, and you can follow a short (250m) circular botanical and geological trail.

## Geopark Visitor Centre

Tues–Sun 9am–4pm • €3 • ☎ 22952043, ⓦ troodos-geo.org

One of the Troodos region's newest and most interesting ventures is the **Geopark Visitor Centre**, some 6km east of Troodos Square and clearly signposted from the B9 road to Nicosia. Opened in 2015 in the abandoned Amiantos asbestos mine (don't worry, visitors are assured that it's quite safe), it's a recognition of the global significance of the Troodos Massif as a uniquely important geological playground, a magnet for academics and students from around the world. The centre, in a converted school, offers a fifteen-minute visual presentation on the geology of the Troodos Mountains, and a series of displays distributed between five rooms covering the geology and ecology of Cyprus, and its copper and asbestos mining industries. Future plans include visitor entry into the open-cast works of the asbestos mine. Geology may seem something of a niche interest, but if you're intrigued by the huge variation in rock formations you can see as you pass through the Troodos Mountains, then the centre is well worth a visit.

## Troodos Botanical Garden

Mon–Fri 9am–2pm all year, Sat & Sun: Apr–Sept 10am–4pm, Jul–Aug 9.30am–5pm, Oct–Jan Sun only 10.30am–3pm • Free • ☎ 25550091, ⓦ amiandos.eu

Occupying part of the same asbestos mining complex as the Geopark Centre, and with a clearly signposted entrance just off the B9 Troodos to Nicosia road, the **Troodos Botanical Garden** does for plants what the Geopark Centre does for rocks. It offers an excellent introduction to the main trees, shrubs and plants of the Troodos Mountains and, though it's still a little raw, it will be a lovely spot when it's bedded in

## WALKS AROUND TROODOS VILLAGE AND PLATRES

### THE MYLLOMERIS TRAIL

The easiest walk in the area, the 1.5km **Myllomeris Trail** is a one-hour return stroll which starts opposite and just north of the church at the bottom end of Pano Platres to the base of the Myllomeris Falls, an attractive cascade when the river contains enough water.

### THE KALEDONIA TRAIL

Accessible either at the top end from Troodos village or from the bottom near the *Psilo Dendro* trout farm/restaurant, halfway between Platres and Troodos, the 3km **Kaledonia Trail** follows the Kryos Potamos River (one of the few in Cyprus that flows year-round) and takes in the eponymous waterfall which, at 15m, is the highest on the island. The trail is well signposted, and drops down from the Presidential Summer House (built by the British as a summer residence for the High Commissioner), crossing the river along log bridges or sets of stepping stones, and passing through a variety of woodland. Pick up the pamphlet detailing the walk from the Forestry Department visitor centre. Allow one to two hours each way. To avoid retracing your steps, start at the bottom end, then return instead of climbing on to Troodos.

### THE ARTEMIS TRAIL

A 7km route whose start from a car park off the road to the summit is signposted from Troodos village, the **Artemis Trail** is particularly satisfying as it circumnavigates Mount Olympos at around 1850m and offers tantalizing views (including interesting rock formations and the remains of several Venetian fortifications), yet doesn't involve much climbing. Again, a pamphlet produced by the Forestry Department explains everything in detail, including exactly what you can see from the various viewpoints. There's no water along this trail, so bring your own. Allow two to four hours, depending on fitness and how long you stop to admire the views.

### THE ATALANTE TRAIL

Similar to the Artemis Trail, but at 1750m the **Atalante Trail** is slightly lower (and therefore longer by a couple of kilometres). It has the advantage of starting right in the centre of Troodos village, and passes a spring with drinkable water. It's not, however, a fully circular route.

### THE PERSEPHONE TRAIL

A there-and-back 90min to two-hour 3km hike to the top of Makria Kontarka Hill, the **Persephone Trail** offers extensive views.

– informative and attractive, with great views of the mountains from its vantage points, it's a botanist's heaven and a great place to have a picnic.

## Platres

Seven kilometres south of Troodos village is **PLATRES**, an archetypal hill station left behind by the British. It's split into two sections – Kato (Lower) and Pano (Upper) Platres, with hotels dotted around both. If you're used to high-end accommodation, you might find it wanting, but you should still enjoy its faded air of imperial grandeur and its beautiful tree-shaded ambience. At the height of the season Platres can become very crowded, with its facilities creaking under the strain, but off-season it has the feel of any Cypriot village, where everybody seems to know everybody else.

On the main square is a post office, a police station, the main CTO tourist office for the region, a bike rental office and, just below, a small amusement arcade (grandly called "Lunar Park"). Look out, too, for the **Chocolate Workshop** (☎99766446, ⓦcypruschocolate.com; book in advance; €50). Here you can spend an afternoon crafting your own luxury confections (at a suitably luxury price). Platres is a good base for exploring the mountains, and offers a couple of popular and easily manageable walks.

## Sparti Platres Adventure Park

50 Phaneromenis Street • Opening times vary throughout the year and depend on daylight hours, best check by phoning. Closed in February. Book by phone in advance • €14–40 depending on age, €5 extra for the zip wire • ☎ 99100003, ⓦ spartipark.com

Opened in 2015, the French-designed treetop ropes, ladders, walkways and zip wire of **Sparti Platres Adventure Park** provide a range of white-knuckle experiences in a safe environment. All participants wear safety harnesses, and different parts of the layout are available to different age ranges, from 3 upwards (their oldest customer to date was 78). There's a log-cabin style cafeteria and ample parking. This is a welcome addition to an area which is undoubtedly beautiful but, apart from walking, perhaps is short of family things to do.

## Foini

A worthwhile short (4km) excursion to the west of Platres is the meandering village of **FOINI**, famous for its **pottery** and its *loukoumi* (see page 124) or "Foini Delight" as it's known here. There's a lovely viewpoint on the way into the village, which provides a

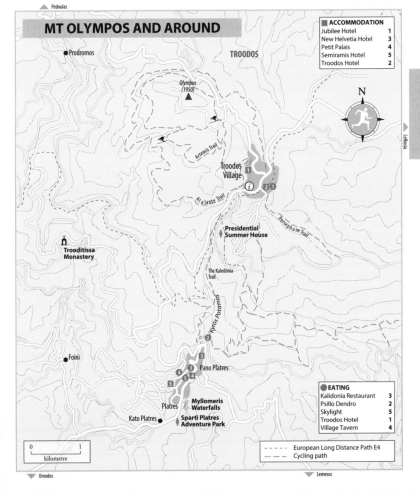

MT OLYMPOS AND AROUND

Pedoulas

Prodromos

TROODOS

Olympus (1950)

Artemis Trail

Troodos Village

Atalante Trail

Persephone Trail

Presidential Summer House

Trooditissa Monastery

The Kaledonia Trail

Kryos Potamos

Foini

Pano Platres

Platres • Myllomeris Waterfalls

Kato Platres • Sparti Platres Adventure Park

| ACCOMMODATION | |
|---|---|
| Jubilee Hotel | 1 |
| New Helvetia Hotel | 3 |
| Petit Palais | 4 |
| Semiramis Hotel | 5 |
| Troodos Hotel | 2 |

| EATING | |
|---|---|
| Kalidonia Restaurant | 3 |
| Psillo Dendro | 2 |
| Skylight | 5 |
| Troodos Hotel | 1 |
| Village Tavern | 4 |

N

Lefkosia

4

0          1
kilometre

- - - - - European Long Distance Path E4
— — — Cycling path

Omodos                                    Lemesos

good map of the surroundings. Foini is a busy little community, dotted with traces of the past – you'll see *pithoi* wine jars decorously positioned throughout, and there are pretty **medieval bridges** to the west of the village.

To try the local *loukoumi*, ask for the **Pilavakis** family who welcome visitors to their small home factory, which is located in the northern outskirts of Foini. They also run the **Pilavakion Museum** (summer: daily 9am–5pm, winter Mon–Sat 9am–5pm; €1), which is housed in a venerable 400-year-old house (signposted as the "pottery museum", or "Finoi Local Folk Art Museum"), and crammed with artefacts from the village's past. The curator will be happy to talk about the contents at considerable length. If you have got time, it's also worth taking the narrow road north from the top of the village to the **Chantara Waterfalls** and eventually, after a tortuously winding route, to Trooditissa Monastery.

## Trooditissa Monastery

Open (church only) daily 9am–noon & 2–4pm • Free

Just west of Troodos village, off the Platres to Prodromos road, is the **Trooditissa Monastery**, which at 1200m is the highest working monastery in Cyprus. Scenically set amid orchards and pine groves, its buildings, though not spectacularly ancient (they're mainly eighteenth century), are pretty and harmonious, with tiled roofs, triangular dormers and gables, and much use of timber and stone.

The story of how the monastery was founded is even more outlandish than most, and tells of an **icon of the Virgin Mary** floating over from Asia Minor in the tenth century to escape destruction by the iconoclasts, finding its way into a cave and then being discovered thanks to its heavenly glow. The monastery grew up around the icon (hence its full name "Panagia Trooditissa"), which developed a reputation for helping childless women conceive; in the past there was a tradition that any male born from the Virgin's intervention would become a monk. You can visit the **cave** in which the icon was found – it's signposted up a short climb off the main road about 200m east of the turning down to the monastery.

Incidentally, don't be put off by the sign at the entrance to the monastery saying "Entry is not allowed to tourists". During the 1990s there were concerns about the influx of coach parties disturbing the monks who are part of the same austere sect as at Stavrovouni (see page 78). Individual visitors are welcomed with great charm (indeed, even the odd coach tour is granted permission to drop by).

### ARRIVAL AND INFORMATION

### TROODOS VILLAGE AND AROUND

**By bus** The Troodos region is served by buses from Lefkosia (Mon–Fri 5.45am and noon, Sat and Sun 8am and 2pm, returning Mon and Fri 7.30am and 2pm; Sat and Sun 10am and 4pm) and Lemesos (daily 9am, return 3.30pm); both services are to Troodos Square.

**Tourist offices** There is a tourist office on the main square in Pano Platres (4B Olympus Street; ☎ 25421020, ⊚ mytroodos.com) and the Troodos Environmental Information Centre (Troodos Square; ☎ 25420145, ⊚ moa.gov.cy/forest) is also a good source of information and maps.

### ACCOMMODATION

#### TROODOS VILLAGE

**Jubilee Hotel** Troodos Square ☎ 25420107, ⊚ jubilee hotel.com; map p.151. Named after King George V's jubilee in 1935, when the hotel was built, the *Jubilee* is all about location: it's the highest hotel in Cyprus, about 500m from Troodos Square (and therefore clear of the coach-tour crowds), and is close to the ski slopes. Rooms are pretty basic, though all have central heating and en-suite facilities. There's a bar/café, a pool table, and that's about it – most guests are out all day hiking, mountain biking or skiing. €95

★ **Troodos Hotel** Troodos Square ☎ 25420000, ⊚ troodoshotel.com; map p.151. A low modern building with stone walls and green-tiled roof facing the main square, the *Troodos Hotel* has open log fires and rooms with clean minimalist lines. Its terrace overlooks the shops and restaurants of the square and there are great views to the rear. Facilities include a lounge, cafeteria-bar and restaurant. Again, it's mostly aimed at outdoor enthusiasts. €80

**PLATRES**

**New Helvetia Hotel** 6 Helvetia St ☎25421348, ⓦnewhelvetiahotel.com; map p.151. The *New Helvetia* is all about location, with its mountain setting overlooking dense forest. Though the decor is a little dated, everything is clean, staff are friendly and helpful, there's an attractive terrace and, when necessary, a wood fire. Open all year, it's cool in summer and warm in winter. **€75**

**Petit Palais** Pano Platres ☎25421723; map p.151. A balconied chalet-type building slap-bang in the centre of the village. Warm, welcoming and used to catering for families. All rooms have balconies, most with views of the wooded valley below the village. There's also a shaded terrace restaurant (burgers €6, mixed grills €14) where you can watch the world go by. **€65**

**Semiramis Hotel** 55 Spyrou Kyprianou ☎99756796, ⓦsemiramishotelcyprus.com; map p.151. Small, quiet hotel in a quirky, architecturally interesting Edwardian building, renovated in 2006 to provide modern facilities and decor. Agreeable multilevel terrace that is atmospherically lit after dark. **€70**

**EATING**

**TROODOS VILLAGE**

**Troodos Hotel** Troodos Square ☎25420000, ⓦtroodoshotel.com; map p.151. Plain, wood-clad restaurant right on Troodos Square with outdoor terrace front and back. Good range of sandwiches, pasta dishes, pizzas and grilled fish and meat. Most main courses €12; trout and steak more expensive. Barbecue on Sundays. Daily 7am–10pm.

**PLATRES**

**Kalidonia Restaurant** ☎25421019; map p.151. On the main road up through the village, the *Kalidonia* offers the usual Greek dishes of *souvlakia* and *mezédhes*; the presence of numerous Greek Cypriots appears to vouch for its authenticity. Main courses from €12. Daily: 10am–11pm.

★ **Psilo Dendro** 13 Aedonion ☎25813131, ⓦpsilodendro.com; map p.151. Restaurant attached to a trout farm between Platres and Troodos – follow the signs from the bottom end of the Kalidonia Trail. As you'd expect, the charcoal-grilled trout is excellent (around €15), though the rest of the menu is pretty standard. There's a large indoor room as well as an outdoor eating area under the trees, loud with the sound of the water running through the fish tanks. Daily 9am–5pm (closed Nov–Feb).

**Skylight** 524 Arch. Makariou III ☎25422244, ⓦskylight.com.cy; map p.151. On the left as you climb up towards the main square, the *Skylight* offers the usual range of Cypriot and international meat and fish dishes (main courses from €10) in cool but warmly lit indoor surroundings and on a roofed terrace. Its USP, though, is the swimming pool just outside, which customers can use for free. Daily 9am–11pm all year.

★ **Village Tavern** 26 Arch. Makariou III ☎99663772; map p.151. Just west of Pano Platres village centre, this is a traditional tavern offering hearty Greek-Cypriot food, served quickly and with a smile. Mezé recommended, and it sells its own wine. Mains from €10, mezé around €35 per couple. Mon–Sat 9am–6.30pm, Sun 9am–5pm.

# Marathasa

The **MARATHASA** region, lying north and west of Mount Olympos and the Troodos region, is dotted with villages and is relatively unspoilt. As well as its three painted **Byzantine churches** in successive villages along the Marathasa River, it hosts the richest and most famous **monastery** on the island at Kykkos. It is also famed for its cool-weather fruit, particularly cherries and apples, and is particularly attractive in spring when the trees are in full blossom.

## Prodromos

On travelling north into the Marathasa, the first village of any size you reach is **PRODROMOS**. The village was named after John the Baptist (or the "forerunner") and, at 1400m above sea level, is officially the highest village in Cyprus. A former hill resort, the jewel in whose crown was the massive *Berengaria Hotel*, the hotel catered for the glitterati from the 1920s onwards, but has been derelict since the 1980s. These days, Prodromos (the top end of the village at least) is now essentially a cluster of restaurants, a bank and a petrol station gathered around a roundabout, there to service pilgrims on their way to the monastery at Kykkos.

## TROODOS FESTIVALS

Villages in the Troodos Mountains celebrate all the usual religious festivals, plus a few devoted to local produce. Because of the weather up in the mountains, those worth seeing tend to be concentrated into the spring/summer/autumn.

### MAY

**Agros Rose Festival** (mid-May) Displays, activities and demonstrations coinciding with the blossoming of the village's rose bushes. On sale are perfumes, rose water, rose brandy and even rose-based sweets.

**Korakou Herb Festival** Celebration of herbs, whether used in food, medicine, perfume or aromatherapy. Free buses run to Korakou from Germasogeia in Lemesos.

### JUNE

**Sports and Fun Festival** (last weekend of June). Cycling, rock climbing, downhill racing, archery and much more, in Platres. Open to all.

### JULY

**Cyprus Herb Event** (late July). Similar to Korakou Herb Festival but held in Pano Platres.

### AUGUST

**Pano Platres Festival** (mid-Aug). Music, dance, drama, craft and farming exhibitions in and around the village.

**Dormition of the Virgin Mary** (Aug 14–15). This big religious celebration takes place across the republic, but is particularly worth seeing at the big three Troodos monasteries – Kykkos, Machairas and Trooditissa.

### SEPTEMBER

**Raising of the Cross** (Sept 13–14). A particular feature in Omodos and Platanistasa.

**Local Products Festival** Held in Galata to celebrate bread, sweets and other local produce. Not exactly a snappy title, though.

### OCTOBER

**Apple Festival** (mid-Oct) Displays, exhibitions and tastings, all apple-related, held in the villages of Amiantos, Dymes and Kyperounta, accompanied by much music and dancing.

### NOVEMBER

**Kakopetria Festival** Choral festival, but with plenty of other music, singing and dancing.

**Zivania Festival** (early to mid-Nov). Displays on the way in which this fierce firewater is distilled, together with the opportunity to drink some of it. Held in the villages of Alona and Pelendri. Inexperienced drinkers beware.

**4**

# Pedoulas

In the Marathasa Valley north of Prodromos, **PEDOULAS** is an attractive place, whose buildings tumble down the hillside in a series of terraces – a view only slightly marred by a scattering of rusted corrugated-iron roofs. The village, notable mainly for its painted church, was established during the Byzantine period by refugees fleeing Arab coastal raids, though the origin of its name is somewhat in doubt – perhaps it refers to the shoe and sandal makers who once plied their trade here ("pedila" being the word for sandal). Pedoulas packs in all the services you might need. Like many settlements in these mountains, its serpentine lanes are something of a maze – probably the easiest way to get orientated is from the huge white **Church of the Holy Cross** in the centre (not the painted church for which the village is famous). As you explore, look out for the statue of **Archbishop Makarios III** on the main (upper) street, the large monument to **Aristides Charalambous**, a local man who died during the independence struggle, and in particular (you can't miss it – it dominates the skyline above the village) the white 25m-high **Cross of Fithkia**, which stands next to a modern chapel.

## THE PAINTED CHURCHES OF THE TROODOS

In its stock of simple but exquisitely **painted rural churches** the Troodos Mountains is truly blessed. You can come across these little gems across the region, but especially on the north slopes of the range, sometimes in villages, sometimes in remote wooded areas. They are modest in construction, with steeply sloping wooden roofs (to shed snow during the winter) above stout rough stone walls. Inside, they are decorated with wonderful frescoes (and in some cases mosaics) which offer a glimpse of life and beliefs during the almost thousand years of the Byzantine Empire. Ten of these churches are collectively included on **UNESCO's World Heritage List** (below are those churches that are most easily visited from locations covered in the Guide).

Photography is not allowed inside the churches, but most sell guidebooks and/or postcards of the most notable paintings. For in-depth background get hold of *The Painted Churches of Cyprus* by Andreas and Judith A. Stylianou (see page 264), which gives detailed descriptions and illustrations of the wall and ceiling paintings of all the Troodos churches (and many others across the island).

**Agios Nikolaos tis Stegis, Kakopetria** (see page 160)
**Monastery of Agios Ioannis Lampadistis, Kalopanayiotis** (see page 157)
**Panagia Forviotissa (Asinou), Nikitart** (see page 162)
**Panagia, Moutoullas** (see page 157)
**Archangelos Michaelis, Pedoulas** (see below)
**Timios Stavros, Pelendri** (see page 164)

### Archangelos Michaelis Church

Daily 9am–6pm • Free

Pedoulas's **Archangelos Michaelis Church** (accessed down a steep lane from the Church of the Holy Cross) is one of the ten "painted churches of the Troodos Region" that have been declared by UNESCO as being a collective World Heritage Site. Distinctive because of its tiled roof, which on one side sweeps down almost to ground level, the church is easy to date – a dedication over the north door says that it was built by "the most honourable priest Lord Basil, son of Chamades" and painted in 1474. The dedication also seeks forgiveness of sins for Basil, his wife and two daughters – a portrait of them donating the church to the Archangel provides an illustration of the fashions of the time. A further dedication (on the beam across the west wall) reveals that the artist was "Menas from Myrianthousa" (ie the Marathasa Valley). As is usually the case in these churches, the walls are divided into a lower zone populated by a host of individual saints and an upper one illustrating scenes from the Bible, including the Birth of the Virgin, Her Presentation to the Temple, the Annunciation, the Birth of Christ, His Baptism, Betrayal, Crucifixion and so on. The more you know your Bible, the more you'll appreciate the murals, but even the non-religious can't help but be impressed by the vividness of the colours, despite some fading over the centuries.

### Folkloric Museum

Holy Cross Street • Tues–Sun 9.30am–4pm • Free (donations welcome) • ☎ 22952140

Centrally located behind imposing Holy Cross Church is the **Folkloric Museum**, better than many of its ilk. Its low stone and timber house contains exhibits which illustrate the history of Pedoulas, and include the interior furnishings of a typical dwelling, local costume and displays on the work of the villagers: the farmer, the winemaker, the blacksmith, the tanner, the boot-maker and more.

---

**EATING** PEDOULAS

**To Vrysi** 38 Pelopida ☎ 22952240. A small family restaurant on a backstreet near the main road. Home cooking, local wine. Try the wild trout if available, and the home-made cherry-and-brandy pie. Mains from €6. Daily 7am–9.30pm.

★ **Platanos** Vasou Hadjiloannou ☎ 22952518. Next to the Folkloric Museum, the *Platanos* is a traditional *estiadorio*, with a terrace canopied by large plane trees (hence the name). Much frequented by locals, who drink coffee, play *tavli* and eat Cypriot food. A shady place to see local life and watch the world go by. Main courses from €7. Daily 10am–6pm.

# Moutoullas

Some 4km north of Pedoulas stands **MOUTOULLAS**, another hillside village of tiled and corrugated-iron roofs, balconies and terraces. This one is known for its mineral water (sold all over Cyprus), and in the past for producing carved wooden objects, particularly feed troughs, bread boards and threshing sledges. Moutoulla's crowning glory, however, is the church of Panagia tou Moutoulla.

## Panagia tou Moutoulla Church

Winter Mon–Fri 7.30am–3pm, summer Mon–Fri 8am–3pm, Sat & Sun 9am–3pm • Free • ☎ 22952677

**Panagia tou Moutoulla** is the oldest of the painted Troodos churches, with a steeply pitched, tiled roof which covers not only the nave, but also a covered walkway around the building. Not easy to find, the church stands next to the cemetery at the highest (northern) point of the village, up a paved ramp that climbs from the signposted dirt road. As is common in many of the Troodos churches, an inscription and portrait (in this case on the north wall) tells us who stumped up the cash and when – John (son of Moutallas) and of his wife Irene, on the fourth of July in 1280 AD. The wall paintings follow the usual pattern – saints on the bottom half, stories from the Bible above, though the small size of the church means that the latter have been cut to a minimum. It's interesting to note that some things haven't changed for over seven centuries – Joseph, watching the approach of the Magi, is sitting on a donkey saddle of a type which you can still see in use today. Some of the paintings have suffered the ravages of time, others were damaged by British soldiers during a 1950s raid against EOKA fighters.

**4**

# Monastery of Agios Ioannis Lampadistis

Church daily: Sept–Apr 9am–1pm & 3–5pm, May–Aug 9am–1pm & 4–6pm • Free, but donations suggested • ☎ 22953460; Museum daily: Oct–Feb Mon–Sat 10am–3.30pm, March–May Mon–Sat 9.30am–5pm, June–Aug Mon–Sat 9.30am–6pm, Sept Mon–Sat 9.30am–5pm • €1• ☎ 22932414

Below Moutoullas is the village of **KALOPANGIOTIS**, known for its fine old buildings and bridges and its sulphur springs. Located here is the third and best of the Marathasa's ecclesiastical treasures, the UNESCO-listed **Monastery of Agios Ioannis Lampadistis**. The monastery is accessible from the main street via a new "elevator" (a cross between a lift and a funicular railway), inaugurated in 2015, then across a bridge in the valley's floor. Altered over the centuries, the main building consists of the eleventh-century Church of St Herakleidius to the south (which you enter first), the Church of Agios Ioannis Lampadistis in the middle, the common narthex (entrance lobby) to the west, and what is thought to be a Latin chapel to the north, all of it under a massive second timber-and-tile pitched roof. The interior walls of these buildings are a riot of Byzantine art and cover many New Testament stories. The most vivid of the paintings include: the *Triumphal Entry of Christ into Jerusalem* (in the western vault of St Herakleidius); *Christ Carrying the Cross along the Via Crucis* and *The Entombment* (in the northern vault); the series in the east wall of the narthex depicting *Christ Healing the Sick* (the paralytic, the man with the dropsy, the blind man); and the Italian-influenced paintings in the Latin Chapel. There's also an on-site bookshop and a Byzantine Museum.

# Kykkos Monastery and around

Daily: June–Oct 10am–6pm; Nov–May 10am–4pm • €5 • ☎ 22942742

The monastery of **Panagia tou Kykkou**, widely known simply as "**Kykkos**", is the most famous in Cyprus. Located on the far edge of the Troodos area, 15km west of Pedoulas and the Marathasa valley, it's often dismissed because its buildings are relatively modern, but it will tell you more about Greek Cypriots and their religion today than all the more venerable churches of Troodos put together. With its mixture of religious observance and commercial enterprise, the presence of national hero President

## THE ICON OF THE VIRGIN AT KYKKOS

According to tradition, the **Kykkos Monastery** was established in the twelfth century AD by a hermit called Esaias, who lived a life of simple piety in the region's woods. One day the Byzantine governor of Cyprus, Manuel Voutoumites, was hunting in the area and got lost. Coming across Esaias, he asked the way, only to be ignored by the holy man, whose mind was on higher things. As you might expect, the politician took offence at the perceived slight, berating the hermit, or even, according to some versions, giving him a good hiding. Having returned to Lefkosia, Voutoumites contracted a terrible disease and, surmising that this was his punishment for his maltreatment of the holy man, appealed to God to cure him so that he could seek forgiveness. This wish met with divine agreement, but when Voutoumites finally tracked down the hermit and apologized, Esaias set him a task. A famous **icon of the Virgin Mary**, painted by the Apostle Luke while the Virgin was still alive, and lodged in the Imperial Palace at Constantinople, must be brought to Cyprus. The governor and the sage set off for Constantinople on what Voutoumites considered to be a wild goose chase – he could see no way in which the emperor would accede to the request. But the almighty intervened again. The emperor's daughter contracted the same disease that had laid Voutoumites low, and he was forced to agree to the icon's export to Cyprus in order to save her. The icon has been lodged in the monastery ever since.

Makarios's tomb and the nearby EOKA hideouts, it's a must-visit for anybody trying to get a handle on modern Cyprus.

The original monastery was established at the end of the eleventh century by the Byzantine Emperor, though none of the original buildings has survived the numerous fires that have swept through the region. Nothing in the current monastery pre-dates the last fire in 1831, and much of it is later than that, though the famous icon of the Virgin Mary seems to have miraculously survived.

The Kykkos Monastery is the richest on the island and it shows. Its buildings are pristine and immaculately maintained, its murals vivid and bright, its monks numerous. This wealth grew partly because of the pulling power of the icon, and partly because, during Ottoman times, many people chose to donate their money to the church rather than see it whittled away by heavy Ottoman taxes. On entry, through a highly decorated porch, you walk into a handsome courtyard with a museum at the far left and, above the monastery roof, a wooded hillside with a recently built bell tower. Beyond the main courtyard the visitor is free to explore a series of passageways and flights of steps and paved courtyards that can't seem to muster a right angle between them.

### Monastery Museum

Daily: May–Oct 10am–6pm; Nov–April 10am–4pm • €5 • ☎ 22942736, ⓦ kykkos.org.cy

**The Monastery Museum**, up a flight of steps from the main courtyard and unexpectedly huge, is organized into antiquities (pre-Christian artefacts) and documents (on the left as you enter), vessels, vestments and ornaments from the early Christian and Byzantine periods and after in the main room, then icons, frescoes and woodcarving (on the left), and manuscripts, documents and books (on the right). Though of limited lay interest, nobody could fail to be impressed by the comprehensiveness of the collections and the lush complexity of the exhibits.

### The church

The **monastery church** is opulent even by Greek Orthodox standards, and is lined with icons, including the famous one of the Virgin, in its own silver, tortoiseshell and mother-of-pearl protective case that is usually busy being kissed by a line of supplicants. Nearby is a brass arm, the result of a punishment, it is said, meted out by the Virgin to a Turk who had the temerity to light a cigarette from one of the sanctuary lamps. There's also the blade of a swordfish, presented by a sailor who was saved from drowning by the Queen of Heaven. The church and the courtyard outside it often become packed with people at weekends – some attending weddings or christenings, some making pious pilgrimage, others simply having a day out.

### Tomb of Archbishop Makarios III

Above Kykkos Monastery is the **tomb of Archbishop Makarios III**, Cyprus's most famous son and the first president of the Republic (see page 161). As you follow the road that climbs up beyond the monastery, past the bell tower, the Troodos Mountains open up around you. After a couple of kilometres you reach a car park and a huge statue of Makarios welcomes you to the summit of Throni (the "throne" of the Virgin). In his youth Makarios served time as a novice at Kykkos, and this is where he chose to be buried. A paved path loops upwards from the car park, lined with mosaics of numerous saints, then doubles back to the tomb, guarded by a small military post. Twists of paper and pieces of cloth are attached to several bushes ("wish trees") as supplications for help and intervention from the saints. The tomb, just below the summit of the hill, is a simple slab of black marble on a stone plinth, with a picture of the archbishop before it, flanked by cut flowers, the whole protected by a low, arched stone roof. On the actual summit, a few hundred metres above the tomb, a new church was, at the time of writing, in the process of being built.

### EOKA hideouts

As you leave Kykkos Monastery, you'll see a sign about 3km back along the main road that points leftwards to "**EOKA Hideouts** 2km". There's a good road as far as the water bottling plant, but from then on it's a rough track. The hideouts themselves are little more than holes in the ground with, up a steep and rather unstable path, a "headquarters", simply a larger hole, above them. But their proximity to Makarios's tomb and to Kykkos Monastery, where units of the Gordon Highlanders were stationed during anti-EOKA activity in 1956, emphasizes the strong links between the political and military fight for independence and the Orthodox Church.

### Xistarouda picnic site

Some 6km east of Kykkos, on the right of the E912, lies one of the picnic sites at which the Troodos Mountains excel. **Xistarouda** has a roofed barbecue area, numerous picnic tables on a series of stone-faced terraces under tall and shady trees, and toilets. Because it's on the main route to the Kykkos Monastery, it gets very busy, especially at weekends, with families erecting gazebos and portable barbecues and setting themselves up for the afternoon.

# Solea

East of Marathasa, the **SOLEA** region straddles the main road to Lefkosia, ensuring its popularity as a day-trip and weekend destination for the capital's residents. Progressively less hilly the further north and east you travel, the region is mainly popular for its village life, and for its wealth of painted churches. The main village, **Kakopetria**, has enough hotels, restaurants and services to make it a good base from which to explore.

## Kakopetria

**KAKOPETRIA** sits astride the Karyotis River on the main B9 road to Lefkosia, 50km from the capital. The village centre has all the necessary conveniences of modern life, while beyond it is a pretty (and now protected) old town of alleys and tottering houses. One of the larger Troodos communities, it has a soundtrack of whispering or roaring waters, depending on where in the village you are.

The name "Kakopetria" means "bad stones", deriving, it is said, from the numerous large rocks swept down from Olympos in primordial times, which you can still see in the foundations of some of the houses. One such stone ("the Stone of the Couple") had a reputation for bringing good luck to newlyweds: they would walk around its base, climb onto it, and make a wish. That reputation was somewhat dented when the stone shifted, killing a young couple in the process (it has since been underpinned by concrete and stone).

### Agios Nikolaos tis Stegis

Tues–Sat 9am–4pm, Sun 11am–4pm • Donations welcomed • ☎ 22922583

Just a couple of well-signposted kilometres southwest of Kakopetria along the F936 stands another of the region's ten UNESCO World Heritage Site churches, **Agios Nikolaos tis Stegis** (St Nicholas of the Roof). Make sure you visit during opening hours – it's completely fenced off, and you won't get even a glimpse of it from the road. The church building has a rough-and-ready, lopsided look, prompting speculation that the eleventh-century masons who built it weren't quite up to the job. The steep-pitched roof, added to protect the early cross-in-square building from the harsh winter weather, led to the name. The church was once part of a monastery, which had ceased to function by the late nineteenth century, and the rest of the buildings disappeared as the weather and locals scavenging for building materials took their toll. The paintings range from the eleventh to the seventeenth centuries and therefore represent a remarkable history of the development of Byzantine art. The oldest paintings (for example, the *Transfiguration* and the *Raising of Lazaros*, both early eleventh century) may not look as impressive and colourful as later ones, but they are of great historical importance because so few have survived from this period. Note the number of life-size saints in the nave and the narthex, and the larger-than-life-size St Nicholas in the entrance to the diaconicon (the chamber to the south of the apse in which the books and vestments used in the services are kept). Look out, too, for the painting of St Peter on one of the east piers supporting the dome, and in particular for the graffito (in ink) written by Russian monk and early travel writer **Basil Moscovorrossos** in 1735 in which he outlines his recent travels in the region – vandalism, it's true, but interesting vandalism nonetheless.

### ACCOMMODATION
KAKOPETRIA

★ **Linos Inn** 34 Palea Kakopetria ☎ 22923161; ⓦ linosinn.com; map p.148. A labyrinthine complex of old houses in the heart of Kakopetria's old town, the *Linos Inn* was restored with the help of the CTO, and falls under the umbrella of agrotourist accommodation, though it is actually big enough to be considered a hotel. It offers a range of rooms, studios and suites, all with a traditional feel yet modern facilities, some with four-poster beds, some with jacuzzis. Take a look at what's available before committing – the range of facilities varies from room to room. Its atmospheric restaurant offers international and Cypriot food. €40

★ **The Mill Hotel** 8 Mylou ☎ 22922536; map p.148. Across the river and overlooking the centre of Kakopetria, *The Mill Hotel* incorporates bits of an ancient water mill within a large modern building. Its size disguises the fact that the accommodation is quite limited – at thirteen rooms, it's half the size of the *Linos Inn*. There's an on-site restaurant and sauna. Wood and stone rooms are clean and chunkily furnished, en-suites adequate, though balconies have lovely river views. €82

### EATING

**Argentina Tziellari Cyprus Restaurant** 72 Palaias Kakopetrias ☎ 22922522; map p.148. Owned and run by an Argentinian/Cypriot couple, this popular restaurant offers a fusion of each country's cuisine, with mezé, steaks and *asado* (barbecued meats and sausages) specialities. Traditional interior with a small terrace. Main courses from €8. Jan–July & Sept–Dec Fri 7–10pm, Sat 12.30–4pm & 7–10pm, Sun 12.30–4pm; Aug Mon 7–10pm, Tues–Sun 12.30–4pm & 7–10pm.

**Linos Inn** 34 Palea Kakopetria ☎ 22923161, ⓦ linosinn. com; map p.148. Rustic restaurant attached to the hotel of the same name. Deceptively large (it seats a hundred indoors and another seventy on the terrace), it has a widespread reputation for both Cypriot (at the associated *Mesostrato Tavern*) and international cuisine. Hugely popular, so you must reserve a table. It's not cheap – mains cost from around €13, although there are cheaper options such as sandwiches, pasta and burgers. Restaurant daily 10am–midnight; tavern Fri & Sat 10am–10pm, Sun 10am–1pm.

★ **Mylos Restaurant** 8 Mylou ☎ 22922536, ⓦ cymill hotel.com; map p.148. With open fires in winter, great views across the village from the balcony and a traditional feel, this hotel restaurant is a firm favourite. The menu is extensive and wide-ranging, with Cypriot specialities and

## MAKARIOS – PRIEST, POLITICIAN AND PRESIDENT

Born into poverty on August 13, 1913, in the village of Panagia in eastern Pafos district, **Makarios** (then known as Michaelis Mouskos) became a novice at Kykkos Monastery at the age of 13, before continuing his education at the Pancyprian Gymnasium in Lefkosia. After graduation, he went on to study in Greece and Turkey (hence his rather unexpected facility with the Turkish language), and finally Boston in the US.

In 1948 he became Bishop of Kition (Larnaka), and two years later **Archbishop of Cyprus**. It was at this time that he took the clerical name of **Makarios III**. He was now not only the religious leader of the Greek-Cypriot community in Cyprus, but their de facto political leader. One of his first actions was to carry out a plebiscite on union with Greece ("**enosis**") – 96 percent of Greek Cypriots voted in favour. It goes without saying that the Turkish-Cypriot community were against enosis from the start, fearing for their position if the island became a province of Greece.

As the 1950s progressed, the so-called "**Cyprus Problem**" became increasingly high profile, with EOKA (the right-wing organization led by George Grivas) carrying out a guerrilla war from April 1, 1955 within Cyprus, and the Greek government pushing hard in the UN for an end to British rule and unification with Greece. Makarios, strongly identified with this opposition to British rule, was eventually exiled to the Seychelles in March 1956. After a year, he was released with the proviso that he did not return to Cyprus. He settled instead in Athens, from which base he travelled the world, drumming up support for his cause, particularly among non-aligned countries and the Soviet Union.

In 1959, amid continued violence across the island, Makarios accepted an offer of **independence** from the British, but without enosis. This provoked predictable disgust and fury among EOKA, and accusations that he had sold out, even that he'd been blackmailed into acceptance by the British Secret Service. No such scenario is needed, though, to explain his actions. Faced with a choice of leading a distant province of Greece or a proudly independent country, it really was a no-brainer. Makarios was duly elected **president** of the **new Republic of Cyprus** on 14 December.

As the new decade dawned, Makarios realized he was presiding over an unenviable situation. Turkish Cypriots, supported by Turkey, would accept no move towards enosis, while the Greek-Cypriot right, supported by Greece, would accept nothing less. The imposition of a virtually unworkable constitution didn't help either. He also had little control over the hawkish General Grivas who was intent on military action against Turkish-Cypriot armed enclaves, which were becoming almost a state within a state. Finally, when a right-wing junta seized power in Greece in 1967, the left-leaning Makarios came out openly against enosis, explaining that it would be beneficial to have two Greek voices at the UN rather than one. He began to try to build bridges with the Turkish Cypriots.

Between 1970 and 1974 there were numerous attempts by the junta and the CIA to assassinate Makarios (Nixon allegedly called him "Castro in a cassock"). Finally, on July 15, 1974, the National Guard and EOKA B rose up in rebellion, deposed Makarios (who fled abroad), and set up a right-wing administration. This provoked the catastrophic response of a full-scale **Turkish invasion** of the north, and partition. When the dust had settled, Makarios returned from abroad to resume as president of a now divided island. He died suddenly of a heart attack in August 1977.

Makarios undoubtedly made many mistakes during his period of office, though it seems unlikely anyone could have managed the ticking time bomb that he inherited. Certainly, blame for the 1974 Turkish invasion could not be laid at his door. His pragmatism, his undoubted political skills and above all his commitment to the people of Cyprus have ensured that he is held in widespread and lasting affection in the modern republic, something which cannot be said of his militaristic rival George Grivas. On the other hand, unsurprisingly, he was not popular among Turkish Cypriots. While his body was lying in state in Agios Ioannis Cathedral in Lefkosia, the capital suffered an unprecedented August downpour. Greek Cypriots quoted an old Greek saying – "God cries when a good man dies". Turkish Cypriots came back with one of their own – "When an evil man dies, the heavens try to wash away his crimes".

4

international food, though it's best known for its trout. Mains from €15. Advance booking of at least four days is required. Mon–Fri 12.30–10.45pm, Sat & Sun noon–3.30pm & 7.30–10.45pm. Closed for the month running up to Christmas.
**Zoumos Restaurant** ☎ 22923004, ⬚ bit.ly/Zoumos.;

map p.148 The *Zoumos*, in the centre of the village, might not look like much, but the food is fresh and well cooked, the wine is local and plentiful, and the service is good. Sit out on the rear balcony if you can – it overlooks the Karkotis River, which flows through the village. Main courses around €10. Daily 11am–10pm.

## Panagia tis Asinou Church

Mon– Sat 9am– 4pm, Sun & hols 11am– 4pm • Free • ☎ 22852922; if closed, contact Father Kyriakos Christofi on ☎ 99830329

Compared with the other painted Troodos churches, **Panagia tis Asinou** (you'll sometimes see it called Panagia Forviotissa) is rather isolated, but it's worth the extra effort because of the beauty of its setting. At the top of a slope in the northeastern Troodos foothills, surrounded by wooded hills, it lies about 4km southwest of the village of Nikitari, off the main B9 Lefkosia to Troodos road.

A great clutch of the church's wall paintings (about two-thirds of the original decoration) dates from when it was built in 1105. Note in particular the picture over the nave's south entrance of the church's founder Ischyrius handing over a model of the church to Christ via the Virgin Mary. It is noticeable that the model lacks a narthex (western entrance hall), which indicates that this was a later addition. The paintings – saints on the bottom half of the walls, scenes from the scriptures on the top half and ceilings – are amazing in their rich use of colour. There's also a touch of macabre humour – look out for the murals depicting the fate of the renegade monk and nun, the thief, the slanderer, the dishonest miller, the woman who refuses breast milk to infants, the one who diverts water from another's land, all of whom are pictured, in almost cartoon form, in chains being tormented by serpents. The whole church is a reminder of one of the purposes of religious art: to provide a biblical education to a largely illiterate population, and to warn them of the wages of sin.

Panagia tis Asinou is one of the best of a brilliant bunch of Troodos decorated churches. But it's not just the church that draws visitors. Just before you get to it the **Asinou Picnic Site** offers the opportunity of alfresco dining, with shaded seating and a small playground. Directly across the road from the church is a well-set-up **restaurant** *Estiatorio Stavros tis Asinou*, and the start of a hiking trail to Agios Theodoros is just beyond. Lunch, a walk, a visit to the church – it makes for a splendid day out.

| **EATING** | **ASINOU** |
|---|---|
| **Estiatorio Stavros tis Asinou** Asinou ☎ 99352500. A great spot for some alfresco Greek-Cypriot food served in a | lovely wooded area. There's also a more formal restaurant indoors. €10–15. Daily 11am–5pm. |

# Pitsilia

Mountainous **PITSILIA** is one of the remotest parts of the Troodos Massif. Spreading eastwards from the main B9/B8 Lefkosia to Lemesos road that loops through the mountains, the region is sparsely forested, with large areas of hazel and almond trees and grapevines. Little visited or known, it has a character and charm all its own, and is beginning to make attempts to attract tourists, with a small but growing number of places to stay and eat. Like other parts of the Troodos Mountains, Pitsilia is associated with the struggle for independence and enosis, memorials to EOKA fighters are encountered in many villages, and the Greek (as opposed to the Cypriot flag) is still much in evidence.

## Agros

**AGROS**, the main village of Pitsilia, is an attractive spot, its red-roofed houses (many of which are on stilts) cupped by the mountains at the head of the **Agros valley**. It's known across the island for its **rose petal products**, sold at several shops along the serpentine main street (try Venus Rose at 12 Triantafillou ☎ 25521893, ⊛ venus-rose. com). During the first half of May the area's dedication to roses is celebrated in the **Rose Festival**. You'll also find several tavernas raucously popular with locals and shops selling the village's **traditional sweets** (try Nikis at 5 Triantafillou, ☎ 25521400, ⊛ nikisweets.com.cy). Just across from the main square are two churches – one, **Panagia Eleousa**, built at the beginning of the twentieth century, the other, **Timon Sprodromos**, slightly older and encased in modern stone walls and a wooden roof.

---

**THE LONELIEST RAILWAY STATION**

As you travel north on the B9 from the heart of the Troodos Mountains towards Lefkosia, a string of villages presents itself, sitting on the slopes of sharp-crested hills, their houses deep in trees or perched on ridges – particularly **GALATA** with its numerous old balconied houses and several old churches, all worthy of note but of interest mainly to enthusiasts. A further 6km brings you to **EVRYCHOU**, a sizeable village just off the main road, unique on the island for having a railway station. Evrychou Station is in fact one of the few remains of the **Cyprus Government Railway (CGR)**, built by the British authorities to link the port of Famagusta to Lefkosia and the copper mines of the northwest. The 2ft 6in gauge line was not an economic success, and was progressively wound down between 1932 and 1951. Odd buildings and bits of equipment remain, mostly in Northern Cyprus, but the only substantial survival of the CGR is the station at Evrychou. Clearly signposted from Evrychou village and accessible via a new road, Evrychou Station is a railway enthusiast's dream. Now a museum (daily: summer 9.30am–5pm; winter 9.30am–4pm; free; ☎ 22933010) dedicated to the CGR, it contains a wealth of photographs, models and memorabilia, and outside, a length of track and a couple of pieces of rolling stock.

---

Agros feels remote, yet is eminently accessible, being thirty minutes from Lemesos along the E110 and twenty minutes from Troodos east of the B9. And the surprising presence of a very large hotel, sited high on the hill with extensive views both south across the village and north across the mountains, makes it the perfect base for exploring the region.

### Frangoulides Museum

Aug daily 10am–noon & 5–7pm or by appointment • Free • ☎ 25521333

Situated in the undercroft of Panagia Eleousa is the **Frangoulides Museum**, dedicated to the work of a well-known artist, Solonas Frangoulidis, who lived in Agros for two years in the 1930s. Lots of his pictures adorn the church above, and the museum, once the local cinema, has rough drafts and sketches and additional finished work by the artist.

## Agridia

About halfway between Agros and the B9 lies **AGRIDIA**. The village is little-visited but really well worth a stop. It's a typical mountain settlement, untidy yet appealing, with a large modern church, a small ecclesiastical museum and a preserved olive mill. However, the things which really makes it worth a visit are its **picnic site** and **viewpoint**, both well signposted in the area. The picnic site, on the right as you enter the village from the south, climbs up a steep-sided little gorge, and has wooden tables, little picket fences, a stream with a wooden bridge, a playground, water fountains, a toilet, and even a small modern amphitheatre. Above the site, a steep but driveable concrete road leads to the little **Chapel of Profitis Ilias**. This pretty church, built in 1998, is usually open, and the modern icons within and mosaics around the door positively glow. Sharing the hilltop (1090m) with the church is a **viewing point** with a (free) telescope through which you can see the tops of Mounts Olympus, Madari and Papoutsa, the villages of Agridia, Dymes, Chandria and Kyperounda, and on a good day Akrotiri Bay.

## Spilia

East of the main B9 route through the Troodos region, on the F929, is **SPILIA**, a small village dominated by a large war memorial consisting of four full-sized statues of **EOKA fighters**. Oddly, the statues – showing men brandishing automatic weapons – seem to be dedicated to some hapless bombmakers who blew themselves up, rather than commemorating one of EOKA's greatest victories over the British which happened in the hills nearby. In December 1955 the cream of EOKA fighters, including its leader

General Grivas (see page 165) and its second-in-command Grigoris Afxentiou (see page 167), were caught in a pincer movement by British troops advancing from the north and the south on their mountain HQ. As the Cypriots retreated towards the summit, a fog descended, under cover of which they avoided the closing trap by marching quickly to the west. When the British troops reached the mountain top, each group believed the other to be EOKA paramilitaries, and in the fog and confusion opened fire, suffering a number of casualties (Grivas claimed around fifty, the British admitted to three). Spilia today is a sleepy and peaceful village, with a small hotel and a single restaurant, *Marjay Inn* (see page 165) – a relaxing base, perhaps, for walking in the surrounding hills.

## Pelendri

About 7km along the E806 southwest of Agros lies the village of **PELENDRI**, which in **Timios Stavros** has not only one of the best of the region's **painted churches**, but also one of the most accessible. The only other thing likely to grab your attention as you enter Pelendri is the inevitable **monument** to local heroes, consisting of full-sized sculptures of local men – Sotiris Tsaggaris who died in 1957 during the EOKA struggles, and Nikos Karasamani who died in 1974, presumably during the Turkish invasion. Neither is well served by their representations: the former looks distinctly nerdy, the latter has a flamboyance that the sculptor surely didn't intend.

### Timos Stavros Church

As you enter the village, the **Timos Stavros Church** is clearly visible a few metres left off the main road – it stands between a reservoir and gardens and vineyards. Although usually locked, the key-holder lives in the cottage next to the church, and he's likely to rush out to open up as soon as he sees that there are visitors.

When built in the twelfth century, it was a single-aisled domed church, but all that remains of the original building is the apse, the west wall and some of the colonnades. An unknown catastrophe destroyed the rest of it in the early fourteenth century. It is, though, the wealth of wall paintings that is the glory of the church, especially some rare **twelfth-century paintings** that were discovered in the early 1970s, having previously been over-painted. These are in the apse, and consist of a "deisis" (Christ with the Virgin Mary on one side and St John the Baptist on the other) and portraits of six prelates with an altar and chalice between them. Inscribed above the apse window is a note from one of the artists, "the sinful and humble servant Monmachos", and the date "6686" (1178 AD according to the modern calendar). Thought to be the work of four artists, the paintings are pretty crude and have sustained some damage, but their survival at all is a miracle. The excellent guidebook to the church by Dr Nektarios Zarras (€10) gives a detailed account of all the paintings (140 are listed).

## Monuments of Heroes

Tues–Fri 9.30am–1.30pm, Sun 10.30–1pm • Free

Signposted in Greek just after Aminatos on the Pelendri road – look out for the words "EOKA 1955–1959" – the activities of EOKA in this part of Pitsilia are comprehensively commemorated in the **Monuments of Heroes** (full title "The Monument of the Liberation Struggle of EOKA"), a heavily symbolic clutch of linked memorials in a woodland setting. Entrance is through the "Porticos", which places the fight against the British against the backdrop of Greek history, and includes portraits of Makarios and Grivas, together with marble rolls of honour. This is followed with the **Room of the Fighters**, which has artwork and a big-screen film presentation, and the **108 Steps of Freedom**, each representing a fallen EOKA fighter. The steps lead up to a large paved hilltop capped with the **Monument of Freedom** and the little **Chapel of Panagia Eleftherotria**, representing the large part played by the Greek Orthodox Church in the struggle. Though the memorial might make uncomfortable viewing for British visitors, and it may seem a little florid to modern taste, nobody would argue today about Cyprus's right to fight for independence, nor their courage in doing so. The memorials to the dead, the huge mural in the Room of the Fighters, and the serenity of the hilltop setting, are very affecting whatever the nationality or political orientation of the visitor.

## ACCOMMODATION                                                    PITSILIA

**Marjay Inn** 2841 Spilia ☎22922208, ⊛marjay.com; map p.148. Small, comfortable hotel owned and run by a married couple in the centre of Spilia, near the EOKA memorial. There are six rooms, each different, with one on two levels, all en suite and (important in winter and on cool spring or autumn nights)

centrally heated. The food is good too – the *Marjay* started as a restaurant and expanded into accommodation. **€66**

★ **Rodon Hotel** 4860 Agros ☎25521201, ⊛rodonhotel.com; map p.148. An unexpectedly vast hotel at the top of Agros, about 1km from the centre, the *Rodon* comprises

---

### CYPRUS'S OLD WARHORSE: GENERAL GRIVAS

Together with Archbishop Makarios III, **General George Grivas** (whose nom de guerre was "Digenis") is the person most associated with the "Cyprus Problem" between the 1950s and 1970s. Born in Trikomo (now Iskele) in northeast Cyprus on May 23, 1898, he, like Makarios, studied at the Pancyprian Gymnasium in Lefkosia. When he graduated he fled to Athens, apparently to avoid an arranged marriage, and it was here that his military education began. Having joined the **Greek army** as an officer, he served in the catastrophic campaign in Asia Minor which ended with the expulsion of the Greeks from Turkey in 1922. Despite this setback, Grivas gradually moved up the ranks, making captain by 1925 and major by 1935.

During the German occupation, Grivas was involved in what can only be described as the murky deeds of the far-right organization "Khe" – the Greek letter usually represented as an "X" – which he founded and led. It was said to be far more concerned with attacking Greek communist guerrillas than the occupying forces. Indeed, there have been accusations of collaboration with the Nazis – at many times during his career, Grivas's political hatred of the left seems to have outranked his patriotic Hellenistic pride.

After the war Grivas played a significant part in the Greek Civil War (1946–49), fighting for the government against the communists. He stood unsuccessfully in the Greek elections of 1951, one of several times when his attempts to turn to politics failed, perhaps owing to a distinct lack of the common touch. Following his dream of enosis (unification of Cyprus with Greece), he returned to his homeland. He met Makarios, and the two of them, together with other supporters, formed **EOKA**, the Ethniki Organosis Kyprion Agoniston or "National Organization of Cypriot Fighters", which pledged to the overthrow of British rule in Cyprus and union with Greece. If there was any disagreement between the two men at this stage, it was that Grivas favoured full-scale armed rebellion, while Makarios wanted to limit action to the destruction of property.

In November 1954, Grivas landed in a caïque loaded with arms and explosives on the west coast of Cyprus, near Pafos, and on April 1 the start of the **armed struggle** was announced by explosions all over the island. Grivas led the rebellion from a series of hideouts, in Lemesos, and later, the Troodos Mountains, attracting a price of £10,000 on his head. After Makarios was exiled in March 1956, Grivas led both the military and the political struggle from a hideout back in Lemesos. Finally, when the archbishop accepted a British offer of independence without enosis in 1959, Grivas decamped in disgust to Greece – his exile was part of the final agreement. In Greece he was deliriously greeted as a hero, and promoted to general.

The deteriorating situation in the new Republic of Cyprus attracted Grivas back to the island in **1964**, where he led Greek hardliners in the National Guard and a division sent by Greece. Attacks on leftists and on Turkish Cypriots became increasingly outrageous, until the massacre of 27 Turkish Cypriots, many unarmed civilians, in Kofinou and Agios Theodoros caused worldwide revulsion. The Greek division, and Grivas, were withdrawn. The general returned once more to Cyprus in 1969, and re-established EOKA, now called EOKA B, whose aim this time, in addition to achieving enosis and suppressing Turkish-Cypriot opposition to it, was to combat the Greek-Cypriot left. Virtual civil war broke out between **EOKA B** and the left, while Turkish Cypriots formed heavily armed enclaves. Finally, in January 1974 and still in hiding in Lemesos, Grivas died of a heart attack, thus avoiding the disastrous Turkish invasion that his actions had done so much to precipitate.

123 double rooms as well as studios, family suites, executive suites, and one presidential and one honeymoon suite, all in a village of under a thousand people. All rooms have full facilities, central heating and a/c, and access to veranda or balcony, while public areas include a gym, saunas, swimming pools (one for adults, one for children) and tennis courts. Plenty to do then, and also ideal for exploring Pitsilia. **€95**

# Machairas

East of Pitsilia, the **MACHAIRAS** region feels even more remote, a fact that is reflected in its total lack of hotels – even villages are few and far between. It is, however, a favourite day-trip destination for Lefkosians, and does have a number of attractions, including a monastery very much associated with EOKA, and a museum village, while its mountains and forests have more of an alpine feel than anywhere else in the Troodos range.

Macharias is signposted along the E902 from Strovolos on the outskirts of Lefkosia, from where an invigorating forest drive via Politiko and Pera brings you to its monastery via the extensive picnic grounds at Mandra Kambiou.

## Panayia tou Machaira Monastery

Nov–April Mon–Fri 8.30am–5pm, Sat & Sun 6.30am–5pm, May–Oct Mon–Fri 8.30am–6pm, Sat & Sun 6.30am–6pm • Free • ☎ 22359334

Lying in the forests southeast of the village of Lazanias, and commanding wonderful views of the surrounding mountains, **Panagia tou Machaira Monastery**, like Kykkos, is very well maintained and exudes a sense of prosperous decorum. The story of its foundation follows the usual formula – a miraculous icon, one of seventy painted by the Apostle Luke, was brought here from Asia Minor by an unknown ascetic during the iconoclastic period. Hidden in a cave, it was discovered by two hermits who'd arrived in the area from Palestine. To reach it, they needed to hack away the undergrowth, and a divine hand kindly provided the sword or "machairi". Ignatios founded the church in 1172 AD, which later expanded into a monastery. Fire destroyed the buildings in 1530 and 1892, but the icon, encased in silver, survived.

The monastery also played a role in the fight for Cypriot independence. EOKA's second-in-command, **Gregoris Afxentiou**, hid here, disguised as a monk, and eventually met a martyr's death at the hands of the British (see page 167) – the cave in which he was trapped lies about 1km below the monastery, and is marked with a flag and commemorative tablet. There's a small **museum** dedicated to his short life (it's to the right of the ramp that leads down to the monastery terrace from the road), and on the terrace itself stands a gigantic statue of the man and the bird (an eagle) from which he derived his nom de guerre. Dashing and heroic though Afxentiou certainly was, he is perhaps ill-served by the huge and flamboyant statue erected in his honour on the monastery terrace.

## Fikardou

The carefully conserved mountain village of **FIKARDOU** lies northwest of Panagia tou Machaira Monastery, and can be approached from there via Lazanias or from the west via Gourri. Either way, you enter the village on the E916. Though somewhat "preserved-in-aspic", it provides an excellent idea of what a Cypriot mountain village of the eighteenth or nineteenth century would have looked like.

The first building you encounter when you finally climb up into the village is the **Church of the Apostles St Peter and St Paul** on the left. A pretty little stone and clay-tile-roofed building, it is set into the hillside below the road. In front of it lie graves which must have some of the best views in Cyprus. Across the road, on the hillside and with equally fine views, stands a memorial to four local men who died during the 1974 invasion. Immediately ahead is the village's coffee house and restaurant *Yiannakos*, tucked into a steep hairpin bend. Two-storey

## GRIGORIS AFXENTIOU: THE GENTLEMAN SOLDIER

While the names of Archbishop Makarios III and George Grivas loom large in the fight for Cypriot independence, within the Greek-Cypriot community **Grigoris Afxentiou** is probably the man held in the greatest honour and affection. Even his notional enemies in the British Army held him in high regard – one British officer is reported as saying to Afxentiou's father, "I want to congratulate you on having such a splendid son". Grigoris Afxentiou is a clear-cut, old-fashioned popular idol whose early death at the age of 29 in a heroic last stand against the occupying forces is the stuff of legend.

Afxentiou was born on February 22, 1928 in the village of Lysi (now in the north and called Akdogan) and became committed to Cypriot independence and enosis from an early age. He joined the Greek army as a volunteer in 1949, and reached the rank of second lieutenant. When he heard that **EOKA** were recruiting, he joined up. His intelligence and potential were immediately recognized by Grivas, who took him under his wing and personally saw to his training in guerrilla warfare. Afxentiou was entrusted with blowing up the Cyprus Broadcasting station in Lefkosia during the night of simultaneous explosions that kicked off the fight against British rule on April 1, 1955. Having been recognized, he went on the run with a group of fighters in the Kyrenia mountains where he became Grivas's second-in-command.

For the next two years Afxentiou moved around the Troodos Mountains, training guerrillas and attacking British positions and convoys. He became one of the British Army's "most wanted", with a price of £5000 on his head. He narrowly evaded capture at the Battle of Spilia (see page 163), and again at Zoopigi a year later. His time ran out in March, 1957, when he was tracked down to the **Machairas Monastery**, where, with the help of the abbot, Irineos, he had been living disguised as a priest. Below the monastery in an underground hideout, he ordered the four men who were with him to surrender, but decided to fight to the death himself. Unable to capture him without serious losses, the British soldiers finally poured petrol into the hideout, ignited it, and followed up with explosives. Afxentiou had finally been killed.

His widespread popularity among Greek Cypriots since his death can be explained by a number of factors. Compared to Grivas, he was a careful strategist, planning actions to minimize loss of life. He was even understanding towards informers, refusing to execute one man on the grounds that his wife had recently had a baby. His commitment to the cause of freedom and union with Greece was simple and straightforward, without the ferocious hatred of the left that consumed Grivas. And finally, by dying when he did, his reputation was never compromised by the sorts of fudges that post-independence politics invariably required.

**4**

traditional houses are stacked up the hillside, each with straw-flecked mud walls and capped by mellow red/brown tile roofs. (The ground floor was used for making and storing wine and other farm produce, while the first floor housed the people.) The organic nature of the village speaks for itself – the buildings seem to grow out of the hillside.

Two of Fikardou's old houses have been opened to the public – the **House of Katsiniorou**, named after its last owner and owing its plan and features to the sixteenth century, has been turned into a rural **museum** (daily mid-April to Oct 9.30am–5pm, Nov to mid-April 8.30am–4pm; €2.50; ☏22634731). Furnishings, tools and utensils from the past are on show, together with photographs, plans, drawings and texts illustrating the process of preservation. The **House of Achilleas Dimitri** (daily: April–Oct 9am–5pm; Nov–March 8am–4pm; €2.50) has been furnished as a weaver's workshop and also acts as a guest house.

### EATING                                                               FIKARDOU

★ **Yiannakos** Fikardou ☏22633311. Stone-built two-storey building with roof terrace overlooking the village. The decor is also traditional (as you'd expect, the restaurant specializes in Greek-Cypriot cuisine, with mezé at around €15/person, and main courses like *stifado* and *koupepia* at €10. It's wise to book – if it's full, as it often is, there is no alternative in the village. Mon–Thurs 9.30am–7pm, Fri 9.30am–2am, Sat & Sun 9am–9pm.

# Lefkosia (South Nicosia)

LEFKOSIA ROOFTOPS

**5**

# Lefkosia (South Nicosia)

The city of Lefkosia (still widely known as south Nicosia by locals) is by far the largest settlement on Cyprus, though by international standards it is still pretty small, with a total population, in the part controlled by the Government, of 246,400. Until 1974 Nicosia was the capital of the unified island; now the southern half, Lefkosia, forms the capital of the republic while the northern half, known as Lefkoşa (see page 196), is the capital of the Turkish-occupied, self-styled TRNC – when the Berlin Wall fell, Nicosia became the last divided capital in the world.

A political and financial centre, not just for the republic and the Eastern Mediterranean, but for the whole of the Middle East, Lefkosia is less dependent on tourism than anywhere else on the island. Yet there is still a great deal to see and do in the southern, republic-controlled half of the city, as well as in the Turkish-controlled northern half (see page 196). Within the forbidding **Venetian Walls** of the old city are the excellent **Cyprus Museum** and the **Leventis City Museum**, as well as the **Shacolas Tower** which offers unparalleled views to the north. You'll also find some of Cyprus's best restaurants and its most sophisticated shopping. There's also many interesting sights in the newer parts of the city and beyond – especially the **Police and Coinage museums** and the **Cyprus Handicrafts Centre** in the suburbs, and the ancient city of **Tamassos**, a short drive to the south.

While the capital remains divided, the opening of **checkpoints** between the republic and the occupied north (the most accessible being **Ledra Street**) enables you to sample two cultures in a single day. The division is still "in your face", particularly in the derelict areas of the Buffer Zone, and a journey between south and north offers you a real insight into the Cyprus Problem.

### Brief history

Thought to have originated in a small town (Ledra) established by Lefkonas, son of Ptolemy I in 300 BC, Nicosia grew significantly under the Byzantines. Its inland position, protected by the island's two main mountain ranges, kept it safe from attack from the sea, and well placed for the political and religious administration of the country. The Lusignans fortified the city and it was under them that Nicosia experienced a "**golden age**" during which numerous palaces, churches and monasteries were built. This has left an impressive, if patchy, legacy of Gothic Crusader remains. Lusignan prosperity, however, ended with a series of **attacks** – by the **Genoese** in 1372 and the **Mamelukes** in 1426, and finally, after the **Venetians** had hastily thrown up the massive walls you see today, by the Ottomans who sacked the city in 1570. There then followed a period of three centuries when, although the population were better off financially than they had been under the Venetians, the city settled into a kind of quiet decrepitude, interspersed with bouts of extreme violence – in 1764 Turkish riots against rule from Constantinople led to the death of a particularly hated governor; in 1821 the authorities indulged in mass executions of leading Greek citizens to discourage support for the Greek War of Independence.

In 1870 the **British** took over the island and continued with Lefkosia as capital. It was during their watch that the city finally burst out of the Venetian battlements, especially after World War II when colonial administrative offices moved outside the walls. During the fight for independence the city's **Pancyprian Gymnasium** was a hotbed of EOKA involvement and sympathy among teachers and students. While the fight against the British intensified, intercommunal violence built up to such an extent that, even before the Turkish invasion of 1974, de facto **partition** was well under way, with the north of the city becoming mainly Turkish, the south mainly Greek. In 1963 the British bowed to the inevitable and made the

# Highlights

**❶ Laiki Geitonia** The old city's quaintest area, all narrow alleys and overhanging old buildings, is perfect for window-shopping and aimless wandering. See page 173

**❷ Venetian walls** These beautifully preserved walls may have failed to stop the Ottoman advance but are well worth exploring today, not least for their impressive views. See page 173

**❸ Cyprus Postal and Philatelic Museum** Hidden down a side-street, this diminutive museum is a little gem, whether or not you're into stamps. See page 173

**❹ Shacolas Tower** Though it no longer offers the frisson of peering over the Green Line into

forbidden territory, the Shacolas Tower still offers fabulous views of both sides of the city. See page 176

**❺ Cyprus Museum** By far the best museum on the island, this is a world-class attraction whose rather fusty presentation in no way detracts from its spectacular contents. See page 179

**❻ Archbishop Makarios III Cultural Centre** Part of the sprawling Archbishop's Palace, the Byzantine Museum and Art Gallery is rich in colour and atmosphere. See page 182

**❼ Royal Tombs, Tamassos** Wonderfully atmospheric burial chambers dating from the time of Homer. See page 191

**HIGHLIGHTS ARE MARKED ON THE MAPS ON PAGES 172 AND 178**

### THE LEFKOSIA MASTER PLAN

Ever since the Turkish invasion of 1974 and the partition of the island, peace plans have foundered on the opposition of one or other of the communities. However, behind the scenes, a number of initiatives have gone ahead, involving north–south cooperation. The best example of this is the **Lefkosia Master Plan**. Beginning with a distinctly pragmatic agreement for the construction of a common sewerage system in 1978, it quickly flowered into a more general agreement on a development plan for Lefkosia. In 1981 a "bi-communal multidisciplinary team" was set up to further the plan. Efforts were concentrated on the old city contained within the walls. Neighbourhoods on both sides of the Green Line were designated for restoration, shopping and artisan zones identified and traffic improved. A start was even made on rescuing the many imposing buildings stuck in the Buffer Zone, which have been decaying for nearly forty years. Though the Lefkosia Master Plan has concentrated on a clutch of practical initiatives, it implies that reunification is, in the long term, the only sensible solution for both the city and the island.

division official – a line (in green pencil, hence the name) was drawn on the map of the city, dividing it into Greek and Turkish areas. The 1974 invasion simply confirmed the division and caused an influx of refugees from the north. As a result, there was extensive further development of the area outside the walls to house displaced Greek Cypriots.

Over the years various practical initiatives have tried to cope with the fact that the city is split in half. In 1979 a joint sewerage plan was drawn up, followed in the 1980s by the **Lefkosia Master Plan**, promoted by both the UN and the EU, under which planners from both sides have started to cooperate on such things as renovating buildings along the Green Line and pedestrianizing streets in the city centre. Much of this is based on the assumption of the eventual **reunification** of the city; and the opening of the Ledra Street crossing in 2008 has gone at least some way towards achieving this.

# Ledra Street and around

Within the walls, South Lefkosia's main tourist area lies between **Ledra Street** (also known as Lidras), which runs north from the D'Avila Bastion to the checkpoint into

**HIGHLIGHT**

7 Royal Tombs, Tamassos

**LEFKOSIA (SOUTH NICOSIA) DISTRICT**

Buffer zone

Limit of full northern control

Limit of full southern control

0    10
kilometres

north Cyprus (see page 177), and **Aischylou**, which parallels it to the east. Much of this area is pedestrianized, and contains the touristy **Laiki Geitonia** traditional quarter, the **Leventis Museum**, the **Shacolas Tower**, within which is the Ledra Museum and Observatory, the **Bank of Cyprus Cultural Foundation and Museum**, and the **Faneromeni Church**. Just to the east of Aischylou is the **Cyprus Postal and Philatelic Museum**.

## Laiki Geitonia

**Laiki Geitonia** is the focus of tourist Lefkosia. Pedestrianized during the 1980s as part of the Lefkosia Master Plan, this area to the east of Lidras Street and north of the D'Avila Bastion is a mishmash of alleys and lanes, where the tables, chairs and parasols of bars and restaurants have colonized the spaces between the buildings and racks of tourist souvenirs spill out of shops onto the pavements. This creates a veritable rabbit warren where, thankfully, given how hot Lefkosia can become, the sun barely penetrates.

### Leventis Museum

15–17 Ippokratous • Tues–Sun 10am–4.30pm • Free • ☎ 22661475, ⓦ leventismuseum.org.cy

The **Leventis Museum** (one of the many projects of a foundation named after Cypriot philanthropist Anastasios Leventis) provides a brilliantly organized introduction to the history of the republic's capital. Housed in a stunning Neoclassical mansion in the heart of Laiki Geitonia, it starts with three rooms which give a broad sweep of nine thousand years of world history and an outline of the city's development from prehistoric times to the present day. This is followed by a chronological series of galleries covering the Byzantine years, the Frankish period and so on up to the British period, and is interspersed with well-presented, varied exhibits dealing with particular subjects, from Gothic architecture and maps to jewellery and pottery). If you're pushed for time, check out the museum's "mini guide" which promises to introduce you to all the important stuff in less than an hour. Photography is allowed (ask for a permit), but you mustn't use a flash.

## Cyprus Postal and Philatelic Museum

Agiou Savva • Mon–Fri 9am–3pm, Sat 9am–1pm • Free • ☎ 22304711

Housed in an unassuming little building tucked away down a side street to the east of Aischylou, the **Cyprus Postal and Philatelic Museum** is surprisingly interesting, even for those who find the attractions of philately inexplicable. Although it covers postal services on the island since Venetian times, the bulk of the exhibits refer to the period of British rule, when a modern mail system was established, and the period since independence. Brits will find some of the exhibits (the Victorian post boxes, for example) very familiar. But then there are the stamps themselves, which, as well as showing what Cyprus considered worth commemorating (the great Pafos mosaics, for example, or the indigenous mouflon), are also miniature works of art in their own

---

**ORIENTATION AND THE CITY'S VENETIAN WALLS**

The principal aid to orientation in Lefkosia is the **Venetian walls** – an aerial view of the city shows their absolutely regular star or snowflake shape punctuated by eleven bastions. What it doesn't show is the eyesore of the Buffer Zone – dilapidated buildings with boarded-up windows, barricaded streets, weeds growing everywhere – that separates South Lefkosia from the Turkish-occupied north. Taking the whole of the walled city, the Green Line cuts it into two roughly equal parts. As a general rule of thumb, most of the old city lies within the walls, which remain relatively complete, and most of the modern sprawl created by the city's expansion during British rule and then after independence lies outside. The scale of the city is such that you don't need to worry about getting around – it's easily walkable, apart from a couple of suburban sights.

5

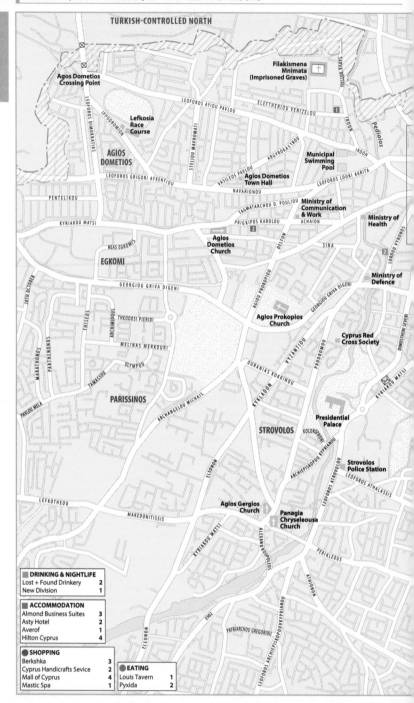

**TURKISH-CONTROLLED NORTH**

Agos Dometios Crossing Point

Filakismena Mnimata (Imprisoned Graves)

LEOFOROS AYIOU PAVLOU

ELEFTHERIOU VENIZELOU

Lefkosia Race Course

**AGIOS DOMETIOS**

Municipal Swimming Pool

LEOFOROS GRIGORI AFXENTIOU

Agios Dometios Town Hall

NAVARIONOU

LEOFOROS LOUKI AKRITA

PENTELIKOU

TAGMATARCHOU D. POULIOU

Ministry of Communication & Work

PRIGKIPOS KAROLOU

ACHAION

Ministry of Health

KYRIAKOU MATSI

NEAS EGKOMIS

Agios Dometios Church

SINA

**EGKOMI**

Ministry of Defence

GEORGIOU GRIVA DIGENI

THEODOSI PIERIDI

Agios Prokopios Church

MELINAS MERKOURI

Cyprus Red Cross Society

OLYMPOU

OURANIAS KOKKINOU

**PARISSINOS**

ARCHANGELOU MICHAIL

Presidential Palace

**STROVOLOS**

KOLOKOTRONI

Strovolos Police Station

LEOFOROS ATHALASSIS

LEFKOTHEOU

MAKEDONITISSIS

Agios Gergios Church

Panagia Chryseleousa Church

PERIKLEOUS

PATRIARCHOU GREGORIOU

**DRINKING & NIGHTLIFE**
Lost + Found Drinkery ... 2
New Division ... 1

**ACCOMMODATION**
Almond Business Suites ... 3
Asty Hotel ... 2
Averof ... 1
Hilton Cyprus ... 4

**SHOPPING**
Berkshka ... 3
Cyprus Handicrafts Sevice ... 2
Mall of Cyprus ... 4
Mastic Spa ... 1

**EATING**
Louis Tavern ... 1
Pyxida ... 2

# LEFKOSIA (SOUTH NICOSIA)

5

| | Buffer zone |
|---|---|
| | Limit of full northern control |
| | Limit of full southern control |

LEFKOŞA
(NORTH NICOSIA)

LEFKOSIA
(SOUTH NICOSIA)
OLD TOWN

PALLOVRIOTISSA

POULIOU - KAPOTA

MARKOU DRAKOU

B16

B16

LORDOU VYRONOS

VASILEOS PAVLOU

ATHANASIOU DIAKOU

TRIKOMOU

AGIOU ILARIONOS

SPYROU CHRISTODOULOU

HOMER AVE

OMIROU

LEOFOROS SALAMINOS

EVAGOROU

FOR DETAIL SEE "LEFKOSIA CENTRE" MAP

LEOFOROS LARNAKOS

IKON POLYTECHNIOU

THEMISTOKLI DERVI

DIGENI AKRITA

LEOFOROS ARCHEPSKOPOU MAKARIOU III

LEOFOROS KALIPOLEOS

**Tamassos
Tours**

NATIONAL
FOREST PARK
OF THE
PEDAGOGICAL
INSTITUTE

JOHN KENNEDY

25TH MARTIOU

RIGA FEREOU

GLAFKOU

ESPERIDON

ARSINOIS

LEOFOROS ACROPOLIS

ARMENIAS

IFIGENIAS

IFIGENIAS

STASINOU

SANS SOUCI

**Museum of the History
of Cypriot Coinage**

**Cyprus International
Conference Centre**

**AGLANTZIA**

KEFALLINIAS

LEOFOROS AGLANTZIAS

KENTAVROU

AKADIMIAS

ARMENIAS

STASINOU

THERMOPYLON

KEFALLINIAS

AXIOU

KYRENIAS

LEOFOROS

**Cyprus
Broadcasting
Corporation**

**Cyprus Police Museum**

LEOFOROS RIK

LEOFOROS ATHALASSIS

OMIROU

LORDOU VYRONOS

ALEXANDROU PAPADIAMANTI

LEOFOROS IOSIF CHR. CHATZIIOSIF

ANDREA AVRAAMIDI

**Cyprus
Handicraft
Centre**

LEOFOROS LEMESOU

ATHALASSA
NATIONAL
FOREST PARK

N

| 0 | 500 |
|---|---|

metres

**5**

right. Stamps bearing portraits of President Makarios inevitably loom large and are used as a case study to illustrate "How a stamp is born". The curator (Ploutis Loizou) is happy to talk on all things stamp-related for as long as you've got, and you can of course buy packets of stamps and commemorative issues.

## Shacolas Tower Observatory

171–179 Lidras • Daily Apr–Oct 10am–6pm, May–Sept 10am–7pm, Nov–March 10am–5pm • €2.50

The eleven-storey **Shacolas Tower**, owned by multi-millionaire philanthropist Nicos Shacolas, is the tallest building in Lefkosia. Once used to peer over the Buffer Zone into northern Cyprus, this function has now been rendered somewhat redundant by the easy access to the occupied part of the city. However, the views from the tower's eleventh-floor **observatory** are still remarkable, and detailed information boards tell you precisely what you're gazing down on (you can borrow binoculars if you want a closer look). It's the best place from which to view the gigantic and inflammatory TRNC flag painted on the hillside to the north of the city. A fine aerial photo of the city provides orientation and there's an introductory video about the history of the city. The first five floors are occupied by Debenhams, while on the sixth floor is the *Venue Cafeteria*, a good place to have a coffee while continuing to enjoy the views. Note that you can't reach the observatory via the department store – a separate entrance can be found down the side street to the right.

## Bank of Cyprus Cultural Foundation

86–90 Faneromenis Street • Daily 10am–7pm • Free • ☎ 22128157, ⊕ boccf.org

The **Bank of Cyprus Cultural Foundation** is more interesting than it sounds. Just off Lidras, to the east, it contains two museums – a **Museum of Coinage**, on the ground floor, and the **George and Nefeli Giabra Pierides Collection** on the mezzanine. The former is an elegantly mounted collection of Cypriot coins; the latter, equally well displayed, covers pottery, ceramics and sculpture from 2500 BC to the sixteenth century AD. Don't miss the hi-tech "digital archeological explorer" in the Pierdes collection where you can place an artefact on a rubber membrane and an explanation pops up on a screen.

## Faneromeni Square

**Faneromeni Square**, which is worth a little wander around, lies between Lidras and Aischylou, and was the centre of pre-1974 Lefkosia. It has several buildings of passing interest. **Faneromeni Church** (Apr–Oct Mon–Sat 6.30am–1pm & 4–8pm, Nov–March Mon–Sat 3–6.30pm, Sun 6am–noon; free), the largest in Lefkosia, has no great pretensions to architectural or historic importance, but is notable for the marble mausoleum on its eastern side which contains the remains of the four clerics executed by the Ottoman authorities in 1821. The **Faneromeni School**, whose Neoclassical façade faces the square, was established by Archbishop Makarios I in 1852, and was the first all-girls school in Cyprus. Today it's a mixed secondary school.

## Ledra Street crossing

Open since April 2008, the **Ledra Street crossing** provides pedestrian access to the north Cypriot part of the city (and indeed of the island) with the minimum of fuss. There are no formalities on the part of the republic's officials, except that you might be searched for contraband on your return. On the northern side (all of 20m beyond the southern office) you need to queue at the row of kiosks, fill in a visa form (which you keep, and have stamped as you come back across), and off you go. In the past

**5**

**VISITING THE NORTH FROM SOUTH LEFKOSIA**

Three of the **Green Line crossing points** are in Lefkosia: two pedestrian-only ones at the Ledra Palace and Ledra Street, and one for vehicles and pedestrians at Agios Dometios. This means that Lefkosia is the best place from which visitors can get a taste of northern Cyprus while being based in the south. Red tape is minimal – if you're on foot, all you need is your passport. If you're concerned that having a TRNC stamp in your passport might cause you grief on any future visit to Greece or Cyprus, ask that a separate slip of paper be stamped rather than the passport itself. You can then use this slip for any subsequent forays into the north. The most convenient place to cross on foot into north Lefkosia is the **Ledra Street crossing** from where the whole of the northern part of Lefkosia can be explored on foot.

Though getting into the north by car is a little more complicated, formalities are still minimal – you'll need your passport, plus proof that you have motor insurance which is valid in the north. Some car rental companies will arrange this for you when you pick up your rental car; otherwise, you can get insurance at the border. But it still only takes a matter of minutes. The Agios Dometios crossing point is west of the city centre. It's not well signposted (this is common on both sides of the Green Line) – when driving west along Leoforos Agiou Pavlou, when the road bears sharply to the left (immediately after Lefkosia Racecourse), look out for the crossing on the right. From the Agios Dometios crossing it's no more than half an hour's drive to Girne (Kyrenia), Cyprus's most picturesque town, and to its spectacular mountain backdrop.

there was considerable propagandist posturing at the crossing, but now it's all much friendlier. For example, on the southern side of the crossing a comprehensive display of photographs focuses on joint north–south ventures, such as police cooperation and the clearing of land mines. It's all a far cry from the UN-manned barrier, boarded-up buildings, barbed wire and no-photography signs that used to be here.

# Pafos Gate and around

A short walk west of Lidras, the area around the **Pafos Gate**, where the Green Line and the Venetian walls intersect, has a clutch of minor attractions, both inside and just outside the walls. The **Holy Cross Catholic Church**, the **Maronite Church** and the **Kasteliotissa Hall**, together with the **Cyprus Classic Motor Cycle Museum**, are concentrated in an area which epitomizes the depressing effects of partition – barbed wire, armed guards and no-photography signs. Just outside the walls in this uninspiring corner of the city lies one of its greatest glories – the **Cyprus Museum**, at the edge of a **Municipal Park** which also contains the **House of Representatives** and the **Municipal Theatre**. On the Pafos Gate roundabout look out for the statue of **Markos Drakos**, a hero of the War of Independence.

## Holy Cross Roman Catholic Church

Pafou • Free • ☎ 22662132, 🖾 holy-cross-nicosia.com

Not of any great interest in itself, but something of a curiosity because of its location, the **Holy Cross Roman Catholic Church** is a few metres inside the Pafos Gate, has a façade in South Lefkosia, a body lying in the Buffer Zone, and a rear end that sticks out into the Turkish-controlled north. By agreement, as long as the back door in the north is kept sealed, the church is allowed to function.

## Maronite Church (Cathedral Church of Our Lady of Graces)

Plateia Panagias Hariton

A hundred metres south of the Holy Cross Church stands another reminder of Cyprus's religious diversity, the **Maronite Church**. The Maronites are descendants of a

5

**ACCOMMODATION**
| | |
|---|---|
| Castelli Hotel | 2 |
| Centrum Hotel | 4 |
| Classic Hotel | 1 |
| Sky Hotel | 3 |

**EATING**
| | |
|---|---|
| Aigaio | 1 |
| Casa Vieja | 5 |
| Derlicious | 8 |
| Domus | 4 |
| Fanous | 7 |
| Il Forno | 6 |
| Old Power House Restaurant | 2 |
| Zanettos | 3 |

**HIGHLIGHTS**
1. Laiki Geitonia
2. Venetian Walls
3. Cyprus Postal and Philatelic Museum
4. Shacolas Tower
5. Cyprus Museum
6. Archbishop Makarios III Cultural Centre

**DRINKING & NIGHTLIFE**
| | |
|---|---|
| Brewfellas | 3 |
| Beer Bar | 1 |
| Enallax | 2 |
| Klubd | 4 |
| Versus | 4 |

Buffer zone
Limit of full northern control
Limit of full southern control

**SHOPPING**
| | |
|---|---|
| All Records | 3 |
| Discount Store | 7 |
| Central Municipal Market | 2 |
| Chrysaliniotissa Multicraft Centre | 6 |
| Flexi | 8 |
| Gatapou | 9 |
| Krama | 4 |
| Leventis Museum Shop | 5 |
| Moufflon Bookshop | 1 |
| Ochi Square | 8 |

**LEFKOSIA CENTRE**

N

0 — 100 metres

Christian sect that originated in Syria and was probably brought to Cyprus between the seventh and thirteenth centuries. Having kept their separate identity for more than a millennium and a half, they have tried to stay neutral in the struggle between the Orthodox and Muslim communities on the island. The vast majority of Maronites live in the republic.

## Kasteliotissa Medieval Hall

Agiou Marona • Open during events only – details from the Tourist Information Office or online • ☎ 22800970, ⓦ cyprusevents.net/venues/kasteliotissa-hall/.

Across the road from the Maronite Church, the Gothic **Kasteliotissa Medieval Hall** was originally part of a Lusignan Palace dating from the thirteenth/fourteenth centuries. You can only admire it from the outside unless a concert or some other cultural event is going on inside.

## Cyprus Classic Motorcycle Museum

44 Granikou • Hours can sometimes vary, but are normally: summer Mon–Fri 9am–5pm, Sat & Sun 10am–6pm; winter daily 10am–5pm • Donations appreciated • ☎ 70009000, ⓦ cyprusmotormuseum.com.cy

Established and run by motorcycle-nut Andreas Nicolaou, the **Cyprus Classic Motorcycle Museum** is a true labour of love. Housing over 150 bikes from World War I onwards, its old-school marques are full of romance – Norton, BSA, Harley Davidson, Triumph, Motor Guzzi, Royal Enfield. Cypriot exhibits include a police bike used in President Makarios's motorcade, an EOKA bike used to transport guns and ammunition, and a World War II military bike. This is a real hands-on museum, with not just a gift shop but also an area selling spare parts and leathers.

## Cyprus Museum

1 Mouseiou • Tues–Fri 8am–6pm, Sat 8am–5pm, Sun 10am–1pm. English-language tours: Tues & Fri 10am & noon, Wed 4pm (with an extra evening tour first Wed of the month at 5.30pm) • Entry €4.50; English-language tours free • ☎ 22303112, ⓦ tinyurl.com/cyprusmuseum

Outside the walls and the Pafos Gate, at the top of Mouseiou and to the left of the Municipal Gardens, is the **Cyprus Museum**, the single most important attraction in Lefkosia. Here you'll find a trove of archeological treasures representing the many cultures which have inhabited the island. It's all slightly old-fashioned and the collection is beginning to outgrow the current building – a new, purpose-built museum building has long been promised, but, courtesy of the world financial crisis, has still not arrived.

The first few rooms take you through objects from earliest (Neolithic) times to the arrival of the Romans. As well as local **pottery** you can see Mycenaean, Phoenician and Greek designs, a reflection of Cyprus's trading position between Europe and the Middle East. Highlights from rooms IV to VI include the hundreds of clay figurines and statues from the Sanctuary at Agia Irini, Egyptian and Assyrian finds, and some stunning **Greek and Roman marbles** and bronzes. Room XI, not to be missed, has the rich pickings from the **Royal Tombs of Salamis**, including an impressive, ivory-decorated bed, two thrones, a large bronze cauldron on a tripod and much else. Also from Salamis, in Room XIII, are the sculptures which came from the gymnasium, together with photographs of the excavations from pre-1974 – Salamis is now in north Cyprus (see page 238). An absolute must-see is the semicircle of seventh- and sixth-century BC terracotta figures found at Agios Irini in northwest Cyprus. Over two thousand figures portraying warriors, war-chariots, demon-servants and snakes, from life-size down to 10cm or so, are collected in a crescent-shaped display case which reproduces the positions, gathered round an altar, in which they were

**5**

discovered – tallest at the rear, smallest at the front. Opposite the display is a screen playing an excellent video that traces the long relationship between Cyprus and the Swedish archeologists who carried out most of the excavations on the island, led by Einer Gjerstad. Look out, too, for the superb display and slide show about the Paphos mosaics. A brief summary can't do justice to the richness and variety of the exhibits on show so it's best to take your time and focus on a couple of areas.

# East Lefkosia

The eastern side of Lefkosia has a number of sights, from the Ottoman-era **Omeriye Mosque** and baths to the magnificent **Hadjigeorgakis Kornesios Mansion**. Further east are several attractions key to Greek-Cypriot identity, concentrated on the **Archbishop's Palace**. Continuing east, you come to the imposing Venetian walls and bastions that incorporate some fairly workaday buildings including the post office, public library and the Town Hall, before you reach the florid **Liberty Monument** at the Caraffa Bastion. The areas fringing the walls contain a mixture of public gardens, playing fields, and the best car park (between the D'Avila and Constanza bastions) for access to the city centre. Just outside the Constanza Bastion is the estimable **State Collection of Contemporary Art**.

## Hammam Omeriye

8 Platia Tillirias • Daily, hours vary between 10am and 8.30pm, with some single sex and some mixed sessions • From €55 • ☏ 22460006, ⓦ hamamomerye.com

Originally part of the same fourteenth-century Augustinian church as the mosque across the square, the **Hammam Omeriye** (Turkish Baths) was fully renovated in 2002–2004 as part of the communal Lefkosia Master Plan. It is an interesting building (with characteristic dome), and the Hammam is a fully functioning steam bath with a variety of options from a basic steam (€30/person) to packages such as the "Yavas Yavas" which includes steam, facial, body scrub, massage, wine and snacks and takes over two hours (€230 for two people). What's on offer, and prices, can change, so check the website.

## Omeriye Mosque

Platia Tillirias • Entry outside of prayer times (no shoes or shorts, shoulders should be covered and, as a sign of respect, women might also wear headscarves) • Donations welcomed

The **Omeriye Mosque** started life as the fourteenth-century church of St Mary, an origin that is clear from the Gothic lines of its barn-like main building. It was largely destroyed during the Ottoman invasion of 1570, and rebuilt the following year as a mosque (based on the belief that the Muslim prophet Omer, who came to Cyprus in the seventh century, was buried here). It is used today by Muslim immigrants and visitors from the Middle East (disagreements between some of them led to a violent and widely reported clash here in 2009). You can, with permission and if you've got a head for heights, climb the minaret for views across the city, though they're not quite as good as from the Shacolas Tower (see page 176).

## Municipal Arts Centre

19 Palias Ilektikis • Tues–Sat 10am–9pm • Free • ☏ 22797400, ⓦ nimac.org.cy

The **Municipal Arts Centre**, located since 1994 in the old power house of the Electricity Authority and partly financed by the Pierides Foundation, stands beyond an extensive archeological dig north of Platia Tillirias along Peiraios. The centre puts on a range of exhibitions of modern and contemporary art (check the website for details).

Although the centre is sometimes closed while a new exhibition is being prepared, one installation always available for viewing is "Excess", which consists of what looks like a battered steel Portakabin suspended from the building high above the street, sitting on a polished stainless-steel plinth covered in numbers. The windowed container was used by UN troops as an office or command centre; the numbers refer to the huge number of United Nations Security Council resolutions that have been passed, to little avail, concerning Cyprus. The whole thing is a comment – rather obscure to the uninformed passer-by – on recent Cypriot history. In addition to its exhibitions, the Municipal Arts Centre is also worth visiting for its extremely beguiling ambience. It has a superb restaurant – the *Old Power House Restaurant* (see page 189) – and an on-site shop (same hours as the centre).

## Hadjigeorgakis Kornesios Mansion

20 Patriarchou Grigoriou • Tues–Fri 8.30am–3.30pm, Sat 9.30am–4.30pm • €2.50 • ☎ 22305316

The **Hadjigeorgakis Kornesios Mansion**, a short walk east along Patrarchou Grigoriou from Platias Tillirias, is a wonderful old house, once the property of a famous eighteenth-century "dragoman" or representative of the Greek-Cypriot community in its dealings with the Ottomans. Although billed as the "Ethnographical Museum", its actual contents are really not of much interest, and it shouldn't be confused with the Ethnographic Museum (see page 182). But the airy architecture, the shady arches and courtyard, the covered stairway, the huge rooms with flagstone floors, and in particular the large sitting room with big rug, low-cushioned seating on three sides and central hookah, give a feeling of how the Ottoman elite and their Greek administrators lived.

## Archbishop's Palace

Five minutes' walk north of the Hadjigeorgakis Kornesios Mansion stands a rather grand complex of buildings centred on the **Archbishop's Palace**, official residence and offices of the Archbishop, and closed to visitors. Built in the early 1960s to celebrate independence, and rebuilt in the 1980s following virtual destruction during the 1974 Nikos Samson coup, it exudes a sense of spaciousness that is missing in much of the rest of the city. Until 2008 a gargantuan **statue** of Archbishop Makarios III stood before the palace, but it was moved (perhaps as a result of negative comments about its artistic merit, or as an attempt to signal a willingness to consider reconciliation) and now overlooks the car park at Makarios's tomb (see page 159). The two busts which remain in front of the palace are those of archbishops Kyprianos and Sopronios – the former was executed, together with over four hundred prominent Greek Cypriots, by the Turks in 1821; the latter was in office when the British took over the island, and was the first to articulate the demand for enosis (union) with Greece.

---

### THE GREAT DRAGOMAN

Hadjigeorgakis Kornesios was the **Great Dragoman of Cyprus** from 1779 until 1804. Although the word "dragoman" simply means "interpreter or guide", the Great Dragoman wielded considerable political clout, being the main link between Greek Orthodox subjects and Ottoman authorities. One of the principal responsibilities was the collection of taxes. By creaming off his own cut, being personally tax-exempt and amassing large estates, Kornesios became the richest man on the island. But his comeuppance arrived in 1804 when a revolt against the authorities drove him and his family to seek asylum in Constantinople. From there, he organized troops to put the rebellion down. When he returned to the island, further political skulduggery led to his downfall. He was called back to Constantinople, found guilty of embezzlement and maladministration, and beheaded.

5

## The Archbishop Makarios III Cultural Centre

Plateia Archiepiskopou Kyprianou • Mon–Fri 7.30am–4.30pm, Sat 9am–1pm • €4 • ☎ 22430008

In the northwest wing of the palace is the **Archbishop Makarios III Cultural Centre**, which, apart from a library and a church music school, houses the impressive **Byzantine Museum and Art Gallery** (museum: Mon–Fri 9am–4pm, Sat 9am–1pm; art gallery: Mon–Fri 9am–1pm, sometimes 2pm). This contains the largest collection of icons in Cyprus (the second largest in the world), and includes, in a separate annexe, the famous **Kanakaria Mosaics**, infamously stolen from the church of Panagia Kanakaria in north Cyprus in the late 1970s (see page 246). Vividly coloured, if a little rough in the execution, the occasional sense of distorted perspective is explained by the fact that originally they were mounted on the curved apse of the church, whereas here they are mounted flat. Elsewhere in the museum are 150 icons and numerous frescoes from all over Cyprus and beyond.

### Agios Ioannis Cathedral

Plateia Archiepiskopou Kyprianou • Mon–Fri 9am–noon & 2–4pm, Sat 8am–noon • Free

Within the Archbishop's Palace precinct is the church of **Agios Ioannis**, which doubles as the city's cathedral. In its scale and simplicity it seems to put to shame the extravagant architecture of the palace itself. Built in 1662 on the site of a previous Lusignan Benedictine abbey, it wasn't actually promoted to cathedral status until 1720. The interior is as splendid as its exterior is modest, boasting an original set of frescoes (including one from St Barnabas's tomb in Salamis), a carved and gold-leaf-adorned iconostasis and four large icons, all dating from the eighteenth century. The cathedral contains the throne on which the archbishop is crowned, together with seating for the president and the Greek ambassador to be used on state occasions.

## Ethnographic Museum

Plateia Archiepiskopou Kyprianou • Tues–Fri 9.30am–4pm, Sat 9am–1pm • €2.50 • ☎ 22432578

Once called the Cyprus Folk Art Museum (and still named as such on the sign outside), the **Ethnographic Museum** is housed in a mellow galleried and colonnaded two-storey structure. Built as a Benedictine monastery in the fourteenth century, it became the Archbishop's Palace, and, when the new palace was built, was donated to the Society of Cypriot Studies for use as a museum. Displays include a wide range of Cypriot folk art and decoration from the nineteenth and early twentieth centuries – carved wood and leatherwork, metalwork, lace, tapestry and embroidery, basketry, woven fabrics, pottery and regional costume, and rustic art. Outside the museum are some giant *pithoi* (earthenware jars), a millstone and a two-wheeled wagon.

## National Struggle Museum

Agiou Ioannou • Mon–Fri 8am–2.30pm • Free • ☎ 22305878

In a newish building next to the Ethnographic Museum is the **National Struggle Museum**, dedicated to those who fought for independence from the British during the period 1955 to 1959, and to highlighting the brutality of the oppressors. As such it can make for an uncomfortable half-hour for the UK visitor. Items on display include photographs of British soldiers searching old women and schoolchildren, the personal belongings of EOKA fighters (including leader Grivas), weaponry, details of torture methods used by the British authorities, full-sized mock-ups of a guerrilla hideout and a prison cell (containing a fighter awaiting execution), plus the gallows used to execute nine men in Lefkosia's central prison in 1956 (see page 185). English labelling is patchy, but this really doesn't matter – the museum's displays rely on visual impact to get their message across. Outside is a Hillman car which once belonged to a police officer, and which was used to ferry Grivas around during the struggle for independence.

**5**

## Pancyprian Gymnasium

Agiou Ioannou • ☎ 22466014

Across the road from the National Struggle Museum stands the imposing edifice of the **Pancyprian Gymnasium**, a secondary school which has had a huge influence on Cypriot history. Established in 1812 by Archbishop Kyprianos, it has educated generations of prominent Cypriots – both Grivas and Makarios attended (at different times), and other illustrious alumni include former presidents Tassos Papadopoulos and Grafkos Clerides. English author Lawrence Durrell taught here in the 1950s, when the school was beginning to earn a reputation as a hotbed of EOKA membership. It is still a functioning secondary school, with no entry for casual visitors.

## Pancyprian Gymnasium Museum

On the corner of Agios Ioannou and Thisseos streets • Mon, Tues, Thurs & Fri 9am–3.30pm, Wed 9am–5pm, Sat 9am–1pm • Free • ☎ 22466014

Close to the city centre, the **Pancyprian Gymnasium Museum** (don't try to get to it through the school, the entrance is around the corner) is one of Lefkosia's hidden gems. Its beautifully displayed collections, the result of donations by staff, pupils, parents and friends, cover not only the history of the school, the lives of its students and education in general, but also science, natural history, archeology, coins, weapons, maps (including the large and famous one created by a young Lord Kitchener) and the national struggle for independence. Though this fusing of educational and national narrative might seem a little odd, it is totally successful – it uses the history of Cyprus's most famous school as a key to unlock the more general history of the island as a whole. It deserves to be far more visited than it is.

## Famagusta Gate

Athina Avenue • Oct-Apr Mon–Fri 9am–1pm & 4–7pm, May–Sept Mon–Fri 10am–1pm & 5–8pm, depending on what's on • Free • ☎ 22797660

Northeast of the group of buildings around the Archbishop's Palace, next to the Caraffa Bastion, stands the squat and solid **Famagusta Gate**, the best preserved of Lefkosia's Venetian gates. Constructed by Guilio Savorgnano in 1567 and an approximate copy of one in Iraklion on Crete, it has now, after a long period of neglect, been tidied up, and is used as a venue for concerts and as an exhibition space. The building consists of an inner and outer gate, joined by a long passageway or tunnel with, about halfway along, a cupola to admit natural light. During the long Ottoman occupation which immediately followed its construction only Muslims were allowed through the gate on horseback – everybody else had to walk – and the gates were locked on Fridays.

## Liberty Monument

Dominating the Podocataro Bastion is the **Liberty Monument**, erected in 1973 to commemorate the release of EOKA prisoners in 1959 in preparation for independence. A female statue representing Liberty stands above two EOKA fighters hauling on chains to open the prison gates below, out of which stream figures representing Cypriot fighters, civilians and clergy. The triumphalism of the statue was rather overtaken by the events of the year following its construction, and it's now considered a bit of an embarrassment by many Greek Cypriots.

## Bayraktar Camii

On the Constanza Bastion stands the **Bayraktar Camii** – "the Mosque of the Standard Bearer" – which throws light on two separate eras in the capital's history. The mosque was built where a soldier bearing the Ottoman colours was killed by defenders (and subsequently buried), having clambered up onto the bastion during the 1570 siege. The mosque and tomb figured in the intercommunal violence that followed independence in 1960 – bombs in 1962 and 1963 damaged the building. The assumption was that these were EOKA atrocities, but it has since been established that they were carried out by Turkish-Cypriot agents provocateurs. The mosque precincts are now kept locked, to prevent any further trouble.

## State Gallery of Contemporary Art

Leoforos Stasinou and Kritis • Mon–Fri 10am–4.45pm, Sat 10am–12.45pm • Free • ☎ 22458228

Next to the Constanza Bastion, but outside the walls, stands the **State Gallery of Contemporary Art**. Its interestingly convoluted Neoclassical building houses a collection of paintings and sculptures by twentieth-century Cypriot artists. There are also one or two modern art pieces in the grounds.

# The suburbs

Most of the things that are worth seeing in the capital are inside or just outside its Venetian walls, and within walking distance of each other. However, the **city suburbs** also merit a visit – the area of Strovolos, for example, wasn't established until 1986, yet is now almost as big as Lemesos. Dotted around these recently developed outskirts are a number of attractions worth visiting, but realistically you'll need a car or taxi to get around.

## Filakismena Mnimata (The Imprisoned Graves)

Intersection of Korytsas and Norman • Mon–Fri 8am–4pm, Sat & Sun 8am–1pm • Free • ☎ 22406000

West of central Lefkosia stands the city's grim Central Prison, somewhere most visitors to Cyprus (and indeed Cypriots) would wish to avoid. However, within its confines are the **Filakismena Mnimata** or "Imprisoned Graves" – those wishing to visit them should ask for directions at the main gate. In a small patch of land, next to what had been cells and gallows, are buried thirteen Greek-Cypriot fighters – nine (all aged between 19 and 24) hanged by the British between May 1956 and March 1957, and four who died during or shortly after fire fights with the British Army. The latter includes Gregoris Afxentiou, Grivas's second-in-command (see page 167). In order to prevent the funerals of these men, widely considered by Greek Cypriots to be martyrs, to become the focus of demonstrations and riots, their bodies were hurriedly buried in secret in the depths of the prison. Since independence, the "Imprisoned Graves" have become a place of pilgrimage for Greek Cypriots, particularly the young.

## Museum of the History of Cypriot Coinage

80 Kennedy Avenue • Daily 10am–7pm • Free • ☎ 22714100

Though widely known, the **Museum of the History of Cypriot Coinage** is in fact rarely visited. A display put together to celebrate Cyprus's adoption of the euro, it is lodged in the basement of the Central Bank of Cyprus. There's ample parking, and if you announce yourself at the main entrance, you'll be given a temporary badge by security staff and asked to wait until they're able to track down somebody to show you around. The emphasis is on modern coinage so it'll help if you're something of a numismatist – those more interested in ancient coins would be better off visiting the Coin Museum in the Bank of Cyprus Cultural Foundation (see page 176). Collector's issues can be bought via the bank's online shop.

**5**

## Cyprus Police Museum

Evangelou Floraki • Mon–Fri 9am–1pm • Free • ☎ 22808793, ⊕ police.gov.cy

Just east of, and visible from, the main road (Leoforos Lemesou) into Lefkosia from the motorway is the **Cyprus Police Museum**. One of those small specialist museums that can be an absolute delight, the museum is housed in a clean white building with appropriate blue trim which sits inside the main police HQ. You approach from Evangelou Floraki, a small street which runs parallel to the main road – if you can't find the way in, ask at the main gate and they'll give you directions. When you get to the entrance, just ring the bell. The museum was founded by the British in 1933 as the "Criminal Museum", and was seen as the Cypriot equivalent of the Metropolitan Police's famous "Black Museum". After independence, it moved around, eventually settling in its current building in 2004. It includes all the sort of stuff you'd expect, from badges, truncheons, helmets, guns, riot shields and uniforms up to motorcycles, Black Marias and armoured cars, and some that you wouldn't – for example, a room full of musical instruments. If you're lucky, the curator – a serving officer and very knowledgeable – will show you around.

## Cyprus Handicraft Centre

186 Athalassa Avenue • Mon, Tue, Thu & Fri 8am–2pm, 4.30–7pm, Wed 8am–2pm, Sat 8.30–1pm • Free • ☎ 22305024 • Bus #16; free parking

Well signposted to the west of Leoforos Lemesou (the main road south towards the A1 motorway) is the **Cyprus Handicraft Centre**, consisting of a range of workshops turning out craft items using traditional methods. Established by the Ministry of Commerce, Industry and Tourism with the support of the UN Refugee Agency, it represents a determined attempt to revive traditional folk art. In a low-key modern building laid out around a shady central garden, craftspeople can be seen hard at work producing clothes, leatherwork, woodwork, basketry, metalwork, pottery, tapestry and embroidery. You can chat to the workers, buy quality-assured items without fear of being ripped off, and feel that you are supporting a worthwhile enterprise. This is the flagship of other such schemes across the island (for example in Larnaka, Lemesos and Pafos), and you'll find plenty of information on Cypriot crafts, such as the traditional pottery of Fini, or Lefkara lace.

## Athalassa National Forest Park

Visitor Centre Mon–Fri 7.30am–3.30pm • Free • ☎ 22805527

Some 2.5km due east of the Cyprus Handicraft Centre and the Police Museum, and again well signposted from Leoforos Lemesou, **Athalassa National Forest Park** represents an invaluable open space only 2km from the city centre. There are two picnic areas, footpaths, bicycle tracks, a children's playground, a kiosk and ample free parking. There's also an Environmental Information Centre, a bird observation point overlooking the Athalassa Dam and a botanical garden. A smaller park-within-the-park, **Agios Georgios**, with its pretty lake and footpath which is lit at night, is particularly charming – you'll find it and all the facilities on the detailed map in the car park.

### ARRIVAL AND DEPARTURE                                                    LEFKOSIA

**By plane** The nearest international airport to Lefkosia is Larnaka (Nicosia Airport, closed in 1974, now languishes in the UN Buffer Zone). A regular shuttle bus runs from Larnaka Airport to the *Philoxenia Hotel* in Lefkosia roughly every hour (€8; 50min). The *Philoxenia* is in the suburbs so you'll most likely need a taxi from there into town (there's a rank nearby).

**By bus** Intercity buses run to Lefkosia from all the republic's main towns. From the bus station in Solomos Square there

are services to Finikoudes in Larnaka (hourly; 1hr), the New Port in Lemesos (hourly; 1hr 45min) and Karavella in Pafos (5 daily; 2hr).

**By car** You're likely to approach the city from the south on the A1 motorway or from the west on the A9. Either way, you will find yourself in a fast one-way system for which your main orientation aid will be the Venetian walls. The most useful car park is the one between the D'Avila and Constanza bastions, from where there's direct access up a

## LEFKOSIA'S FESTIVALS

### APRIL

**Ledra Music Soloists International Festival** (early April) Two-week festival of chamber music held at the PASYDY Auditorium.

### JULY

**International Festival of Ancient Greek Drama** (late July/early August; ⓦ greekdramafest. com) Held in Lefkosia, Lemesos and Pafos.

### SEPTEMBER

**Septemberfest** (mid-Sept) Beer festival held at the Constanza Bastion. As well as a good range of ales there's music and dance, plus children's events.

**Ice Cream Festival** (late Sept) Free ice creams and entertainment to be enjoyed at the Famagusta Gate Moat.

**Cyprus International Film Festival** (late Sept; ⓦ cineartfestival.eu) Established film festival with screenings followed by Q&A sessions with directors.

### OCTOBER

**Pharos International Contemporary Music Festival** (early Oct; ⓦ pharosartsfoundation. org) Twentieth and twenty-first century avant-garde music at the Shoe Factory, the Pharos Foundation's Lefkosia venue.

**Rainbow Festival** (mid-Oct) International music and dance. Festival run by Action for Equality, Support and Antiracism. Also held in Larnaka and Pafos.

---

flight of steps to the main tourist area of the city. Parking is cheap, starting at €1.50 for 2hr then increasing by €0.50 for each additional hour.

**By shared taxi** A shared taxi service (ⓣ 77777474) links Lefkosia and Larnaka (€8.20 one-way) and Lefkosia and Lemesos (€10.90 one-way). Fares are slightly higher on Sundays.

### GETTING AROUND

**On foot** Lefkosia is small enough for you to explore the main city, within the walls, on foot. Walking is also the best way to access North Lefkosia (see page 177).

**By bus** Bus services throughout Lefkosia and the surrounding district are provided by OSEL (ⓦ osel.com.cy) from their terminus on Solomos Square.

### INFORMATION AND TOURS

**Tourist office** 11 Aristokyprou ⓣ 22674264. Located deep within labyrinthine Laiki Geitonia, the tourist office is nevertheless well signposted and easy to find (Mon–Fri 10am–1pm & 4–7pm, Sat 10am–1pm). They offer a range of free walking tours of the city departing Mon & Thurs at 10am.

**Tours** For trips further afield, try Aeolos Sightseeing Tours at 6 Zenas Kanther (ⓣ 22881200, ⓦ aeolos.com), Exp Cyprus at 4 Saronikou (ⓣ 96263177, ⓦ expcyprus. com), or Tamasos Tours 66, Makarios Avenue, Kronos Court (ⓣ 22762683, ⓦ tamasostours.com.cy).

### ACTIVITIES

**Basketball & squash** Eleftheria Indoor Hall, Makariou Athletic Centre Avenue, Engomi. Home to the Cyprus National Basketball team, with facilities also for badminton, gymnastics, volleyball, squash and much else. Also used as a venue for concerts.

**Bowling** Kykko Bowling, Theodosi Pieridi Egkomi ⓣ 22350085. Ten-pin bowling, with the usual fast-food accompaniment.

**Horse racing** Lefkosia Race Club Agios Dometios ⓣ 22782727, ⓦ nicosiaraceclub.com.cy. Horse racing and betting on Wednesdays and Fridays in the summer, and Wednesdays and Sundays in winter.

**Swimming** Lefkosia Municipal Swimming Pool, 4 Loukis Akritas Avenue, Agios Andreas ⓣ 2797646. Olympic-sized outdoor pool open during the summer months (May–Sept).

### ACCOMMODATION

Hotels in Lefkosia are mainly aimed at business customers – despite the city's many attractions, visitors tend to come in for the day rather than to stay over. If you're travelling by car, it's better to avoid the hotels within the walls as parking can be a problem.

**5**

## INSIDE THE WALLS

**Castelli Hotel** 38 Ouzounian ☏ 22712777, ⓦ castellihotel. com.cy; map p.178. The *Castelli Hotel* has a useful location tucked into the southwest corner of South Lefkosia, within a 5min walk of Ledra Street. Part of the *Holiday Inn* chain, customers can use some of the much more expensive mother ship's facilities just along the street. The hotel is beginning to look a little worn, and it can be noisy on lower floors. **€80**

**Centrum Hotel** 15 Pasikratous ☏ 22456444, ⓦ centrumhotelcyprus.com; map p.178. The clue to this hotel's USP is in the name – it's bang in the centre of the Laiki Geitonia district within easy walking distance of shops, restaurants and sights. This, of course, has its drawbacks – it can be noisy into the small hours. Partly occupying an early twentieth-century mansion, its rooms are modern and comfortable, though standard rooms can seem a little cramped. There are coffee- and tea-making facilities (not always the case in Cyprus), and the mini-fridge can come in handy on hot days. **€80**

**Classic Hotel** 94 Rigenis ☏ 22664006, ⓦ classic.com.cy; map p.178. In the same corner of the city as the *Castelli*, the *Classic* offers a good range of in-room and hotel facilities aimed at business customers. It is less suited to families with children. There's a rooftop gym and spa, a bar-café and restaurant, and (oddly) an art gallery. **€77**

**★ Sky Hotel** 7c Solonos St ☏ 22666880, ⓦ skyhotel. ws; map p.178. A good-value choice in the heart of Laiki Geitonia. You won't find luxurious fixtures and fittings, and it can get noisy, but, though badly in need of TLC, it's perfectly comfortable and its restaurant (*Fanous*) is Lebanese/Arabian, which adds interest. **€60**

## OUTSIDE THE WALLS

**Almond Business Suites** 25 March St, Agios Omologites ☏ 22879131, ⓦ almond-businesshotel. com; map p.174. Although intended largely for business people – it's located in an area which contains the bulk of government offices, embassies and consulates – *Almond Business Suites* is also an attractive alternative for other types of traveller. Suites are top-end regarding comfort, all include a well-equipped kitchenette, and decor is cool and modern. Despite being away from the city centre, there are plenty of shops and restaurants within walking distance. **€120**

**★ Asty Hotel** 12 Prince Charles St, Agios Dometios ☏ 22773030, ⓦ astyhotel.com; map p.174. Located in a quiet residential area to the west of the city centre, the *Asty* is, for a city hotel, family-friendly, with a children's play area, mini-golf, a pool table, games room and babysitting services. Rooms are clean and comfortable, and the hotel is just a 5min drive from the Agios Dometios crossing point into north Cyprus. A shuttle service into the city centre is available on request, and there's a good taverna and a 24hr bakery within a 5min walk. **€140**

**Averof** 19 Averof St, Agios Andreas ☏ 22773447, ⓦ averof.com.cy; map p.174. Plus points for the *Averof* are that it's in a quiet residential area yet only a 10min walk from the Venetian walls, its staff are friendly and helpful, and its rates are rock bottom for a hotel in the capital. Currently, its downsides are the lack of a restaurant (though it has a supply of takeaway menus and an area in which you can eat your own food), a fairly minimal bar, and dated decor. Like the *Asty*, it is a 5min drive from the Agios Dometios crossing place into the north. **€55**

**Hilton Cyprus** Archiepiskopou Makariou III ☏ 22377777, ⓦ hilton.com; map p.174. The only five-star hotel in Lefkosia, the *Hilton* is hard to miss on the main approach from the motorway. Though it claims to be within walking distance of the city centre, it's a fair slog, though buses are frequent. There are some facilities which you might not expect in a city hotel – outdoor pool, tennis court – and if you're overlooking the pool, you could almost believe you're in a resort rather than the capital. A word of warning, though: the bar prices are eye-watering. **€299**

## EATING

**Aigaio** 40 Ektoros ☏ 22433297; map p.178. Classy Greek-Cypriot restaurant in the old city with an open-air courtyard that often hosts live traditional music. It's good for a treat (allow around €20 for mezé) and has an excellent wine list. It's popular, so you'll need to book a table. Tue–Sat 7.30pm–1am.

**Casa Vieja** 3 Archangelou Michael ☏ 22673371, ⓦ facebook.com/casavieja.nicosia; map p.178. Smart tapas bar with three dining areas plus patio. Choose from, at the last count, nearly forty tapas dishes and four types of paella. Most dishes are between €4 and €9 (paellas €10–14), with wines from around €15. Warm in winter, cool in summer, and with excellent service. Live Spanish music on Fridays. Daily 7.30–11pm.

**Derlicious** Corner of Ledras and Ippokratous ☏ 22307891; map p.178. One of a chain of fast-food restaurants/take-aways (there are branches in all the Republic's main towns), the atmosphere is casual, the service fast, and the food good. Thronged with young people, but quiet – they're mostly on their mobiles. Daily 9am–11pm.

**★ Domus** 5 Korae ☏ 22433722, ⓦ domusloungebar. com; map p.178. Chic, international cuisine, fine dining restaurant with attached lounge (or vice versa) in a rather sedate old building in the area of the city around the Archbishop's Palace. Slightly self-conscious decor in the lounge with lots of wood and arty photographs, cooler and classier in the restaurant and its attached bar. Reservations necessary for restaurant meals, though there is a bar menu in the lounge. Bar food €3.50–13; restaurant main courses €18–30. Daily 8pm–2am.

★ **Fanous** 7c Solonos ☎ 22666663, ⊛ fanous.eu; map p.178. Lebanese-style restaurant attached to the *Sky Hotel*. You can't miss it – cane tables, chairs and sofas spill out onto and across the alley next to the hotel entrance, where customers smoke hookahs (or *narghiles*), giving the whole place a really Middle Eastern atmosphere. With its long opening hours, it's as good for a quick coffee and a cake as for a full meal (meze €15). You can buy *narghiles*, tobacco and much else in the *Fanous* shop, and on Saturdays there are belly-dancing performances. Daily 11am–midnight.

**Il Forno** 216–218 Ledra St ☎ 22456454, ⊛ ilforno.com. cy; map p.178. Does what the best Italian restaurants do so well – provide comfort food in a warm, busy atmosphere. There's quality pasta and pizza as well as all the staple main courses, and delicious sweets. Not for calorie-counters. Overflows onto Ledra Street in the summer, and is always busy so it is best to book a table (or they do take-away). Main courses (pizzas, pastas) from €11.50. Daily 11.30am–11pm.

★ **Louis Tavern** 84 Agiou Andreou, Pallouriotissa ☎ 99315881, ⊛ louis-tavern-restaurant.business.site; map p.174. Highly rated family-run restaurant east of the city centre. Good grilled meat and fish in convivial surroundings, and a cosy atmosphere – solid rather than outstanding. Main courses from around €10. Mon–Sat

5–10.45pm, Sun noon–2.30pm & 6.30–10pm.

**Old Power House Restaurant** Palia Elektriki ☎ 22432559; map p.178. Attached to the cultural centre next door, this sophisticated restaurant serves a mixture of Cypriot (especially grills) and more eclectic meals (main courses €10–20) in what was once the Nicosia Electricity Authority building. Try to get a table outside in the leafy courtyard. Tues–Thurs 6pm–1am, Fri 6pm–2am, Sat 11am–2am, Sun 11am–5pm.

★ **Pyxida** 5 Menandrou St ☎ 22445636, ⊛ pyxida fishtavern.com; map p.174. Popular fish restaurant offering a nineteen-dish seafood meze and mains featuring everything from swordfish to sardines (mains from €11.50, fish pastas €14). A big patio offers formal alfresco dining, and the interior decoration is suitably nautical. Southwest of the old town, out beyond the Cyprus Museum. Popular, so you'll need to reserve a table. Daily 12.15–3.30pm & 7.15–11pm.

**Zanettos** 65 Trikoupis ☎ 22765501, ⊛ zanettos.com; map p.178. *Zanettos* has been going since 1938, so it's obviously doing something right, particularly its traditional meze, washed down with lashings of wine. Not easy to find (it's just west of the Omeriye Mosque and Hammam), but everybody knows where it is, and it is heavily patronized by locals. Famous for its souvlaki, from around €5 in a pitta. Daily 6.30pm–midnight.

## DRINKING AND NIGHTLIFE

More than in any other large Cypriot town, Lefkosia's nightlife is largely for local youth rather than for visiting holiday-makers. There are lots of bars, pubs and clubs, many of which are contained inside the old town, others along the inner and outer ring roads that follow the walls.

**Brewfellas Beer Bar** 7–9 Pygmalionos ☎ 22 264 00 07, ⊛ brewfellas.com; map p.178. They offer an impressively great selection of beers - and a lot of them on tap, too. Ales, stouts, porters - your head will spin, but the friendly and knowledgeable staff is right there to guide you through it all. Mon–Thurs 6pm–1am, Fri 6pm–2am, Sat 5pm–2am, Sun 3pm–1am.

**Enallax** 16–17 Athinas Avenue ☎ 96440848; map p.178. At the eastern edge of the walled city, near the Famagusta Gate, *Enallax* concentrates on live and recorded Greek music and some rock. Daily 5pm–3am, closed on Sundays.

★ **Klubd** 36 Ammochostou ☎ 99010214; map p.178. Near the Famagusta Gate (close to *Enallax* above), this is perhaps the most sophisticated club on the island –

the main room glories in a "sky" made up of tiny LEDs. Techno with minimalist industrial decor. International DJs sometimes feature. Sat 11.45–5.30am.

**Lost + Found Drinkery** 38 Lord Byron; map p.174. A quirky bar with a wide selection of fun cocktails served in climatic though mismatched decor. It offers very little space so on busier nights there are queues forming hoping to get served. There isn't much to offer in terms of food - some hot dogs at best - but it's not for the food that the bar's become so popular. Mon–Thurs 6pm–12.30am, Fri 6.30pm–1.30am, Sat 7pm–1.30am.

**New Division** 2 Vasilissis Frederikis ☎ 22679957; map p.174. Laid-back and down-to-earth rock bar with the atmosphere of a students' union. Mon–Thurs 8pm–2am, Fri & Sat 8pm–2.30am, Sun 8pm–midnight.

**Versus** 2 Archiepiskopou Makariou III, Capital Centre 3rd floor ☎ 99393009; map p.178. Just south of the D'Avila Bastion. Top-end light and sound systems, progressive, house, dance, some live music. Sat 11.30pm–4.30am.

## SHOPPING

Lefkosia offers the closest you'll get to big-city shopping in Cyprus. Apart from the usual **souvenirs** (leather goods, textiles, jewellery, wines and spirits, lace), you'll find plenty of **designer shops** and a number of modern **shopping centres**. Two areas are particularly worth concentrating on:

the streets either side of Ledra Street, and the area outside the walls to the southwest, on either side of Archiepiskopou Makariou III and Diagorou/Themistocle Dervi. Look out also for Stasikratous, the smartest and most stylish street in the city, which runs between the two. This is the area which

**5**

contains the Louis Vuitton, Versace and Gucci stores. For fruit and vegetables, head for the Central Market.

## BOOKS

**Moufflon Bookshop** 38 Sofouli ☎ 22665155; map p.178. Good general bookshop with extensive English-language section. All aspects of Cypriot life and history are well covered. Mon–Fri 9.30am–7.30pm, Sat 9.30am–5pm.

## CLOTHES, SHOES AND ACCESSORIES

**Bershka** Mall of Cyprus, Shacolas Emporium Park, 3 Verginas St; also other branches ☎ 22472100, ⓦ bershka. com; map p.174. Stylish clothes for teens and young adults at affordable prices in eye-catching surroundings. Another brand from the Spanish Zara/Massimo Dutti group. Mon–Sat 10am–8pm, Sun 11am–7pm.

★ **Flexi** 23 Aphrodites ☎ 22767003; map p.178. Specialist boutique which carries ranges by a number of Cypriot designers who have an international reputation, among them Joanna Louca and Elena Pavlou. Mon, Tues, Thurs & Fri 10am–1pm & 3–7pm, Wed 10am–1pm, Sat 10am–1pm.

**Krama** 3E Arnaldas ☎ 22761655; map p.178. Original designs of necklaces, bracelets, rings and earrings in silver and gold by local designer Skevi Afantiti (ⓦ skeviafantiti. com). April–Oct Mon 5–8pm, Tues–Fri 9.30am–1pm & 5–8pm, Sat 10am–1.30pm; Nov–March Mon 3–7pm, Tues–Fri 9am–1pm & 3–7pm, Sat 10am–1.30pm.

## CRAFTS, GIFTS AND SOUVENIRS

★ **Chrysaliniotissa Multicraft Centre** 2 Dimonaktos ☎ 22347465; map p.178. Intimate little arts and crafts centre, with eight workshops and a coffee shop (the excellent *Ings's Veggie Heaven*) facing a central courtyard. Mon–Fri 10am–5pm, Sat 10am–1pm.

★ **Cyprus Handicrafts Service** 186 Athalassa Avenue ☎ 22305024; map p.174. Tat-free source of genuine Cypriot craft items (see page 186). Mon–Wed & Fri 7.30am–2.30pm, Thurs 7.30am–2.30pm & 3–6pm.

**Gatapou** Stoa 25, Georgiou Papadopoulou ☎ 22667741; map p.178. This shop overflows with ornaments, bookmarks, greetings cards, coasters, key-rings, dress jewellery, photograph frames and more. If efforts to find suitable gifts have come to naught, this is the place to go. Mon–Tues, Thurs–Fri 11am–2pm & 4.30–7.30pm,

Wed 11am–2pm, Sat 11am–5pm.

★ **Leventis Museum Shop** 15–17 Hippocrates St, Laiki Yitonia ☎ 22661475, ⓦ leventismuseum.org.cy; map p.178. The attached shop to one of Cyprus's best museums, selling quality replicas of pottery, jewellery and other items from the collection – ideal for gifts. Tues–Sun 10am–4.30pm.

## HEALTH AND BEAUTY

**Mastic Spa** 42 Themistocles Dervis ☎ 22667771; map p.174. Beauty products based on (the clue's in the name) mastic (the gum from the mastic tree). Clearly all the rage – another shop (Mastiha) across the road offers a similar range. Mon, Tues, Thurs & Fri 9.30am–7pm, Wed & Sat 9.30am–2pm.

## MALLS AND DEPARTMENT STORES

**Mall of Cyprus** Shacolas Emporium Park, 3 Verginas St ☎ 77776255, ⓦ themallofcyprus.com; map p.174. Large shopping mall just east of (and well signposted from) the A1 motorway south of the city. You'll find everything from Accessorize to Zara here, plus a Carrefour supermarket, a five-screen cinema, a food hall and ample parking. Mon–Sat 9.30am–8pm, Sun 11am–7pm (individual stores may differ).

## MARKETS

**Central Municipal Market** Diogenous; map p.178. Rather bleak concrete covered market selling fruit and vegetables, nuts, honey and fish. Under renovation at the time of writing, due to reopen 2019. Mon, Tues, Thurs & Fri 6am–3pm.

**Ochi Square** Constanza Bastion; map p.178. Open-air fruit and vegetable market. Wed 6am–5pm.

## MUSIC

**All Records Discount Store** Chanteclair Building, 30–32 Sefouli ☎ 22663251; map p.178. Good range of music – new releases on the ground floor, together with ethnic, R&B, electronic, easy listening, film soundtracks and Greek music, classical, jazz and blues on the first floor. There's also a wide range of DVDs. This was the first of a chain of music stores (known as "Play" outside Lefkosia) now found across the Republic. Mon, Tues & Thurs 9am–6.30pm, Wed & Sat 9am–2pm, Fri 9am–7pm.

## DIRECTORY

**Consulates and embassies** Australia, Block A, Level 7, Alpha Business Centre ☎ 22753001, ⓦ cyprus.embassy.gov. au; Canada, 15 Themistocles Dervis St ☎ 22775508; Ireland, 7 Aiantas St ☎ 22818183, ⓦ embassyofireland.com.cy; New Zealand, 6 Kondilaki ☎ 22818884; UK, Alexander Pallis St ☎ 22861100, ⓦ ukincyprus.fco.gov.uk; US, Metochiou & Ploutarchou St ☎ 22393939, ⓦ cy.usembassy.gov.

**Medical** Lefkosia General Hospital (A&E) ☎ 22603000. Night pharmacies ☎ 11892, ☎ 90901412 (automatic recording).

**Police** Next to the Ledra Street crossing ☎ 112.

**Post office** The Central Post Office is at Constantinos Palaeologos St, just off Eleftheria Square (on the D'Avila Bastion).

# Around Lefkosia

There is much to see around **Lefkosia**, and it would be a mistake to concentrate solely on the capital. Most of the district's wilder areas of mountain and forest are considered part of the Troodos Mountains, but there are also a few worthwhile sights beyond the (seemingly endless) industrial estates and suburbs to the south and west. The areas to the east and north of Lefkosia, of course, lie in the Turkish-controlled zone, though these are now also easily accessible.

## Panagia Chrysospiliotissa

Kato Deftera • Open all year • Free

Situated on the E903 which strikes southwest of the capital (from the B9), the village of **Kato Deftera** has an oddity which is worth a stop. **Panagia Chrysospiliotissa** (Our Lady of the Golden Cave) is an early Christian cave-church of a type common in the rest of the Middle East but rare in Cyprus. Built either to benefit from peace and remoteness, or perhaps as a response to persecution, its entrance is halfway up a crumbling ochre cliff face above the (usually dry) Pediaios River. Fortunately, it now benefits not only from a modern roofed flight of steps and a couple of benches either side of the entrance on which to rest after the climb, but also a new lift grafted onto the cliff face. The cave, which is air conditioned, consists of two main chambers connected by tunnels, the whole being at once in good order but also slightly eerie. There are modern icons and church furnishings, but the original frescoes have been largely washed away by flooding – appropriately, this is the place to pray for rain. The Virgin here also helps to find husbands for unmarried women. The church is not easy to find, however, despite a brown and yellow sign opposite Kato Deftera's village church. The road it points down is rough enough for you to think you're lost. Keep going, and look out for a large cross at the top of a cliff – the entrance is directly below. There's ample parking, a fountain and plateia, and even a small seasonal food and drink kiosk, all at the base of the cliff.

## Politiko and Ancient Tamassos

On the same road (the E903) as Kato Deftera but 7km further south is the large modern village of **POLITIKO**, which stands on the site of the ancient city-state of **Tamassos**. A mention of "Temessis" in Homer's *Odyssey* is thought to refer to it, and other sources indicate a large and prosperous city whose wealth was based almost entirely on the production of copper. The study of Tamassos is very much a work in progress, with German excavations during the 1970s having unearthed a sanctuary dedicated to Aphrodite next to the remains of early copper production. Finds from the area include the "Chatsworth Head" – a bronze head of Apollo, purchased by the Duke of Devonshire (and named for his residence) and now in the British Museum – and a group of six large limestone statues of sphinxes and lions now on display in the Cyprus Museum (see page 179).

### Royal Tombs

Mid-April to mid-Sept Mon–Fri 9.30am–5pm; mid-Sept to mid-April Mon–Fri 8.30am–4pm • €2.50 • ☎ 22622619

The star attraction of the Tamassos remains is its pair of **Royal Tombs**, dating from the sixth century BC and first excavated towards the end of the nineteenth century, which stand on the northeastern edge of Politiko, their entrance steps protected by wood-and-tile louvred structures. Once down the steps and through modern Perspex doors, the simplicity of the design of the tomb chambers and the quality of the stonework give them the feel of the interior of Egyptian pyramids. This minimalism is slightly misleading – the tombs undoubtedly had great piles of statuary, gold and other goods,

**5**

long pinched by grave-robbers (in one of the tombs there's a still-visible hole in the roof). Look out, too, for the skilful carving of the stone to simulate wood. The site itself is on raised ground, which gives views of fields, poplars, cypresses and vineyards of the surrounding areas.

### Agios Irakleidios

Daily: April–Oct Mon–Fri 8.30am–12.30pm & 3.30-6pm, Sat & Sun 6am–6pm; Nov–March Mon–Fri 8.30am–12.30pm & 2.30pm–sundown, Sat & Sun 6am–sundown • Free, but donations accepted • ☎ 22623950

On the other side of Politiko from the Royal Tombs is the convent of **Agios Irakleidios**, a popular destination for Greek Cypriots. Irakleidios was the son of a pagan priest ordained by Cypriot Christianity's two founders Saints Paul and Barnabas. Martyred at the age of 60, he was buried in the cave in which he'd lived. In 400 AD a monastery was erected over his grave. This was then subsequently much destroyed and rebuilt – the present one dates from 1773. The monastery has been occupied by nuns since 1962. Entry is through a gatehouse trustingly decked with modern icons, beyond which a drive curves up across vineyards and olive groves to the convent itself. Between the usual bright mosaics of saints, the entrance leads through a pointed arch to the cloisters and cells arranged around a verdant garden, in the centre of which is a medieval chapel built over the tomb of Irakleidios himself. The main church contains some early frescoes and the skull of the saint in a jewelled reliquary. The whole atmosphere of the convent is one of self-contained peace and quiet.

## Cyprus Museum of Natural History

Carlsberg Breweries • Mon–Fri 8.30am–1pm. Though usually visited by tour groups rather than individuals, it is possible to gain access by arrangement: it's always better to phone ahead, to make sure that the curator is in • Free • ☎ 22585834, ⊛ natmuseum.org.cy

The privately run **Cyprus Museum of Natural History** requires a determined effort to visit – it's in a brewery complex deep in a business park east of the A1 motorway. Exit at Junction 6 and, at the first set of lights east, turn left. The brewery is about two or three kilometres along this road, on the right. The location of the museum is thanks to its benefactor, Cyprus Carlsberg, who helped set up the cultural foundation to which it owes its existence. Indeed, a visit usually includes a guided tour of the brewery. The first hall contains a comprehensive treatment of the geology of Cyprus, the second a similarly thorough account of the island's marine life. Further halls deal with fossils, insects and rural life with a specific exhibit on Pafos Forest and Larnaka's salt lake. There are also collections of semi-precious stones, corals and shells, and, in the surrounding gardens, a group of replica dinosaurs.

## Ancient Idalion

Dali • Mon–Fri 8.30am–4pm • €2.50 • ☎ 22444818

In the angle between the A1 and A2 motorways halfway between Lefkosia and Larnaka lies the city of **Ancient Idalion** which was, it is said, established by Chalcanor, one of the Greek heroes who besieged and in due course destroyed Troy. Although there is evidence of occupation of the area going back to 1800 BC, the city itself dates from around 700 BC, and flourished from then until around 500 BC when it was captured by the Phoenicians under Kition. There's no longer a huge amount to see on the ground – the remains of walls, the ground plans of buildings – the most important parts of which are now protected by wooden canopies. This is partly because it was so thoroughly looted in the past, particularly by **Luigi Palma di Cesnola** (see page 118), who boasted that he had excavated (plundered, that is) 10,000 graves here. The archeological investigation of Idalion continues, especially of several sanctuaries discovered recently. The site **museum** provides a fine introduction to the city's development, featuring the results of excavations old and new. It does, alas, rely on photographs for the more illustrious finds, the originals having long found their way abroad. A second gallery deals with the Phoenician conquest and administration of the city.

# Early Industrial Workshop of Agia Varvara

Agia Varvara • Wed & Sat 8am–1pm, Sat also 3pm–6pm, other visiting times can be arranged by appointment • Donations welcome • ☎ 22521715

A good example of efforts made by idealistic young people to conserve local history can be found in the village of Agia Varvara, just west of the A1/A2 motorway junction. The **Early Industrial Workshop of Agia Varvara** (clearly signposted from the main village street) is a collection of tools, contraptions and workshops that once belonged to a certain Gregoris Theocharous (1887–1991). The well-travelled Theocharous became a sort of pioneer industrialist, having learned to build and repair machines in Egypt and Greece. On his death at the age of 104, his house, its contents and a variety of inventions (including a water recycling pump) were bequeathed to the community and are preserved by a local history group. You can learn more at ⓦtinyurl.com/industrialworkshop.

# North Cyprus

GIRNE (KYRENIA) HARBOUR AND CASTLE

# North Cyprus

For many visitors, crossing into Turkish-controlled north Cyprus is akin to time travel. Gone are the busy resorts, malls and familiar international chains of the south, replaced by remote villages and a slower place of life – "the Mediterranean as it used to be" in the words of the local tourist board. This sense of suspended animation can be dated precisely to the Turkish invasion of 1974, when the north, stripped of its Greek Cypriot population, became cut off from the rest of the world, a self-styled republic recognized by no one but Turkey itself (see page 203).

The Republic's government has done all in its power to limit relations between north Cyprus and the outside world, and the issue of Turkish-Cypriot (and indeed Turkish) occupation of property owned by Greek Cypriots in the north continues to be a major stumbling block in any movement towards reunification. The republic's stance on "legal" entry points and property ownership hasn't changed, and is very clear (see page 24). Nevertheless, it is now commonplace for Greek Cypriots in their thousands to cross into the north, both on day-trips and for overnight stays. This is largely due to the gradual opening up of the **Green Line**, the de facto dividing line between the two communities – there are now seven crossing points, and two more are under discussion. The process of entering the north from the south has been made even simpler since Mustafa Akinci became President in 2015 – one of his first acts was to get rid of irksome visa requirements. Consequently, it is perfectly feasible for travellers staying in the south to see as much of the north as they wish, with many attractions little more than half an hour's drive away from the south's major resorts. Others choose to spend their whole trip in the north, though this necessitates travelling via Turkey.

There is certainly plenty to draw you here. North Cyprus boasts two of the island's best-looking **towns** (Girne and Gazimağusa), half the **capital city** (Lefkosia/Lefkoşa), three of its mightiest **Crusader castles** (St Hilarion, Buffavento and Kantara), and arguably the island's most significant archeological site at **Salamis**. Its wilderness areas, particularly the **Kyrenia Mountains**, are a hiker's paradise, and many of its **beaches** remain mercifully free of high-rise resorts. Furthermore, any visit to Cyprus which includes both sides of the island offers the unique experience of two very different cultures: Orthodox, Greek Cypriot, and Muslim, Turkish Cypriot. There's also the small matter of **cost** – being outside the Eurozone, the north can feel considerably cheaper than the south, and its tourist infrastructure, though inferior, is gradually improving.

As for sightseeing in the north, you might find that many **museums** and other places of interest seem rather neglected and old-fashioned, while its **hotels** and **restaurants** lack the sophistication of the south. You might also come across a cavalier attitude to published **opening times** – if something's really important to you, try to phone ahead or check with the tourist office. Finally, if you haven't had a chance to obtain **Turkish Lira**, don't worry: euros and dollars are widely accepted.

## Lefkoşa (North Nicosia)

**LEFKOŞA** (the northern half of what was, before 1974, Nicosia) is the capital city of north Cyprus. As with its southern counterpart, the old town is hemmed by Venetian walls (see page 173), with the majority of Lefkoşa's modern buildings and administrative machinery located outside the walls, and most tourist attractions to be found in the old town within the walls. Compared to the southern part of the city,

BÜYÜK HAN

# Highlights

**❶ Mevlevî Tekke Museum, Lefkoşa** Learn about the origins and beliefs of the "whirling" Dervish sect in the setting of a seventeenth-century monastery. See page 201

**❷ Büyük Han (Great Inn), Lefkoşa** Take refreshment and shop for souvenirs at this beautifully renovated traveller's inn. See page 205

**❸ Girne Harbour** People-watch while strolling around the prettiest harbour in Cyprus, or while sitting in one of its many cafés and restaurants. See page 212

**❹ St Hilarion Castle** Clamber around this fairy-tale Byzantine/Lusignan castle, while imagining the medieval courtly life it played host to. See page 220

**❺ Bellapais** This bustling village, the setting for Lawrence Durrell's travel classic *Bitter Lemons*, is a lovely spot to while away an afternoon. See page 223

**❻ Soli** A well-excavated Roman town with a Byzantine basilica famous as the site of St Mark's christening. See page 228

**❼ Gazimağusa old town** Relish the unique ambience of this delicately ruined old town surrounded by crumbling Venetian walls. See page 234

**❽ Salamis** Marvel at the remains of one of Cyprus's greatest ancient cities, followed by a visit to the equally significant Royal Tombs. See page 238

**HIGHLIGHTS ARE MARKED ON THE MAPS ON PAGES 198 AND 200**

Lefkoşa has noticeably less vitality, with the air more of a sleepy provincial town than a national capital. While the city feels safe, wandering in areas away from the centre is best avoided at night.

Foreign tourists usually enter from the south through the **Ledra Street crossing** (see page 177). Once across, you're faced with an attractively **pedestrianized area** packed with shops, cafés and restaurants. Clear signposts indicate where the nearest attractions lie. Beyond here the main street – **Girne Caddesi** – leads north to the **Girne Gate**, the best place to start a walking tour of North Lefkoşa. If you're short of time, though, it's probably worth heading straight to the **Büyük Han**, a beautifully renovated sixteenth-century merchants' inn. **Museums** to look out for include the Mevlevî Tekke and Lapidary museums and the Derviş Paşa Mansion, each worth an hour or so of your time. Other places of interest include the **Samanbahçe Quarter**, an early experiment in social housing, and the dishevelled but improving **Arabhmet Quarter**. Religious sites include the huge **Selimiye Mosque**, visible north and south of the Green Line. Beside it is the ornately Gothic **Bedestan**, once a Christian church, now a performance venue. Other sights, among them the **National Struggle Museum**, the **Museum of Barbarism** and of course the **giant flags** looming on the hillside behind the city, provide uncomfortable reminders of the island's division.

## Girne Gate and around

Of the various entrances into the walled city on the northern side, the **Girne (Kyrenia) Gate** is the best preserved, and has been used by the Venetians, the Ottomans and the British, all of whom have left inscriptions that adorn its exterior. In 1931 the British demolished parts of the wall on either side to allow traffic into the city. As a result, the gate is now stranded in the middle of a dual carriageway, with worthy statues to the

**HIGHLIGHTS**

3 Girne Harbour
4 St Hilarion Castle
5 Bellapais
6 Soli
7 Gazimağusa old town
8 Salamis

**NORTH CYPRUS**

## LEFKOŞA (NORTH NICOSIA)

**● SHOPPING**
Gloria Jean's Coffees ........ 2
Hasder Folk Arts
Institute Craft Centre ...... 3
Mentes Ozsakir .............. 1

**■ ACCOMMODATION**
City Royal ..................... 2
Golden Tulip Hotel ......... 3
Merit Hotel ................... 1

**■ DRINKING**
Cadi Kazani .................... 1

**● EATING**
Biyer ........................... 1
Boghjalian ..................... 3
El Sabor Latino ............... 2
Old Mosaic .................... 4
Sedirhan ....................... 5

**HIGHLIGHTS**
① Mevlevi Tekke Museum
② Büyük Han (Great Inn)

Buffer zone
Limit of full northern control
Limit of full southern control

**CROSSING POINTS, VISAS AND TRANSPORT**

There are seven **crossing points** between south and north Cyprus (and 4 more planned at the time of writing this book) – some for pedestrians only, some for vehicular transport, some for both (see page 27). There has been a suggestion that two more points might be opened up, giving access to the Kokkina enclave, though at the time of writing this still hadn't happened.

Citizens of the EU, the USA, Canada, Australia, New Zealand, Mexico, Israel, Japan, Singapore, Switzerland, Iceland, Norway and Turkey do not need **visas**, as long as their passports have six months or more to run.

**Transport** in north Cyprus is ever improving, and consists of service taxis, minibuses, buses and rented cars.

Note also the need for a **map** using Turkish place names. We have used these names throughout this chapter, giving original Greek names also where relevant.

Remember too that if you think having a **TRNC stamp in your passport** might cause you problems, you can ask for it to be recorded on a separate piece of paper, which you can continue to use until it's full. For more information, see the entry requirements section of Basics (see page 37).

north (Ataturk) and south (Dr Küçük, with adoring little girl), and an open space on all sides – **Inonu Square** – which now sometimes becomes the focus of political rallies and demonstrations.

## National Struggle Museum

Musalla Bastion • Summer Mon–Fri 9am–2pm, Winter Mon–Fri 9am–1pm, 2–4.45pm • Free

Just east of the Girne Gate, on the Barbaro (or Musalla) Bastion, and situated inside an army camp, is the **National Struggle Museum**, which, while inevitably partisan, does offer considerable insight into the Turkish-Cypriot (and Turkish) perspective on events since the 1950s. You will need to show photo ID to the soldiers who guard the site (that is, if you can attract anybody's attention to let you in, and if you can get them to understand that you wish to view the museum). Opened in 1989, it might be seen to be a response to its namesake museum in the south (see page 182), though of course with a different agenda: focusing on the struggle of Turkish Cypriots against Greek Cypriots, especially between the Turkish TMT and the Greek EOKA in the 1960s. Artefacts on display include guns and improvised weapons, broadcasting equipment used by Radio Bayrak, gung-ho artwork, and, outside, some military vehicles and ordnance. The invasion (or "Peace Operation") of 1974 is, of course, covered in detail.

## Mevlevî Tekke Museum

Girne Caddesi • Summer Mon–Fri 9am–4pm, Winter Mon–Fri 9am–1pm, 2–4.45pm • €7

Just south of the Girne Gate on Girne Caddesi is the **Mevlevî Tekke Museum**, devoted to the Muslim sect widely known as the **Whirling Dervishes** and housed in what is left of a seventeenth-century dervish monastery. The Mevlevî Order was founded in Konya in Turkey by the Mevlana Jelal al-Din Rumi (1207–73) and quickly spread through Asia Minor. Central to their beliefs was the *sema* – the characteristic whirling dance, thought to achieve a transcendental forgetting of the self and communion with God, a process that UNESCO has declared to be a "masterpiece of the oral and intangible heritage of humanity". The museum depicts the *sema* in its central hall where a set of mannequins in traditional dress are frozen in time, spinning to a mannequin band above. Beyond here are the tombs of past Mevlevî Sheiks, archive photographs, prayer beads and other ephemera, as well as a few gnomic quotations that give you pause for thought: "A stingy Vizier is forced to pay a high price to a poor potter" or "The candle Mevlana lights is smaller, but keeps burning long after the others have melted away". One sums up the whole point of the dervishes – "Mevlana whirls in humble reverence".

## Dr Fazil Küçük Museum

Girne Caddesi • Daily: April–Oct 9am–1pm & 2–4.45pm; Nov–March 9am–2pm (opening hours can be unreliable; if apparently shut, try banging on the door) • Free

Housed in a 1920s-era building, the **Dr Fazil Küçük Museum** gives an insight into one of the key figures in Cypriot politics (see page 202). Dr Küçük is held in the same respect by Turkish Cypriots as Archbishop Makarios is by Greek Cypriots, and his home and surgery have been converted into a diverting museum containing plenty of photographs and personal possessions which help to bring the man to life. A brief pamphlet of notes is available on request from the custodian.

## Tekke Bahçesi Şehitlği

East of Girne Caddesi and a few metres south of the Dr Fazil Küçük Museum is the **Tekke Bahçesi Şehitlği**, a graveyard which contains the remains of Turkish Cypriots who died during the troubles in 1963 and the invasion of 1974 – it's signposted "Tekke Bahçesi Şehitlği Martyrdom". It's an affecting spot, which draws attention to the cost of political upheaval and war, but its overt agenda can be off-putting with the photographs of the corpses of men, women and children and the inflammatory language of the dedication.

## Samanbahçe Quarter

On the other side of Girne Caddesi from the Tekke Bahçesi Şehitlği is an interesting example of early town planning – the **Samanbahçe Quarter**. Built in a grid pattern from the 1890s onwards on land which was once a market garden called "Straw Field", and financed by a Muslim religious trust or *vakif*, the quarter provided social housing for the poor, and consisted of 72 dwellings made of mud brick with tile roofs. With uniform white walls and green shutters and doors, the houses are arranged along five parallel stone-paved streets with a domed stone fountain at the centre. Unlike, say, London mews flats which once housed lowly grooms and are now the preserve of the well-heeled, the Samanbahçe Quarter is still reserved for low-income families whose pride in their houses is reflected in the profusion of potted plants that line its lanes.

# Ataturk Square

**Ataturk Square (Meydani)** is the nearest thing to a hub that North Lefkoşa has, with its large paved and pedestrianized central island, fitted out with benches, around a circular wall surrounding the fenced-off Venetian Column (which was pilfered from Ancient Salamis by the Venetians in 1489), overlooked by the stately British Law Courts. Incidentally, if you ask for directions to "Ataturk Meydani" you're likely to

---

### DR FAZIL KÜÇÜK

In contrast to many of the leaders of both north and south Cyprus, **Dr Fazil Küçük** was an engaging, larger than life figure, a journalist and bon viveur much given to bad language, carousing with friends, and playing practical jokes. Born in Nicosia in 1906, he trained as a doctor in Turkey, Switzerland and France, returning to practise in Cyprus in 1938. As friction between Greek and Turkish Cypriots developed, he emerged as a leader of the **Turkish-Cypriot community**, setting up his own political party, establishing the first Turkish trade union and launching a newspaper – *Halkin Sesi* – which is still published today. He led the Turkish-Cypriot faction during talks leading up to independence, and became the first **vice president** of the republic. He was increasingly eclipsed by Rauf Denktaş (see page 206) as the intercommunal strife of the 1960s progressed, and was replaced by him as the leader of the Turkish Cypriots in 1973. He died in London in 1984. True to character, his last request was that a glass of his favourite tipple be regularly poured onto his grave.

**THE STATE WITHIN A STATE**

The **Turkish Republic of North Cyprus** (TRNC), as it has called itself since 1983, is still in many ways a pariah state, and this lack of international recognition continues to starve it of investment. Global chains such as McDonald's and Starbucks are conspicuous by their absence and its tourist industry is still dwarfed by that of the south. In part this is self-inflicted: the shabbiness of many of its museums and attractions contrasts markedly with the magnificence of its totalitarian-style military monuments, and the regular sight of Turkish troops and bases, often incongruously close to tourist attractions, can be a jolt to the senses. The empty shells of Orthodox churches and monasteries that dot some parts of the landscape are also an uncomfortable reminder of the wonton destruction that followed the invasion or "intervention" as the Turks put it. While the north remains in political limbo, its future seems to hang on demographics – with Turkish settlers now outnumbering Turkish Cypriots, north Cyprus increasingly feels like an offshore province of Turkey rather than the independent state that it claims to be.

be met with blank stares – all the locals call it **Sarayönü** after the palace ("saray") that once stood on the square, the same derivation appearing in the nearby Moorish-style **Sarayönü Camii** and the ugly, 1960s-built *Saray Hotel*, which does at least offer fine views from its roof terrace.

# The Arabahmet Quarter

Some 600m west of Ataturk Square is the **Arabahmet Quarter**, named after Arab Ahmet Paşa who governed the city from 1584 to 1587. A warren of narrow streets and alleys, old houses with balconies and arched doorways, the area is now being renovated bit by bit and gradually being settled by mainland Turks. Many houses are therefore in immaculate condition while others, mostly still inhabited, look about to fall down. Indeed, if you get off the beaten track, and see families sitting out in the backyards of tumbledown houses, you might well feel as if you've been transported to an Anatolian village. It's good for a quick wander (though don't expect too many cafés or restaurants) and there are several attractions worth seeking out.

### Arabahmet Mosque

Muftu Ziyai Effendi • Free access outside prayer times

The **Arabahmet Mosque**, which serves the quarter, was probably built in the late sixteenth century on the remains of a Lusignan church – the floor of the mosque is partly made up of Lusignan tombstones. It was heavily restored in the mid-nineteenth century, and is of interest more for its lush and peaceful graveyard than for the building itself.

### Derviş Paşa Mansion

Belig Pasa Sk • Mon–Fri 9am–1pm, 2.30–5pm, Sat 9am–1pm • €7

In the Arabahmet Quarter, two minutes' walk south of the Arabahmet Mosque, is the **Derviş Paşa Mansion**. The two-storey house with overhanging upper floor was built at the start of the nineteenth century for one Derviş Paşa, the editor of *Zamam* or "Time", Cyprus's first Turkish-language newspaper. Since 1988 it has been a museum which, like the Hadjigeorgakis Kornesios Mansion in the south, offers an insight into Ottoman-era living. Set in palm-fringed gardens, the house is cool and colonnaded, with steps leading up to a first floor furnished in contemporary style. There's plenty of decorative glassware, rugs, pottery, swords and the odd mannequin. As well as a dining room and bedroom there's what's billed as the "main room", a large area for entertaining, with bench seating around the outside, rugs on the floor and hookah pipes and coffee cups dotted around.

## A POLITICAL LANDSCAPE

From the Shacolas Tower in Lefkosia or the *Saray Hotel* in Lefkoşa (and indeed, from any other vantage point which has a clear view north) you can't help but see two enormous **flags** on the nearest south-facing hillside. One represents the TRNC (red crescent and star on a white background with red bar above and below), the other Turkey (white crescent and star on red background). The story behind them is rather dispiriting for those who would like to see the island reunited. Officially created to honour the great Turkish leader Ataturk (the slogan below the Turkish flag – "How happy is he who can say he is a Turk" – is attributed to him), the position of the flags seems to indicate that this explanation is disingenuous. A more believable version says that the Turks created the flags by painting boulders at night, turning them face down during the day, then, on the eve of August 15, a national holiday in the Greek-Cypriot calendar but also the anniversary of the 1974 Tochni massacre of Turkish Cypriots, turned them face up so that they could be seen in the south. In other words, a taunt or a memorial, depending on your point of view.

### Armenian Church

On Salahi Sevkai Sk, just before a barrier across the road marks the Green Line, is the **Armenian Church**, a ruin that is gradually being restored. Until the troubles in the mid-twentieth century, the Arabahmet Quarter was largely populated by Armenians. In return for their support of the Ottomans during the sixteenth-century invasion, they were given an old Benedictine monastery to use as their place of worship. In 1963, having been perceived as favouring the Greeks during that troubled year, the Armenians were expelled by the TMT and their church fell into disrepair. Based on the initial renovation work financed by the UN, the front aspect now seems to be complete, but the rear is still shrouded in scaffolding. It should be a splendid addition to the Quarter when complete.

### Arabahmet Cultural and Art Centre

80 Mehmet Akif Caddesi · For activities and opening hours, ask at the Tourist Information Centre

Next to the Armenian Church in a beautiful group of old houses is the **Arabahmet Cultural and Art Centre**, renovated by Girne American University and opened in 2014. It contains an exhibition hall, a theatre, a toy museum and an art gallery.

## South of Ataturk Square

South of Ataturk Square, and north of the pedestrianized shopping streets that greet you on passing through the Lokmaci Gate (that is, the Ledra Street crossing from the south), is an area of busy traffic and impressive buildings, survivals from the city's Byzantine, Lusignan and Ottoman past which have seen many changes of function over the years.

### Büyük Hammam

Irfan Bey Sk · Tues–Sun 9am–9pm, with single-sex and "touristic" mixed sessions · Entry €40, treatments from ¨100 · ☎ 8300881, ⓦ grandturkishhammam.com

It's easy to identify the **Büyük Hammam** (Great Baths) – it's a fine stone building that looks as if it has sunk into the ground (whereas, of course, it's the ground that has risen up from its original medieval level as successive layers of building have taken place). The baths were converted by the Ottomans from a Lusignan church, St George of the Latins, whose front portal is still the main entrance, and is approached down one of two flights of stone steps. After a period of closure it's now thoroughly restored and fully operational. Not cheap, but an intriguing experience.

## Kumarkilar Han

A minute's walk east of the Büyük Hammam is the **Kumarkilar Han**, or "Gamblers' Inn". Also called "The inn for merchants using donkeys" and "the inn for travelling musicians", the Kumarkilar Han, until recently in a sad state of neglect, is now approaching full renovation, though still boarded off in parts and surrounded by rubble. Built around 1700, with 44 of its original 56 rooms surviving, its likely use after renovation is not clear – proposals that it become a casino have been rejected, while other suggested uses have been (in keeping with its original function) as a hotel, or as a mixed shopping and restaurant attraction.

**6**

## Büyük Han

Arasta Sk • Opening hours variable, but core hours seem to be Mon–Fri 8am–7pm, Sat & Sun 8am–4pm

The **Büyük Han** (Great Inn) is a graceful and harmonious building which is somehow more affecting because it was built not to glorify God or the power of princes but as practical lodgings for traders and merchants. Appropriately, this is not a frozen-in-time relic, but a vibrant collection of shops, restaurants and small businesses that do its origins proud. It was built on the orders of the first Ottoman governor general of Cyprus, Mustafa Paşa, in 1572, just after the conquest. Used by the British as a prison, and later to house destitute families, it was sensitively restored between 1992 and 2002. The two-storey building consists of 68 rooms on two vaulted galleries looking onto a courtyard, and ten shops which open outwards to the street. In the centre of the courtyard a *mesjid* (miniature mosque) stands on columns under which is a *sadirvan* (fountain) used for ritual ablutions. There are two entrance gates to the east (the main one) and west, and inside the courtyard stone stairways lead to the upper floor (once used for accommodation and now housing, among other things, the "Traditional Cyprus Turkish Shadow Theatre", a sort of Middle Eastern Punch and Judy featuring its main character, "Karagoz"). The courtyard of the Büyük Han is an ideal place to sit in the shade, have a drink or a meal and, on Tuesday or Friday evenings, listen to live music (see page 210).

## Selimiye Cami

Kuyumcular Sk • Open to visitors outside prayer times • Free

East of the Büyük Han, the **Selimiye Cami** is not only Lefkoşa's biggest mosque, but also one of its most historically significant. Built by the Lusignans between 1208 and 1326 as the Roman Catholic St Sophia's Cathedral, it was adapted into a mosque shortly after the Ottoman invasion by the addition of the two impressive minarets (between which, these days, Turkish and TRNC flags are suspended). This combination of Lusignan and Ottoman architecture is best appreciated in detail from the café in the garden or as a whole from some distance away – there's a particularly good view of it from the Shacolas Tower in South Lefkosia.

The Selimiye Mosque (it was renamed in 1954 after **Selimiye II**, sultan at the time of the Ottoman conquest) is still a working place of worship. The whitewashed interior is simple and spacious (all the Roman Catholic furnishings were removed immediately after the Ottoman conquest) except for an elaborate and flamboyantly painted *mihrab* (prayer niche) in the southern wall, and a green-painted *minbar*, or pulpit, in the north transept. The south transept has a women's gallery. The cathedral was used for coronations during the Lusignan period, and several royal tombstones are incorporated into the floor, now obscured by the Mecca-orientated carpets. Around the back of the mosque is a splendid, roofed *sadirvan* (ablution fountain) in its own courtyard.

## The Bedestan

Kuyumcular Sk • Mon–Fri 10am–3pm, Sat 10am–1pm • €3

Right next door to the Selimiye Mosque is the **Bedestan**, a building which even by Cypriot standards has had a chequered past. Starting as a twelfth-century Byzantine

## "MR NO" – RAUF DENKTAŞ

Turkish-Cypriot leader **Rauf Denktaş** was born in 1924 in Pafos. He studied law in England and returned to practise as a solicitor in 1947. He quickly became involved in politics, helping to found the Turkish resistance movement the TMT during the 1950s. He rose to further prominence during the troubles that followed independence in 1960, became known for strong-arm tactics, even against fellow Turkish Cypriots with whom he disagreed, and finally replaced his mentor Dr Fazil Küçük as the leader of the Turkish Cypriots in 1973. In 1974 he welcomed the Turkish invasion, became head of the "Turkish Federated State of Cyprus" and oversaw the foundation of the Turkish Republic of North Cyprus in 1983. His uncompromising support for a **"two-state solution"** (he once claimed that there were no such things as Greek and Turkish Cypriots, saying that the only true Cypriots were the island's donkeys) made him the darling of the Turkish military and the Turkish-Cypriot community and the bane of a succession of Greek-Cypriot, UN and US negotiators (he became known as "Mr No" for his intransigence). However, during the early years of the twenty-first century his unchanging views began to look outdated, with Turkish Cypriots in the north becoming increasingly frustrated by their isolation from the rest of the world, a situation only exacerbated by the republic's accession to the European Union. Even Turkey began to find his inflexible views difficult as the north started to experience serious economic problems, and as Turkey began to nurture their own hopes of joining the EU. Though Denktaş reluctantly presided over the easing of restrictions on crossing the Green Line, he looked more and more out of touch, and finally left politics in 2005. He died in January 2012.

church, it was reincarnated as St Nicholas Roman Catholic Church during Lusignan times, became an Orthodox church during the Venetian occupation, and under the Ottomans was converted into a covered food and textiles market by subdividing the internal space. Towards the end of the Ottoman period the Bedestan fell into disrepair, but was revived as a market under the British. Only part of the north face of the building, including a magnificent Gothic entrance, was preserved complete, though the whole edifice is currently being renovated using EU funding. The Bedestan is now used as a venue for performances and for exhibitions, including, for example, Whirling Dervish displays (Mon–Sat noon, 2pm & 5pm; 30min; €22).

### Bandabuliya/Belediye Pazari
Mon–Sat 8am–6pm

Around 100m east of the Büyük Han is the **Bandabuliya** or covered market, a handsome building of great character; its Art Deco entrance gate has the official title of "Belediye Pazari" engraved on its lintel and the date 1932 worked into the decorative ironwork below. Closed for renovation for a considerable time, it is now once again up and running, with a range of produce on sale, from fruit, vegetables and meat, to clothes, bags and rugs, in a distinctly Middle Eastern atmosphere (though those who knew it before the renovation say that it has lost something in the transition).

### The Eaved House
Mon–Fri 8am–3.30pm • Free • ☏ 2277547

Stretched out along Kutuphane Street/Yeni Cami, the road that heads north after threading its way between the Bedestan and the Bandabuliya, are several establishments that are worth visiting, the first of which is the **Eaved House**. Now an arts and cultural centre which mounts periodic exhibitions, its eaves are indeed noticeable, jutting out far enough beyond the walls to require wooden struts to support them. The ground floor was built by the Lusignans, the first floor added during Ottoman times. Though its restoration in the 1990s was so thorough that there's not much of architectural consequence to see (the only inscribed date is 1932), the graceful arches, galleries, verandas and white painted walls make it at the least a cool refuge from the heat of the day and, at best, a fine venue for exhibitions.

## Lapidary Museum

Kirlizade Sokak • Mon–Fri 8am–3.30pm • €7

A minute's walk north of the Eaved House is the tiny **Lapidary Museum**, contained in a perfect little fifteenth-century Venetian house and courtyard. Featuring a hotchpotch of stone carvings and architectural details from all over Cyprus assembled by the British, it offers an irresistible hint of times past and a sense of crumbling grandeur. A valiant attempt has been made to categorize and contextualize the exhibits, so that, for example, a jumble of pieces of window tracery and archways in the courtyard have design outlines above them, and exhibits inside the house, on two floors, are accompanied by notes and sketches.

**6**

## Haydarpaşa Camii

Kirlizade Sk • Open during exhibitions Mon–Fri 9am–1pm & 2.30–5pm, Sat 9am–1pm • Free

The **Haydarpaşa Camii** is most notable for its mixed architectural ancestry – it has a tall, Gothic, clearly Lusignan nave (part of what was formerly the fourteenth-century St Catherine's Church) with, at its prow, a minaret added by the Ottomans. The whole building is out of proportion – too narrow, too high for its length – presumably because of bits that have been demolished, and as with many converted churches, the minaret just doesn't look comfortable. The mosque was earmarked for renovation with UNESCO funding, but this was withdrawn after the Turkish invasion of 1974, so it never went ahead. It is now a private art gallery open only during exhibitions.

## The Lusignan House

Mon–Fri 8am–3.30pm • €7

An impressive fifteenth-century **Lusignan House**, not a mansion but obviously the abode of somebody of singular wealth, can be found a short walk beyond the Haydarpaşa Camii. An arched gateway boasting several Lusignan coats of arms leads into a secluded courtyard, from which stone steps lead up to an immaculate first floor with, again, an arched entrance into the building. Though over 500 years old, few of us in the twenty-first century would object to living in it. Though the house was closed for renovation at the time of writing, staff have no objections to visitors looking around the outside.

## Yeni Cami

North of the Lusignan House, on the street named after it, lies the **Yeni Cami** ("new mosque", which gives its name to the surrounding district). Its interest lies not in the new mosque itself, but in the ruins of the old mosque that stands in its grounds. An eighteenth-century governor, so the story goes, had a dream that the original mosque (which was itself a Lusignan church) had treasure buried beneath it, so he had it demolished in order to secure the riches for himself. Not only was there no treasure, but local indignation at the desecration of the mosque provoked the sultan into having the delinquent paşa executed. His tomb stands next to the minaret which survives from the mosque he destroyed, together with a Gothic arch from the original church. The "new mosque" stands a few metres away in the gardens. Incidentally, the domed old Turkish tombs nearby are those of the family of the first Ottoman chief judge.

# Museum of Barbarism

Irhan Sokak 2 • Mon–Fri 8am–3.30pm • Free

Outside the walled city, in the northwestern suburbs of Lefkoşa, stands an unassuming suburban bungalow, once the home of a Dr Ilhan, a major in the Turkish Army. It has been converted into the **Museum of Barbarism** to commemorate the fate of his unfortunate family. In December 1963, while the doctor was on duty, armed Greek-Cypriot irregulars burst into the house and gunned down his wife, three children and a next-door neighbour. With graphic descriptions and photographs, bullet holes and bloodstains, this is not a

**6**

museum for children or the faint of heart. Its purpose is to draw attention to the sort of terrorism that was perpetrated by EOKA during the period after independence in 1960. You can't help feeling the simple memorial in the garden outside is a more fitting reminder.

## ARRIVAL AND DEPARTURE — LEFKOŞA (NORTH NICOSIA)

**By plane** Ercan Airport (📞 6005000, 🌐 ercanhavalimani. com; see page 23) is located 12km east of the city, to which it is linked by a good dual carriageway. Scheduled airport buses provided by Kibhas (12/day to Lefkoşa, 7/day to Güzelyurt and Lefke, 9/day to Magusa) are cheap (€7–12) but they sometimes don't coincide with flights, so you may be better off renting a car or taking a taxi (around €30 to Lefkoşa or Girne).

**By bus** The long-distance bus station in Lefkoşa is on the intersection of Ataturk Caddesi and Gazeteci Kemal Asik Caddesi, due north of the old city. Note that there are no

through buses to the south.

**Destinations** Gazimağusa (every 20min; 1hr); Girne (several per hour, but departs when full; 30min); Güzelyurt (every 30min; 45min).

**By car** Wherever you are arriving from by car, you will end up at the Girne Gate. Once in the city, on-street parking is relatively easy, and there are several car parks.

**By service taxi and minibus** Service taxis and minibuses travel to Gazimağusa and Girne, from the main bus station and from stops within the old city.

## GETTING AROUND

**On foot** Lefkoşa is small enough to explore on foot – there really is no need to use taxis or buses.

**By car** For car rental, try Sun Rent a Car (📞 2272303,

🌐 sunrentacar.com) or Rent a Car North Cyprus (📞 8705300, 🌐 rentacar-northcyprus.com).

## INFORMATION

**Tourist office** The main office is in the Girne Gate, at the northern end of the main north–south street, Girne Cad (Girne Gate, Mon–Fri 9am–5pm, Sat & Sun 9am–2pm; 📞 2275051). There's also a kiosk at Ercan Airport and the

Ledra Street crossing, where you can pick up the "Nicosia Walled City: Walking Route Map" published by the Lefkosia Master Plan (see page 172).

## ACCOMMODATION

There are no hotels that can be unreservedly recommended in Lefkoşa – they tend to be rather dated and in need of renovation, and the fact that they offer casino facilities can attract the odd unsavoury character. Consequently, most who wish to visit stay south of the Green Line and cross over to shop or see the sights.

**City Royal** 19 Kemal Asik Cad 📞 2287621, 🌐 city-royal. com; map p.200. North of the old town, about a 20min walk from the centre, near the bus station. A slightly monolithic business and gamblers' hotel, with full range of services, casino, gym and pool (closed in winter). Ask for a room away from the main street. **€65**

**Golden Tulip Hotel** Dereboyu Street 📞 6105050, 🌐 goldentulipnicosia.com; map p.200. North of the city

centre, the *Golden Tulip* offers decent accommodation in a fairly central location, and a good range of facilities – bar, restaurant, pool, fitness suite, saunas and the inevitable casino. Aimed more at the business market than at tourists, and with some doubt about the level of training and spoken English of its staff, it's still a reasonable option for those wishing to explore Lefkoşa. **€144**

**Merit Hotel** Bendrettin Demirel Street 📞 3903030, 🌐 merithotels.com; map p.200. Northwest of the city centre, about a 20min walk. A substantial tower block with a Byzantine/Ottoman feel and a casino inside. Rooms are well appointed, bathrooms spacious, food good, and there's a pleasant fountain and terrace. Sweeping views from the fourteenth floor. **€150**

## EATING

Many of the most popular restaurants in Lefkoşa are in the old city, within the walls. Otherwise try the Dereboyu district to the northwest.

### OLD CITY

**Boghjalian** Salahi Sevket Sokak 📞 2280700, 🌐 twitter. com/BoghjalianKonak; map p.200. Beautiful restored building, once owned by a rich Armenian, in the Arabahmet

area on the western edge of the city. High banqueting hall and courtyard in the Turkish style. Kebab-style dishes, especially mixed kebab and meze. Good-quality food, highly popular. Meze around €10 a dish. Mon–Sat 11am–midnight.

★ **El Sabor Latino** Selimiye Meydani (next to the mosque) 📞 2288322, 🌐 twitter.com/ElSaborLatino2; map p.200. *El Sabor Latino* offers Italian food with an additional strangely eclectic mix of tapas and Chinese.

**6**

## NORTH CYPRUS FESTIVALS

Whatever the festivals are called, in north Cyprus they usually include a wide variety of activities and events, not all directly relating to the subject contained in the title. So the tulip festival includes a pinball competition, an olive festival a darts competition. And many also throw in a beauty contest for good measure.

### MARCH

**Tepebasi Tulip Festival** (mid-March) Walks and displays to celebrate the Cyprus tulip (*Tulipa cypria*) and a wide range of activities – including bicycle tours, dancing and a pinball competition, in villages near Lapta.

### MAY & JUNE

**International Bellapais Music Festival** (end of May/early June) (ⓦbellapaisfestival.com) A festival of chamber and choral music and dance in Bellapais Abbey, one of north Cyprus's most beautiful settings.
**International Famagusta Art and Culture Festival** (ⓦmagusa.org) Huge music, theatre, ballet and visual arts festival held at various venues in Gazimağusa.

### JUNE & JULY

**Girne Living Culture and Art Festival** (whole of June) Turkish and Cypriot drama and music festival held in Girne's amphitheatre.
**Iskele International Folk Dance Festival** (end of June) Week-long festival where folk dancing groups from all over the world take part, staging a series of nightly performances.
**Lapta Tourist Festival** (June) Huge range of competitions aimed at and put on by the expat community – pool, table tennis, remote-controlled boats – there's even an "alcohol-drinking competition" (details at ⓦcyprusscene.com).
**Lefke Walnut Festival** (June) Festival of walnut-based sweets in the village in the western part of north Cyprus.

### AUGUST

**Gecitkale Hellim (Halloumi) Festival** A variety of events and demonstrations revolving around the Cypriot cheese halloumi – cooking, photography (not just photographs of cheese), beauty and fashion competitions.

### OCTOBER

**International Girne Olive Festival** (ⓦgirnebelediyesi.com; early Oct) Dance and drama, music, food (with an olive theme) and drink, shooting and darts competitions. Starts in Kyrenia Castle, then moves to the village of Zeytinlik.

---

The setting is fashionable – open kitchen, wood, leather, hanging lamps, photographs on the walls, there's live jazz on Wednesdays and Fridays, and the coffee is famous. Though much frequented by tourists, it is also popular with locals from both sides of the Green Line. Mains around €12–15. If there's any criticism, it's that service can be a little slow. Claims to be open "always", but more realistic opening hours are Mon–Sat 10am–midnight.

**Old Mosaic** Selmiye Meydani ☏2279551; map p.200. In the centre of the city, with shady tiled courtyard festooned in bourgainvillea, *Old Mosaic* serves a wide range and acceptable quality of meze. There's a bar across the street under the same management. Expect to pay around €30. Daily 9am–midnight.

★ **Sedirhan** Büyük Han ☏2287760, ⓦtwitter.com/ SeridhanCafe; map p.200. Good selection of traditional Turkish snacks and meals served in the beautifully restored Büyük Han. Don't be put off by the picture menu – it's very useful if you don't know the cuisine. Most meals around €20. Even if you're not hungry, stop for a drink – it's such a marvellous setting. Mon, Wed & Fri 9am–5pm, Tues, Thurs & Sat 9am–1pm, but hours can vary – restaurant stays open if there's live music on.

### DEREBOYU DISTRICT

**Biyer** 61 Mehmet Akif Cad (opposite Califorian Grill) ☏2293025, ⓦtwitter/CarsidaBiyer; map p.200. A good-value restaurant for the younger crowd, modelled perhaps on the sort of street cafés you might get in Istanbul. Turkish food with the emphasis on kebabs and cold and hot meze, accompanied on some days (usually Wed & weekends) by live music. Takeaway on offer. Mains from €15. Mon–Sat 10am–midnight.

## DRINKING AND ENTERTAINMENT

Lefkoşa is not known for its nightlife. Apart from eating and drinking, the main entertainment is gambling – all three of the hotels listed (see page 208) have casinos attached. Casinos also put on entertainment, though this can often resemble a kind of "north Cyprus's got talent". Otherwise, it's a matter of looking out for live music in bars and other venues – *Sedirhan*, for example, has live music on most Tuesdays and Thursdays.

★ **Cadi Kazani** 77 Tanzimat Sokak ☎2292371; map p.200. A bar tucked away in the up-and-coming Arabahmet area on the western edge of the old city, *Cadi Kazani* is owned and run by an artist whose paintings decorate the walls. Gentle background music, mellow atmosphere. Mon–Thurs 6pm–1am, Fri & Sat 5pm–2am.

## SHOPPING

Serious shoppers tend to stick to Lefkosia. However, quite a few head north in search of bargains – especially cheap copies of designer goods on sale on the other side of the Ledra Street crossing. The renovation of the covered market on Uray Sokak, the Bandabuliya, was completed in 2012, with, it has to be said, the loss of much of its character, but it's still a good place to go for clothing, fruit and vegetables. Büyük Han, too, is a good place for all sorts of souvenirs and arts and crafts objects. Bear in mind that there are restrictions on what you can bring back into the south: 40 cigarettes, 1 litre of alcohol and no more than €260 worth of other goods.

**Gloria Jean's Coffees** Girne Cad 22–26 ☎2283506; map p.200. Although now one of a well-known international chain of coffee shops, this was once bookshop Kemal Rustem, and still sells books. Decent range of English-language books, new and second hand, together with magazines. It's opposite the *Saray Hotel*. Mon–Thurs & Sun 8am–midnight, Fri & Sat 8am–1am.

★ **Hasder Folk Arts Institute Craft Centre** Selimiye Square ⊕hasder.org; map p.200. Excellent range of craft output from basketry and glassware to lace and furniture. Mon–Wed 8am–12.30pm & 1.30–5pm, Thurs–Fri 8am–7.30pm, Sat 8am–1pm.

**Mentes Ozsakin** Devlet Hastanesi Karsisi ☎2232940; map p.200. Fashion shoes and accessories, including boots and shoes with the highest heels you've ever seen. Mon–Sat 8.30am–7.30pm.

## DIRECTORY

**Banks and exchange** There are numerous currency exchange offices (including one at the Ledra Street crossing) and banks with ATMs in the city, especially on Sarayönü and Girne Cad. But don't forget that, if you're crossing from South Lefkosia, euros are widely accepted in the north. Bank opening hours are Mon–Fri 8am–5pm in winter, but vary from bank to bank in the summer.

**Consulates and embassies** Turkey is the only country that recognizes the TRNC, and therefore has a full embassy: Bedreddin Demirel Cad ☎6003100. Other countries have liaison offices: Australia, 20 Guner Turkmen Sokaki 20 ☎2277332; Germany, 29 Mehmet Akif Cad ☎2275161; UK,

Mehmet Akif Cad 23 ☎2283861; USA, 6 Serif Arzik Street ☎2273930; EU, Sarayonu ☎2287907.

**Emergencies** Ambulance (☎112), Fire Brigade (☎199) or Police (☎155).

**Internet** Though wi-fi is getting more and more available, it is still not as common as in the south. If you can't find wi-fi in a hotel or restaurant try the *Fistik Net Café* on Şht Salih Cibir Sokak 15 ☎2273727. Failing that, ask at the tourist office.

**Medical** Burham Nalbantoglu Devlet Hastahanesi (☎2285441).

**Post office** Sarayönü Sokak just off Ataturk Meydani (Mon–Fri 8am–1pm & 2–5pm, Sat 8.30am–12.30pm).

# Girne (Kyrenia)

**GIRNE** (still widely known by its Greek name **Kyrenia** or *Keryneia*) is the most beautiful town in Cyprus, owing to its ravishing harbour, mighty Venetian castle, and a backdrop of sharp and craggy mountains. It even has a pleasant climate, courtesy of those mountains, which bring cooler air and a greener landscape than in the rest of Cyprus. Following a lengthy period of street development and road works, Girne is now an easy city to navigate – the main approach road from the motorway ends in a central roundabout which is next to the main square Belediye Meydani and a large car park. It's also the main public transport hub. From this roundabout, the city's two main streets head east and west. In addition to road improvements, the whole city centre and harbour area have been tidied up, with clutter removed, buildings painted and streets cobbled or block paved. Girne is a place that all visitors to the island should try to take in, for the day if not longer.

Apart from the harbour and the castle, there's much else hidden away among Girne's steep serpentine alleys. The Anglican Church, the **Cafer Paşa Camii**, the **Ottoman Cemetery** and the **Chrysopolitissa Church** attest to the spiritual life of the town, the tiny **Folk Art Museum** and **Icon Museum** to its cultural life, and the **Bandabuliya** together with a host of shops to its commercial side. Finally, Girne's numerous **cafés** and **restaurants** offer the opportunity to eat, drink and socialize with friendly locals, or just enjoy the views and the chance to people-watch in comfort.

### Brief history

Girne was established in the tenth century BC by the first Greek invaders of Cyprus, the **Mycenaeans**, and can therefore claim to be the settlement with the longest history of continuous occupation anywhere on the island. During the time of Classical Greece it was one of the ten kingdoms of Cyprus. In the seventh century AD, **Arab raids** led to the building of a castle by the **Byzantines**, possibly on the site of an earlier Roman fort, later added to and strengthened by the **Lusignans** and then the **Venetians**. Although the castle was never taken by force of arms, it was starved into surrender by the **Ottomans** in 1570. During the occupation that followed, Girne declined and stagnated, but saw something of a renaissance during the **British period** as the new rulers built roads and developed the harbour. It became a busy port, exporting carob pods, importing goods from Greece and Turkey, and building ships. Prosperous and with a delightful climate, it was no wonder that British civil servants, streaming back from the collapsing empire, saw it as a paradise to which they could happily retire. However, this Levantine Shangri La changed as Cyprus gained its independence in 1960, and was then riven by intercommunal friction. Girne was one of the first places to fall during the 1974 Turkish invasion. With properties being looted, and then confiscated during the early post-invasion years, British expats left in droves, their number falling from 2500 to a couple of hundred. The spaces left by them, and even more by departing Greek Cypriots, were filled by Turkish Cypriots relocating, mainly from Lemesos, and by Turks coming in from the mainland. Since then, the **Brit expat community** has burgeoned once more, though issues over property ownership in the north have stifled the second-homes market.

## Girne harbour and around

Busy with excursion boats, laced with wooden pontoons and bristling with masts, Girne's medieval **harbour** is one of the most picturesque in the Mediterranean. Almost perfectly circular, its western side is dominated by the massive Girne castle, while the harbour entrance is now protected by a long breakwater built after independence. The horseshoe-shaped quay is taken up with restaurants and small hotels, some in converted carob warehouses, others in modern buildings, with balconied upper storeys and canopied ground floors. Nearby is the **Customs House**, converted by the British from a medieval tower to which, during troubled times, a chain was slung from the castle to prevent access to the harbour. It is now occupied by the tourist office. There's an even

---

**VISITING GIRNE FROM THE SOUTH**

The best place to cross over from the south if travelling to **Girne** is at the **Agios Dometios checkpoint** west of Lefkosia city centre. It's not well signposted – drive west along Leoforos Agiou Pavlou, and when the road bears sharply to the left immediately after Nicosia Racecourse, look out for a sharp right turn. The crossing is a few metres up this side street. Once across, you're in Metehan, and it's no more than a well-signposted half hour's drive to Girne. But do memorize the route after the crossing so that you can find your way back – the signposts are for Metehan, and there's no mention of it being a crossing point.

**GIRNE (KYRENIA)**

MEDITERRANEAN SEA

FOR DETAIL SEE MAP BELOW

KORDONBOYU CADDESI

Harbour

SAHILBOYU SOKAK

SERAP

SHT. EEDAL AKÇA

Folk Art
Museum

GOKSU SOKAK

CANBULAT SOKAK

AĞA CAFER PAŞA

Girne
Castle

Ağa Cafer
Paşa Camii

Ancient
Harbour

Bandabuliya

ERSIN AYDIN SOKAK

Byzantine
Tower

Belediye
Meydani

ZIYA RIZKI CADDESI

BOZKIRLI SOKAK

MUSTAFA CAGATAY CADDESI

MERSIN CADDESI

KORUTURK SOKAK

ATATURK CADDESI

TURKMEN SOKAK

NAMIK KEMAL CADDESI

4 BIS SIMAV

MARM

KARACA S.

ECEVIT CADDESI

SEDAT SIMAVI CADDESI

INONU CADDESI

MUCAHITLER CADDESI

FEVZI CAKMAK CADDESI

ISKENDERUN CADDESI

0    200
metres

Korineum Golf Club & 3

6

---

0    200
metres

Northwest
Tower

Lusignan
Tower

KORDONBOYU CADDESI

Harbour

SERAP

SHT. EEDAL AKÇA

Entrance to
Castle

Tomb Finds
Gallery

Castle

KORDONBOYU CADDESI

KUPDEMIR SOKAK

West Wall

Shipwreck
Museum

SAHILBOYU SOKAK

CANBULAT SOKAK

ATILLA SOKAK

BOZOKLAR SOKAK

Folk Art
Museum

Lusignan
Dungeon

GOKSU SOKAK

BAFRA SOKAK

AĞA CAFER PAŞA

Ağa Cafer
Paşa Camii

Venetian
Tower

EFELER SOKAK

EFELER SOKAK

Bandabuliya

Byzantine
Tower

ZIYA RIZKI CADDESI

Belediye
Meydani

Ottoman
Baldoken
Cemetery

Ferry offices

Bus Station and Post Office

older, ancient harbour immediately to the east (you can see it from the Venetian tower of the castle) and a much newer, modern one even further east beyond that.

## Girne Castle

Daily: April–Oct 8am–7pm, Nov–March 9am–5pm •€12

**Girne Castle** has a confusing architectural history, having been adapted, destroyed, rebuilt and improved so many times. The Byzantines first built a castle here, perhaps on the remains of an earlier structure, in the tenth century AD. Rectangular in shape, it was reinforced and extended during the Lusignan era, with the addition of living quarters and a moat. Its present form took shape under the Venetians in the sixteenth century, with the addition of the west and south walls and the construction of three new bastions. The British used the castle as a prison and as a police academy, and, during the late 1950s, to incarcerate EOKA fighters.

Never taken by force (though it was almost destroyed by the Genoese in 1373), the castle did succumb to the Ottomans in 1570. It is said that the Venetian commander of the castle negotiated a truce with the Ottomans until it became clear how the siege of Nicosia turned out. When the Ottomans presented him with the severed head of his Nicosian counterpart, he promptly surrendered.

### The entrance and courtyard

The entrance to the castle is across a stone **bridge**, which can be approached either from the central square **Belediye Meydani** through the police station yard, or up (clearly signposted) steps from the quayside. Either way, you need to buy tickets just before crossing the bridge. Once through the entrance gate, a tunnel brings you to the **central courtyard**, with its bits of broken masonry, palm trees, piles of stone catapult ammunition and, in the northeast corner, the rather pleasant *Kybele Cafe* and a souvenir shop from where all the castle's attractions are signposted. Be sure to take the steps up to the **viewpoint** over the harbour from where you can see as far as St Hilarion Castle. Notice, too, the twelfth-century **Byzantine Chapel of St George**, which was swamped by the castle as it expanded.

### Lusignan Tower

The **Lusignan Tower** standing at the northeast corner of the castle contains two floors of displays illustrating the medieval history of the castle. On the lower floor there are drawings by English academic William Dreghorn, mannequins dressed in armour and various weapons (crossbow, cannon, even an early sort of machine gun), clearly labelled by period – Lusignan, Venetian, Ottoman. There are also details of some of the political prisoners held in the castle by the British.

### Tomb Finds Gallery

To the east of the entrance to the Lusignan Tower is the **Tomb Finds Gallery**, showcasing Neolithic and Bronze Age objects found in excavations at **Vrysi** (Agios Epiktitos), 10km east of Girne, **Kirni** (near modern Pinarbasi) and **Akdeniz** (Agia Irini). The highlight is a reconstruction of an underground tomb on the top floor.

### Shipwreck Museum

The fascinating **Shipwreck Museum** is located in rooms that originally housed the royal guard. The chief exhibit is a 15m-long Greek merchant ship dating from 300 BC. The wreck was discovered by a local sponge diver off the coast of Girne in 1965 and raised by marine archeologists from the University of Pennsylvania. Among the cargo were 400 wine amphorae, thousands of almonds preserved in jars and 29 millstones which also served as ballast. Archeologists were able to deduce that the ship, made of Aleppo pine sheathed in lead, had a crew of four, and had docked at Samos and Rhodes on its final voyage. As well as the ship itself, the museum has exhibitions of the goods found on board, artists' impressions and a life-sized cross section to show how it was built, and is worth the price of admission to the castle on its own.

Venetian Tower

In the southeast corner of the castle, a gallery slopes down into the depths of the **Venetian Tower** to show a mock-up of a Venetian cannon crew in action. There are also more Dreghorn paintings.

Lusignan Dungeon

Halfway along the western wall, between the southwest bastion and the exit, lies the entrance to the **Lusignan Dungeon**. Waxwork displays show some of the types of torture used in the dungeons in the early 1300s when a purge of royalty and nobility was carried out. These displays include a particularly graphic model of a naked man being stretched on a wheel. The detail on the victims is grisly in itself – for example, Joanna L'Aleman, who was tortured while pregnant, and one John Visconti, who wound up starving to death in Buffavento Castle.

## Ağa Cafer Paşa Camii

Ağa Cafer Paşa Street • Open to visitors outside prayer times • Free

Just uphill from the waterfront west of the castle is Girne's main mosque, the **Ağa Cafer Paşa**. Dating from 1589, it has been renovated and adapted many times, most recently after an EOKA-B bomb damaged it in the 1950s. Although the minaret is fairly short and stumpy, it's remarkable how visible it is from wherever you are in the harbour area. The mosque contains three main rooms, each with an air of simplicity and space. Outside is the unused yet lavishly named "Hasan Kavizade Huseyin Effendi Fountain", built in 1841.

## Folk Art Museum

Mon, Tue, Wed & Fri 9am–2pm, Thurs 9am–4pm • €7

On the waterfront facing the harbour, is the **Folk Art Museum** (Harup Ambari Ve Kibris Evi), which stands in a fine Venetian-era house, once used as a carob store and donated to the city by a British expat in 1966. The building has been beautifully preserved and is distinctly more impressive than the contents – a motley collection of kitchen utensils, textiles and a few items of contemporary furniture.

## Icon Museum

Canbulat • Closed for renovation at the time of writing (usual hours Mon–Sat 8am–3.30pm, Thurs 8am–5pm) • €7

Located on the western arm of the harbour up steep steps from Canbulat Sokak, the **Icon Museum** is housed in what was the church of Archangelos Michaelis. The church is a sad sight, with rendering falling off the walls, a bell tower, long a landmark for sailors, festooned in scaffolding. Before closing, the largely seventeenth- to nineteenth-century icons, gathered from unnamed churches and stored in the castle until 1991 when the museum was opened, were displayed on three floors in the church, built in 1860 with the blessing of the Turkish authorities, and with a bell donated by a local Muslim. Across the road to the steps up to the entrance are some Greco-Roman **rock-cut tombs**, a rare sight in Girne as many others have been built over.

# Belediye Meydani and around

If the harbour is the tourist face of Girne, **Belediye Meydani** (Town Hall Square) reflects its ordinary Turkish Cypriot life. It's only a couple of hundred metres up the hill from the waterfront, yet it has a totally different feel – buzzing with pedestrians and traffic, and with a shopping centre joining it to the main shopping street, **Ziya Rizki Caddesi**. If you raise your eyes above the bustle, you can see the snaggle-toothed outline of St Hilarion Castle in the distance. The only thing to spoil the atmosphere is the very building that gives the square its name – an ugly modern municipal town hall, plonked right in the centre.

## Ottoman Baldoken Cemetery

With busy Belediye Meydani on one side and a large car park on the other, the little **Ottoman Baldoken Cemetery**, all that's left of a once huge graveyard, looks a little overwhelmed. It started as a place outside the castle to bury soldiers killed during the Ottoman siege, and later, during the seventeenth century, began to take civilians. It has also, at different times, been known as the Islamic Graveyard or the "Graveyard of the Forlorn". At its heart is a **domed tomb** called the Osmanli Baldoken Mezarligi. Given its location in the centre of a busy town, it is a surprisingly serene place in which to relax.

## Byzantine Tower

Walking west from Belediye Meydani along Ziya Rizki Caddesi, you'll see the **Byzantine Tower**, squat and ancient-looking, with a busy café at its base and the "Round Tower Art Gallery and Craft Centre" shop upstairs. It's worth a visit to see the inside of one of the remaining city wall towers. If you spot souvenirs to buy, that's a bonus.

## Bandabuliya

Next to the Byzantine Tower, with the main entrance on Canbulat Sokak, the **Bandabuliya** is another old building that's been dragged into the twenty-first century. Once the town's bazaar, it's now an upmarket shopping mall with cafés, restaurants and gift shops.

### ARRIVAL AND DEPARTURE

GIRNE (KYRENIA)

With excellent roads connecting it to the south, west and east, Girne is an easy place to get to, wherever you're staying on the island.

**By bus** The long-distance bus station can be found just off Halim Hocadglu Cad, southwest of the medieval harbour. Shared minibuses (*dolmuş*) set off from the central square, Belediye Meydani.

Destinations Gazimağusa (every 30min; 75min); Lefkoşa (every 20min; 20min).

**By car** Girne is connected to Lefkoşa by a dual carriageway,

and to Gazimağusa and Güzelyurt by good main roads. On arrival, head for the car park next to the central square, Belediye Meydani, or look out for (often more expensive) private car parks on waste ground. Away from the old town, on-street parking is also a possibility.

**By ferry** Ferries connect Girne with Tasucu on the Turkish mainland, and run to and from the new harbour, east of the medieval harbour. Check out ⓦ northcyprusonline.com for times; tickets can be booked online at ⓦ ferries-turkey.com.

### GETTING AROUND

**On foot** Girne is best explored on foot. Other places worth visiting in the region (St Hilarion, Buffavento and so on) will need a car, or can be visited using service taxis (from the bus

station) or on tour buses.

**By car** For car rental try Cyprus Pines Rent a Car (ⓣ 8686779, ⓦ cypruspines.com) or Ship Inn Rent a Car (ⓣ 8156701).

### INFORMATION

**Tourist office** The tourist office is located at the back of the Old Customs House at the western end of the medieval

harbour (daily 8am–6pm; ⓣ 8152145).

### ACTIVITIES

**Golf** Korineum Golf Club (Esentepe, Girne ⓣ 8887575, ⓦ korineumgolf.com) is a newish par-72 golf course – the first full golf course in north Cyprus. It has a golf academy, driving range, spa and gym, pro shop, and even accommodation. Green fees: low season €50, high season

€85, plus a range of equipment to rent.

**Paragliding** Tandem paragliding (no experience needed) is offered by Highline Tandem Paragliding, Old Harbour, Girne (ⓣ 8709292, ⓦ highlineparagliding.com). Experienced paragliders are also catered for.

**Walking** There's good walking in the Kyrenia mountain range just south of Girne – ask for a trail map at the tourist office, or consult ⓦkyreniamountaintrail.org, where you can buy downloadable GPS files for your mobile phone and a range of paper maps. As ever in Cyprus, the best walking weather is in spring and autumn, though the altitude in the mountains makes even summer hiking a pleasure.

**Water sports** Numerous water sports, boat trips and fishing trips are advertised around the harbour. There's

usually no need to book. Options include: African Queen ☎8763666 (six-hour boat trips, with stops at beach clubs for water sports); Aphrodite Boat Trips and Water Sports ☎868 09 43 (boat trips, fishing trips); North Cyprus Fishing ☎8258333 (fishing trips); Ladyboss ☎8709222 (offshore fishing).

**Scuba diving** Blue Dolphin (☎8515113, ⓦblue dolphin.4mg.com) offers a full range of scuba diving and tuition, based at the *Jasmine Court Hotel*.

**6**

## ACCOMMODATION

Girne has a growing stock of hotels, villas and apartments split between the town and big package resorts along the coast. Another option is to stay in Bellapais village in the hills above town.

### GIRNE TOWN

**British Hotel** Kyrenia Yacht Harbour ☎8152240, ⓦbritishhotelcyprus.com; map p.213. Boutique-style hotel in the centre of town with fine views from the roof terrace, and from some upstairs rooms (though you'll have to pay €20 extra). All rooms have plush interiors (deep purple throws and chairs add a bit of colour) with bath or shower, and there's a bar, restaurant and 24hr room service. **€65**

★ **The Colony** Ecevit Cad ☎8151518, ⓦthecolony cyprus.com; map p.213. Back from the harbour area, this is a smart hotel which aims at a classy ambience, with a choice of restaurants and bars, rooms and suites. Facilities include the inevitable casino, a fitness suite and spa (personal trainers are available) and a rooftop pool and terrace. Mostly aimed at Turkish business clientele rather than holiday-makers, but a good choice if you fancy a splurge. Minimum stay seven nights. **€135**

**Dome** Kordon Boyou ☎8152454, ⓦdome-cyprus.com; map p.213. Just out of the central harbour area, on the western promontory, within easy walking distance of the castle, this is the most famous colonial hotel in Girne. It dates back to the 1930s, and was where Lawrence Durrell stayed when he first arrived here. Stately public areas are complemented by comfortable modern rooms. There's a smart bar with sea view, and both freshwater and seawater pools. The staff are well trained and friendly. Minimum stay two nights. **€140**

**Nostalgia** 7 Cafer Paşa Sokak ☎8153079, ⓦnostalgia boutiquehotel.com; map p.213. Old-fashioned (hence the name) hotel in the centre of Girne – behind the Bandabuliya and the Byzantine Tower. Facilities include a/c and en-suite bathrooms in all rooms (though en suites can be a bit basic), and there's a small pool, and a restaurant and bar. The hotel occupies two townhouses, one slightly more

modern than the other, so check the room on offer if this matters to you. This is a hotel with a slightly eccentric feel – you'll either love it or hate it. And there's a fair amount of street noise. **€50**

**Onar Village** Girne–Lefkoşa Road ☎8155850, ⓦonar village.com; map p.213. Nicely set hotel on the hill above Girne, with rooms in two wings plus villas around the pool, in lush gardens. There's a sauna/Turkish bath, solarium, indoor pool, restaurant, bar, library, even a small museum. Villas have full kitchens, so can be self-catering. There's a free daily shuttle into town (essential as it's several kilometres from the town centre up a steep hill). The coastal and mountain views are lovely. **€92**

★ **Pia Bella** Iskeriderun Cad ☎6505000, ⓦpiabella. com; map p.213. Clean, attractive modern family-run hotel with caring friendly staff. Quiet gardens with palm trees and mountain backdrop, pool, restaurant, café and several bars (though pool bar sometimes not open). Rooms are comfortable and have central heating and a/c, mini-bar and coffee-making accoutrements. Three nights' minimum stay high season. **€76**

**White Pearl** 23 Eftal Akca Sokak ☎8150430, ⓦwhite pearlhotel.com; map p.213. Well-placed small hotel (ten rooms with heating, a/c and en suite facilities) on Girne harbour, with great views from room balconies and a roof terrace bar/restaurant which is open April till October. Rooms vary in size, so ask to see first if this is an issue. **€70**

### BEACH HOTELS

**Acapulco Holiday Resort** Çatalköy ☎6504500 ⓦacapulco-cyprus.com; map p.213. Large resort hotel (200 rooms, 230 bungalows) with casino. The *Acapulco* has a good range of facilities, including a beach restaurant, children's funfair and mini water park, kids' club, fitness and health centre. It claims to have the biggest pool in north Cyprus. Main restaurant uses locally sourced food, and there are several bars (including an "English Pub"). Good sandy beach, though the army camp on the western promontory is a bit intimidating. Free daily shuttle bus to Girne. Four nights' minimum stay in high season. **€135**

## EATING

**Canli Balik** Eski Liman ☎8152182; map p.213. This is a good fish restaurant down by the harbour (roughly halfway

**6**

around, below the Folk Art Museum) and cheaper than many. The menu includes a wide selection of main courses, including lamb shank, sea bass and sea bream, kebabs, *kléftiko*, omelettes, egg and chips and burgers, together with set menus. Main courses around €30, and a meze for twelve dishes for €40. Daily 10am–12.30am.

**Carob** Eski Liman ☎ 8633333; map p.213. As the name implies, this restaurant is accommodated in a converted carob warehouse on the dock. Italian and Turkish cuisines are on offer – eat or drink downstairs, or enjoy the commanding views of the harbour from the balcony (full meals only). There's live music on Fridays and Saturdays. Around €15–27 main dishes, with a three-course set menu at €49. Daily 9am–midnight.

★ **Chimera** Eski Liman (on the harbour side, at the castle end) ☎ 8454394; map p.213. French and Turkish cuisine served by attentive, friendly staff. Expect to pay €40/person for three courses and wine. They also serve English breakfast and there is occasional live music. Daily 9am–midnight.

**Jakaranda** 2 Cafer Paşa Sokak ☎ 8156008; map p.213. Right next door to the Cafer Paşa Mosque, the *Jakaranda*, once the *Set Italian*, has now become the restaurant of the *Kyrenia Palace Hotel*, though it retains its name on the

door. It is set in a beautiful little terraced courtyard, with access either end. Classic Italian set menu of pasta, seafood and steaks (€32–55), with a set menu at €80/person. Food 9am–midnight.

**Niazi's** Kordon Boyn Cad ☎ 8152160 (take away ☎ 8158460), ⊛ niazis.com; map p.213. Hugely popular with locals and visitors, *Niazi's* (there are also branches in Lefkoşa and Gazimağusa) is famed for its "full kebab" (€25) which packs in *kofte*, *şeftali* (north Cypriot sausage), plus a lamb chop, and comes served with accompanying meze and sweets from the open buffet. They also do takeaway. Daily noon–midnight.

**Set Fish** Eski Liman ☎ 8152336; map p.213. In an attractive stone building with balconies, on a terrace above the harbour road, this good-value fish restaurant used to be the sister restaurant to *Set Italian*, which is now *Jakaranda* (see above). Main courses €30–55, with set meze menu at €60/person. Daily 10am–11pm.

**Stonearch Restaurant** 13 Efeler Sokak ☎ 8154753; map p.213. Well-reviewed restaurant with a pleasant ambience in a traditional stone house up the hill from the harbour. Beef and chicken dishes range in price from €30–55, with wine from €37–98. Daily 6–11.30pm.

## DRINKING AND NIGHTLIFE

Girne is no Agia Napa, though there are numerous bars around the harbour area and even a beach club (a rarity in north Cyprus). Otherwise nightlife and entertainment revolve around hotel casinos – with over twenty in the area, Girne is the casino capital of the north.

★ **Escape Beach Club** Yavuz Cikartma Plaji, Alsancak ☎ 8218330, ⊛ escapebeachclub.com; map p.213. Set right on the beach 5km west of Girne, the *Escape* is a bar/club/restaurant complex. Music veers between RnB, hip-hop and Turkish. Thurs–Sat 10pm–4am.

**Ice Lounge** Yavuz Cikartma Plaji ☎ 8893333; map p.213. Just outside Alsancak, above Cikarma Beach, west of Girne. Drinking, dancing and a decent sound system, and, during the summer, international DJs. Wed, Fri & Sat 10.30pm–5am.

**Losers Club** 9 Namik Kemal ☎ 8627662, ⊛ facebook.com/losers.club.girne; map p.213. If you prefer socializing rather than deafening beats, this is the place to go. A quiet, cosy bar in pleasant surroundings. No food served. Daily 7pm-3am.

## SHOPPING

There's not much in the way of exciting shopping available in Girne, though a couple of places offer a good range of souvenirs and gifts in interesting historical surroundings.

**Bandabuliya** Corner of Canbulat Sk and Aga Cafér Pasa Street; map p.213. The old indoor market (see page 216) is now a place to source souvenirs and gifts, from handbags and textiles to pottery and jewellery. There's also a restaurant, juice bar, coffee shop, and sometimes live

music. Mon–Sat 8am–6pm.

**Round Tower** Ziya Rizki Cad; map p.213. Good place to get art and craft goods like pottery, jewellery and pictures, in the setting of a Lusignan tower. You can also buy books. Published opening hours are approximate, may be shorter on Sundays, and it may be closed for brief periods with a note on door. Daily: March–Nov 10am–6pm, Dec–Feb 11am–5pm.

## DIRECTORY

**Banks and Exchange** Turk Bankasi, Ziya Rizki Cad; Is Bankasi, corner of Ziya Rizki Cad and Ataturk Cad.
**Emergencies** Ambulance (☎ 112), Fire Brigade (☎ 199) or Police (☎ 155). Girne Hospital (☎ 8152266).
**Internet** *Café Net*, Efeler Sokak ☎ 815 92 59; *Bright Star*

*Internet Café*, Vakifler Paşaji 7 ☎ 8449333.
**Post office** M Cagatay Cad, off Belediye Meydani (Mon–Fri 8am–12.30pm & 1–4.15pm, Thurs 8am–12.30pm & 1pm–5.30pm).

# Around Girne

Although there's plenty to see in Girne, after a few days you may want to explore further afield. Fortunately, its sandy coastline offers some excellent beaches, while inland are some heavyweight sights including St Hilarion Castle and Bellapais village. Indeed, it shouldn't be forgotten that Lefkoşa and Güzelyurt are also within easy reach.

## Karaoğlanoğlu (Agios Georgios)

Landings monument and cemetery open access; museum: Mon–Fri 8am–6pm • Free

About 8km west along the coast from Girne is the village of **Karaoğlanoğlu** (previously the Greek village of Agios Georgios), now a run-of-the-mill resort and also home to the campus of the American University (and thus busy with students during term time). It's mainly notable as the place where the **Turkish forces landed** on July 20, 1974.

The landings are commemorated by a **monument** and museum west of town – stay on the main road, straight through three roundabouts (the first and third of which have signs for Karaoğlanoğlu pointing off to the right), and the monuments and museum are on the right. A large paved area leads to a small **Muslim cemetery** in which the 71 Turkish soldiers who died during the landing are buried, backed by a modern sculpture and the flags of Turkey and the TRNC. Karaoğlanoğlu was named in honour of an infantry colonel who was killed on the beach – his photograph and biography are mounted on a plinth.

Next to the plinth and cemetery is the **Peace and Freedom Museum**, a small collection of uniforms and photographs with some military vehicles on show outside. The actual **landing point** is marked by a huge concrete monument, nicknamed "the Turkish erection" by locals. The beach where it all happened was called "Five Mile Beach" by the British, presumably because it's five miles from Girne. It's one of the more attractive in the area, with the *Ada Beach Hotel* on one side, and on the other a pretty cove with golden sand and a little offshore island.

## Hazret Omer Tekke

Mon–Thurs 9am–4pm • Free

On a rocky shore, 10km east of Girne, sits the **Hazret Omer Tekke**, built to house seven Muslim martyrs. It's not easy to find – despite being a major attraction for both tourists and the faithful, it merits only a tiny sign left off the main road east of Girne – look out for it 1.8km after the massive *Port Gratos* hotel complex, and immediately before a "Tempo" supermarket. The story goes that the seven (the commander Omer and six of his men), now regarded as saints, were killed in the seventh century, and their bodies put in a cave. Centuries later, after the Ottoman conquest, their bodies were discovered, still in a miraculous state of preservation, and moved to a mosque and mausoleum specially built to receive them – their tombs are to the right as you enter. The beautifully designed mosque is in a spectacularly pretty setting, with views across a bay towards the mountains, but the effect is somewhat spoilt by the towering modern lamppost above it and intrusive modern toilet in the car park. The mosque itself, however, once rather the worse for wear, having been battered and buffeted by wind and rain each winter, has been given a face-lift.

## Alagadi Protected Area

Daily 8am–8pm • Free • W seaturtle.org/mtrg/projects/cyprus

East of Acapulco Bay is a beach of a totally different type. An otherwise rather bleak spot, **Alagadi** is a "Protected Area" because of the green and loggerhead turtles that nest here. As well as sea turtles, the area is home to a variety of plants, lizards and

**6**

> ## DASTARDLY DEEDS AT ST HILARION
>
> On January 17, 1369, **Peter I, King of Cyprus**, was stabbed to death as he slept in his palace in Nicosia, supposedly by three of his own knights. He was succeeded by his son, Peter II. **Queen Eleanor** – now the Queen Mother – became convinced that her husband had been killed on the orders of Peter's brother, **Prince John**. Despite rumours of her infidelity in the king's absence she vowed to avenge his murder. John had taken up residence in St Hilarion Castle, which he held with a force of Bulgarian mercenaries, while Peter's other brother James held Kyrenia. A Genoese invasion, possibly at Eleanor's instigation, led, in 1374, to the surrender of Kyrenia, and James ended up as a prisoner in Genoa. Eleanor now turned her attention to John. Having persuaded him that all was forgiven, she warned the prince that his Bulgarian forces were planning to overthrow him. John responded by throwing several of them to their deaths from Prince John's Tower. Eleanor's accusations were almost certainly untrue – a Machiavellian plan aiming to both bring him closer and weaken him. The drama concluded when Eleanor invited John to dine with her and the young king in Nicosia. They ate in the very room where Peter I was murdered and, when the final dish arrived, she dramatically flung back the cloth to reveal her dead husband's blood-stained shirt. This was the signal for retainers to appear and stab Prince John to death in his turn.

butterflies. During July and August a visitor centre (bear right after the *St Kathleen Café*), established by Exeter University and staffed mainly by Exeter students who have volunteered or are studying for their doctorates, operates and offers a variety of activities depending on the season. Although there are signs to deter litter and driving on the beach, a barrier which is shut overnight, and attempts to limit bathers to certain parts of the shore, there is often rubbish strewn across the sands.

## St Hilarion Castle

Daily: April–Oct 9am–6.30pm, Nov–March 9am–4.30pm • ☎ 2272994 • €9

Of the three magnificent castles in the Kyrenia mountains, by far the most accessible, popular and most complete is **St Hilarion**. Dramatically sited on a rocky crag with elegantly ruined turrets, towers and windows, it certainly fires the imagination – in writer Dame Rose Macaulay's words it's a "picture-book castle for elf kings" – and formed the template for both the fairy-tale castles of King Ludwig in Bavaria and Walt Disney's Magic Kingdom. If possible, visit in spring when the surrounding landscape is a riot of wild flowers. The views from the snack bar are to die for.

To reach the castle from Girne you need to drive south along the Lefkoşa motorway as it climbs up into the mountains, and just before it gets to the top of the pass and begins its descent to the Mesaoria plain, follow the yellow signpost off to the right. A 3km side road snakes up through a **military camp**, past a large statue of a soldier in battledress at its entrance. (The firing range on the left was once the site for medieval tournaments.) Up a sharp hill, you arrive at a small car park outside the castle gate. The whole trip from Girne takes about twenty minutes. On this road bear in mind that you're in a restricted military area, and not allowed to stop, let alone take photographs. This is a pity because it's as you approach the castle that you get by far the best view.

### Brief history

St Hilarion was originally a **monastery** dedicated to an obscure fourth-century Syrian hermit who lived in a cave on Mount Didymus ("Twin peaks"). An ascetic of the most extreme kind, **Hilarion** reputedly never washed and built up a following thanks to banishing demons and performing miracles. The monastery's strategic position, commanding the pass through the Kyrenia mountains and overlooking the northern coastal plain, was not lost on the Byzantines. Facing repeated Arab raids, they converted it into a castle, probably sometime in the eighth century AD. The

Lusignans improved and strengthened it in the thirteenth century – most of what you can see today was built in 1228 by John d'Ibelin – and it became not only a military stronghold but also a **palace** for Lusignan royalty, nicknamed "Dieu d'Amour", loosely translated as Cupid's Castle. This was the castle's heyday, an era of tournaments, knights and courtly intrigue, especially under the rule of **King Peter I** and **Queen Eleanor of Aragon**.

St Hilarion continued to be a castle of importance during the latter Lusignan period, but when the Venetians took over in 1489 it fell into disrepair and became the ruin it is now, only to see action during the mid-twentieth-century troubles, when the Turkish TMT occupied it.

**6**

### The site

Once through the castle entrance – which includes a barbican – you will find yourself in the large **outer bailey** originally built by the Byzantines. Follow the sign to the right for the first of many wonderful views then continue upwards along the "Main Road". It's a well-made path with occasional steps, and as you climb you'll see a watchtower and, to your left, the impressive curtain wall that rises steeply to the upper parts of the castle. This outer bailey was the area into which peasants and livestock could be withdrawn when the castle was under attack.

The castle stables are now used as a small **visitor centre** which offers lots of sketches, and information about the Lusignans. Beyond the stables, the path winds steeply upwards to the tunnel-like gate of what is described as the "second section", perhaps the **Lower Ward**. It's a warren of alleys, buildings and rooms opening off a central tunnel, some of which were part of the original tenth-century monastery. The first structure, up to the right, is the monastery **church**, now open to the elements, but with a well-preserved apse. North of here is the **Great Hall**, now home to the *Café Lusignan*. Along one side of the hall is a wooden balcony hanging over a staggering view of the coast below – on a clear day you can see Turkey, some 100km away.

Beyond the hall is a group of rooms which serviced it – **kitchen**, **buttery** and **privies** – and a **belvedere**, a shaded vaulted terrace with picnic tables and arches, again with those superb views. To the left (west) of the hall are more workaday rooms and the **castellan's quarters**, which contain displays with mannequins illustrating medieval life. Continuing along the path, which tunnels through this clutch of lower ward rooms, you emerge into the sunlight to signs pointing one way (off to the right) to the **barracks**, and **Royal Apartments**, and the other way, onward and upward, to the third section.

You pass a very large cistern which appears to have been built rather than hewn out of the rock (it has stone buttresses), and then the path, partly steps, partly rock-strewn tracks, soars upwards. Just before you reach the top, a fork leads left to the isolated **Prince John's Tower**, where several of John's Bulgarian mercenaries were murdered (see page 220). Turning right instead of following the path to Prince John's Tower brings you to the main gate of the **Upper Ward**. Once through the gate, there are, in succession, a Byzantine tower, a kitchen, a cistern and a group of subsidiary buildings. Beyond them are a further set of Royal Apartments and the famous **Queen's Window** at which Queen Eleanor is said to have sat. From here glorious views to the west open out, with, in the foreground, the village of Karmi. All that remains to be seen is the **Western Tower** and the **Zirve** (summit) of the mountain.

## Buffavento Castle

Open access • Free

**Buffavento Castle** is the second of the three great fortresses that are strung out along the Kyrenia Mountains – the third is Kantara, far off to the east (see page 245). Whereas St Hilarion is easily accessible, Buffavento is more remote, with the result that you may well be the only visitor – a major plus in terms of atmosphere. However, don't expect refreshments, information leaflets or the like – there's not even a ticket kiosk. Part of the excitement of the visit is the wild tortured landscape of the "five fingers" mountain through which you pass, and the winding mountain road up to the castle, which reveals views across the whole island (see page 223).

### Brief history

Though never a monastery, Buffavento, like St Hilarion, was a Byzantine fortification built during the Arab raids, much developed and improved by the Lusignans. Indeed, it was the surrender of Buffavento to Richard the Lionheart by the daughter of Isaac Comnenos, the then ruler of Cyprus, that signalled the end of resistance to the English King and, a year later, the beginning of the Lusignan age. The castle had some high-profile residents – **John Visconti**, for example, who was the knight who informed King Peter I that his wife Eleanor was having an affair and was incarcerated for his pains, first in Girne Castle then at Buffavento, where he starved to death. Another story tells of a woman (variously identified as a Byzantine queen or the Lusignan **Eschive of Montbeliard**) who locked herself away in the castle to prevent others being infected with her leprosy. Her only companion was her dog (which also had the disease). The mutt started to go missing for a time every day, and miraculously began to get better.

**THE ROAD TO BUFFAVENTO**

The **castle** is accessed from the main coast road east of Girne. Look out for the sign ("Buffavento 6km") on the right, past Acapulco Beach. From Lefkoşa, take the main Gazimağusa road east, then take a left (signposted "Girne") at a roundabout after 14km. Ignore earlier signs for Buffavento via Taskent – you're better off sticking to the main roads. After the turn-off, a good road climbs for 13km up towards an impressive blade of a mountain (called Pentadaktylos because its five peaks look something like a hand) past a large quarry – you may have to overtake heavily laden lorries grinding along at barely walking speed – to the Buffavento turning.

The mountain road to the castle looks narrow and uninviting, and is easy to miss, but it's well surfaced (not gravel, as is sometimes reported) and meanders fetchingly off into the mountains. It doesn't, as some guidebooks say, require four-wheel drive. There are stretches where there are steep drops to the left and no guardrail, and in places you might have to dodge rocks that have fallen off the cliffs to the right, but it's easy enough driving if you ignore the amazing views and keep your eyes on the road. After 6km a clear sign points up a steep hill to the castle car park.

**6**

One day she followed him to a natural spring, where he splashed in the water. She too bathed in the spring and was cured. In thanks, she built a church over the spring – **Agios Ioannis Chrysostomos** – and around it grew a monastery. It's still there (though deconsecrated) below the castle, but can't be visited, since it's well within one of the area's military camps.

### The site

Though at 940m above sea level the highest of the three castles, Buffavento is also the smallest and worst preserved, more a romantic Gothic ruin than a sturdy fortress. The castle was much damaged by the Venetians to prevent its future use, and badly eroded over the centuries by the elements (though its name means "not yielding to winds").

From the car park a path and steps rise steeply towards the ruins, which you can see lining the clifftop high above. Bear in mind that it requires a fair bit of hard climbing (though there are plenty of hand rails) and there's little shade (if you get into trouble, dial ☏155). As you climb, the views south are particularly impressive. As at St Hilarion, the hillside is carpeted with flowers in spring.

Incidentally, in the car park is a sad little **monument**, almost completely demolished by vandals. It commemorates the victims of an **air crash** in February 1988 when a Boeing 727 chartered by a Turkish airline heading for Ercan Airport hit the mountain here. All fifteen people on board were killed. The vandalism has been the subject of numerous complaints from visitors, but nothing has yet been done, either to remove or repair the ruined monument.

# Bellapais

Almost exactly halfway between St Hilarion and Buffavento is the flower-bedecked village of **Bellapais**, a tangle of narrow lanes and steep hills, with fine views down to Girne's modern harbour. The village is synonymous with its **medieval abbey**, one of the most beautiful in the eastern Mediterranean. Yet, it's not just the abbey that makes Bellapais so popular – one of its principal cheerleaders was English author **Lawrence Durrell**, who lived here in the 1950s and included detailed descriptions of the village and its inhabitants in his book *Bitter Lemons*. Bellapais is one of the principal tour-stops on the island, so it is often packed. Try to avoid high season and late morning/early afternoon. Despite being such a popular attraction, Bellapais is not easy to find. Travelling east on the main road from Girne, turn right at the Bellapais-signposted "peace" roundabout (with its two figures holding olive branches), and, a few hundred metres along, take the first (unsignposted) main turning left. At the top of the hill turn left at the (unsignposted) roundabout, and continue on to the village. Or just stop and ask.

### Brief history

Bellapais abbey was founded by the second Lusignan ruler **Aimery** to house Augustinian monks expelled from the **Church of the Holy Sepulchre** when Jerusalem fell to Saladin in 1187. Known as the "Abbaye de la Paix" or the Abbey of Peace, most of what remains dates from the period 1267–84, with the cloisters and refectory being added in 1324–59. In its early years the monastery adopted strict Premonstratensian beliefs, but as time went on it started to earn a name for a variety of **corrupt practices**, where monks ate and drank to excess, took wives (sometimes two or three), had children, and would then only accept their own sons into the monastery as novices. Though it built up considerable wealth, its treasure was plundered by the **Genoese** in 1373. After the **Ottoman Conquest** in 1571 the abbey became derelict, and was raided for its dressed building stone – only the church escaped, as it continued to be used for worship by the local Greek Orthodox community. Vandalization of the monastery continued under the British, who even used the refectory as a rifle range.

### Bellapais Abbey

Daily: June–mid-Sept 9am–7pm, mid-Sept–May 9am–5pm •€9

**Bellapais Abbey** stands on a small square with trees, lawns, flowerbeds and park benches. Having bought tickets, you can walk through the **entrance gateway** whose ruins indicate that it was once heavily fortified. Nearby is the enviably sited *Kybele Restaurant* (see page 225), which occupies the abbey's kitchen court, and a set of steps to the abbey's lofty **medieval tower**, topped by the vivid red and white of the Turkish and TRNC flags; despite signs warning that it's not safe to climb, the tower is far too seductive a photo opportunity for most visitors. Beyond here a tree-shaded **courtyard** leads to the **church**, the most complete part of the monastery. Unlike Western monasteries it is flat roofed, with a rather dark, gloomy interior. To the north of the church are the **cloisters**, the most atmospheric part of the abbey, three sides of which are in reasonable condition, but the fourth (western) side is ruined. The four rather large poplar trees in the quadrangle, planted in 1940, are home to a loud flock of sparrows. To the north of the cloisters, with access through a superb doorway with dog-tooth edges and three Lusignan coats of arms, is the **refectory**. Some 30m long, 10m wide and 12m high, it is covered by a single-span stone vaulted roof, an architectural triumph considering that it stands right at the edge of a cliff. At the far end (the end with the small rose window) stood the Abbot's high table, with, along the length of the north and south walls, the long tables of the ordinary monks. On the north wall is a small **pulpit** from where scriptures would be read to the diners silently munching below. Outside the refectory is a fountain where the monks would wash their hands before eating. If you look carefully you can make out the Roman sarcophagus into which it has been incorporated.

### Lawrence Durrell's House

Aci Limon Sokak • Not open to the public except for some days in September from time to time

Lawrence Durrell lived in Bellapais from 1953–56, detailing his experiences in *Bitter Lemons* (see page 263). To find his home, walk up from the abbey square along Aci Limon Sokak, which climbs past the Tatlisulu market – there is a small hand-painted sign "Bitter Lemons 400m up on left" attached to a telegraph pole and pointing skywards. Another sign further up indicates that you're nearly there but should really visit the *Gardens of Irini* guest house. **Durrell's house** (dated 1893) is large and yellow, with brown doors and window shutters and a wooden-fenced roof terrace. In case you were in any doubt, there's a ceramic plaque above the door. Across the road is the public water fountain (marked "ER 1953"), which played a prominent part in the tortuous and hilarious process of buying the house – the purchase takes up a whole chapter in the book.

Another chapter of the book is devoted to the "**Tree of Idleness**" that stands opposite the abbey. Durrell was warned never to sit under it because, "its shadow incapacitates one for serious work", a belief that arose from the idle hours spent by many villagers under the tree. It is now the centrepiece of a rather good restaurant.

**6**

**ACCOMMODATION AND EATING**                                                                                                          **BELLAPAIS**

★ **Bellapais Monastery Village** Bellapais Yolu ☎ 8559172, ⊛ bellapaismonasteryvillage.com. Within walking distance of the village of Bellapais, this collection of Byzantine/Ottoman-style modern buildings offers rooms, suites and "mini villas" all with a/c and en-suite facilities. There's a sun terrace, indoor and outdoor pool, rooftop restaurant and bar – and the views are great throughout. A hotel that prides itself on peace and quiet (therefore no children under 12). **€87**

★ **Gardens of Irini** Bellapais ☎ 8152820, ⊛ twitter. com/gardensofirini. Run by long-term expats (one of them an artist whose paintings decorate the place), the *Gardens of Irini* is located at the top of Bellapais village – head for Lawrence Durrell's house, and you'll see the sign. Tiny and

delightful, the guest house consists of a small converted cottage and a studio backing onto a lovely garden. **€75**

**Kybele Restaurant** Bellapais Abbey ☎ 8157531, ⊛ kybele.biz. Stunningly located within the grounds of Bellapais Abbey with views of the Abbey and the sea beyond, the *Kybele* offers a wide range of seafood, grills and pastas from around €30. Daily 11am–11pm.

★ **Tree of Idleness** Bellapais ☎ 8153380. Good-quality Turkish food in a restaurant through which grows the "Tree of Idleness" immortalized by Lawrence Durrell (though there is another pretender to the title elsewhere in the village). The stairs to the first floor climb up through its branches. Main courses €20–30. Live Turkish music on Fridays and Saturdays. Daily 10am–midnight.

# Güzelyurt and the west

The western part of north Cyprus is not much frequented by visitors, yet it's easy to access following the opening of more **crossing points from the south** (see page 27). The region's main town, **Güzelyurt**, is worth a brief wander for its archeological museum and the Agios Mamas Church. But it's the twin ancient sites of **Soli** and **Vouni** that are the real draw.

## Güzelyurt (Morfou)

**GÜZELYURT** (called Morfou before 1974, a name that is still widely used), 40km west of Lefkoşa, is the principal town for the western part of north Cyprus. Once hugely prosperous, it has suffered badly, first from the demise of the copper-mining industry and, subsequently, the impact of the 1974 invasion which devastated the surrounding citrus groves and strawberry fields, once tended by Greek-Cypriot farmers – still a cause of immense bitterness in the south. The fruit farms are, at last, recovering and the main impression that you get now as you approach is a sea of orange and lemon trees stretching as far as the eye can see.

On the way into town on the Girne road, look out for **Engine No 3** of the Cyprus Government Railway. A saddle engine, it was built in the USA in 1924, and looks a little sorry for itself compared to Engine No 1 in Gazimağusa. Rearing up on the town's main roundabout (along with a memorial to Turkish Cypriots killed by EOKA) is the imposingly large, white **Fatih Camii** mosque, built with Saudi Arabian money. Nearby is the **archeological museum** and the town's main highlight, the church and monastery of **Agias Mamas**. The rest of Güzelyurt, with its prosaic buildings and heavy traffic, is simply somewhere to pass through on your way to the attractions further north or west.

---

### VISTING GÜZELYURT FROM THE SOUTH

There are two crossing points in the Güzelyurt region. The **Astromeritis/Zodia crossing**, opened in August 2005, is one of the better-signposted and is also one of the quietest crossing points. Astromeritis is a fast 30km west on the A9/B9 motorway/dual carriageway from the outskirts of Lefkosia. Once across into Zodia, it's only 3km to Güzelyurt. The **Yeşilirmak/Limnitis/Kato Pyrgos crossing** (see page 27) is the most recent, built jointly by the north and south and opened with great fanfare in October 2010. Again, it is easy to find – a ten-minute drive east from Kato Pyrgos brings you to the crossing point, after which it's a scenic 32km drive to Güzelyurt. This makes possible a number of enjoyable routes through the north. Lefkosia–Girne–Güzelyurt–Kato Pyrgos, for example, is certainly feasible in a day, in either direction, or try Astromeritis–Güzelyurt–Kato Pyrgos.

---

### Museum of Archeology and Nature

Main Square, Güzelyurt • April–Sept Mon–Sat 9am–6pm; Nov–March Mon–Sat 8am–3.30pm • €7

Güzelyurt's **Museum of Archeology and Nature** is housed in an impressive white colonial building that stands just behind the main roundabout. Broadly, the ground floor contains the "nature", the first floor the "archeology". The former consists of a miscellany of stuffed animals (including a frankly disturbing lamb with two heads), plus a small collection of mounted butterflies and geological samples. Upstairs things start to look up. **Neolithic** and **Bronze Age artefacts** occupy the first room; the next two are devoted to finds from Tumba tou Skuru, and the last two display objects from the Archaic to the Byzantine eras. Particularly fine is a nicely mounted gold diadem (though with no indication of its provenance), finds from Salamis and some votive figures from the seventh century BC. Around the back of the museum are some lovely **gardens** (a perfect spot for a picnic), behind which the church of Agios Mamas and the minarets of the mosque rise in a becoming fashion.

### Agios Mamas Church and Monastery

Main Square, Güzelyurt • Key available from Museum of Archeology and Nature • Free with ticket to the museum

To the left of the Museum of Archeology and Nature is a gate offering direct access to the cloisters of **Agios Mamas**. The story of St Mamas is a colourful one. A hermit who lived in a cave, he refused to pay taxes to the Ottomans. Soldiers were sent to bring him before the authorities. As they took him to Nicosia, they came upon a lion attacking a lamb. Mamas commanded the lion to spare the lamb, then hopped on the lion's back and (lamb safely in his arms) rode the beast all the way to the governor's palace. The governor, much impressed by the manner of his arrival, granted Mamas immunity from local taxation for the rest of his life. Some accounts say that the grateful saint then gave the lamb to the governor.

Today the monastery and church are unused (except for intermittent permission for the saint's name day to be celebrated) but are in very good condition compared with many such Orthodox sites in the north, and host an icon museum. Cool colonnades surround a paved courtyard in the centre of which is the church which contains, partly inside and partly outside, the sarcophagus of St Mamas. Inside the church a rather good iconostasis survives, as does an ornate 1711 pulpit. The star of the show, though, accessible from both within and without, is the saint's marble sarcophagus on the left of the north entrance. A scented nectar is said to ooze out of it on occasion, and is apparently excellent for curing earache – hence the ear-shaped votive offerings – and for calming stormy seas.

## The Koruçam Peninsula

Due north of Güzelyurt, separating the north Cypriot coast from Morfou Bay, is the **Koruçam Peninsula**, similar in size to the Akamas to the west. Though it offers superb sunsets, a dramatic, rock-strewn and wave-lashed coastline (often, alas, heavily littered) and beautiful views back to the Kyrenia mountains, there's not much here to tempt the passing tourist, though a point of interest is the age-old **Maronite community** that still keeps a precarious toehold in the area.

You can access the peninsula via the loop of road (mostly in good condition) that leaves and rejoins the Girne to Güzelyurt route just before the garrison town of **Çamlibel** (Myrtou). The only landmarks on the coast road are **Horseshoe Beach**, which has a few basic facilities on a bluff above a stony shore, **Kayalar (Orga)**, with its regimented villas, **Sadrazamkoy (Livera)**, a clutch of white houses and a café and the last village on the peninsula, and beyond that a dirt track to the tip, with little **Kormakitis Island** beyond. On the inland road the only settlement is **Koruçam/Kormakitis** itself, dominated by its large Maronite church and the gaunt frame of a modern, and abandoned, school.

## Çamlibel (Myrtou) and around

**Çamlibel (Myrtou)**, inland from the Koruçam Peninsula and about 20km from Güzelyurt, is best used as a navigation aid rather than as a place to visit in itself. It's at the heart of an extensive series of **Turkish army camps**, and any attempt to navigate through it will founder on barbed wire and sandbagged entrance gates. However, a couple of places around it are worth a look.

### Pigades Shrine

Open access • Free

Just off the main Çamlibel to Lefkoşa road, about 2km past the turn-off for Güzelyurt, is **Pigades**, a Bronze Age shrine which it might just be worth slogging along a 250m path to see. There is a sign on the main road, though it's easy to miss, and you can identify where the shrine is by the clump of trees in the middle of a field. It's an open site, the remains of a temple that dates from 1600–1050 BC, the centrepiece of which is a pyramidal stone altar topped by Minoan-style stone bull-horns. The rest of the temple consists of two blocks of rooms, one around a garden, the other around a hole in the ground.

### The Blue Villa

Tues–Sun 9am–4pm • €0.5

A little way west of Çamlibel is the clearly signposted **Mavi Kosk** or **Blue Villa**, a bizarre 1970s pleasure palace now within a Turkish military area. You need to hand over your

---

### THE MARONITES OF THE KORUÇAM PENINSULA

A **Maronite** community has existed on the **Koruçam Peninsula** for at least nine hundred years, though it has now shrunk to a few hundred people. Maronite Christian beliefs originated in Syria and the Lebanon, and arose from an arcane seventh-century dispute about the nature of Christ. The Maronites lost the argument, were declared heretical, and had to take to the hills. They came to **Cyprus**, it is said, on the coat-tails of the Crusaders: they'd helped their fellow Christians against the Muslims in the Holy Lands (though one theory postulates that they were simply joining a Maronite community which was already on the island). The Maronites congregated on the Karpaz and Koruçam peninsulas – the former disappeared through emigration and intermarriage; the latter are, just about, still there. During the troubles of the 1960s the Maronites sided with the Greeks, and following the Turkish invasion in 1974, were harassed, issued with identity cards, and refused citizenship. Most left for the south, or went abroad. Since the progressive opening up of the Green Line since 2003, however, Maronites who had made their lives in the south can now visit freely. The future of their distinctive language, a fusion of Aramaic and Arabic, is less rosy, and its demise as a living language is predicted within a few decades.

passport to the guards at the gate in order to drive up to the house (no getting out and walking) – note that if you're in a rented car from the south, you will be politely but firmly turned away.

The villa was built a year before the Turkish invasion by Greek-Cypriot **Byron Pavlides**, a successful car dealer with friends in high places (particularly high in the case of Archbishop Makarios III). Something of a playboy (he had a sunken pool built in the lounge and a secret tunnel to his bedroom), rumour has it that he also dabbled as an EOKA gun-runner and chose this location, with its unimpeded views out to sea, in order to keep an eye on his contraband boats. Having relocated from the equally fabulous "White House" near St Hilarion when that area became predominantly Turkish Cypriot, Pavlides was forced to flee once again as the Turks invaded and commandeered the Blue House in 1974 (he died in mysterious circumstances in Italy in 1986). Aside from its sense of intrigue, the house has a gorgeous blue-themed interior and offers some unbeatable ocean views.

## West of Güzelyurt

The main road west from Güzelyurt to Yeşilirmak and the Kato Pyrgos crossing is of good quality all the way along its length, whatever your map says. It gets to the coast just before Gemikonaği – a quick detour up to **LEFKE (Lefka)** is worthwhile, for its lush vegetation, old Turkish houses and colonial British storehouse. Back on the coast you reach **GEMIKONAĞI (Karavostasi)**, which, with its derelict ore-handling jetties, has an appealingly shabby air. Beyond Gemikonaği are the unmissable archeological sites of **Soli** and **Vouni**.

### Ancient Soli

Daily: April–Oct 9am–6pm, Nov–March 8am–3.30pm • €7

The site of the ancient city of **SOLI** has few equals in north Cyprus, possibly on the whole island, thanks to its instant comprehensibility and the quality of information provided. It offers a detailed picture of life in late Roman and early Byzantine times, in a city set on a hillside overlooking the Mediterranean.

You'll find the site just after leaving Gemikonaği, travelling west on the coast road. Look out for a small sign pointing to the left just after the announcement that you're in Yedidalga (Potamos). The sign is easy to miss, but the huge roof covering part of the site isn't.

#### Brief history

Soli was originally settled in the eleventh century BC – its first mention in written records is as "Si-il-lu" in an Assyrian tribute list. According to legend, it was named after the Athenian philosopher **Solon**, who, while visiting his friend King Philocypros, suggested he built a new capital here, pointing out the excellent natural harbour and fertile soil. Soli soon flourished, though siding with the Ionians against the Persians led to it being sacked in 498 BC. Biblical scholars will also recall Soli as the site of St Mark's baptism by St Auxibius, and it soon became an important **Christian centre**, particularly once the Edict of Milan (313 AD) had legalized the religion throughout the Byzantine empire. By the seventh century, however, the harbour was silting up, and a succession of Arab raids, especially the one in 653 AD, led to a gradual decline, such that by the ninth century AD Soli had been abandoned.

#### The site

Soli is vast, and only part of it has been excavated. Once you've parked and bought your ticket (get hold of a plan) you'll see the ruins of the third-century AD Roman town down the hill to the right – the agora, a portico, the remains of a nymphaeum – and immediately ahead the remains of the great **Byzantine basilica**, protected by a roof, and with wooden walkways to allow visitor access. In fact, the remains you can see are of two basilicas – Basilica A, dating from the fourth century, and Basilica B from the sixth century. **Basilica A** had a wooden roof supported on stone columns, and had **mosaic floors**, some geometrical, others with the figures of birds and dolphins. The most famous of these representations is of a swan against a blue background, with flowers, dolphins and a duck. In the apse is a dedication: "Jesus, protect those who had these mosaics made". **Basilica B** was built entirely of stone, and instead of mosaics made of cuboid tesserae was floored with opus sectile tiles (larger pieces specifically shaped for the job). Though the mosaics take pride of place, other parts of the basilicas are also explained – a presbytery, an atrium, a column which still lies where it fell in the eighth century AD, and the "**Mystery of Soli**" – a staircase or ramp leading down to what's thought to be a tomb dedicated to St Auxibius or even a treasure house (unfortunately sealed off).

**6**

ANCIENT SOLI

0    200
metres

N

Kambos River

Vouni

Ancient Port

MEDITERRANEAN
SEA

Necropolis
of
Classical
Period

City Wall

Agora

Nymphaem

Basilica

East Gate

Roman
Theatre

Saray
Palace

Temple of
Athena

Necropolis of
Roman Period

Necropolis of
Hellenistic &
Roman Period

Necropolis of
Geometric &
Archaic Period

Lefkoşa (Nicosia)

Up the hill behind the basilica is an early third-century AD **Roman theatre**, extensively renovated and sometimes still used for performances. There's very little left of the original masonry – the British pilfered most of it for use in the building of the Suez Canal and Port Said.

## Palace of Vouni

Daily: April–Oct 9am–6pm, Nov–March 8am–3.30pm • €7

Crowning the summit of a hill 5km west along the coast from Soli (look out for the sign pointing up a steep drive) is the mysterious **Palace of Vouni**. It's mysterious because, despite its size, there are no known references to it in ancient documents. Even the name tells us nothing – it simply means "hilltop". Archeologists have surmised that the palace was built in the early fifth century BC, and followed a design common throughout the Middle East. From this it has been suggested that it was originally built by a king sympathetic to the Persians to keep an eye on nearby Soli. Vouni was eventually destroyed by fire in around 380 BC.

You'll have to use your imagination to visualize the "palace". However, you're given an excellent pamphlet with annotated ground plan, photographs and notes when you buy your ticket. Each part of the site is labelled – entrance hall, main room, cistern, courtyard, bathrooms, storerooms, private rooms and so on. In the centre of the courtyard is a very distinctive piece of masonry, which looks like a time-worn statue. It is located above the entrance to the cistern, and was in fact intended to hold a windlass for raising water – the slots for the handles are there, but the intended decoration of a goddess is unfinished, leading to the conclusion that the palace was destroyed before it could be completed. At the top of the site are the remains of a Temple of Athena, indicating that the palace had been adapted to Greek taste at some point in its history.

Despite being a little underwhelming in terms of its remains, the views towards the little island of Petra tou Limniti, the surrounding countryside and back towards Gemikonaği, are spectacular.

# Gazimağusa (Famagusta)

The charming city of **GAZIMAĞUSA** (Famagusta) is second only to Girne in the north's tourism league table. Like Girne, it boasts an atmospheric old town surrounded by crumbling Venetian walls, a legacy of its strategic position facing the Middle East. Its shops, restaurants and cafés are threaded between the photogenic remains of **churches**

---

### VISITING GAZIMAĞUSA FROM THE SOUTH

To get to Gazimağusa from the south, there are two convenient crossings, both in the Dekhelia Sovereign Base area. The first is the most useful if you're staying in Larnaka, and is known variously as the **Pyla/Beyarmudu/Pergamos crossing** (see page 27). From Larnaka, take the coast road or the A3 motorway towards Agia Napa, and follow the signs off to the left, signposted Pyla. Drive through Pyla, and up the hill on the other side. The crossing is a couple of kilometres along this main road. Once across, you're in the village of Beyarmudu – remember the name, since you'll need to head towards it on your return. Drive for 9km to an intersection, cross it, and continue for another 9km till you join the main Lefkoşa–Gazimağusa highway. Turn right, and you hit the dual carriageway all the way to Gazimağusa. On your return, make sure you don't miss the turn off the highway towards Beyarmudu.

The second option, which is especially handy if you're staying in the Agia Napa/Protaras area, is the **Agios Nikolaos/Akyar/Strovilia crossing**. Drive through Paralimni and head for Derynia. Continue through Derynia, heading for Frenaros along the main E305 road, then follow the signpost right to Vrysoulles. Turn right at the T-junction, and the crossing point is about 3km beyond. Once across, Gazimağusa is just 5km beyond.

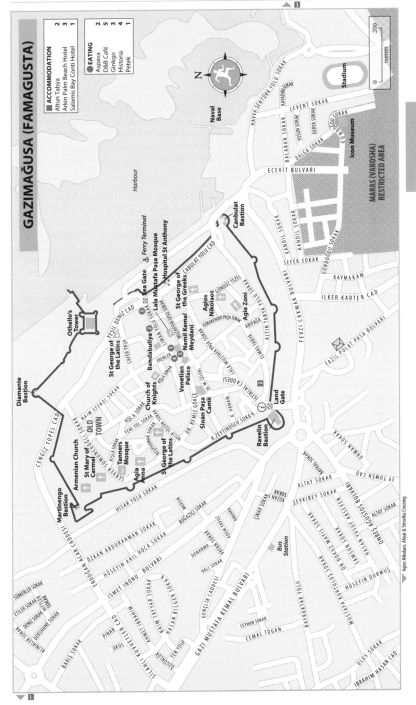

# GAZIMAĞUSA (FAMAGUSTA)

| ■ ACCOMMODATION | |
| --- | --- |
| Altun Tabya | 2 |
| Arkin Palm Beach Hotel | 3 |
| Salamis Bay Conti Hotel | 1 |

| ● EATING | |
| --- | --- |
| Aspava | 2 |
| D&B Café | 5 |
| Ginkgo | 3 |
| Historia | 4 |
| Petek | 1 |

Othello's Tower

Diamante Bastion

Martinengo Bastion

Canbulat Bastion

Naval Base

Harbour

Sea Gate & Ferry Terminal

Lala Mustafa Paşa Mosque

St George of the Greeks

Hospital St Anthony

St George of the Latins

Agios Nikolaos

Agia Zoni

Bandabuliya

Namik Kemal Meydani

Church of Knights

Venetian Palace

Sinan Paşa Camii

Armenian Church

St Mary of Carmel

Tanners Mosque

Agia Anna

St George of the Latins

Land Gate

Ravelin Bastion

Icon Museum

Stadium

MARAS (VAROSHA) RESTRICTED AREA

Bus Station

ECEVIT BULVARI

OLD TOWN

▶ Agios Nikolaos, Alnyar & Strovilia Crossing

0 — 200 meters

6

destroyed or damaged during the Ottoman siege of 1570–71. Immediately to the south lies the ghost town of **Varosha**, once the heart of Famagusta's tourist trade, now isolated by the Turkish invasion of 1974. To the north lies a clutch of historically important sites – ancient **Enkomi/Alasia**, the monastery of **Apostolos Varnavas**, the **Royal Tombs**, and above all ancient **Salamis** – and the many kilometres of beaches that line Gazimağusa Bay.

Confusingly, Gazimağusa is known by a host of different names. The city was renamed Gazimağusa (sometimes shortened to **Mağusa**) by the Turks in 1974, having been known as **Famagusta**, from French (Famagouste) and Italian (Famagosta), since Lusignan/Venetian times. In Greek it is known as **Ammochostos**. If that weren't puzzling enough, the name Famagusta/Ammochostos is also used by the republic for the district across the Green Line to the east, of which the city is the notional capital.

### Brief history

The current site of Gazimağusa was established during the Byzantine era by refugees from Salamis, after that city was destroyed by Arab raids. The new city reached its zenith under the Lusignans, especially after the Fall of Acre to the Saracens in 1291 AD brought an influx of Christian merchants and craftsmen. When the pope banned direct economic ties with the infidel, Gazimağusa became a major entrepôt for the whole of the Middle East, famous for its wealth and as a melting pot of different cultures and beliefs – hence the huge variety and number of churches (one, it was said, for every day of the year). It went into something of a decline from the late fourteenth century onwards, but was fortified under the Venetians as they tried to meet the growing threat from Ottoman expansion. As at Girne and Lefkosia, this did them little good – the city fell in 1571 after a nine-month siege, thus completing the Ottoman conquest of the island. It is said that 100,000 cannonballs crashed into the city during the siege and, since no attempt was made by the Ottomans to repair the damage, the remains still stand today. Three years after the siege, Greek residents were expelled from within the walls. Many of them resettled just to the south, creating what later became Varosha. During the 1960s and early 1970s, Varosha and its beaches were at the heart of massive tourist development, only to be frozen in time by the Turkish invasion.

## The city walls

Originally built by the Lusignans, Gazimağusa's **city walls** owe their present impressive dimensions and design to the Venetians, who spent half a century up to 1540 remodelling them for medieval battle; for example, building ramps up which to haul cannons, and making square towers round, so that they were proof against artillery fire. A dry moat was cut around three of the four sides – the fourth faces the sea. The northwest section of wall and the Martinengo Bastion, with a group of places of worship, were until recently a restricted area because of the presence of an army camp, but this has now been abandoned, and the whole area, and indeed the walls as a whole, are again open to visitors – British officers in the 1930s even played golf along the top of the walls.

### The Land Gate and Ravelin Bastion

In the southwest corner of the walls is the **Land Gate**, one of the two original main gates (the other being the Sea Gate) to the old town. The Land Gate offers the best approach to the city centre, both on foot and by car, because of the presence of the Tourist Information office inside the gate and the clear signposting from there to places of interest throughout the city centre, in which there is ample parking throughout. As you approach across the bridge, look to the right for a good view of the stretch of wall to the first "Santa Napa" bastion. Once inside, you'll find the tourist office to the left. The **Ravelin Bastion** (or Rivettina Bastion) in front of the gate was heavily involved in

## THE SIEGE OF FAMAGUSTA

Fresh from its victory over Nicosia and the surrender of Kyrenia, the Ottoman army approached Famagusta in confident mood in September 1570. Before them lay a small garrison of Venetians, no match it would seem for thousands of battle-hardened Turkish troops. Having blockaded the port (thus preventing relief from the Venetian navy), the Ottoman commander **Mustafa Paşa** ordered his artillery to pound the city while his engineers built trenches and a huge earth ramp to scale the walls. The Venetian defenders, hopelessly outnumbered, put up a gutsy resistance under the command of **Marcantonio Bragadin** and his lieutenant **Lorenzo Tiepolo**, cunningly moving soldiers about so that the invaders were tricked into thinking them a far more formidable force. The Venetians managed to hold out for ten months, before the citadel was breached in July 1571. Bragadin agreed to a negotiated surrender where all civilians could leave the city and his soldiers could sail for Crete.

Things went largely to plan until during the hand-over ceremony when Mustafa Paşa, up until then courteous towards his opponent, suddenly exploded with rage, killing several Venetian officers and cutting off Bragadin's ears and nose. A **massacre** of the remaining Christians in the city followed. Bragadin, after several weeks' imprisonment, was publicly **executed**, his body quartered, and his skin, stuffed with straw, sent riding on an ox through the town before being sent to the sultan in Constantinople. The treatment of Bragadin so incensed the Venetians that it was said to inspire their forces at the Battle of Lepanto a couple of months later, halting Ottoman expansion in the Mediterranean. Bragadin's flailed skin was rescued from Constantinople in 1596 and returned to Venice, where it still rests in the Basilica di San Zanipolo.

the Siege of Famagusta, and when it finally seemed bound to be taken by the attackers, the Venetians blew it up, killing, it's said, a thousand Ottoman soldiers and a hundred of their own. This was also where the white flag of surrender was flown, prompting the victors to rename it Akkule, or "White Bastion". They built a new entrance to the city, and incorporated a mosque to meet the religious needs of the garrison (now occupied by the Tourist Information Office). The innards of the bastion, a warren of passages, rooms and flights of steps, are open to the public as the "Akkule Oren Yeri" attraction (Mon–Fri 8am–3.30pm; €7), but even when this is closed, you are free to clamber up the steep inclines (designed to allow cannons to be hauled up to the battlements) and explore the top of the bastion and its adjoining walls.

### The Canbulat Bastion

Mon–Fri 9am–12.30pm & 1.30–5pm • €7

As you circle the walls in an anticlockwise direction, after the Ravelin Bastion, the next major bastion – the **Canbulat Bastion** – is in the southeast corner. It is named after one of the Turkish heroes of the 1571 siege of Venetian Famagusta by the Ottomans, Canbulat (pronounced "Djambulat"), the Bey of Kilis. Faced with a fearsome defensive device consisting of knives attached to a rapidly rotating wheel, Canbulat rode his horse full tilt into it, killing both himself and his steed, but jamming the wheel and making it ineffective. His tomb, which is in the bastion, once had a fig tree growing out of it, whose fruit, if eaten by young women, would not only ensure conception, but also that the resulting children would be as brave as Canbulat. There's a small museum displaying artefacts associated with the siege, ranging from costume and artillery to ship models and weapons. Look out particularly for the "memorial" tomb of Canbulat, and the reconstruction of a sixteenth-century Ottoman tent. The collection is well displayed, and a steep flight of stone steps gives access to further exhibits and views of the walls from the roof of the bastion. Just beyond the entrance to the museum, through an archway, the entrance to the port which stretches along the eastern wall of the city is marked by a large ceramic mural of the Ottoman conquest of Famagusta.

## The Sea Gate

After the Canbulat Bastion, the walls swing north, parallel to the sea. Note, to the left of the wall, the remains of the **Hospital of St Antony**, which was built using stone taken from the ruins of Salamis. Beyond them is the **Sea Gate**, which once provided access from the port. A squat and solid-looking fortification with a signature statue of a Venetian lion at its base, it has massive iron-clad wooden gates, Ottoman in origin, and a heavy Venetian iron portcullis (both shrouded in tarpaulin at the time of writing). The top of the Sea Gate is accessible via a steep flight of steps from inside the town at the end of Liman Yolu; the views across the town one way, and the port the other, are worth the climb. Looking north from the Sea Gate, you can see a variety of ships in the harbour, many of them Turkish naval vessels (which is why the northern parts of the walls are off limits). Incidentally, a local myth says that the Venetian lion opens its mouth once a year, giving bystanders the chance to plunge their hands down its throat to retrieve treasure.

## Othello's Tower

Yesil Deniz Cad • April–Oct Mon–Fri 8am–7pm; Nov–March Mon–Fri 8am–3.30pm • €9

Beyond the Sea Gate stands the massive **Othello's Tower**. The name is a little fanciful, bestowed by the British on the strength of the locations mentioned in Shakespeare's play: "A seaport in Cyprus" and "a hall in the castle". Indeed, its alternative name, "**The Citadel**", is a better description. Above the entrance in the southwest corner is a large relief of the Lion of St Mark, the Venetian emblem. Despite its Venetian exterior, you can still make out the original Lusignan fortress beneath: the large central courtyard on the north side is the Great Hall. The views from the battlements are as good as those from the Sea Gate, and offer prospects of the citadel itself, as well as of the port, snuggled up to the eastern wall of the city. Othello's Tower has been renovated in a combined Greek- and Turkish-Cypriot initiative, driven by the Technical Committee on Cultural Heritage. The fabric of the building is now in good order and is open to the public, but much remains to be done – in particular, the almost liquid sand underfoot in the Great Hall can be treacherous. As you explore the tunnels and passages of the Tower, look out for the ventilation shafts designed to clear smoke from the cannons inside the tower; a few of these were filled in with rubble, prompting rumours that the Venetians had buried their gold here rather than see it fall into the hands of the Ottomans.

# The old town

Within the walls, the **old town** of Gazimağusa is an appealing jumble of ruined churches, odd bits of medieval masonry, cafés, restaurants and shops, tree-shaded and flower-bedecked and much of it pedestrianized. The best approach, once you've entered through the Land Gate and perhaps visited the tourist office, is to head up the main street **Istiklal Caddesi** towards the central square, **Namik Kemal Meydani**, perusing shops and cafés as you go. East and south of the main square is a maze of narrow streets and alleys, good for souvenir hunting, and overlooked by picturesque ruins. You can imagine a similar scene in medieval times, though with the great Gothic churches intact, rising above people's homes.

## Sinan Paşa Camii (Church of St Peter and St Paul)

Open access • Free

As Istiklal Caddesi bends to the right, just before the central square, the first of Gazimağusa's ruined churches sails into view. A great lump of Lusignan architecture, **Sinan Paşa Camii**, originally the **Church of St Peter and St Paul**, is impressively massive, with wide flying buttresses shoring up its bulk. It was built in the mid-fourteenth century and financed, it is said, by a merchant from the proceeds of a single transaction. As one of the few larger buildings to survive the 1570 Turkish bombardment relatively intact, it has gone through a number of reincarnations – under the Ottomans as a mosque, under the British as a potato and grain store, and more recently as a public library and performance venue. At the time of writing it was locked up, its future uncertain. In its precincts are several tombs – one is of Yirmisekiz Mehmet Cheleb, who was the first Ottoman ambassador to France.

### The Venetian Palace
Open access • Free

Just as you enter the square, you'll see on the left what remains of the **Venetian Palace** which housed the governor. There's not a lot to see – the east façade consisting of a couple of two-storey-high walls, and three arches supported by four columns taken from Salamis. This was the palace in which the ill-fated Bragadin lived, and in front of which he so horribly died (see page 233).

### Namik Kemal Meydani
Namik Kemal Museum: April–Oct Mon–Fri 8am–5pm; Nov–March Mon–Fri 8am–3.30pm • €7

At the heart of old Gazimağusa is the central square **Namik Kemal Meydani**. Surrounded by mellow, ruined buildings, it is dotted with cannons and piles of cannonballs (the iron ones were fired, the stone ones flung from catapults), and lined with the tables, chairs and parasols of several cafés – a delightful spot to stop for refreshment. The square is named after dissident Turkish poet and playwright **Namik Kemal** (1840–88) who was exiled to Cyprus when one of his plays, performed in Constantinople, was considered seditious. He was imprisoned from 1873 to 1876 in the small building that faces into the square. His "dungeon" is now a small museum consisting of the room in which he was imprisoned on the ground floor and, up a flight of steps, a small display which includes copies of his works, a model of his tomb, a succession of portraits of the great man submitted for a "Namik Kemal Art Contest" organized by the Ministry of Education and Culture. There's also an impressive bust of the man in front of the cathedral.

---

### ECCLESIASTICAL GEMS – A WALKING TOUR

Dotted around the old town are numerous minor churches, often in a poor state of repair but full of interest. A good place to start is just off Namik Kemal Meydani, on Kisla Sokagi opposite the distinctive glass-dotted dome of a hammam, where, next to each other, two little fourteenth-century churches stand. They are invariably identified as the churches of the **Knights Templar and Knights Hospitaller**, the latter based on the Hospitaller coat of arms above the western door. One is now a cultural centre and art gallery, the other, surprisingly, is a bar. A short walk northwest, by the Othello Tower, is the ruined **St George of the Latins**, one of Gazimağusa's oldest churches. Based on the height off the ground of its surviving windows, and the presence of a parapet, it has been speculated that it was a fortified church predating the Lusignans. There's little left now but a single wall with large lancet windows, precarious but undoubtedly romantic. Beyond St George of the Latins, a walk along Gengiz Topel Cad then left onto Server Somuncuoglu Sokak brings you to the northwest corner of the town. Here the churches of **Agia Anna** and **St Mary of Carmel**, the **Armenian Church** and the converted **Tanners Mosque** are clustered together in the angle between the walls that meet at the Martinengo Bastion, which, following the abandonment of the military camp that once controlled the area, is now open to the inquisitive tourist. Back at Namik Keymal Beydani, a stroll due south brings you to **St George of the Greeks**, which is (or was) a large Byzantine Orthodox church (all that remains are three apses and a flying buttress at one end and the entranceway on the other) – while a little further southeast you'll find **Agios Nikolaos** and **Agia Zoni**, which are small and pretty, the first a ruin, the second pretty much intact.

### Lala Mustafa Paşa Mosque (St Nicholas Cathedral)
Namil Kemal Meydani • Open to visitors outside prayer times • Free (donation requested)

On the eastern side of Namik Kemal Meydani, and dominating all around it, is the impressive bulk of **Lala Mustafa Paşa Mosque (St Nicholas Cathedral)**. Though badly damaged during the siege, its western façade is still largely intact, looking like a cathedral lifted out of northern France and dropped here in the Levant. Built during the first half of the fourteenth century, and designed by architects brought from France (it's said to be modelled on the "royal" cathedral at Reims), it was an ostentatious celebration of the huge wealth of the town after the influx of merchants fleeing the fall of Acre. Once the site of Lusignan coronations, its twin towers were destroyed by the Turkish shelling and by later earthquakes. While converting it into a mosque, the victorious Ottomans ripped out its interior Christian decorations and memorials, and added a rather inconsequential minaret to the northwest corner. Inside, it is cool and spacious and impressively simple. Outside are two typical **Ottoman shrines**, those of Mehmet Omer Efendi and Mustapha Zuhtu Efendi, both past imams, the bust of Namik Kemal and, beside the mosque, the Famagusta **medrese** dating from around 1700. Also worth noting is the huge **fig tree** (allegedly *in situ* when the cathedral was built, making it over 750 years old), and the **Venetian loggia** which now houses the ablutions fountain.

### Bandabuliya

Just north of the cathedral/mosque, across Liman Yolu, is the old covered market or **Bandabuliya**, restored and painted a delicate shade of yellow; it contains cafés, restaurants, stalls and a stage – look out for the elegant arches down one side.

## Maras (Varosha)

If the old town of Gazimağusa is full of ruins dating from the Ottoman siege, the "new town" of **Varosha**, now officially **Maras**, is a sad reminder of a more recent conflict. Having been expelled from the old town in the 1570s, the Greeks established a prosperous settlement here, surrounded by orange groves. Over the years the population of the new town eclipsed that of the old and in the twentieth century its beach area, **Glossa**, became an upmarket **resort**, "The Monte Carlo of the Middle East", visited by the likes of Elizabeth Taylor and Paul Newman. During the 1974 invasion, the Turkish army seized Varosha in its entirety, forcing its Greek population to flee to the south. Today, sealed off by fences, barbed wire and checkpoints, it festers in the sun, its high-rise hotels crumbling, its cracked tarmac claimed by weeds and scrub. You can walk or drive down Fazil Polat Paşa Bulvari (once Independence Avenue) to see the ruins. On the way you'll notice a little black tank engine (dating from 1904 and the first locomotive imported into Cyprus) standing outside what was the Famagusta terminus of the **Cyprus Government Railway** (see page 163). The street ends abruptly at a barrier, beyond which can be seen the ruined buildings that mark the beginning

---

### VAROSHA – A BRIDGE TO PEACE?

For almost forty years the fate of **Varosha** has been a painful source of resentment among Greek Cypriots and a strong bargaining tool for the Turks who have deliberately avoided any development of the resort. Various proposals have been put forward to end the impasse – the latest to turn the town into a UN-administered buffer zone which would allow Greek Cypriots to return as an act of goodwill, rather than a prelude to reunification. This would, it is thought, help grease the wheels of Turkey's accession to the EU. In August 2012 President Demetris Christofias said Varosha "can, as in the past, be a bridge of peace, hope, cooperation and cohabitation", and it has been one of the issues mentioned in ongoing negotiations during 2015 and 2016.

of derelict Varosha. The converging street of Ilker Karter Caddesi and the streets east of here offer views of Varosha, as do the streets around the Dr Fazil Küçük Stadium, though it's probably best seen as a whole from the Cultural Centre of Occupied Famagusta (see page 70) across the Green Line.

## ARRIVAL AND DEPARTURE

### GAZIMAĞUSA (FAMAGUSTA)

**By bus** The bus station (☎3666347) is on Gazi Mustafa Kemal Bulvari, the main road that heads northwest from the Victory Monument roundabout – it's a 5min walk from the Land Gate. Minibuses leave from the Itimat bus station on the south side of Yirmisekiz Ocak (☎3666666).
Destinations Girne (every 30min; 1hr 10min); Lefkoşa (every 30min; 1hr). You can also pick up minibuses to Lefkoşa and Girne from the large roundabout outside the Land Gate.
**By car** All roads into Gazimağusa lead to the old town. This

area is mostly pedestrianized, so you can park outside the walls and walk in. However, if you wish to drive into the old city, there's plenty of free parking. From the south, two crossing points are convenient (see page 230).
**By ferry** Ferries sail three times a week between Gazimağusa and Mersin on the Turkish mainland. The ferry port is right next to the Old Town's Sea Gate. Tickets available from Cyprus Turkish Shipping (☎3665995) or at the passenger terminal.

## GETTING AROUND

**On foot** Most of what you'll want to see in Gazimağusa is within the walls and mostly within a pedestrianized area, so all you'll need to get around is your feet.

**By taxi** If you want to go further afield, look to the taxi rank next to the Sea Gate.

## INFORMATION

**Tourist office** The tourist office is located just inside the Land Gate, on the left (Istiklal Cadis; daily: April–Oct 8am–

6.30pm, Nov–March 8am–5pm; ☎3662864).

## ACCOMMODATION

With a few notable exceptions, most of Gazimağusa's hotels languish in a kind of 1970s time warp and are aimed principally at Turkish visitors. In general you are better off staying in Girne (see page 217).
**Altun Tabya** Altun Tabya Sokak ☎3665995; map p.231. One of the very few hotels within the walls of the old town – follow the signs from the Land Gate. Rooms are distinctly down at heel, though they do at least have en-suite facilities, and you can elect to have a/c for an extra charge. It's on a busy street, though, so don't expect peace and quiet. €62
**Arkin Palm Beach Hotel** Nadir Yolu, Deve Limani ☎3662000, ��arkinpalmbeach.com; map p.231. Recently renovated large hotel, just southeast of the walled city. There are helpful staff and good facilities – pool,

beach club, fitness suite, restaurants, bars, health club and so on. Rooms are modern and comfortable, decor classy and understated. The elephant in the room, though, is its position right next to ruined Varosha (some guests, perhaps those who don't realize its location, want to leave as soon as they've arrived). And don't take photos of the devastation – it's forbidden. €175
**Salamis Bay Conti Hotel** ☎8507070101, Ⓦsalamis bayconti.com; map p.231. Beachside luxury hotel 10km north of Gazimağusa. Good range of rooms and suites with full facilities, three bars and a main restaurant, kids' club, sports facilities, evening entertainment, and casino (though what's offered may be restricted out of season – check with the hotel). It's a bit isolated, though – it's a 45min walk to the site of Ancient Salamis. €145

## EATING

The best area to eat in Gazimağusa is in and around the central square – Namik Kemal Meydani. There is very little in the way of nightlife and entertainment except that put on by hotels and casinos.
**Aspava** 19 Liman Yolu Sokak ☎3666037, Ⓦtwitter. com/AspavaRestauran; map p.231. The Aspava looks out onto the main town square and mosque and offers not only grills and meze, with food served in a shady garden, but is a prime people-watching site. Kebabs €10–15. Mon–Sat noon-midnight.
**D&B Café** Namik Kemal Meydani ☎3666610,

Ⓦfacebook.com/dbcaferestaurant/; map p.231. One of the many restaurants on the main square, D&B has ample seating outside, and an upstairs terrace. It advertises "world cuisine" – lots of pizzas, pastas, burgers and grilled meats (€17–40). The clientele is young, with many students from the local university. Mon–Sat 10am–10pm.
**Ginkgo** 1 Liman Yolu Sokak ☎3666660; map p.231. Next door to the mosque, housed in buildings that were partly the old Catholic building and partly a Muslim madrasa, the menu includes pasta, salads, fish and meat, and famously huge home-made burgers. Or they're happy

for you to have just coffee and cake. There's often live music, too. Daily 10.30am–midnight.

**Historia** Namik Kemal Meydani ☎8621199; map p.231. A good range of meals is provided by the *Historia*, which faces the main square, and therefore is also a good place to watch the world go by. Options include: omelettes (€14–20), burgers (€15–17), kebabs (€24–35) and chicken dishes (€27). Mon–Sat 9am–9pm, Sun 10am–6pm.

★ **Petek** 1 Yesil Deniz Sokak (where it intersects with Liman Yolu Sokak, opposite the Sea Gate) ☎3667104, ⊕petekpastahanesi.com; map p.231. Part of a chain of patisseries (or *pastahanesi*), *Petek* offers a wide range of sweets, Turkish Delight, baklava, ice cream and various types of cake, most involving combinations of honey, chocolate and nuts. From €5. Housed in an odd-shaped building with terrace, balcony and potted plants, an attractively cluttered interior and a tempting cake counter beyond. Daily 10am–11pm.

## SHOPPING

Gazimağusa is not known for its shopping. However, there are a number of attractive shops along Liman Yolu, mainly selling clothes, postcards, sunglasses, hats and souvenirs. Otherwise head for the narrow tangle of lanes southeast of Namik Kemal Meydani and Istiklal Cad where you'll find music, jewellery and accessories.

## DIRECTORY

**Banks and exchange** The most convenient ATM to use is right in the central square, Namik Kemal Meydani – it's the HSBC one at the back of *D&B Café*'s outside seating area. Also in the square, right next to the HSBC ATM, is another, in a branch of Turkiye Bankasi.

**Emergencies** Ambulance (☎112), Fire Brigade (☎199) or Police (☎155). Gazimağusa Hospital (☎232000000).

**Post office** Fazil Polat Paşa Bulvari (Mon–Fri 8am–3.30pm).

# Around Gazimağusa

Some 8km north of Gazimağusa, and signposted from both the coast road to Boğaz and the main road to the capital, is a group of ruins which are among the most important and impressive in all of Cyprus. By far the most famous and most photographed are the remains, largely Roman, of **Ancient Salamis**. But within a couple of minutes' drive of this colossal seaside site are the **Royal Tombs**, the **Monastery of St Barnabas** (now a museum), and the prehistoric remains of **Enkomi-Alasia**. Allow a day for a full inspection, or half a day for edited highlights.

## Ancient Salamis

Daily: April–Oct 9am–6pm, Nov–March 9am–5pm • €9

One of the most significant archeological sites in the Mediterranean, **Salamis** is notable not only for the richness and extent of its remains but also for its agreeable beachside setting. The site itself is huge and, despite almost a century of archeological digging, has still not been completely uncovered. The approach to the site is along a road beside a huge picnic area, and the first thing you'll see is a restaurant (*Bedi's*) with a recently added beach bar and pier and a fine sandy beach. You can park either behind the restaurant or in one of the archeological site's two car parks. A plan of the site at the entrance (clearly signposted from Gazimağusa) offers **two walking routes**, one short, one long. Luckily the most important and most comprehensively investigated buildings are very close together just beyond the entrance. If you intend to view every single part of the city, it'll involve a lot of walking so come prepared.

## Brief history

Founded around 1075 BC by Greek and Anatolian settlers and reinforced by refugees as Enkomi-Alasia was abandoned, Salamis was an important cultural centre throughout **Classical Greek and Roman** times, becoming the richest and most important city on the island for around 1700 years. Its kings claimed descent from its founder, the Trojan War hero Teucer, brother of Ajax and son of the King of Salamis, the island to the

**GYMNASIUM & BATHS**

1 Columned Courtyard
2 Stoa
3 Latrines
4 Stoa
5 Swimming Pools
6 Cold Rooms (Frigidaria)
7 Medium Hot Room (Tepidarium)
8 Hot Water Baths (Caldarium)
9 Sweating Room (Sudatoria)
10 Stoking Room (Praefurnium)
11 Latrines
12 Aqueduct

N

**STADIUM/ AMPHITHEATRE**

**THEATRE**

Orchestra

Stage & Prosenium

Seating

**ANCIENT SALAMIS**

0       20
metres

south of Athens (hence the name). Destroyed by earthquakes in 332 and 343 AD, the city was rebuilt by Byzantine **Emperor Constantine II**, who modestly renamed it Constantia. But the harbour silted up, there were further earthquakes, and the *coup de grâce* was delivered by the **Arab raids** which plagued Cyprus from the seventh century AD onwards. The inhabitants of Salamis moved south to where modern Gazimağusa now stands.

### The site

The first impressive group of remains are the **Gymnasium and Baths**, built originally by the Greeks and substantially modified by the Romans and Byzantines. At the heart of the building is the huge open courtyard surrounded by columns, with the remains of a plinth in the centre. This is the **palaestra**, where people exercised or stood gossiping in the shade of the surrounding colonnaded *stoa*. Much of the tessellated marble flooring remains, with clearly legible inscriptions in places. To the west of the palaestra are the remains of a number of shops. To the east are the **baths** with the usual series of rooms of escalating heat – from *frigidarium* to *caldarium*. In places the floor has collapsed, revealing the hypocaust (underfloor heating system) beneath. Plunge pools stand at either side of the baths; the northern one (through which you enter the site) is rectangular and surrounded by headless statues. There are also latrines, several octagonal pools, and an aqueduct for bringing in the water.

Leaving the baths via the south plunge pool, a column-lined path leads to the sketchy remains of an amphitheatre/stadium. Beyond here is the much more impressive **theatre**, one of the highlights of the site. Built during the reign of Augustus (27 BC–14 AD), it has the standard Greco-Roman semicircular layout, though built upwards in the Roman manner rather than fitting into a hillside as the Greeks were wont to do. As you enter it from the north, the seating curves sharply to your left around the semicircular orchestra, the stage and proscenium straight ahead. Much restored (the new seating is easily distinguished from the original – it's white instead of red/brown), it could originally accommodate 15,000 spectators in fifty rows of seats. In the orchestra was an altar to Dionysus, and the stage was backed by statues.

When you leave the theatre, the short route swings round through the second car/coach park back to the entrance. The long route continues south, past the remains of the largest **basilica** in Cyprus, founded by **St Epiphanius** in the fourth century AD – his empty marble-lined tomb can be seen at the end of the south aisle – to a large Byzantine **cistern** or vouta in which water, brought via an aqueduct 50km away, was stored before being distributed to the baths. Beyond this is the large Roman forum or **agora** (of which there's not much left apart from a single column) and the few remains of a **temple to Zeus**. Returning back past the St Epiphanius basilica, then turning off towards the sea, brings you past another Byzantine building called "**The Olive Press**" on the plans, but whose original purpose is unknown – it was used to house an olive press in the Middle Ages. Beyond this is the Byzantine **Basilica of Kampanopetra**, a slightly later, fifth-century AD building.

## Royal Tombs of the Kings

Mezarlik Alani • Mon–Fri 9am–3.30pm • €7

The eighth- and seventh-century BC **Royal Tombs of the Kings** should be considered an adjunct to any visit to Salamis, since they represent a part of the vast necropolis in which the dead – not necessarily kings but certainly the very wealthy – from the ancient city were interred. Despite centuries of looting and treasure hunting, several finds from the site have caused great excitement in the world of archeology. However,

the most stunning aspect about the graves is that they reveal **burial customs** virtually identical to those described by Homer in the *Iliad*. The dead were carried to the tomb on a horse-drawn hearse accompanied by ceremonial chariots before being burnt on a funeral pyre or *propylaeum*, the remains collected, put into jars, and stored inside the tomb. The horses were sacrificed as well as the occasional human according to the *Iliad*: "The mourners made a pyre and on it … laid the body. Four horses he (Achilles) laid on the funeral pyre. Twelve noble young Trojans he slew without mercy. Then he applied the relentless fire …. When the fire had been quenched with wine, they set up a circle of stone slabs … and shovelled earth within."

### The site

When you return to the main road from the entrance to Salamis, turn left at the roundabout, then right at the next roundabout. The Royal Tombs of the Kings are to the left off this road a few hundred metres west: look out for the yellow sign – it's easy to miss. There's a small ticket office and a **museum** which includes some good reconstructions of some of the most startling finds, for example bronze chariots and horse armour still attached to equine skeletons. Outside, the tombs (each with a number) are dotted around a grassy plain, and are clearly signposted.

Within a minute's walk of the ticket office are tombs 47, 50 and 79. **Tombs 47 and 79** have a clearly defined *dromos* (the ramp down which the hearse was dragged) and *propylaeum* (the platform on which the dead were burnt). The incongruous-looking glass structures on the ramps are there to protect the skeletons of the sacrificed horses. **Tomb 50**, also known as St Catherine's Prison, is an oddity in that the original structure was adapted by the Romans to create a chapel in which, local legend maintains, St Catherine was imprisoned and martyred. Walking the other way from the ticket office brings you to **Tomb 1** (with steps instead of a ramp), **Tomb 2** (classic in structure but smaller than usual) and **Tomb 3** (very large and protected by a modern roof). A few hundred metres to the southeast of these tombs is the **cellarka**, a warren of small rock-cut chambers with truncated ramps, the burial ground of poorer Salamians, used between 700 and 300 BC. Finally, a long walk south brings you to **Nicocreon's Cenotaph**, which isn't a tomb at all, but a memorial to King Nicocreon who, under siege by the army of Ptolemy I in 311 BC, opted for suicide rather than the dishonour of surrender. His wife Axiothea decided that first all their daughters should be killed (and persuaded the wives of Nicocreon's brothers to do likewise). If that weren't tragic enough, the palace was then set ablaze. When the cenotaph was excavated in 1965, clay figures (presumably of the doomed royals) were found on a circular platform surrounded by steps.

## Monastery of St Barnabas

Mon–Fri: April–Oct 9am–7pm, Nov–March 9am–5pm • €9

Continuing along the road west from Salamis, within another kilometre or so of the Royal Tombs (and built on the western edge of the necropolis), takes you to the **Monastery of St Barnabas**, once one of the most important Christian sites on the island, now an archeological and icon museum. This handsome monastery, said to have been built as the result of a divinely inspired dream (see page 243), consists of the church of St Barnabas, behind which lie the monastery cloisters: a colonnade of pillars on three sides of a lush and well-tended garden. An extension – further colonnades and a campanile – though modern, fits in pretty well with the rest of the building. The **archeological museum**, housed in rooms that look out into the garden, is less than impressive – a miscellany of Neolithic axe-heads, Bronze Age pottery and Ottoman artefacts; the **Icon Museum**, housed in the church of St Barnabas, is a somewhat perfunctory collection of icons lit by domestic light bulbs. A few bits of the Orthodox furnishings remain in place – the pulpit, a chair, the iconostasis. Look out in particular

## ST BARNABAS AND THE CHURCH OF CYPRUS

One of the great figures of early Christianity, **St Barnabas**, was a Jew, born in Salamis, who became one of the earliest converts to the new religion and founded the Cypriot Church. Together with his cousin **Mark the Evangelist** and the pivotal **St Paul**, he travelled extensively in both Cyprus and Asia Minor, spreading the gospel. In fact Barnabas was so successful that the Jewish elders in Salamis had him stoned to death around 75 AD. Mark retrieved his body and buried it secretly in a cave to the west of the city. Over time, the location of the cave was forgotten.

Four hundred years later the Cypriot Church under **Archbishop Anthemios** was faced with a takeover bid by **Antioch**, the patriarch of which claimed suzerainty over the island's Christians – a claim supported by Byzantine Emperor Zeno. In 478 AD, when all seemed lost, Anthemios was visited in a dream by the spirit of St Barnabas, who told him where his body was buried – beneath a distinctive carob tree on the western edge of Salamis. Here Anthemios discovered a skeleton along with a copy of **The Gospel of Mark**. Anthemios shot off to Constantinople, donated the good book to the emperor and the Church of Cyprus was triumphantly granted autonomous or "autocephalous" status. Zeno also paid for a monastery to be built over the saint's final resting place. The independence of the Cypriot Church was to become particularly important over a thousand years later when it was able to use its privileged position to shelter its flock from the worst excesses of Ottoman occupation.

**6**

for the four **frescoes** to the right of the entrance which tell the story of the finding of St Barnabas's body. Before leaving, take a look at what is said to be the **tomb of the Apostle Barnabas** himself, contained in a 1950s-built mausoleum. The tomb is along a short track that heads east from the car park, past excavated rock-cut tombs, to the mausoleum's modern steps.

## Ancient Enkomi-Alasia

Mon–Fri: April–Oct 8am–7pm, Nov–March 8am–3.30pm • €7

The archeological site of **Enkomi-Alasia** lies on the same road as the Monastery of St Barnabas, less than 1km further west. When you get to a T-junction, you'll see the rather inconspicuous entrance across the road, just to the right.

One of the earliest settlements on the island, Alasia (the "Enkomi" bit refers to the nearest Greek village) is thought to have been established around 2000 BC and is mentioned in clay tablets from ancient Egypt, Syria and Anatolia. When the city was excavated (by the British Museum from 1896 and by successive French, Swedish and Cypriot teams up to 1974), much evidence of copper smelting was discovered. Boosted by the arrival of Achaean migrants in the thirteenth century BC, Alasia was of impressive size, made up of straight streets on a grid pattern, with public buildings of dressed stone and with a stone-paved central square, all surrounded by massive walls. The town was levelled by invaders from the sea in 1200 BC, and most of what can be seen today arose from its rebuilding. Alasia never truly recovered, and when its river harbour silted up and it was rocked by an earthquake in 1075 BC, its people left, possibly to establish a new city at Salamis.

Despite its historic significance, **the site** is relatively underwhelming, especially after a visit to Salamis. A path slopes down to some jumbled masonry walls overgrown with grass and other vegetation. There are no explanatory information boards, but the single-page information sheet, available from the custodian, helps with navigation. As you work north from the south, a series of "houses" is identified by what was found in them – the **House of the Bronzes**, the **House of the Pillar**, the **House of the Horned God** (all to the left as you approach along the path) and the **Sanctuary of the Ingot God**, another house in which many bronze objects were found. Further north is the main site of the extensive **copper works**. The best view of the site is from the air – if you can't afford to hire a helicopter, take a look on Google Earth.

# The Karpaz Peninsula

Famous for its wild donkeys and relatively little else, the **Karpaz Peninsula (Kirpaşa)** stretches for 70km, a tapering finger of land pointing northeast towards Turkey and Syria. One of the most sparsely settled places on the island, road improvements have now made it more readily accessible and holiday villages are springing up along its otherwise pristine beaches. Greek Cypriots also make pilgrimages here to visit **Apostolos Andreas Monastery**, near the peninsula's tip. There is no fixed view on where Karpaz begins, but we've defined this area as east of **Iskele/Boğaz** on the south coast, and **Kaplica** on its north coast. On this basis the atmospheric castle of **Kantara** falls within its boundaries.

The only convenient way of exploring the peninsula is **by car**. Buses are infrequent and the route from Gazimağusa extends only to Yenierenköy.

## Iskele

Just 3km inland off the main coast road from Gazimağusa, **ISKELE** is the administrative centre for the Karpaz Peninsula. For centuries called Trikomo, a name that reflected its creation by the amalgamation of three villages, it was renamed Iskele after the place in the south from which many Turkish Cypriots were resettled after 1974. There's not much to detain you – even its own tourist information map can muster only two places of interest, both churches. **George Grivas** was born in Trikomo, but you wouldn't expect much to be made of that in north Cyprus.

## Boğaz

Continuing 4km up the coast road from the Iskele turn-off brings you to **BOĞAZ**, which is much more worth visiting. A pretty little harbour lined with fishing boats and pleasure craft, it has a well thought out pedestrianized area, numerous bars and restaurants, and a sandy beach. It also boasts a couple of hotels, making it a feasible base for exploring the peninsula.

**ACCOMMODATION**                                                                                    **BOĞAZ**

**Boğaz Hotel** Boğaz ☎3712558, �🌐bogazhotel.com. *Boğaz Hotel* is set around a private beach backed by a pleasant restaurant terrace. Though simple and rather basic, the *Boğaz* has been much improved by recent renovation, and now offers extremely good value for money on the edge of the very pleasant little harbour town. **€40**

**Exotic** Boğaz ☎3712885, �🌐exotichotel.net. For a smallish hotel away from the big towns, the *Exotic* offers a lot – adult and child pools with water slides, views of the sea from all rooms and decent facilities. The hotel's not

---

### THE WILD DONKEYS OF THE KARPAZ

At the easternmost end of the Karpaz Peninsula, beyond Dipkarpaz, hundreds of **wild donkeys** roam free. Though seemingly native to the region, their wild status goes no further back than the Turkish invasion of 1974 when thousands of domestic donkeys, the mainstay of peasant agriculture on the island, were abandoned. The new administration of the north herded them together and let them loose on the Karpaz Peninsula, whose covering of marquis was felt to be ideal for their sustenance. The donkeys, however, preferred the more succulent crops being grown by local farmers, and made a thorough nuisance of themselves, even jumping fences to get at the crops. Understandably angry, the farmers put pressure on the authorities to do something about them, but a proposal to relocate the animals to mainland Turkey caused a storm of environmental and animal-rights protest. So the donkeys remain, and the farmers take what measures they can to keep them out. Perhaps five hundred to a thousand feral donkeys survive here, and visitors are advised to treat them with respect – they have a notoriously bad temper.

on the beach, though – it's set back on the opposite side of the road – and is beginning to look a little run-down (renovation was promised at the time of writing). All the water sports, bars and restaurants of Boğaz are right on its doorstep. **€70**

## Kantara Castle

Mon–Fri: April–Oct 9am–5pm; Nov–March 9am–3.30pm • €7

**Kantara Castle** is the third of the great mountain fortresses built originally by the Byzantines along the Kyrenia Mountains, the others being St Hilarion (see page 220) and Buffavento (see page 222). Kantara Castle is worth visiting not only for its Gothic architecture and atmosphere, but also for its views – from here, you can see both coasts of the Karpaz Peninsula stretching off to the east, and on a clear day the mountains of mainland Turkey. The first mention of Kantara Castle is in 1191 AD when, legend has it, Richard the Lionheart captured Isaac Komnenos here. Lusignan prince John, brother of King Peter I (see page 220), is said to have hidden out here from the invading Genoese in 1373. Later, his brother James I of Cyprus refortified the castle – the origin of much of the stonework that remains today. The nearby **village of Kantara** is a hill station which has seen better times.

The easiest route to the castle is along the north coast road **from Girne** to the Karpaz. At **Kaplica**, a fine, wide new road climbs up from the sea, and within minutes you've covered the 6km to the Karpaz village intersection. From here, there's a clearly signposted and good-quality tarmac road which takes you past a large picnic ground to the castle car park, some 4km from the village. You can also approach **from Gazimağusa**, turning off the east coast road just before Boğaz and following a vertiginous mountain road via Yarkoy and Turnalar. After around half an hour of white-knuckle driving (there are no safety barriers) you reach Kantara village.

### The site

Access to the castle (750m) is up well-graded paths and steps, with a few safety barriers (though higher up the castle, barriers are not always present, so keep an eye on children). Once you're through the main gate, an inner entrance leads between the massive northeast and southeast towers to a path that leads westwards. A succession of **vaulted rooms** with arrow slits, probably the barracks, is followed by a latrine. Beyond here are several more chambers and ruined towers. At the southwest corner of the castle are more chambers and latrines, and a hidden gate. At the top of the castle is a **beacon tower** which could send warning of attack west to Buffavento, which in turn lit beacons to warn St Hilarion.

## Kaplica

You can see **KAPLICA** clearly from the ramparts of Kantara Castle. The village, its white mosque prominent, stands back from two curved sandy beaches on the north coast of the peninsula. On the one to the west stands a large hotel and restaurant and a mobile home/caravan site, the one to the east a small boat harbour. Both beaches are pleasant enough spots to idle away an afternoon, and have fine sand and clear water.

## Yenierenköy and around

Midway between Kantara and the tip of the peninsula is **YENIERENKÖY**, now populated by migrants from the Kokkina Enclave in the west. It has a bank, a petrol station and a tourist information office. Before reaching the village a turn-off some 11km west leads to the villages of **Gelincik** (Vasili) and **Boltasli** (Lythrangomi). Between them lies the church of **Panagia Kanakaria**, made famous by the theft of its mosaics after the 1974 invasion, and even more so by their return in 1991 (see page 246).

**6**

---

**THE KANAKARIA MOSAICS**

The widespread **looting** of religious art treasures from Orthodox churches in the north after 1974 is epitomized by the fate of the **Kanakaria mosaics**, whose story reads like a Hollywood thriller. At some point between 1974 and 1979, thieves raided the church of **Panagia Kanakaria**, about halfway along the Karpaz Peninsula, and made off with four sections of its sixth-century mosaics. In 1988, Indianapolis art dealer Peg Goldberg ("Indiana Peg", perhaps) agreed to buy the mosaics from a Turkish art dealer for just over $1 million. Goldberg soon began hawking the mosaics around museums and art galleries in the US, with a price tag of $20 million. One museum, the Getty, became suspicious, and checked with the authorities in Cyprus. It confirmed that the mosaics were stolen and demanded their return. The Church of Cyprus followed up with a legal claim, and the Indiana Federal Court found in favour of their repatriation. In 1991 the mosaics were returned to the **Archbishop Makarios III Cultural Centre** in Lefkosia, where they can be seen today (see page 182).

The dealer who sold the mosaics, Aydin Dikmen, was tracked down to Munich in 1997 and his flat raided by police. They discovered a huge haul of Cypriot icons, frescoes, bibles and other artefacts worth some $40 million. After a tortuous legal dispute with the German authorities the stolen artworks were eventually repatriated in 2010.

---

East of Yenierenköy are some fine beaches, though the view is now dominated by the luxury **Karpaz Gate Marina** (Ⓦ karpazbay.com). Seemingly aimed at superyacht-owning oligarchs, the marina was opened in 2011 and boasts a 200-seat restaurant, dive centre and a 33m infinity pool among its attractions.

On the edge of the village of **SIPAHI**, to the right off the main road about 5km after Yenierenköy (follow the yellow sign), are the remains of an impressive early Christian basilica, **Agia Trias** (daily: summer 9am–5pm; winter 9am–3.30pm; €5), dating from the fifth century AD. Particularly remarkable are its large geometric mosaics, with, at the northern and southern end, inscriptions acknowledging the men who financed the church. Further along the main road (8km from Yenierenköy) and occupying a terrace on the shore is the old stone church of **Agios Thyrsos**, in the crypt of which is a sacred spring said to have healing powers.

## Dipkarpaz (Rizokarpaso) and around

Fifteen kilometres beyond Agios Thyrsos is **DIPKARPAZ**, the last village on the peninsula and your last chance to fill up with petrol. It's a prosaic kind of a place, reflected in the preponderance of vans and pick-up trucks on its streets, and is mainly notable for the fact that there are still Greeks living here among the largely Turkish incomers. In the centre is an Orthodox church overlooked by a very large mosque, and behind them arcaded shops. Around Dipkarpaz, to the north (follow the signs for the *Oasis Hotel*), lie the substantial ruins of the twelfth-century **Agios Philon** church, one of the few Orthodox churches in Cyprus built in the Romanesque rather than the Byzantine style (all of which are found on the Karpaz Peninsula). Standing in a cluster of palm trees, the church is characterized by a profusion of blind arches and windows. Beside and around Agios Philon are the remains of Greco-Roman **Karpasia** and a fifth-century AD cathedral built from stone plundered from it. From the beach you can see the remains of the ancient harbour, including a 100m-long breakwater stretching out to sea.

## The tip of the peninsula

Beyond Dipkarpaz there's a real feeling that you're approaching the edge of the world. This is a land of roaming donkeys, open country, isolated beaches and wild geological formations. Along the north coast are the ruins of **Aphendrika**, one of the largest cities of Ptolemaic Cyprus, marked now only by the ruins of three later churches – Panagia

Chrysiotissa, Agios Georgios and Panagia Asomatos. Along the south coast (turn right at the mosque in Dipkarpaz) a good-quality highway turns, after about 5km, into a rough and bumpy road and remains so for the 17km to Apostolos Andreas monastery, which is amply signposted. Look out for herds of sheep and goats, and for the famously importunate wild donkeys. Side roads strike off to the right, giving access to several south coast beaches, including one of the finest in Cyprus – **Nangomi**, or **Golden Sands Beach**. Backed by substantial dunes, the beach is some 6km long, with a hill at the end of the western promontory, and consists of fine sand and shallow pellucid water. Besides being a fine bathing beach, Nangomi is also a **sea turtle nesting site** where the security of the eggs is ensured by particularly aggressive sand flies. It is also, as is the whole tip of the peninsula, part of the "Milli Parki" protected area.

**6**

### Apostolos Andreas Monastery
Dawn to dusk • Donations requested

A couple of kilometres beyond **Galounopetra Point**, at the eastern end of Golden Sands Beach, is one of Cyprus's greatest pilgrimage destinations, the **Apostolos Andreas Monastery**. A kind of Cypriot Lourdes, its reputation for miracles comes from the tale of the **Apostle Andrew** who is said to have run aground here on his way to Palestine. St Andrew went ashore, the story goes, and struck a rock with his rod, causing spring water to gush out. The ship's captain was blind (perhaps this was why the ship ran aground), but bathing his eyes in the spring water cured him. A chapel was built on the spot in the fifteenth century, followed by a church in the eighteenth century, and the monastery buildings in the nineteenth.

The monastery's miraculous reputation was boosted in 1895 by the story of Anatolian Greek **Maria Georgiou**, whose son had disappeared seventeen years earlier. She was told in a dream to visit the monastery to pray for her son's return. On the boat over she told her story to a young dervish, who asked how she would identify her son after all this time. She said that he had distinctive birthmarks on his shoulder and chest, at which point he threw his cloak back to reveal identical marks, prompting a tearful reunion (and, of course the reversion of the son to the Orthodox faith).

The monastery was the site of frenetic mass pilgrimages on the saint's name days, August 15 and November 30, until the events of 1974 caused its closure. Since the opening of the Green Line in 2003 it has been growing in popularity again, not only with the religious, but also as a general tourist attraction. The long-awaited renovation of the monastery complex, partly financed by the United Nations and seen as a step towards reconciliation of Greek and Turkish Cypriots, is now well under way. Before renovation started, it consisted of a huge plaza surrounded by lodgings and stalls selling souvenirs and religious items with, towards the sea, monastery buildings surrounding a church topped by a bell tower. Inside, in addition to the usual icons, were numerous votive offerings. From the church, steps led down to the chapel and the holy well. As with many monastery buildings in Cyprus, the whole place was overrun by cats. At the time of writing, renovation was taking place; in due course the monastery, restored to its former splendour, will be well worth visiting.

### Zafer Burnu (Cape Apostolos Andreas)

A further 4km from Apostolos Andreas Monastery brings you to **Zafer Burnu (Cape Apostolos Andreas)**, which has a rocky shore and a small archipelago offshore – the Kleides ("Keys") Islands. A rock, hollowed out by caves and bearing Turkish and TRNC flags, marks Cyprus's northernmost and easternmost point.

ROMAN MOSAIC, PAPHOS

# Contexts

# History

The turbulent history of Cyprus arises directly from its geographical position in the Eastern Mediterranean (the "Levant") – a crossing point and melting pot between the three continents of Europe, Asia and Africa. This has resulted in successive waves of invaders each leaving behind traces of its culture in a complex patchwork of ancient burial sites, pagan temples, Byzantine churches and medieval castles, often built on or adapted from what has come before. What follows, therefore, is a simplification. It should, however, offer a framework through which to interpret and appreciate the many historical sites described in the Guide. For a comprehensive history of Cyprus, try some of the books mentioned in the reading list (see page 263).

## Prehistoric Cyprus

The earliest stone implements in Cyprus date from around 8000 BC and indicate the presence of a hunter-gatherer society who slowly developed the use of domestic animals and farming. Small amounts of copper started to be used for making ornaments, tools and weapons, probably by incomers, from around 4000 BC to 2400 BC, often called the **Chalcolithic Age** from the Ancient Greek "chalcos" – copper. They also used the serpentine mineral picrolite for making jewellery, in particular, small cross-shaped human figures. The people of this period lived in circular single-roomed dwellings and continued to use stone tools, drinking vessels and pots. They grew and ate cereals, raised domesticated animals (sheep and goats, but no cattle) for meat, milk and skins, and buried their dead within their settlements, usually under the floors of their huts. Two outstanding sites originating in this period can be visited in Cyprus – Tenta (see page 74) and Choirokoitia (see page 75).

## The Bronze Age (2400–1050 BC)

During the **Early Bronze** (2400–1900 BC) and **Middle Bronze** (1900–1650 BC) Ages, dwellings became oblong, and contained several rooms. Farming was revolutionized by the use of ploughs, copper jewellery became common, and the dead were buried in separate cemeteries. As the island moved into the **Late Bronze Age** (1650–1050 BC), domestic life was increasingly dominated by bronze implements, drinking vessels, pots and pans. Weapons could also be fashioned out of the new material. The **mining of copper** (the main constituent of bronze) and other metals became more widespread, and the large reserves of copper found in the Troodos Mountains attracted envious looks from across the region as demand for the metal exploded. Coastal towns developed, and trading contact was made with all three nearby continents. Partly arising from these outside contacts and driven by the needs of commerce, a **written script** appeared – old inscriptions have been found on pottery shards and loom weights, for example, and a complete text on a sixteenth-century BC tablet from Enkomi-Alasia, just north of

| c.7000–5000 BC | c.4000–2000 BC | c.2400–1900 BC | c.2400–1650 BC |
|---|---|---|---|
| First settlers arrive and establish Tenta and Choirokoitia. | Copper starts to be mined and used to make tools. | Beginnings of the use of bronze. | Bronze jewellery becomes common (Early and Middle Bronze Age). |

Famagusta. The script, possibly a version of the Minoan script from Crete (and therefore called Cypro-Minoan), and consisting of eighty characters, is yet to be deciphered.

From the latter part of the thirteenth century BC, waves of **Mycenaean Greeks** came to the island, probably driven out of their cities in the Peloponnese by invaders from the north. They established cities – for example, Maa-Palaiokastro and Kition in the west and Salamis in the east – and brought with them the Greek language and Mycenaean pottery.

## The Iron Age (1050–480 BC)

During the **Iron Age**, bronze was progressively replaced by the much harder, stronger and more effective iron, at first only in jewellery, later in the making of tools and weapons. At the same time, the Bronze Age Mycenaean cities disappeared, probably destroyed by earthquakes, or replaced or taken over by new **city kingdoms** established, according to legend, by Greeks returning from the Trojan Wars, or more probably by a late wave of Mycenaean incomers. These cities included Salamis, Kition, Idalion, Amathus, Kourion, Paphos, Marion and Soli. Whatever the truth regarding these developments, this was when Greek language and traditions became really firmly entrenched on the island. Links, too, with other Greek islands grew, particularly Evvia and Crete.

The Iron Age is often divided into two eras, according to the type of pottery they produced – **Geometric** (1050–750 BC) and **Archaic** (750–480 BC). These two eras coincide with the incursion of two different groups of outsiders. From the Geometric era's first two centuries very little has survived, which is why the period is sometimes called a "Dark Age". But thereafter, from about 850 to 750 BC, Kition (Larnaka) was colonized by the **Phoenicians** from nearby Lebanon, and this sparked a renaissance in that part of the island. Setting up influential trading posts in other Cypriot towns, the Phoenicians introduced an alphabet for the first time.

The subsequent **Archaic era** saw conquest by the **Assyrians**, who had no interest in colonizing the island, but only in extracting tribute. The existing cities (Salamis, Kition, Amathous, Kourion, Idalion, Palaipafos, Marion, Soli and Tamassos) retained effective independence, and continued in what was, economically and culturally, something of a golden age. Further incursions by the Egyptians (under the Emperor Amasis 568–525 BC) and the **Persians** (under Cyrus, from 525 BC) followed.

## Classical Cyprus (480–323 BC)

The **Classical period** in Cyprus was contemporary with, though not as illustrious as, that of mainland Greece – Cyprus's main contribution being the establishment of the Stoic school of philosophy by **Zenon of Kition** (see page 51). Politically, because of its geographical position, Cyprus was piggy in the middle during the **Greco-Persian Wars**, with some Cypriot cities supporting Persia, some Greece. Dominated at first by the Persian Empire, parts of Cyprus were freed briefly (450–449 BC) by the victory of the Athenian fleet under Kimon and the subsequent relief of Marion (Pafos) and of Kition (Larnaka). However, Kimon was killed during the siege of Kition, and Cyprus reverted to Persian rule, retaining, though, a fair degree of autonomy so long as tribute was paid. The Persians in no way diluted the island's Greek personality – it was during this period that the pantheon of **Greek gods** was adopted, and in particular that the Middle

| c.1650–1050 BC | c.1200–1050 BC | c.1050–750 BC | c.750–480 BC |
|---|---|---|---|
| Cypro-Minoan script developed. | Mycenaean Greek settlers bring Greek culture, art, language and religion, and establish cities. | New city kingdoms established, according to legend, by Greeks returning from the Trojan Wars. | Assyrian conquest followed by Egyptian and Persian incursion. |

Eastern goddess of Astarte, long worshipped on the island, was Hellenized to become **Aphrodite**, the goddess with which Cyprus is most associated.

## Hellenistic Cyprus (323–31 BC)

Persia's domination of Cyprus was emphatically ended by **Alexander the Great**'s defeat of the Persian Empire, but after his death in 323 BC Cyprus became a bone of contention between his generals. The War of the Diadochi ("successors") from 323 BC until 280 BC was, as it affected Cyprus, between two of the successor states: the Egypt of Ptolemy and the Seleucid Empire in the Middle East, with **Ptolemaic Egypt** prevailing. There followed two hundred years of relatively peaceful rule from Alexandria, during which Hellenization progressed apace as the new rulers exploited the island's timber, olives, wheat and above all copper. They also used the island as a military base.

## Roman Cyprus (31 BC–330 AD)

In 58 BC Cyprus was annexed by Rome, then reverted several times to Egyptian rule, finally becoming a full **province of the Roman Empire** in 31 BC. As with many other parts of the empire, the Romans' main interest was in exploiting natural resources – in this case copper (this is when Cyprus first got its modern name, being known by the Romans as "cuprum", the Latin for copper). However, unlike earlier rulers of the island, the Romans left a positive legacy: the building of new roads and harbours, the expansion of trade, economic growth, greater prosperity and three hundred years of relative peace and stability. It was during the Roman hegemony that the island embraced what has come to be regarded as one of the cornerstones of Greek-Cypriot identity – Christianity. The island was converted to the new religion by St Paul and St Barnabas (see page 243) from 45 AD onwards.

## Byzantine Cyprus (330–1192)

In 330 AD the capital of the Roman Empire was moved by the Emperor Constantine to the new city of Constantinople (modern-day Istanbul) on the Black Sea. In 395 AD the declining empire was divided in two, the western half ruled from Rome, the eastern half from Constantinople. Cyprus fell firmly into the latter half, the so-called **Byzantine Empire**. This period, which was to last, with interruptions, for well over eight hundred years, left a a rich legacy of Christian art, architecture, ritual and legend on the island. Although the Cypriot Church was ruled nominally from Constantinople, it was in reality independent, a status that was formalized by the granting of autocephalos status by the Emperor Zeno (see page 243).

The early churches were simple wooden-roofed buildings based on the Roman basilica model, not dissimilar to those in much of Western Europe. But over time domes and arches were added, giving the more Levantine or Middle Eastern outline of modern Cypriot churches. Many were adorned with beautiful frescoes and mosaic **icons** (see page 253), as well as plenty of gold and silver plate, contributing to the opulent appearance of many Orthodox churches on the island today. Examples include the early frescoed, wooden-roofed **churches in the Troodos Mountains**, the gold and

| c.480–323 BC | c.323–31 BC | 31 BC |
| --- | --- | --- |
| Cyprus is caught in the conflict between Greece and the Persian Empire. | The (Greek) Ptolemies of Egypt succeed in struggle between the heirs of Alexander the Great and rule Cyprus. | Roman rule in Cyprus begins, bringing relative peace and prosperity. |

silver plates discovered in Lambousa and now in Nicosia's **Cyprus Museum**, and the three surviving early **Christian mosaics** in Kiti, the Karpas Peninsula and Livadia.

In addition to this great flourishing of Byzantine art, **new cities** developed as others declined or were destroyed, often by earthquakes. The capital moved from Pafos to Salamis, and Ammochostos (Famagusta) grew up nearby. Lemesos (at first called Neapolis or Nemesos) was established, Lefkosia (Nicosia) replaced Ledra, and was eventually to become the capital in the eleventh/twelfth centuries.

Economically, the great innovation of the period was the introduction of the **silk industry**, based on secrets stolen from the Chinese and developed from the sixth century AD. Shipbuilding, gold and silversmithing all flourished.

There were, however, setbacks. The island was sacked in 649 by a Saracen army, with a garrison being left from 653. Periodic **raids by Arab pirates** drove the population away from the coast to seek safety in inland villages. A Byzantine/Arab agreement brought a sort of peace between 688 and 965, after which the intruders were cleared out by Emperor Nicephorus Phocas, re-establishing full Byzantine control. Add to all this a succession of earthquakes, plagues and famines, and it becomes clear that the great artistic successes of the period were achieved in the face of considerable misfortune.

The Byzantine Empire's hold on Cyprus ended in a welter of political intrigue. In 1184 **Isaac Komnenos**, King of Cyprus, declared the island independent of Constantinople, a move which might have been popular among his subjects had it not been for the king's substantial personal failings. His short reign was characterized by pointless cruelty and political ineptitude, which ended with the first incursion into the story of Cyprus by a country at the opposite end of Europe – England.

## Lusignan (Frankish) Cyprus (1192–1489)

The successors to the long period of Byzantine rule arrived on the island almost by accident, courtesy of political chaos caused by the Third Crusade, started in 1187. A gaggle of European kings led by **Richard the Lionheart** of England, infuriated by Saladin's successes in the Middle East, set out to restore Christian access to the Holy Lands. Richard was on his way to the Middle East when his sister and his wife-to-be were shipwrecked on Cyprus. Isaac Komnenos took them hostage and tried to extract ransom from the English king. Angered by this impertinence, and mindful of how useful Cyprus would be for future Crusader activity, Richard invaded and conquered the island and imprisoned Komnenos. Not wishing to be sidetracked by the need to keep Cyprus in subjugation, Richard promptly sold the island to the **Knights Templar**. Their rule was short and not very sweet, so the island was in turn off-loaded to one **Guy de Lusignan**, a Frankish knight who had helped Richard conquer the island in the first place. It was this unlikely and rather disreputable chain of events that inaugurated the three hundred years of Frankish, or **Lusignan**, rule of the island.

The Lusignans, originally from Poitiers in France, introduced a feudal system of government which was in essence common to many countries in Western Europe – for example, that imposed by William the Conqueror on England from 1066. Numerous **knights** of French origin came in as the new ruling class, the island was divided between them, and the peasantry was expected to provide labour and military service in return for land on which to grow crops. The knights were allowed to build themselves fortified

| **45 AD** | **330** | **468** | **647** |
|---|---|---|---|
| St Paul and St Barnabas begin the conversion of the island to Christianity. | Cyprus becomes part of the Byzantine Empire. | The Church of Cyprus is granted autonomous status. | First of numerous Arab raids on coastal cities. |

## ICONOGRAPHY: RELIGIOUS ART IN CYPRUS

Most visitors to Cyprus will find themselves looking at **icons** in churches, monasteries, or in one of the island's many Byzantine **museums**. Though the word "icon" can cover a variety of types of religious image, its most common use is for figurative religious art consisting of representations of biblical figures and scenes, either painted on a simple wooden board, sometimes embellished with gold and silver, or made of small pieces of pottery or glass organized into mosaics.

Few icons date from before the eighth/ninth century AD. This was because, during the years between 725 and 842, the Byzantine Empire was split by a vicious struggle between **iconoclasts**, who considered icons to be idolatrous, and "iconodules", who viewed them as aids to worship rather than things to be worshipped. The iconodules eventually triumphed, but not before the iconoclasts destroyed icons in their thousands.

Icon painters in Cyprus adhered strictly to the formal style established in Constantinople – figures appear flat against a plain background, facing the viewer, with emphasis on eyes and hands. Although the influence of Italian Renaissance art can be detected in the later output of the **Cypriot School**, their loyalty to the traditional approach over many hundreds of years makes Cypriot icons hard to date. While many of the icons produced today are just cheap reproductions made for the tourist market, others are of high quality, such as those produced in Stavrovouni Monastery.

After the **Turkish invasion** of 1974, many of the north's religious icons were looted and ended up either on the black market or auctioned off to collectors. The Church of Cyprus has been successful in repatriating only a small proportion of the art (for images of stolen icons see ⓦ churchofcypruseu.com). In 2011 the singer Boy George returned an icon that he had bought in London in the mid-1980s. The authorities in the north have belatedly made some attempt to preserve the artworks in their care, for example setting up museums in Girne and Gazimağusa. However, their failure to prevent what amounts to the greatest large-scale theft of art since World War II remains a continued source of resentment in the south.

towers, for example the ones at Pyla, Alaminos and Kiti, while the great fortresses of Nicosia, Famagusta, Paphos, Limassol, Kyrenia, St Hilarion, Buffavento and Kantara were reserved for the royal family. These towers and **castles** are among the main survivals of the Lusignan era. Another change was the imposition of **Roman Catholicism**, although the Orthodox Church continued to worship in secret. As might be expected, the ruling class and the Catholic Church did very well during this period, the Cypriots and the Greek Orthodox Church less so. The ruling family themselves were an unprepossessing lot, long on luxurious living, short on political ability (see page 254).

When, in 1291 Acre, the Crusaders' last major stronghold in the Kingdom of Jerusalem, fell to the Muslims, Cyprus became the only Christian land in the Eastern Mediterranean, and therefore even more important militarily and commercially. **Genoa** and **Venice** competed fiercely for favours, and both were granted trading rights by the Lusignan authorities. The cities of Nicosia and Famagusta flourished, as did production and export of sugar, wine, textiles (especially asproploumia, an early type of lace) and ceramic ware.

## Venetian Cyprus (1489–1571)

The continuing rivalry between Genoa and Venice finally ended in 1489 when the island was ceded by the Lusignans to the **Venetian Republic**. They immediately

| 649 | 649–965 | 965–1191 | 1191 | 1192 |
| --- | --- | --- | --- | --- |
| Island invaded by Saracen army. | Conflict between the Christian Byzantine Empire and the forces of Islam. | Second period of relative peace within the Byzantine Empire. | Richard the Lionheart conquers Cyprus. | Richard sells Cyprus first to the Knights Templar, then to his lieutenant Guy de Lusignan. |

**MEET THE LUSIGNANS**

The **Lusignans**, rulers of Cyprus for nearly three hundred years from 1192, were more colourful than the austere ruins of their castles and churches might lead one to expect. As James of Vitry described them (quoted by Colin Thubron in *Journey into Cyprus*), "They were brought up in luxury, soft and effeminate, more used to baths than battles, addicted to unclean and riotous living, clad like women in soft robes". Supposedly devout Christians, they garnered a reputation for being debased in lifestyle and treacherous in politics, much given to extravagant feasting and endless hunting trips. Women of the court wore scandalously low-cut gowns in expensive materials beneath the black capes worn to symbolize mourning for the loss of Jerusalem. Contrasting with this decadent elite, the poverty of the ordinary people continued: as Thubron puts it, "All this brilliance, of course, lay sugar-like on the rotting cake of Greek peasantry". The best place to imagine this vibrant but debauched lifestyle is at the castle of St Hilarion, central to some of the most devious goings-on of the Lusignan period.

began to develop it as an entrepôt for their activities in the eastern Mediterranean. Conditions for ordinary Cypriots became, if anything, worse, with the island being viewed by its new rulers as little more than a military base and a source of tax revenue. Commercially, the island's main exports were sugar, wine, olive oil, wheat, barley and cotton, and it was this period that saw the beginning of the production of the intricate and expensive type of lace for which Lefkara became famous. The bulk of these exports was funnelled through **Famagusta**, which became by far the island's main port.

The **fall of Rhodes** to the Ottoman Empire in 1522 led to a feverish military building programme, with the Venetians rightly suspecting that Cyprus would be next. New walls were thrown up around Nicosia, and the existing walls of Famagusta were greatly strengthened. The onslaught didn't come immediately, but all these preparations in the end proved of little avail. **Nicosia fell** to the Ottomans after a seven-week siege in 1570, and Famagusta, after heroic resistance lasting almost a year, in July 1571. The cruelty meted out to the Famagusta's defenders – their leader, **Marcantonio Bragadin**, was flayed alive – boded ill for the island's future.

A perhaps apocryphal but amusing story says that the Ottoman invasion of Cyprus occurred partly because the splendidly and aptly named **Sultan Selim the Sot** was eager to get his hands on the source of the sweet Commandaria wine of which he was excessively fond. It was a case of be careful what you wish for: under the influence of the wine he fell in his bathroom, fractured his skull, and died.

## Ottoman Cyprus (1571–1871)

**Ottoman rule** was initially welcomed by the local population. And indeed, things started well enough, with the new regime recognizing the Cypriot Orthodox Church. This was, however, more to do with greed than tolerance – the easiest way to collect taxes was through the Church's established network. Administrators – among them dragomen (see page 181) – had to pay the authorities hefty bribes to secure their posts, and were badly paid, the expectation being that they would make a profit by extracting as much money as they could from the population. When the tax burden became too great, there were periodic **rebellions** (such as in 1680, 1764, 1821 and 1833) which were put down with

| 1192–1489 | 1489–1571 | 1522 | 1571 |
|---|---|---|---|
| Lusignan rule – Cyprus becomes a Crusader state. | Venetian rule – Cyprus becomes a commercial trading base. | The fall of Rhodes to the Ottoman Empire leads to the fortification of the island against possible Muslim attack. | Siege of Famagusta completes the Ottoman conquest of the island. |

ferocious cruelty – the rebellion of 1821, for example, led to the execution by hanging or beheading of five hundred prominent Greek religious leaders in Nicosia.

Some Cypriots, often those descended from the remnants of the previous Venetian occupation, were aware that Muslims enjoyed a variety of privileges, and converted, at least outwardly, while maintaining most of their Christian beliefs in private – many of today's "Turkish" Cypriots are descended from these "**Linovamvakoi**" (see page 106). Others emigrated, many of them to the Anatolian region of Turkey or elsewhere in the Balkans. Yet more looked to Greece, particularly after the end of Ottoman rule in 1823.

The **Greek War of Independence** had widespread, albeit implicit, support from **Great Britain**, the ascendant power of the time, whose ruling classes had often been schooled in ancient Greek philosophy and language. Yet despite their Philhellenic tendencies, the British preferred to keep the status quo in Cyprus. The rise of nationalism across the Balkans and Eastern Mediterranean and the weakening of the Ottoman Empire, known as the "**sick man of Europe**", threatened to create a power vacuum. Mindful of Russian designs on Cyprus as a useful warm-water port, Britain continued to support the ailing empire, fighting alongside the Ottomans in the Crimea.

Despite the ill-governance of the Ottomans, Cyprus flourished as the nineteenth century progressed, with European traders establishing themselves in the main ports, and consular offices opening on the island, particularly in Larnaka. Cypriots were becoming increasingly educated and urban, and the seeds of "**enosis**" – union with Greece – began to flower. At the same time, Britain's continued support for the Ottomans on the international stage was recognized by London's increasing influence over the sultan, and, after British military support in the 1877–78 Russo-Turkish War, was formalized in the **Cyprus Convention** of 1878. This allowed Britain to occupy Cyprus, with extensive administrative powers, though it stopped short of outright sovereignty. British forces landed in Larnaka in July, 1878, and the period of British rule began.

## British Cyprus (1878–1960)

The **British takeover** of Cyprus was popular with Greek Cypriots, who hoped that their new rulers would view eventual union with Greece more favourably than the Ottomans. The Cypriots had every reason to be optimistic – after all, Britain had ceded the Ionian islands to Greece fourteen years earlier. For a variety of reasons, however, this didn't happen, despite the reduction in Cyprus's strategic importance after Britain's occupation of Egypt and the Suez Canal in 1882. When Britain finally offered to hand over Cyprus to Greece during World War I (in return for Greek entry into the war), the Greeks refused – the Greek king, Constantine I, being pro-German. The offer was one of cynical wartime political expediency, with a return to normal service (opposition to enosis) once the war was over.

Having ended up on the losing side in World War I, the Ottomans were forced to renounce all claims to Cyprus and the rest of their empire under the **Treaty of Lausanne** in 1923, in return for recognition of the new Turkish state. Two years later Cyprus became a full **British colony**. The British authorities continued to tax the population fiercely, and refused to countenance demands for enosis. In October 1931 there was a serious uprising which was harshly put down. Cypriots did their bit for Britain during **World War II** – six thousand Cypriot volunteers joined the newly formed Cyprus Regiment which fought in the Greek campaign. Greek Cypriots were hopeful that they

| 1572 | 1821 | 1878 | 1925 |
|---|---|---|---|
| Building of the Büyük Han (Great Inn) in Nicosia by Mustafa Paşa. | Rebellion is violently suppressed, with over five hundred prominent Greek Cypriots being publicly executed in Nicosia. | Period of British rule begins. | Cyprus becomes a Crown colony. |

would be rewarded by being allowed to join Greece, but again their hopes were dashed, though an offer of limited self-rule was made and turned down in 1947.

It is in some ways difficult for outsiders to understand the passion of Greek Cypriots for **union with Greece** – a country which was impoverished, chaotic and, at that time, right wing. It was, perhaps, an affair of the heart, not the head. The opposition of Turkish Cypriots, who made up around eighteen percent of the island's population, was easier to grasp. Whatever the practicalities, the demand for enosis reached new heights: on January 15, 1950 an unofficial referendum organized by the Church was held among Greek Cypriots, who voted overwhelmingly (95.7percent) for enosis. The British authorities paid no attention, their resolve reinforced when Britain moved its Middle East Command to strategically significant Cyprus from newly independent Egypt in 1954. Armed **rebellion** against British rule began the following year.

### EOKA and the fight for independence

The leader of the political movement for enosis was the head of the Greek Orthodox Church in Cyprus, **Archbishop Makarios III** (see page 161), while that of the military opposition to the colonial power was **George Grivas** or "Digenis" (see page 165), leader of right-wing paramilitary organization **EOKA**. Weapons and explosives were smuggled onto the island along the west coast north of Pafos, and British military installations and personnel were targeted, together with Turkish Cypriots and even left-wing or anti-enosis Greek Cypriots.

Violence, and British responses, escalated. In 1956 Makarios and two of his associates were **exiled** to the Seychelles, and in the same year nine EOKA fighters were executed, causing widespread demonstrations on the island and in Greece. In 1958 an explosion outside the Turkish press office in Nicosia sparked further intercommunal violence (though it was actually thought to have been caused by Turkish-Cypriot agents provocateurs, not by Greek Cypriots). The British authorities recruited special constables exclusively from the Turkish-Cypriot community, a move widely condemned as provocative. At the height of the disturbances, around 1200 EOKA guerrillas, located mainly in the Troodos Mountains, were tying down 25,000 British regulars and 4500 special constables. Finally, hostilities ended in 1959 when **independence** (though not enosis) was granted.

## Independent Cyprus (1960–present)

The independent **Republic of Cyprus** came into being on August 16, 1960, with Archbishop Makarios as its first president, and the Turkish-Cypriot leader **Dr Fazil Küçük** vice president. Cyprus took its place at the United Nations, the Commonwealth and the Council of Europe, and became a member of the Non-Aligned Movement. The settlement was based on a hugely complicated formula which tried to secure the rights of both communities (a 1960 census revealed a population of 442,138 Greek Cypriots and 104,320 Turkish Cypriots), while Britain retained two sovereign military bases – Dhekelia and Akrotiri, totalling 158 square kilometres. Among several agreements made at the time of independence was the **Treaty of Guarantee**, by which Britain, Greece and Turkey were empowered to take action if the terms of independence were violated.

| 1942 | 1955–59 | 1957 | 1959 | 1960 |
|---|---|---|---|---|
| British soldiers discover the Pafos mosaics. | EOKA fights for union with Greece (enosis). | *Bitter Lemons* by Lawrence Durrell is published. | Independence granted and elections held. | Archbishop Makarios III elected president. |

Suspicion between the Greek-Cypriot and Turkish-Cypriot communities was if anything exacerbated by independence, and divisions within the Greek-Cypriot community also appeared, between the left and the right, and between those who were happy with independence and those who still wanted enosis. Grivas, rightly suspecting that Makarios's fervour for enosis had cooled, went into self-imposed exile in Greece.

### Intercommunal violence and the beginnings of partition

The provisions of the new constitution never really worked, and in 1963, when Makarios suggested a number of changes, Turkish Cypriots and Turkey rejected them, and the Turkish-Cypriot contingent withdrew from government and set up a "temporary Turkish Cypriot administration". Intercommunal violence (involving paramilitaries on both sides) escalated to the extent that the UN sent in a peacekeeping force in 1964.

Despite the presence of UN troops the violence continued, and a series of heavily defended **Turkish-Cypriot enclaves** was set up, with their own administration, police forces and radio stations. Nicosia became a divided city, separated by the **Green Line** (so-called because it was drawn by the British commander in green crayon on a map of the city) into northern Turkish-Cypriot and southern Greek-Cypriot halves. An enclave centred on the village of **Kokkina** on the northwest coast became a landing point for men and supplies coming in from the Turkish mainland. In 1964 the Cypriot National Guard, led by the newly returned Grivas, attacked the enclave, despite pleas from Makarios not to do so. This almost provoked all-out war as Turkish air-force jets bombed and strafed the Greek positions and the nearby town of Polis. Far from preventing men and supplies coming in via the enclave, it subsequently became a Turkish military base. De facto partition was happening.

### Coup d'etat and the Turkish invasion

By 1974 Makarios had lost the support of the military junta that had been ruling Greece since 1967, and of the Greek-Cypriot right, including EOKA-B (the later incarnation of the EOKA), neither of which believed that he still wanted union with Greece. He was also opposed by the US, who considered him to be too left wing and too close to the USSR. All this came to a head in **1974** when on July 15 an extreme

---

### THE CYPRIOT "COSTA DEL CRIME"

A combination of Cyprus's historic links with Britain, the camouflage offered by its large expat community, and the presence of the unrecognized Turkish Republic of Northern Cyprus, which has no extradition treaty with the UK, just minutes away, makes Cyprus particularly attractive to members of the British criminal fraternity. In 2012 a UK Police campaign "**Operation Zygos**" targeted a list of the nine "most wanted" hiding out on the island. That said, the experiences of tycoon **Asil Nadir** will be both an encouragement and a warning to felons hoping to use Cyprus to evade justice. Having fled to north Cyprus from the UK in 1993 following accusations of false accounting and theft arising from the collapse of his Polly Peck International company, Nadir enjoyed a life of luxury in the north for seventeen years. Yet the restrictions on his freedom to travel anywhere apart from Turkey eventually led him to risk prosecution by returning to the UK in 2010 to face trial. He duly had his day in court, was convicted in August 2012, and sentenced to ten years in prison.

---

| 1963–64 | 1964 | 1974 | 1983 |
|---|---|---|---|
| Intercommunal violence in Cyprus leads to intervention of UN troops. | The Kokkina Incident almost leads to all-out war; Green Line across the capital established. | Turkish invasion leads to conquest of northern Cyprus, de facto division of the island. | The "Turkish Republic of North Cyprus" is established. |

right-wing member of EOKA-B, **Nicos Sampson**, led a **coup d'etat** with the backing of the Greek junta (and, it is claimed, the CIA). In response, **Turkey invaded** the island on July 20, landing just west of Kerynia (near the village now called Karaoğlanoğlu), justifying the action by referring to the Treaty of Guarantee.

The Turkish military intervention ended both Sampson's brief rule in Cyprus and that of the longer-lived junta in Greece. A new government took office in Cyprus under President **Glafkos Clerides**, removing the ostensible reason for the invasion. But during the ensuing cease-fire, Turkey continued to pour reinforcements into the island and advanced further inland. By the time hostilities ended – because of international pressure but also because Turkey had got what it wanted – 37 percent of the island had been occupied. Turkey established a border between the north and the south (the **Attila Line**, commonly called the **Green Line**, since it was an extension of the one drawn initially in 1964). In order to prevent further incidents, a United Nations "**Buffer Zone**" was set up, with block-houses, barbed wire, and regular patrols. By this stage around 200,000 Greek Cypriots had been forced out of the northeastern occupied zone, and 50,000 Turkish Cypriots moved into it. In 1975 the occupied zone declared itself the "Turkish Federated State of Cyprus" and finally, in 1983, the "Turkish Republic of Northern Cyprus".

## Solving "the Cyprus Question"

Today many Cypriots have no memory of a united island. Since the invasion there have been numerous **UN resolutions** condemning the illegal regime in the north, all of which have been ignored. According to one British diplomat, the intractable nature of the problem was that "no Turkish Cypriot could ever forget the period between 1963–74, and no Greek Cypriot could remember it". Though a flippant remark, it goes some way to summing up the impasse in which the minority Turkish Cypriots fear Greek domination while Greek Cypriots will never forget or forgive the invasion of 1974 (for the Cypriot government position see ⓦmfa.gov.cy, and for the Turkish see ⓦmfa.gov.tr).There have, however, been some signs of movement on the "**Cyprus Question**". In April 2003 restrictions on crossing into north Cyprus imposed by the Turkish-Cypriot regime were suddenly relaxed, allowing thousands of Greek Cypriots from the south to visit the homes and villages from which they'd been expelled. On May 1, 2004 the Republic of Cyprus became a member of the **European Union**, leading to a bizarre situation where a part of the EU is being occupied by a foreign power.

Pressure on and in north Cyprus has been growing. Turkish Cypriots in the north have become irate at being treated increasingly as a province of Turkey, and have taken exception to the large number of immigrants coming in from the Turkish mainland. Faced with increasingly open discontent, the Turkish-Cypriot regime cracked down hard on dissidents, starting with the arrest of the editor of an opposition newspaper in July 2000. Faced with increasing discontent with unemployment and living standards in the north, the Turkish-Cypriot leader **Rauf Denktaş** (see page 206) poured scorn on the idea that there could be a united, federal state of Cyprus. In 2003 he claimed that there were Turks who lived in Cyprus and Greeks who lived in Cyprus – "the only true Cypriots are its donkeys".

In 2004, at the instigation of the Secretary-General of the United Nations, a new attempted solution – the **Annan Plan** – proposed a "United Republic of Cyprus" as a

| 2003 | 2004 | 2008 | 2008 |
| --- | --- | --- | --- |
| First crossing point on the Green Line established. | Republic of Cyprus joins the European Union. | Cyprus adopts the euro while the north persists with the Turkish Lira. | Demetris Christofias elected president of the Republic. |

## CYPRUS DOWN BUT NOT OUT

With a population of less than a million, Cyprus was always a minnow in economic terms. However, the island was confident that it could ride out the recession. It was capitalizing on its geographical position, to become a financial hub for the region, and tourism seemed to be going from strength to strength. There was even hope that ongoing **natural gas exploration** might turn the Eastern Mediterranean into a new North Sea.

At the start of the twenty-first century this confidence evaporated. The explosion at the Vasilikos naval base in 2011 (see page 73) severely damaged the republic's economy, while Greece's economic woes had a knock-on effect on Cyprus. The continuing stalemate over the de facto division of the island, aggravated by disagreements over drilling rights, does neither side any favours as regards inward investment. Add all this to the effects of the global financial crisis, with Cypriot private and public debt spiralling, and something had to give. In June 2012 Cyprus became the fifth EU member to request a **bail-out** and has concluded the assistance programme successfully in 2016.

That said, Cyprus's debt was small compared to bigger European players. And Russian money continued to flood into the country, in the form both of big-spending tourists and expats. The election of pro-austerity President Nicos Anastasiades in 2013, the continued natural gas exploration, and the surprise election of Mustafa Akinci to the presidency of the north in 2015 held out hope for a surge in economic and political progress. The tourism-based economy picked up fairly quickly and is now among the best faring in the Mediterranean area.

federation of two states. In a **referendum** on the plan, in the north two to one were in favour, despite Denktas's opposition; in the south three to one were against. However, political changes on both sides of the divide added rekindled hope of a settlement – in 2008 the left-wing Demetris Christofias was elected President of the Republic, and Mustafa Akinci, founder of the pro-unification Peace and Democracy Movement, became President of the north in 2015, one of the planks of whose campaign was the refurbishment of Varosha by contractors from both sides. Both men expressed optimism about the future, and Mustafa Akinci made a number of encouraging moves – he lifted visa restrictions on people crossing from the south into the north, and began attempts to increase north Cyprus's independence from Turkey.

However, the election of centre-right president **Nicos Anastasiades** in the Republic in 2013 indicated that reunification had slipped down the political agenda, with Anastasiades stating that "the most urgent task is to face the financial crisis". The situation seemed to have arrived at stalemate, though many hoped that Turkey's long-held ambitions to join the EU might be a possible catalyst for new talks between the two sides.

At the World Economic Forum in Davos in January 2016, and later in Nicosia, Akinci and Anastasiades met – "We have the same vision" said the former, while the Republic's president called the meetings "extremely constructive". The hope was short-lived, however, and the entire process broke down in 2017. In 2018 Austria, as the next president of the EU council, offered to host the possible future negotiations. Meanwhile the Turkish activity both in the Aegean and the Eastern Mediterranean Sea meant to interfere with the Cyprus exploitation of their own natural resources has forced the European Council to call on Turkey to cease their illegal actions.

| 2012 | 2013 | 2015 | 2017-19 |
|------|------|------|---------|
| In London, Pavlos Kontides wins Cyprus's first ever Olympic medal – a silver in the Laser sailing event. | The presidents of the Republic of Cyprus and North Cyprus begin peace talks. | Negotiations halt and the talks break down. | Discussions regarding possible reunification take place. |

# Geology and wildlife

Whether you're walking across the sands of Fig Tree Bay, trekking in the Troodos Mountains, driving through the vineyards of Lemesos or Pafos districts or exploring a spectacular Crusader castle, you can't help but be aware of Cyprus's varied geology and its influence on the landscape. Likewise, the island's diverse flora and fauna has been influenced primarily by Cyprus's geographical position between Europe, Asia and Africa.

## Geology

Cyprus in its present form has its origins in the collision of the African and Eurasian tectonic plates about ten million years ago – the same geological pile-up that created the Alps. For millennia Cyprus consisted of **two islands** – one centred on the Troodos Massif, the other on the Kyrenia Mountains, separated by the primordial Athalas Sea. Slowly the two islands were joined as the floor of the Athalas Sea rose and progressively silted up, creating the Mesaorian Plain. Over time the relatively soft, water-soluble **limestone** of the Kyrenia Massif to the north became weathered into its present spectacularly tortured shapes, while the more extensive and higher Troodos Mountains to the southwest lost their limestone covering to erosion, revealing the much harder and older **igneous rock** beneath. This was not only far more impervious to erosion (hence the rounded shape of the mountains) but also contained a wealth of minerals, particularly **copper**. The significance of the region's geology was further emphasized in the late 1960s when undisturbed samples of **ophiolite** – oceanic crust and its underlying mantle – were identified, proving that the Troodos Massif was created by the sea floor spreading and the collision of the African and European tectonic plates. In recognition of the geological importance of the Troodos Massif, the Troodos Geopark Visitor Centre was opened in 2015 in an abandoned asbestos mine near Troodos village (see page 149).

## Human geography and environmental concerns

The people of Cyprus have long adapted to the geology and topography of their environment. In fertile Mesaoria, and to a lesser extent elsewhere on the coastal plain, the principal activity is **arable farming**, supplemented or in some places replaced by fishing. The southern foothills of the Troodos Massif are carpeted in **vineyards** and dotted with wineries, while the higher hills and mountains of both Troodos and Kyrenia ranges are the haunt of sheep and goats. Copper and asbestos were until recently widely extracted from the Troodos range. The western end of the Mesaorian Plain, around Güzelyurt, is dominated by the production of **soft fruit**, particularly oranges and lemons. In most parts of the island **olive trees** are a source of fruit and oil.

The expansion of the tourist industry, especially in parts of the republic but also increasingly in the north, has provided a much-needed additional source of income but has thrown up a number of **environmental concerns**, particularly on the otherwise pristine peninsulas of Akamas and Karpaz. Historically, the greatest cause of natural disasters has been earthquakes, as witnessed by the histories of virtually every town and city on the island. Increasingly, though, water shortages, industrial pollution and the incursion of saltwater into freshwater supplies have become common. Since the devastating explosion at the island's principal power station in 2011, a shortage of electricity has also been a problem.

# Wildlife

The range of flora and fauna to be found in Cyprus is wide, partly because it is an island with **endemic species** that have evolved in isolation, and partly because its geographical position between Europe, Asia and Africa has made it a major intersection for **migrating birds**.

## Plants

Cyprus in the past was heavily forested, but its stock of trees became severely depleted as man cut timber for fuel, to build ships and to make charcoal for copper smelting. Reforestation proceeded apace from the British occupation onwards – mostly in the Troodos and Kyrenia mountains, and in the great **forest of Tiliria** – and woodland now covers about seventeen percent of the island. Upland forests contain Aleppo and black pine, the charmingly named "stinking juniper", cedar and many more, with much of the rest of non-agricultural land having a dense covering of scrub or **"maquis"** consisting largely of Phoenician juniper, rock rose, lentisk, terebinth, myrtle, storax and golden oaks. **Cypress trees** and fig trees also abound. Along the coastal plain numerous imported species flourish, among them palm trees, eucalyptus, mimosa and **bourgainvillea**, and cacti such as prickly pear. Cyprus also has a wide enough variety of flowering plants to keep a botanist happy for a few lifetimes – around 1800 different species, of which about seven percent are endemic. For **wild flowers**, the best time to visit is in spring, when a carpet of multicoloured blooms makes a brief but glorious appearance – crocus, vetch, buttercup, marigold, tulip, poppy, fennel, gladioli and many more. Autumn too has its glories as the first post-summer rains bring narcissus and hyacinth varieties into bloom, followed by cyclamen, anemone and crocus. Most famously, Cyprus has a wealth of **orchids**, especially around Larnaka's Salt Lake, the Akamas Peninsula and the Kyrenia Mountains. The variety of the flora of the Troodos Mountains has been recognized by the establishment since 2014 of the Troodos Botanical Garden near Troodos village (see page 149).

## Animals

Cyprus has a relative paucity of **mammals**, compensated for by a huge range of reptiles and amphibians. As the fossil records show, it was once home to dwarf elephants and hippopotamuses, both of which were spared the need to grow to intimidating size by the lack of natural predators. The largest mammal on the island today is the **Cypriot mouflon** (*Ovis orientalis ophion*) or wild horned sheep – your best chance of seeing these shy creatures is in the special enclosure attached to the Stavros tis Psokas forest station in Tiliria. Also of interest are the island's fourteen or so species of **bat**, among them the Egyptian fruit bat (Cyprus being its only European habitat). Despite their protected status, bats are often considered pests and are shot in rural areas.

As might be expected in such a hot and rocky country, Cyprus has a large range of **reptiles** (25), including nine species of snake, of which three are venomous (though only the rare blunt-nosed viper is really dangerous). The island's most popular reptiles, though, are its two types of **sea turtle** (green and loggerhead), which come ashore to lay eggs on certain beaches on the west and north coast, and on the Karpaz Peninsula. Of the many **lizard** species, the largest is the starred agama, resembling a diminutive dinosaur, the most common are the little sand lizard and gecko, and the most interesting is the chameleon. Amphibians include the tree frog, the marsh frog and the green toad.

Of more specialist interest are the numerous species of **insects** – butterflies, moths, spiders, scorpions and centipedes – and the teeming **marine life** which you can observe while snorkelling or diving, through the glass bottom of a tour boat, or on the quayside when fishermen bring in their catch.

### Birds

Given the island's position between Europe and Africa, up to 250 million birds visit Cyprus on their way south in autumn and north in spring. In total, **370 bird species** have been spotted on the island, of which two are endemic (the Cyprus pied wheatear and the Cyprus warbler); four more are endemic subspecies. Because of this, the island can be an ornithological paradise. The best times to see birds in Cyprus are March to May for the north-bound migration and August to October for the reverse flow to the south. Significant species include the **griffon vulture** with its 2.5m wingspan, numerous owls and raptors including Bonelli's eagle, found particularly in the Kyrenia Mountains, **flamingos**, which visit the salt lakes of Larnaka and Akrotiri between October and March, and the bee-eaters, **golden orioles** and strikingly multicoloured **hoopoes** that you might see between April and September. For more information, contact BirdLife Cyprus (☎22455072, ⊛birdlifecyprus.org), and the North Cyprus Society for the Protection of Birds (Kuskor; ⊛kibrisbirds.net).

Sadly, many Cypriots regard birds either as a threat (so farmers often shoot or poison birds of prey) or, far more destructively, as a resource to be exploited. Small songbirds like blackcaps, thrushes and robins are regarded as a great delicacy and are grilled, pickled or boiled and eaten whole. The appetite for this "**ambelopoulia**" leads to millions of songbirds being captured and killed. The birds are attracted by tape lures (recordings of birds), trapped in mist nets or on birdlime-covered sticks hidden among the trees, then killed, often by a toothpick to the throat. The practice has been illegal in the republic since 1974, but enforcement has been at best patchy, and many restaurants still openly have *ambelopoulia* on their menus. Those who oppose the practice – the Committee Against Bird Slaughter (CABS), for example (⊛komitee.de/en/homepage) – are regarded by many locals as interfering outsiders, trying to stop a traditional practice that has gone on for centuries throughout the Mediterranean. Campaigners point out that the practice is cruel and indiscriminate – many endangered or inedible migratory species die in the nets or on the birdlime, as well as so-called "indigenous" birds. It is estimated that trapping kills around 2.5 million birds a year in Cyprus.

# Books

Despite its diminutive size and its relative obscurity there is a vast range of literature devoted to Cyprus. Before reading anything about the island, the following should be borne in mind. The politics of the "Cyprus Question" are so labyrinthine, the feelings provoked by it so extreme and the vested interests so extensive that personal beliefs, cultural background and political allegiance inevitably colour any writing on the island, whether its politics, travel, history, food and wine, music or any other aspect of life. This could be said of most places of course, but it is particularly acute on an island literally divided along religious and nationalistic lines.

What follows is a personal selection of some of the books which might be usefully read in preparation for such a visit, and which the author has found useful in researching this book. This is not an academic reading list, and therefore only the more accessible volumes are included. A word of warning – since the burgeoning of self-publishing, a lot of personal memoirs and books of guidance regarding Cyprus have appeared. Treat with caution, especially books that do not bear the imprint of a recognized publishing house, and try to preview before buying – the standard of some can be extremely low.

It's worth remembering that places of interest, churches, monasteries, museums and ancient sites in the republic have printed, and often handsomely illustrated, guides on sale. In particular, look out for the excellent editions published by the **Bank of Cyprus Cultural Foundation**. In north Cyprus, guides where they exist are often useful but brief – perhaps a single sepia sheet of A4 with a plan of the site on one side and notes on the other. The best private source of maps and historic books on Cyprus is the **Sylvia Ioannou Foundation**, which provides downloadable extracts at ⓦsylviaioannoufoundation.org.

## TRAVEL BOOKS AND MEMOIRS

**Lawrence Durrell** *Bitter Lemons of Cyprus*. Memoir by the great novelist of his settling in Cyprus in the early 1950s – buying and renovating a house in Bellapais, working part-time in Nicosia, and interacting with locals, whom he paints vividly (if sometimes a little patronizingly) with his pen. Analysis of the island's troubles is clear and opinionated, and put a lot of backs up at the time of publication.

**Lorenzo Warriner Pease** *Diaries 1834–1839*. A fascinating look into the past from an American missionary posted to Cyprus (see page 53). It is perhaps one for aficionados – it costs £150 on Amazon.

★ **Colin Thubron** *Journey into Cyprus*. Account by one of Britain's top travel writers of his six-hundred-mile walk through Cyprus in 1972, providing an erudite and beautifully written snapshot of the island on the eve of the Turkish invasion.

## RECENT HISTORY

**Brendan O'Malley and Ian Craig** *The Cyprus Conspiracy: America, Espionage and the Turkish Invasion*. Written by two British journalists, this book persuasively puts forward the theory that, far from being a failure on the part of US foreign policy as Kissinger claimed, the events of 1974 and the division of Cyprus were exactly what the Americans wanted. It is particularly good on the influence of the Cold War and Cyprus's geographical position and strategic importance.

★ **William Mallinson** *Cyprus: A Modern History*. Published in 2008 and concentrating heavily on events from the mid-twentieth century onwards, this is not a brief survey for the casual reader but a fascinating and illuminating analysis of the complicated realpolitik affecting Cyprus. Few of the participants, in particular the great powers, can take any pride in the part they played – the chapter headings say it all: "The Poker Table", "The Poker Players" and "Keeping the fingers in the pie".

**Dr Stavros Panteli** *The Making of Modern Cyprus: From obscurity to statehood*. Excellent account of Cypriot history, concentrating on the British occupation, the early years of independence and the Turkish invasion of 1974 (though with brief chapters on the previous 10,000 years). Published in 1990, it takes the story only up to the late 1980s.

★ **Yiannis Papadakis** *Echoes from the Dead Zone: Across the Cyprus Divide*. Personal and impressively impartial account by a Greek Cypriot of his growing acceptance that both communities in Cyprus have responsibility for intercommunal breakdown, and that only a change of heart will heal the wounds.

## GENERAL HISTORY AND CULTURE

**Timothy Boatswain** *A Traveller's History of Cyprus*. Coverage of the history of the island, north and south, in the *Traveller's History* series. It contains a useful chronology of events and a gazetteer.

**Eileen Davy** *Northern Cyprus: A Traveller's Guide*. A useful description of northern Cypriot archeological and historical sites, dealt with chronologically rather than in regions, in chapters covering the main historic (and prehistoric) periods. Published in 1994 and therefore in parts a little outdated, it's still a very useful treatment.

**Professor A. Bernard Knapp** *The Archaeology of Cyprus*. Detailed coverage of the archeology of the island by the prestigious Cambridge World Archaeology series. Bang up to date (published 2013), it covers the story of Cyprus from the earliest times to the end of the Bronze Age, and places the island's development in both its Levantine and Aegean context.

★ **Andreas and Judith Stylianou** *The Painted Churches of Cyprus*. Something of a special-interest title and now out of print. But there's an excellent PDF available to download from ⓦ images.icon-art.info (the link is at ⓦ tinyurl.com/unescochurches). Put together by husband-and-wife team Andreas and Judith A. Stylianou, this title is invaluable to anybody who wishes to explore Cyprus's exquisite painted churches, particularly those in the Troodos Mountains.

## FOOD

There are numerous books about Greek food, but not so many about specifically Cypriot cuisine.

**Melek Cella** *Cypriot Barbecue Delights and Side Dishes*. A cheap but useful little book of recipes written by a Turkish Cypriot. Given the title, the emphasis is on kebabs, but there are also chapters on pulses, salads and dips. Not a glossy coffee-table book but none the worse for that.

**Julia Chrysanthou and Xenia Chrysanthou** *Traditional Greek Cooking from Cyprus and Beyond*. Clearly laid out, well-illustrated recipes that are easy to follow.

**Jan Cutler and Rena Salaman** *The Illustrated Food and Cooking of Greece* and *The Complete Book of Greek Cooking*. Clear, practical guides to Greek (not specifically Cypriot) cooking by experienced food writers, one of whom is Greek.

**Tessa Kiros** *Food from Many Greek Kitchens*. A relatively comprehensive introduction to Greek cooking from an author whose background includes a Greek-Cypriot father. The recipes are good, but there are lots of largely irrelevant photographs and the pale blue print is difficult to read.

**Helen Tsanos Sheinman** *Love, Laughter and Lunch: the Evocative Memories of a Cypriot Family's Journey*. Written by a London-born Greek Cypriot, and more a memoir and cultural outline than a cookbook, but includes lots of her family's recipes. It's not cheap, but it can be found at a discount online.

## WALKING

**Brian and Eileen Anderson** *North Cyprus Walk and Eat*. Lots of general advice and information on north Cyprus as well as eleven walks with recommended restaurants.

**Geoff Daniel** *Cyprus Car Tours and Walks*. One of the *Sunflower Landscape* series, this includes seven driving tours and thirty walks, all in the south of the island. The book is somewhat unnecessarily bulked out by bus and service taxi timetables, and is an updated version of a much older book.

**Rolf Goetz and Gill Round** *Cyprus South and North*. Useful addition to the *Rother Walking Guide* series, and covers both sides of the Green Line – something that is not always the case. However, there are some problems arising from the fact that it's translated from the German.

## LEARNING GREEK AND TURKISH

**Alison Kakoura and Karen Rich** *Talk Greek* (book and 2 CDs). Probably the best product for beginners' essentials in print, and for developing the confidence to try them out.

**Asuman Çelen Pollard and David Pollard** *Teach Yourself Turkish*. The usual Teach Yourself course – well structured and relatively cheap, but the quality of the course book could be improved upon.

**BBC** *Greek Language and People*. This is not a formal language course, but it's a good basic introduction to conversational Greek.

**Rough Guides** *Rough Guide Phrasebook: Greek* and *Rough Guide Phrasebook: Turkish*. Current, accurate and pocket-sized, with phrases that you'll actually need and useful two-way glossaries. Free audio samples available at ⓦ roughguides.com.

# Greek and Turkish

Neither Greek nor Turkish is a particularly easy language to learn. There are pronunciation pitfalls with both, while Greek also involves an unfamiliar alphabet. Further challenges can arise from the fact that, in Cyprus, each language has developed separately from its mainland roots, bringing in divergent dialects and accents. Not only can the visitor struggle with the vernacular they're likely to encounter, but Cypriots speak with rapid speed and staccato delivery which can make it difficult to follow. Add to this the fact that most Cypriots speak good English, and it might be thought that only the naturally gifted or preternaturally enthusiastic linguist would make the effort to converse in Greek or Turkish. This would be a mistake. Both Greek and Turkish Cypriots are proud of their history, traditions and language, and will react with delight to any attempt on the part of visitors, however clumsy, to at least make an effort. And certainly knowledge of alphabet and pronunciation, together with a few well-chosen words and phrases, will go a long way to helping you to navigate your way from A to B, chat with shopkeepers and restaurant owners, and generally enjoy your visit to the island. We've included the basics in this section, but for a wider range of words and phrases and an extensive menu reader check out the relevant Rough Guide phrasebook (see page 264).

## Greek

Bear in mind that the **pronunciation** given below is approximate – all you can do is use it as a starting point, then try to copy the locals. Cypriot pronunciation is different from that of mainland Greece. So, for example, the Greeks would pronounce the word for "tea" exactly as it is spelt ("tsai"), whereas the Cypriots would say "chai". But if you pronounce it the Greek way, you'll still be understood (probably with a smile – if a Cypriot pronounced it "tsai", whey would be accused of putting on airs).

### Greek alphabet

**A/α** alpha (a as in cart)
**B/β** beta (v as in very)
**Γ/γ** gama (somewhere between y as in yacht and g as in grow)
**Δ/δ** delta (th as in they)
**E/ε** epsilon (e as in sherry)
**Z/ζ** zeta (z as in zebra)
**H/η** ita (ee as in tree)
**Θ/θ** thita (th as in thumb)
**I/ι** yiota (ee as in tree)
**K/κ** καρα (k as in book)
**Λ/λ** lamda (l as in bog)
**M/μ** mi (m as in mat)
**N/ν** ni (n as in not)

**Ξ/ξ** ksi (x as in fax)
**O/o** omikro (o as in fox)
**Π/π** pi (somewhere between p as in pot and b as in box)
**P/ρ** ro (r as in right, but with the r rolled slightly)
**Σ/σ/ς** sigma (s as in say)
**T/t** taf (somewhere between t as in tap and d as in dog)
**Y/υ** ipsilo (ee as in tree)
**Φ/φ** phi (ph as in photograph)
**X/χ** hi (ch as in lock, but slightly further forward on the palate)
**Ψ/ψ** psi (ps as in dipstick)
**Ω/ω** omega (o as in fox)

## Combinations

The pronunciation of some letters can be different if they're combined with others, or according to where they come in the word. Therefore:

**AI/αι** e as in fey

**AY/αυ** av or af, depending on what consonant follows them

**EI/ει** ee as in tree

**EY/ευ** ev/ef depending on what consonant follows them

**OI/οι** ee as in tree

**OY/ου** ou as in tourist

**ΓΓ/γγ** ng as in bangle

**ΜΠ/μπ** b as in boat at the start of a word, mb as in Cumbria elsewhere in the word

**NT/nt** d as in dam at the beginning of the word, nd as in pandemonium elsewhere in the word

**ΣΙ/σi** sh as in shambles

**ΤΣ/tσ** ch as in char

**ΤΖ/tz** ts as in cats

## GREEK WORDS AND PHRASES

### BASICS

**Hello** Yiassou/yiassas (plural)

**Good morning** Kalimera

**Good evening** Kalispera

**Good night** Kalinihta

**Today** Simera

**Tomorrow** Avrio

**Please** Parakalo

**Thank you** Evharisto

**Yes** Nai (ai pronounced as e sound as in egg)

**No** Ohi

**OK** OK/entaxi

**Excuse me** Signomi (to get past); meh sinkhoriteh (to say sorry)

**How are you?** Ti kanis?

**My name is...** Me lene...

**I'm English** Imeh Anglos/Anglitha (m/f)

**...Scottish** ...Skotsezos/Skotseza (m/f)

**...Irish** ...Irlanthos/Irlantheza (m/f)

**...American** ...Amerikanikos/Amerikana (m/f)

**...Australian** ...Afstralos/Afstraleza (m/f)

**I don't speak Greek** Then milao elinika

**Slowly** Siga siga

**Water** Nero

**Telephone** Tilefono

**Doctor** Yiatros

**Police** Astinomia

**Pharmacy** Farmakio

### TRANSPORT AND DIRECTIONS

**Car** Aftokinito

**Where is?** Pou ine?

**Road** Dromos (d pronounced as th sound)

**Left** Aristera

**Right** Dexia

**Straight on** Efthia/Issia (local dialect)

**Petrol** Venzini/ bezina (local dialect)

**Mechanic** Mihanikos

### ACCOMMODATION

**Hotel** Xenodohio

**Do you have a room with** Mipos exede domatio me

**With a double bed** yia diplo krevati

**Single room** Mono domatio

**Double room** Diplo domatio

**First floor** Proto patoma

**Second floor** Deftero patoma

**Ground floor** Isoyio

**I have a reservation** Eho kratisi

**One night** Mia nihta

---

### POPULAR GREEK DISHES

**Moussaka** layers of minced lamb and aubergine, with a béchamel sauce.

**Souvlakia** cubes of lamb, pork or chicken cooked on a charcoal grill.

**Stifado** rabbit (or sometimes lamb) stew with onions, steeped in wine or vinegar, cooked in a sealed container.

**Kléftiko** lamb or goat dish cooked in an outdoor oven.

**Sheftalia** minced pork or lamb with onions, stuffed into the lining of a lamb or pig's stomach, and grilled over charcoal.

**Keftedes** meatballs.

**Goubes** minced meat and onions encased in cracked wheat and deep fried.

**Koupepia** minced meat and rice wrapped in young vine leaves.

**Two nights** Dio nihtes

**Five nights** Pente nihtes

**Where is the lift?** Pou ine to asanser?

**Do you have wi-fi?** Ekheteh wi-fi?

**What time is breakfast served?** Ti ora ine to proyevma?

**Bar** Mbar

**Toilet** Toualet

**Air-conditioning** Klimatismos

**Shower** Ndous

**Television** Tileorasi

**Key** Klidi

**Pool** Pisina

## AT THE RESTAURANT

**Restaurant** Estiatorio

**Café** Kafeteria, Kafenío

**Can I have the menu?** Mporo na eho to menou?

**What do you recommend?** Ti mou protinede?

**Lunch** Mesimeriano

**Dinner** Vradino

**White wine** Aspro krasi

**Red wine** Kokkino krasi

**Beer** Mbira

**Milk** To gala

**Bread** Psomi

**Can I order please?** Mporo na parakalo?

**Chicken** Kotopoulo

**Beef** Vodino

**Lamb** Arni

**Pork** Hirino kreas

**Chicken** Godopoulo

**Fish** Psari

**Salad** Salada

**More bread please** Ligo psomi parakalo

**A bottle of water/wine** Ena boukali nero/krasi

**please** parakalo

**Knife** Maheri

**Fork** Pirouni

**Spoon** Koutali

**Waiter** Servitoros

**Salt** Alati

**Pepper** Piperi

**I have a reservation** Eho kratisi

**Table for two** Trapezi yia dio

**I don't eat meat** Then trogo kreas

**Can I have a coffee please?** Ena kafe parakalo

**Coffee types** Kafe gliko (sweet), medrio (medium), sketo (no sugar)

**Tea** Tsai

**Dessert** Gliko

**The food was lovely** To fayito itane poli oreo

**What time do you close?** Ti ora klinete?

**The bill, please** To logariasmo parakalo

**I would like to pay with a credit/debit card** Thelo na pliroso me karta

## NUMBERS

1 Ena

2 Dio

3 Tria

4 Tessera

5 Pente

6 Exi

7 Epta

8 Ohto

9 Enea

10 Deka

11 Endheka

12 Dhodheka

13 Dhekatría

20 Íkossi

21 Íkossi ena

30 Trianda

40 Saranda

50 Peninda

60 Exínda

70 Evdhominda

80 Ogdhonda

90 Eneninda

100 Ekato

200 Diakossia

1000 Hilia

## DAYS AND MONTHS

**Monday** Dheftera

**Tuesday** Tríti

**Wednesday** Tetarti

**Thursday** Pempti

**Friday** Paraskeví

**Saturday** Savato

**Sunday** Kyriakí

**January** Yennaris

**February** Fleváris

**March** Martis

**April** Aprílis

**May** Maios

**June** Iounios

**July** Ioulios

**August** Avgoustos

**September** Septemvris

**October** Oktovris

**November** Normvris

**December** Dhekrmvris

## Turkish

**Turkish** is based on the Roman alphabet and most letters are pronounced as in English. There is no "q", "w" or "x" in Turkish and there are some additional characters. The stress usually falls on the first syllable in the word. In the **pronunciation** given below we have tried to find the nearest approximation to the Turkish sounds which are easy for English-speakers to pronounce while still enabling you to be understood.

### Turkish characters

A/a a cross between a long and short **a** somewhere between the **a** in m**a**n and the **a** sound in **a**re.

C/c pronounced **j** as in **j**am

Ç/ç pronounced **ch** as in **ch**urch

E/e a short **e** sound as in **e**gg

G/g is a hard **g** as in **g**o

Ğ/ğ this character is silent but elongates the vowel to either side of it

I/ı pronounced like the **er** in numb**er**

İ/i a short **i** sound as in **i**nk

O/o pronounced as in **o**ff

Ö/ö pronounced as in the **or** sound (with a silent r) in word

S/s is a hissing sound as in s**e**ven

Ş/ş pronounced **sh** as in **sh**ut

U/u pronounced as in the **oo** in c**oo**l

Ü/ü pronounced as in the **u** sound in f**u**se

Y/y is generally used to separate vowels and creates some slightly different sounds in combination as follows: **ay** pronounced **eye**; **ey** pronounced as in **they**; **iy** pronounced **ee**

### TURKISH WORDS AND PHRASES

#### BASICS

**Hello** Merhaba

**Good morning** Günaydın

**Good afternoon** İyi günler

**Good evening** İyi akşamlar

**Good night** İyi geceler

**Please** Lütfen

**Thank you** Teşekkür ederim

**Yes** Evet

**No** Hayır

**How are you?** Nasılsınız? Nasılsın?

**Excuse me** Pardon (to get past) Özür dilerim (to say sorry)

**I'm fine** İyiyim

**I don't speak Turkish** Anlamadım/Türkçe anlamıyoru

**My name is** ...İsmim...

**I'm English** ...İngilizim

**...Scottish** ...İskoçyalım

**...Irish** ...İrlandalıyım

**...American** ...Amerikalı

**...Australian** ...Avustralyalım

**I want** İstiyorum

**When?** Ne zaman?

**Today** Bugun

**Tomorrow** Yarın

**Where?** Nerede?

**Be careful!** Dikkat!

**Pharmacy** Eczane

#### ACCOMMODATION

**Hotel** Otel

**Pension, inn** Pansiyon

**Campsite** Kamping

**Do you have a room?** Boş odanız var mı?

**Single/double/triple** Tek/çift/üç kişilik

**Do you have a double room?** Bir/iki/üç gecelik çift?

**...for one/two/three nights** ...Bir/iki/üç gecelik yataklı odanız var mı

**...for one/two weeks** ...bir/iki haftalık

**...with an extra bed** ...ilâve yataklı

**...with a double bed** ...fransiz yataklı

**...with a shower** ...duşlu

**Hot water** Sıcak su

**Cold water** Soğuk su

**Can I see it?** Bakabilirmiyim?

**I have a booking** Reservasyonum var

**Do you have wi-fi?** Kablosuz var?

**Toilet** Tuvalet

#### AT THE RESTAURANT

**Restaurant** Lokanta, restoran

**Café** kafeh, pastane

**Lunch** To yevma

**Dinner** To thipno

**Water** Su

**Milk** Sut

**Beer** Bira

**Wine** Şarap

**Tea** Çay

**Coffee** Kahve

**Glass** Bardak

**Another...** Başka bir...

**Plate** Tabak

**Knife** Bıçak

**Fork** Çatal

**Spoon** Kaşık

**Bill** Hesap
**Service charge** Servis ücreti
**Spicy kebab** Adana kebap
**Minced kebab** Beyti
**Rotisseried kebab** Döner kebap
**Shish kebab** Şiş kebap
**Meatballs** Köfte
**Lamb** Kuzu
**Beef** Sığır
**Fish** Balık
**Squid** Kalamar

**Swordfish** Kılıç
**Tuna** Orkinos
**Honey and nut pie** Baklava

## TRANSPORT AND DIRECTIONS

**Left/right** Sol/Sag
**Straight ahead** Dogru, direk
**Turn left/right** Sola don/sagta don
**Parking/No parking** Park yapilir/Park yapilmaz
**Slow down** Yavasla

## NUMBERS

| | |
|---|---|
| **1** Bir (beer) | **13** On üç |
| **2** Iki (icky) | **20** Yirmi |
| **3** Üç (ooch) | **30** Otuz |
| **4** Dört (dirt) | **40** Kırk |
| **5** Beş (besh) | **50** Elli |
| **6** Altı (al-ter) | **60** Altmış |
| **7** Yedi (yea-dee) | **70** Yetmiş |
| **8** Sekiz (seck-is) | **80** Seksen |
| **9** Dokuz (dock-uz) | **90** Doksan |
| **10** On (on) | **100** Yüz |
| **11** On bir | **200** iki Yüz |
| **12** On iki | **1000** Bin |

## DAYS AND MONTHS

| | |
|---|---|
| **Monday** Pazartesi | **April** Nisan |
| **Tuesday** Salı | **May** Mayıs |
| **Wednesday** Çarşamba | **June** Haziran |
| **Thursday** Perşembe | **July** Temmuz |
| **Friday** Cuma | **August** Ağustos |
| **Saturday** Cumartesi | **September** Eylül |
| **Sunday** Pazar | **October** Ekim |
| **January** Ocak | **November** Kasım |
| **February** Subat | **December** Aralk |
| **March** Mart | |

# Glossary

**Acropolis** Ancient hilltop, usually fortified.

**Aga** Minor Ottoman rank, commonly used as a term of respect. Comes after the name.

**Agora** Central market area of a town.

**Amphorae** Storage containers with large handles and a pointed base, usually made of clay. Smaller than *pitharia* which they complemented.

**Apse** Curved recess at the eastern end of a church.

**Agios/Agia/Agii** Saint (masculine, feminine and plural). Widely used in iconography and place names.

**Basilica** Colonnaded hall-type church based on earlier Roman types, common in Cyprus.

**Bedestan** Covered market.

**Bey** Like Aga, a minor Ottoman title.

**Cami(i)** Mosque.

**Classical period** In Cyprus, 480–323 BC.

**Conch** Shell-like half-dome above the apse, often decorated with frescoes.

**CTO** Cyprus Tourist Organization.

**Domatia** Rooms (especially for rent).

**Dragoman** Interpreter or guide under the Ottoman Empire (see page 181).

**Dromos** Street, or the ramp leading down into a subterranean tomb.

**Drum** Cylindrical vertical section supporting the dome of a church, often with windows. Also one of the sections from which columns were constructed.

**EOKA** Ethnikí Orgánosis Kipriakoú Agónos (National Organization of Cypriot Struggle), associated with the fight for independence from Britain.

**EOKA-B** A later incarnation of the EOKA, which fought mainly against Turkish Cypriots.

**Forum** Market and meeting place in a Roman town – equivalent to the Greek Agora.

**Frieze** Sculpted figures around a temple.

**Hammam** Turkish Bath.

**Han/Hani** (sometimes Khan) Hostel for travellers.

**Hypocaust** Underfloor heating system.

**Iconoclasm** Eighth- and ninth-century Byzantine movement which declared icons to be idolatrous. Led to the destruction of many icons.

**Ikonostasis** Ornate screen between nave and altar of an Orthodox church, upon which are hung (at least three) icons.

**Imam** Prayer leader in a mosque.

**Kafenío** Café or coffee house, often at the centre of a community, patronized mainly by men.

**Kale** Castle.

**Kastro** Castle or fortified hill.

**Katholicon** Monastery church.

**Kato** Lower, used as prefix for town or village.

**Kilise** Church.

**Krater** A large, often two-handed and ornate, drinking vessel.

**Lusignan Dynasty** Rule by the heirs of Guy de Lusignan, 1192–1489 AD.

**Medrese** School for Islamic religious instruction.

**Mihrab** Niche within a mosque indicating the direction of Mecca.

**Mimbar** Pulpit in a mosque.

**Mitrópolis** Orthodox cathedral of a large town or city.

**Moni** Monastery or convent.

**Mukhtar** Village headman.

**Narthex** Entrance hall or vestibule, often added after a church was built. If there are more than one, the outermost is the exonarthex (the outer vestibule).

**Nave** The main body of a church.

**Necropolis** Literally "city of the dead", made up of above-ground tombs outside the city limits.

**Neos/Nea/Neo** New (masculine/feminine/neuter). Often used in names of towns or villages.

**Nymphaeum** Rear wall of a formal fountain, often with statues.

**Odeion** Small Greek or Roman theatre.

**Paleos/Palea/Paleo** Greek for "Old" (masculine/feminine/neuter).

**Panagia** Virgin Mary.

**Pandokrátor** Figure of Christ with a bible in one hand and the fingers of the other extended in blessing.

**Paşa** (sometimes pasha) Honorary Ottoman title, which follows the name.

**Pitharia** Large earthenware jars used to store wine or olive oil.

**Plateia** Square in a town or village.

**Rhyton** Drinking vessel, often in the shape of a horn.

**Sadirvan** Ablution fountain.

**Stele** Ancient inscribed tombstone.

**Stoa** Colonnaded walkway around the edge of the Agora or Forum.

**Sufi** Followers of an ascetic Sufi Muslim order, of which the best known is that of the dervishes.

**Tavli** Backgammon, which is commonly played in coffee houses.

**Tekke** Sufi gathering place or shrine.

**Tesserae** Cubes of different-coloured stone or glass used in the making of mosaics.

**TMT** Türk Mukavemet Teşkilatı (Turkish Resistance Organization).

**TRNC** Turkish Republic of North Cyprus (also called the KKTC).

# Small print and index

## A ROUGH GUIDE TO ROUGH GUIDES

Published in 1982, the first Rough Guide – to Greece – was a student scheme that became a publishing phenomenon. Mark Ellingham, a recent graduate in English from Bristol University, had been travelling in Greece the previous summer and couldn't find the right guidebook. With a small group of friends he wrote his own guide, combining a contemporary, journalistic style with a thoroughly practical approach to travellers' needs.

The immediate success of the book spawned a series that rapidly covered dozens of destinations. And, in addition to impecunious backpackers, Rough Guides soon acquired a much broader readership that relished the guides' wit and inquisitiveness as much as their enthusiastic, critical approach and value-for-money ethos. These days, Rough Guides include recommendations from budget to luxury and cover more than 120 destinations around the globe, from Amsterdam to Zanzibar, all regularly updated by our team of roaming writers.

Browse all our latest guides, read inspirational features and book your trip at **roughguides.com**.

## Rough Guide credits

**Editor:** Tatiana Wilde
**Author:** Jos Simon
**Updater:** Klaudyna Cwynar
**Cartography:** Carte
**Managing editor:** Rachel Lawrence

**Picture editor:** Aude Vauconsant
**Cover photo research:** Aude Vauconsant
**Senior DTP coordinator:** Dan May
**Head of DTP and Pre-Press:** Rebeka Davies

## Publishing information

Third edition 2019

### Distribution

*UK, Ireland and Europe*
Apa Publications (UK) Ltd; sales@roughguides.com
*United States and Canada*
Ingram Publisher Services; ips@ingramcontent.com
*Australia and New Zealand*
Woodslane; info@woodslane.com.au
*Southeast Asia*
Apa Publications (SN) Pte; sales@roughguides.com
*Worldwide*
Apa Publications (UK) Ltd; sales@roughguides.com
**Special Sales, Content Licensing and CoPublishing**
Rough Guides can be purchased in bulk quantities at discounted prices. We can create special editions, personalised jackets and corporate imprints tailored to your needs. sales@roughguides.com.

## Help us update

We've gone to a lot of effort to ensure that this edition of **The Rough Guide to Cyprus** is accurate and up-to-date. However, things change – places get "discovered", opening hours are notoriously fickle, restaurants and rooms raise prices or lower standards. If you feel we've got it wrong or left something out, we'd like to know, and if you can remember the address, the price, the hours, the phone number, so much the better.

Please send your comments with the subject line **"Rough Guide Cyprus Update"** to mail@uk.roughguides.com. We'll credit all contributions and send a copy of the next edition (or any other Rough Guide if you prefer) for the very best emails.

## Photo credits

(Key: T-top; C-centre; B-bottom; L-left; R-right)

# Index